AF251910

RONALD REAGAN'S WEEKLY RADIO ADDRESSES

The President Speaks to America

Volume 1: The First Term

RONALD REAGAN'S WEEKLY RADIO ADDRESSES

The President Speaks to America

Volume 1: The First Term

Compiled by
Fred L. Israel

With an Introduction by
Senator William V. Roth, Jr.

Scholarly Resources Inc.
Wilmington, Delaware

© 1987 by Scholarly Resources Inc.
All rights reserved
First published 1987
Printed and bound in the United States of America

Scholarly Resources Inc.
104 Greenhill Avenue
Wilmington, Delaware 19805-1897

Library of Congress Cataloging-in-Publication Data

Reagan, Ronald.
    Ronald Reagan's weekly radio addresses.

    Includes index.
    Contents: v. 1. The first term.
    1. United States—Politics and government—1981-
I. Israel, Fred L. II. United States. President
(1981-   : Reagan). III. Title.
J82.E5   1987   353.03′5   87-9461
ISBN 0-8420-2282-1 (v. 1)

CONTENTS

Preface ix
Introduction xiii
Chronology xvii
Highlights in the Life of Ronald Reagan xxxvii

Economic Recovery Program *April 3, 1982* 1
Caribbean Basin Initiative/Student Loans *April 10, 1982* 3
Nuclear Weapons *April 17, 1982* 5
Taxes, Tuition Tax Credits, and Interest Rates *April 24, 1982* 7
Economic Recovery Program *May 1, 1982* 9
Federal Budget/Unemployment *May 8, 1982* 11
Armed Forces Day *May 15, 1982* 13
Federal Budget *May 22, 1982* 15
Federal Budget/Western Alliance *May 29, 1982* 17
Trip to Europe *June 5, 1982* 19
The Economy *August 28, 1982* 21
Labor Day *September 4, 1982* 23
Crime and Criminal Justice Reform *September 11, 1982* 25
Prayer in Public Schools *September 18, 1982* 27
The Economy *September 25, 1982* 29
Federal Drug Policy *October 2, 1982* 31
Solidarity and U.S. Relations with Poland *October 9, 1982* 33
The Economy *October 16, 1982* 35
Economic and Budget Issues *October 23, 1982* 38
Economic Recovery Program *October 30, 1982* 40
Congressional Agenda/The Economy *November 6, 1982* 42
East-West Trade Relations and the Soviet Pipeline
    Sanctions *November 13, 1982* 45
International Free Trade *November 20, 1982* 47
Highway and Bridge Repair Program *November 27, 1982* 49
Caribbean Basin Initiative *December 4, 1982* 51
Production of the MX Missile *December 11, 1982* 53
Economic Recovery/National Defense *December 18, 1982* 55
Christmas Day *December 25, 1982* 58
New Year's Day *January 1, 1983* 60
U.S.-Soviet Relations and the Vice-President's
    Trip to Europe *January 8, 1983* 62
Dr. Martin Luther King, Jr. *January 15, 1983* 64

Domestic Social Issues *January 22, 1983* 66
Fiscal Year 1984 Budget *January 29, 1983* 68
Economic Recovery Program *February 5, 1983* 70
Fiscal Year 1984 Budget *February 12, 1983* 72
Defense Spending *February 19, 1983* 75
Natural Gas Consumers and Regulatory Reform
      Legislation *February 26, 1983* 77
Employment Programs *March 5, 1983* 79
Education *March 12, 1983* 81
House of Representatives' Budget Proposal *March 19, 1983* 83
House of Representatives' Budget Proposal *March 26, 1983* 86
Easter and Passover *April 2, 1983* 88
Federal Income Taxation *April 9, 1983* 90
Withholding Tax on Interest and Dividends *April 16, 1983* 93
Death of Diplomatic and Military Personnel in
      Beirut *April 23, 1983* 95
Education *April 30, 1983* 97
Mother's Day *May 7, 1983* 99
Small Business *May 14, 1983* 102
Armed Forces Day *May 21, 1983* 104
Williamsburg Economic Summit *May 28, 1983* 106
American Red Cross/Williamsburg Economic
      Summit *June 4, 1983* 108
Environmental and Natural Resources
      Management *June 11, 1983* 110
Federal Reserve Board Chairman/Space Shuttle Flight
      and Science Education *June 18, 1983* 113
Education *June 25, 1983* 115
Independence Day *July 2, 1983* 117
Economic and Fair Housing Issues *July 9, 1983* 119
Arms Control and Reduction *July 16, 1983* 121
International Monetary Fund/Organ Donorship *July 23, 1983* 123
Organ Donorship/Reform 88 *July 30, 1983* 126
International Trade *August 6, 1983* 128
Situation in Central America *August 13, 1983* 130
Federal Civilian Employment *August 20, 1983* 132
Situation in the Middle East *August 27, 1983* 134
Soviet Attack on Korean Civilian Airliner/
      Labor Day *September 3, 1983* 136
American International Broadcasting *September 10, 1983* 138
Soviet Attack on Korean Civilian Airliner *September 17, 1983* 141
Peace *September 24, 1983* 143
Economic Recovery and Employment *October 1, 1983* 145

vi

Situation in Lebanon *October 8, 1983* 147
Quality of Life in America *October 15, 1983* 149
Arms Control and Reduction *October 22, 1983* 152
NATO Nuclear Weapons *October 29, 1983* 154
America's Veterans *November 5, 1983* 156
Trip to Japan and the Republic of Korea *November 12, 1983* 158
First Session of the 98th Congress *November 19, 1983* 160
James G. Watt *November 26, 1983* 163
The American Family *December 3, 1983* 165
Situation in Lebanon *December 10, 1983* 167
Drunk Driving *December 17, 1983* 169
Christmas *December 24, 1983* 171
New Year's Eve *December 31, 1983* 173
School Discipline *January 7, 1984* 175
National Bipartisan Commission on Central
    America *January 14, 1984* 177
Economic Recovery Program *January 21, 1984* 179
Goals for Space *January 28, 1984* 181
Budget Deficits/Peace in Central America
    and Lebanon *February 4, 1984* 182
U.S.-Soviet Relations *February 11, 1984* 184
Crime and Criminal Justice Reform *February 18, 1984* 186
Prayer in Public Schools *February 25, 1984* 188
Budget Deficits *March 3, 1984* 190
Economic Recovery *March 10, 1984* 192
St. Patrick's Day *March 17, 1984* 194
Elections in El Salvador *March 24, 1984* 196
Opportunities for Women *March 31, 1984* 198
Foreign Policy Challenges *April 7, 1984* 200
Situation in Central America *April 14, 1984* 201
Federal Income Taxation *April 21, 1984* 203
Trip to China *April 28, 1984* 205
Defaults on Student Loans/Reducing Waste
    in Government *May 5, 1984* 207
Education *May 12, 1984* 209
Summer Jobs for Youth *May 19, 1984* 211
Economic Recovery/National Defense *May 26, 1984* 213
Trip to Ireland/D-Day Anniversary *June 2, 1984* 215
Trip to London/Economic Summit *June 9, 1984* 217
Father's Day/Outlook for Families *June 16, 1984* 219
Economic Recovery *June 23, 1984* 220
Budget Deficits/Drug Abuse *June 30, 1984* 222
Anti-Crime Legislation *July 7, 1984* 224

Environmental and Natural Resources
    Management *July 14, 1984* 226
Private Enterprise in Space *July 21, 1984* 228
U.S. Olympic Team *July 28, 1984* 229
Mondale's Tax Increases *August 4, 1984* 232
Equal Access Bill/Do-Nothing Congress *August 11, 1984* 234
Olympic Athletes/Economic Recovery *August 18, 1984* 236
Goals for the Future *August 25, 1984* 238
Labor Day *September 1, 1984* 240
Education *September 8, 1984* 242
Clear Choice for Voters *September 15, 1984* 243
Help for Steel and Agriculture *September 22, 1984* 245
U.S.-Soviet Relations *September 29, 1984* 247
Mondale's Initiatives to Combat Drugs *October 6, 1984* 249
Clear Choice for Voters *October 13, 1984* 251
Foreign Policy Issues *October 20, 1984* 253
1984 Presidential Campaign *October 27, 1984* 255
1984 Presidential Campaign *November 3, 1984* 257

Index 259

PREFACE

Future dictionaries will include, I think, the noun "Reaganism," defining it as: 1) a conservative philosophy; 2) the disposition to preserve what is established; and 3) the principles and practices of political conservatives, *circa* the latter half of the twentieth century. These radio transcripts are vintage Reaganism, enunciated by its most eloquent spokesman. Few—very few—presidents in this century have been able to convey their thoughts so clearly, making fullest use of the most modern methods of communication.

On April 2, 1982, the White House announced that, on the following day, President Ronald Reagan would deliver the first of ten short, live, Saturday radio addresses. And, on June 5th, the president concluded the series. The broadcasts had been a success. Favorable comments came from every section of the country. The largest newspapers gave these weekly talks excellent coverage, and wire service stories had been picked up by the nation's smaller ones. The White House director of communications described the broadcasts as a "win-win proposition" with no down side to it. Five minutes on the radio, and the president dominated the weekend news. Above all, the president thought that radio was a superb way of reaching his countrymen. "I believed there was so much conflict and confusion coming out of Washington," said Reagan, "it was hard for people to know what was really happening. . . . I thought a weekly radio address would give me an opportunity to explain my decisions and help clarify the picture." And so the live Saturday talks began again on August 28, 1982, and continued until November 3, 1984, three days before the president's triumphant reelection. The Saturday schedule resumed shortly after the second inauguration and, to date, has been continuous.

Radio stations carry these talks on a volunteer basis. Each week, the Democrats give a five-minute response, but their subject usually has nothing to do with the one chosen by Reagan, whose topic is not announced in advance. The president's address and the Democratic response are carried live by the ABC, NBC, CNN, Associated Press, and United Press International radio networks. Since the networks only "feed" the speech to subscribers, however, there is no definitive count of how many stations actually air it. Numerous letter writers have asked why these broadcasts are not heard in a particular area. Therefore, the White House currently is experimenting with a 900 telephone number. The cost for the five-minute presidential talk is $1.90, and the first reports of dialers have been surprisingly good, considering the fee involved.

Oratorical eloquence is becoming a lost political art. Not many possess it. Of those who do, Ronald Reagan must rank among the greatest. In fact, the president's outstanding single skill is his ability to communicate an idea or an emotion. Almost half a century earlier, Franklin D. Roosevelt, also a skillful communicator, had launched a political revolution which transformed the American government from a passive onlooker to an active participant. Reagan has led the counterreformation, the reversal. Always articulate, he believes that interventionist government has run its course. Using a brilliantly effective speaking style honed through the years, Reagan has broken the New Deal coalition which had dominated American politics since the Great Depression.

Communicating has been Reagan's lifelong profession. At 21, he started his first job as a $10-per-game, play-by-play baseball announcer at radio station WOC in Davenport, Iowa. ("Radio has always been part of my life," remarked the president. "I can still remember how exciting it was when I first scratched a crystal with a wire and heard a faint voice saying, 'This is KDKA Pittsburgh, KDKA Pittsburgh.'") Thus began a successful career which has always involved communicating, whether through radio, movies, television, or on the banquet circuit. A highlight of the 1964 presidential campaign was Reagan's October 14th speech on behalf of Republican candidate Barry Goldwater. Brilliantly effective, the speech brought in more than $1 million for Republican candidates, more money than had been raised by any political address up to that time. Washington columnist David Broder called it the best oration since William Jennings Bryan electrified the 1896 Democratic convention. A new political voice had been found—an articulate voice which truly reached its audience.

Reagan's aides say the president often comes up with an idea for the weekly address during his Monday lunch with advisers. A draft is prepared by his speechwriters, and then he reworks it. Observers have noted that the president gazes on the radio microphone before him as if wooing the woman of his dreams, while he blocks out the aides and technicians hovering around him. ("Wherever I am and whatever I am doing," wrote Reagan, "everything stops for my live radio report to the people. And I must admit, even after all these years, I still get a thrill out of sitting down at the microphone. There is something special about radio, and something exciting about a live broadcast.") Through a friendly and reassuring delivery, Reagan's message is projected superbly by his mellow voice. That quality for which he strives, intimacy with his audience, comes through. The president aims his talks for the ear. "He changes those scripts a lot and then practices them and marks them up, so they can be done in five minutes flat," said an aide. As I read these radio transcripts, the image and cadence of Reagan are present. Moreover, the president projects his ideas clearly. "If you start thinking, I am talking to an audience out there of X-million people, you will have an impersonal tone," he noted. Instead, he focuses on talking to someone he knows, to a friend. It works.

No stereotype fits President Reagan. He is a composite of his predecessors—and yet he is someone entirely new. Perhaps closest to Dwight Eisenhower in tone and style, Reagan has brought to the White House an unbounded faith in free enterprise and an utter disdain for the excesses of government. These 125 radio addresses convey the president's way of thinking. How history will judge him, we do not know, but these addresses certainly convey the philosophy of the 40th President of the United States.

Fred L. Israel
City College of New York
February 1987

INTRODUCTION

During the winter of 431 B.C., the Athenian statesman, Pericles, on the occasion of a public funeral for the dead in battle, delivered what today is acknowleged as one of the masterpieces of literature and one of the first political speeches ever recorded. Since that time, the eloquence of politics has been an art sought by many but mastered by few. In America, our own history is sprinkled with the names of men whose rhetoric, style, and delivery expanded political philosophy, advanced personal careers, preserved the Nation, or comforted Americans in challenging times. The words of men like Fisher Ames, John C. Calhoun, Abraham Lincoln, Daniel Webster, William Jennings Bryan, Franklin Delano Roosevelt, and John Fitzgerald Kennedy still stir within our history books and provide a rhythmic record of our past, our thoughts, our concerns, our challenges, and our dreams.

When future historians write the story of the twentieth century, another name will be added to the list of great orators—the name of Ronald Wilson Reagan, a man whose ability to touch the hearts and minds of his audience has made him one of the most popular presidents of all time. Politics aside, whether the audience is ultraconservative or ultraliberal, the rhetorical Reagan is a man the audience loves. His warm and sensitive personality, his quick wit, and his ability to touch his listener one-on-one, despite the size of the audience, are gifts coveted by any politician. They are gifts that have caused him to be dubbed the Great Communicator.

President Reagan understands his strength. He knows he is most effective when he goes directly to the public, bypassing the media, a necessary but obstructive third party that lives on sound bites, stripping the eloquence in search of the essence. For this reason, he initiated the White House radio series on April 3, 1982, a series that, in his own words, "permits me to talk directly to people. There is nothing between us—no editors, no reporters, no third parties of any kind."

Of course, President Reagan is no stranger to the medium. Fifty-five years ago he entered the young but growing field of broadcasting as an announcer for WOC in Davenport, Iowa. Since then, he has called radio a part of his life, feeling as comfortable behind the microphone as he is atop a horse. Like Franklin Roosevelt, whose fireside chats in the 1930s and 1940s encouraged America out of the Great Depression and nursed it through World War II, Ronald Reagan knows the power of radio. His experience has taught him that radio is the theater of the mind, forcing the audience to become a part of the creative process and giving him the ability to open the imagination of his listener and establish a common ground. And besides, he is often quick to remind, no one can argue back.

However, his broadcasts have not been immune to criticism. More than once the president has found himself planted in controversy due to a pre-broadcast joke or an ad-libbed phrase. Whether he called the nation's economy "a hell of a mess," or labeled the Polish government "a bunch of no-good lousy bums," none of his ad-libs caused as furious an explosion of criticism as the infamous joke he told about signing legislation to outlaw Russia forever. "Bombing will begin in five minutes," he said, when the microphone was turned on but he was not yet on the air. The joke was picked up by the radio pool that was preparing to transmit to other stations, and by Monday morning everyone in America had heard it.

I have a special regard for the White House radio series. In the president's first address, delivered at 12:06 P.M. from the Oval Office, he talked about the Roth-Kemp Tax Plan that had passed Congress a few months earlier to cut 25 percent in income taxes for individual Americans over three years. He reported to the nation that, even at that early date, the economic response to those cuts was encouraging: "interest rates have been reduced by 20 percent," he said, and "our greatest success has been in conquering inflation. It's no longer double digit. For the last 5 months, it's been running at 4½ percent."

But in my mind, that was only one of many memorable five-minute broadcasts that I have listened to over the years. Each one—whether it was used to solicit support for his foreign policy initiatives, to report to the nation on the condition of his health, or to clarify what he considered to be misinterpreted news reports—sparked a different emotional response. Sometimes I agreed. Sometimes I did not. But I always understood what he was trying to say.

The president's April 7, 1984 address, outlining America's foreign policy challenges and what must be done to meet them, stands out as one of the best and most easily understood overviews and explanations of an otherwise complex subject. In his optimistic eloquence, he outlined the four challenges: reduce the risk of nuclear war; bring great stability to regions riddled by terrorism and revolutionary violence; deal with an international economy crippled by soaring inflation rates, low growth, and predictions of imminent global depression; and restore bipartisan support for a foreign policy that would allow America to meet its responsibilities. Once outlined, he offered a clear explanation of what was being done by the government to meet the challenges, the progress made, and even the remaining deficiencies.

Another memorable program took place October 2, 1982, when the president was joined by the First Lady, and they turned the nation's mind to the war against drug abuse. He outlined the federal drug policy that coordinated for the first time nine departments and thirty-three agencies within the government that deal with narcotics. "We've decided to do more than pay lip service to the problem," he said. "The results of our task force have been dramatic...drug related arrests [in south Florida where the task force was initiated] are up over 40 percent, the amount of marijuana seized is up about 80 percent, and the amount of cocaine seized has more than doubled. The important thing is we're hurting the traffickers. It's true that when we close off one place they can move somewhere else. But one thing is different now: We're going to be waiting for them. To paraphrase Joe Louis, they can run but they can't hide."

As with all of his speeches, President Reagan is most effective when he allows his warmth and compassion to surface in his effort to make a point. As historians have said of Demosthenes, a man still considered to be one of the greatest orators of all time, he was great not only because of his style but also because of his character. And it is over the radio that the president can allow his character, filled with idealism and patriotism and optimism, to touch the listening audience and provoke the emotional experience which often ends in tears. The human condition has only a bright future when President Reagan speaks. A case in point was his Christmas Day radio address, 1982. In that five-minute span of time, he read a letter from a sailor, aboard the aircraft carrier *Midway,* to his parents. It was a short and simple story about freedom, but it was told with such emotion that the spirit of the broadcast, and more importantly the message, carried throughout the day and lingers even now.

President Reagan speaks not only to be heard but also to be felt. Whether his success is born of his professional training as an actor, by his early years of communicating with the public over radio stations WOC in Davenport or WHO in Des Moines, or from his congenial personality that establishes an immediate bond between himself and those who come in contact with him, he is one of the most skilled political speakers of our generation. And this skill, combined with his weekly radio addresses, has endeared him to his country. And, as he so eloquently puts it, this is good: "after all, a young fellow like me has to keep his name before the public."

William V. Roth, Jr.
U.S. Senator from Delaware
February 1987

CHRONOLOGY

The chronology is provided to enable the reader to relate current events to topics in the radio addresses.

1982

January 7 — President Reagan decides to continue the registration of young men for possible military conscription.

January 8 — The Bureau of Labor Statistics announces that unemployment rose from 8.4% to 8.9% during December. More than 460,000 people were laid off, bringing the total unemployed to 9,462,000. Among blacks, the unemployment figure was 16.1%.

January 26 — In his State of the Union message, President Reagan promises to insist on his tax-cut proposal. He also proposes a major "new federalism" plan under which he would give states and cities more control over federal social programs.

January 28 — The Reagan administration declares that the United States will increase aid to El Salvador. The president certifies, as required by Congress, that the Salvadoran junta government has made progress in protecting human rights.

February 6 — In his budget message to Congress, President Reagan calls for a decrease in the social responsibilities of the government and an increase in the military strength of the nation.

February 11 — The Reagan administration drops its proposal to place the new MX intercontinental missiles in silos reinforced to withstand a nuclear attack.

February 25 — The Labor Department reports that the Consumer Price Index for January showed an increase of only 0.3%, the smallest since July 1980. Although the price of food increased, there were declines in the prices of gasoline, new cars, houses, and clothing.

March 3   President Reagan warns Congress that its proposals to rescind part of his tax cuts would result in a continuation of the recession.

March 5   According to the Bureau of Labor Statistics, unemployment rose to 8.8% during February. More than 9.5 million people were without jobs, an increase of 280,000 since January and 1.8 million more than during July 1981.

March 12   Producer prices fell 0.1% in February, the first drop since 1976.

March 22   The space shuttle *Columbia* is lifted into earth's orbit for the third time.

March 28   Salvadorans hold elections and choose the centrist Christian Democrat party led by Jose Napoleon Duarte.

April 2   Argentina and Great Britain begin a seventy-four-day war over the Falkland Islands.

                 The Labor Department announces that unemployment in March rose to 9%. Nearly 9.9 million people were out of work, the highest number since World War II. The unemployment for blacks was a record 18%.

April 21   The U.S. gross national product (GNP) for the first quarter of 1982 continues to fall, slowing the rate of inflation.

April 23   As a result of reductions in gasoline, food, and housing costs, the Bureau of Labor Statistics announces that consumer prices declined 0.3% in March, the first drop in almost seventeen years.

May 9   President Reagan proposes an arms reduction plan that calls for the United States and the Soviet Union to reduce one-third of their nuclear warheads on land- and sea-based ballistic missiles.

May 18   Soviet leader Leonid Brezhnev says that the Soviet Union is ready for arms reduction talks but that Reagan's plan is one-sided.

May 31   President Reagan announces that the United States and the Soviet Union will begin negotiations in Geneva on June 29 to discuss the limitation and reduction of strategic nuclear arms.

June 1
The unemployment rate rose 0.1% in May to 9.5% of the labor force.

June 2
President Reagan arrives in Paris for a nine-day European visit.

June 6
The Israeli army launches a massive invasion into Lebanon, aimed at eliminating the threat of Palestine Liberation Organization (PLO) terrorism on Israel's northern frontier.

June 12
In New York City an estimated 500,000 persons protest against nuclear arms, the largest demonstration in the city's history.

June 21
John Hinckley, Jr., is found not guilty by reason of insanity on all thirteen charges of shooting President Reagan and three others on March 30, 1981.

June 24
The leaders of the fight to ratify the Equal Rights Amendment (ERA) to the Constitution admit defeat.

June 25
Secretary of State Alexander M. Haig, Jr., resigns. President Reagan nominates George P. Shultz, former secretary of the treasury, to replace him.

July 2
The unemployment rate during June held at 9.5%; among black teenagers it rose to a record 52.6%.

July 19
The Census Bureau reports that the number of Americans officially classified as poor increased by 2.2 million (14%) in 1981, giving the country its highest rate since 1967. As established by the government, an income of $9,287 per year for a family of four is considered poverty level.

August 2
The unemployment rate in July rose to 9.8%, another post-World War II high. An estimated 10,790,000 people were without jobs, and the Bureau of Labor Statistics concluded that another 1.5 million discouraged Americans who have discontinued to job hunt were not included in this figure.

August 19
Both houses of Congress pass President Reagan's $98.3 billion tax bill. More than two-thirds of the revenue raised by this bill over the next three years will come from business, a reversal of the 1981 tax act which had reduced taxes on businesses.

August 20	The Soviet Union accepts the Reagan administration's offer to extend by one year its grain sale agreement.
September 2	The Bureau of Labor Statistics reports that in the week ending August 21 the number of Americans filing initial claims for unemployment benefits rose to 621,000. By mid-August, more than 4 million people had filed for unemployment benefits in 1982.
September 16	Israeli troops seal off the Shatila and Sabra Palestinian refugee camps in West Beirut. In the ensuing two days, hundreds of Palestinian men, women, and children are killed. The massacre followed the September 14 murder of Lebanese President-elect Bashir Gemayel.
October 6	The House of Representatives defeats an administration-backed proposal to amend the Constitution to require a balanced federal budget.
November 11	USSR General Secretary Brezhnev dies at age seventy-five. Yuri Andropov, former head of the Soviet internal security agency (KGB), succeeds him.
November 22	The president announces plans for the "dense pack" deployment near Cheyenne, Wyoming, of the MX missiles in order to modernize U.S. nuclear forces.
November 23	President Reagan agrees to support a $27.5-million program to create jobs by rebuilding the nation's roadways. It will be financed by a federal tax on gasoline.
December 1	Senator Edward M. Kennedy announces that he will not seek the Democratic presidential nomination in 1984.
December 3	The jobless rate climbs to 10.8%; in a labor force of 111 million, about 12 million are unemployed. Congressional leaders of both parties agree that creating jobs is the most important issue before Congress. House Speaker Thomas P. O'Neill and Senate Majority Leader Howard Baker both support a bill allocating $5.5 billion to repair the nation's roads, bridges, and urban transit systems. After almost a month of Senate debate, the bill is passed by both congressional houses on December 23 and sent to the president for his signature.
December 21	General Secretary Andropov proposes to reduce the number of Soviet intermediate-range missiles deployed in Europe. The United States rejects his proposal.

1983

January 3	President Reagan appoints a bipartisan panel to find new ways of basing the MX missile.
January 7	The Labor Department announces that unemployment averaged 9.7% for 1982.
January 11	The Defense Department reports a reduction of $8 billion, or 3%, in the defense budget for the 1984 fiscal year, which nevertheless shows a 14.2% increase over fiscal 1983. Most of the increase is planned for weapons production and research.
January 15	The National Commission on Social Security announces a program for saving the system from bankruptcy.
January 18	The Commerce Department discloses that housing starts declined 2.2% in 1982, to the lowest annual total since 1946, and that personal income rose 6.4% in 1982, the smallest gain since 1963. The GNP, adjusted for inflation, fell 1.8% in 1982, the greatest decline since 1946.
January 21	President Reagan certifies to Congress that El Salvador's government has shown progress in reducing human rights abuses and thus is eligible for additional U.S. military aid.
	Dun & Bradstreet figures showed that in the past year about 25,000 businesses had failed, an increase of 50% from 1981.
January 23	Howard Baker announces that he will not run for the Senate in 1984.
January 24	Price agreements within the Organization of Petroleum Exporting Countries (OPEC) begin to unravel. The prospect that oil prices will fall causes the Dow Jones Industrial Average to drop 22 points.
January 25	President Reagan delivers his State of the Union message.
January 26	The president proposes the abolishment of corporate income taxes.
	The ERA is reintroduced in the Senate.

February 1-6   More than 1,600 U.S. military personnel and 4,000 Honduran soldiers participate with Nicaragua in war games near the Honduran border. Nicaragua claims the exercise is in preparation for an invasion.

February 4   Unemployment in January fell 0.4% to 10.4%, the first decline in eighteen months.

February 7   Iran launches a major invasion of Iraq.

February 10   Vice-President George Bush returns to Washington after a twelve-day European trip. His goal was to obtain support for the projected deployment of U.S intermediate-range missiles in Europe.

February 16   The Commerce Department reports that housing starts in January jumped about 36%, the sharpest increase since records first were kept in 1959.

February 17   Senator Gary Hart announces his candidacy for the Democratic presidential nomination.

February 21   Former Vice-President Walter Mondale announces his candidacy for the Democratic presidential nomination.

February 22   President Reagan pledges border protection to Israel if its troops leave Lebanon.

February 26   The president proposes to decontrol natural gas by 1986.

March 1   Pope John Paul II begins a week-long trip to Central America.

March 2   The Commerce Department reports that sales of single-family homes rose 9.9% in January, the largest increase in twenty-eight months.

March 3   A $4.9-billion jobs bill is voted on by the House of Representatives.

                    The inflation rate for February remained at 10.4%.

March 9   Anne Burford resigns as administrator of the Environmental Protection Agency, while criticism of the agency continues.

March 11   The February unemployment rate remained at 10.2%.

March 14   For the first time in its twenty-three-year history, OPEC agrees to cut oil prices.

March 17 The Senate approves the jobs bill, which is expected to create 400,000 jobs in the construction industry and in public service organizations and to provide day-care and home health-related services.

March 24 The House of Representatives passes the compromise bipartisan bill to rescue the Social Security system from bankruptcy, with the hope that the system now will remain solvent for at least seventy-five years.

April 4 The space shuttle *Challenger* is launched for the first time.

April 11 A commission appointed by President Reagan announces its proposals for the production and basing of the MX missile. The president endorses the commission's proposals, stating that the Soviet Union would have no motivation to negotiate arms reduction agreements unless the United States modernizes its land-based missile systems.

April 18 A massive explosion destroys the U.S. embassy in Beirut, killing forty-seven persons and injuring more than one hundred; sixteen Americans are among the dead. A radical Iranian group claims responsibility.

April 20 The Commerce Department reports a 3.1% rise in the GNP for the first quarter of 1983.

President Reagan signs the Social Security rescue bill into law.

April 26 The Dow Jones average closes above 1200 for the first time.

April 27 President Reagan takes an unusual step and addresses a joint session of Congress on a foreign policy issue. He appeals for approval of his requests for economic and military aid to Central America. The president draws heavy applause when he states that he has no intention of sending U.S. combat troops to the area.

May 6 Israel and Lebanon reach an agreement for the withdrawal of Israeli troops from Lebanon, but Israeli acceptance of the U.S.-mediated plan is conditioned on agreement by Syria.

The Dow Jones average reaches another all-time high of
1232. Economic data released shows that economic recovery continues at a steady pace.

May 13   Syrian President Hafez Assad rejects the U.S. plan and
refuses to remove his troops from Lebanon.

June 2   Meeting in Brussels, NATO defense ministers reaffirm
their commitment to the deployment of U.S. intermediate-
range nuclear missiles in Europe, unless the United States
and the Soviet Union reach an agreement in the arms
reduction talks by December.

June 3   The Labor Department reports that unemployment fell
to 10% in May.

June 10   The Commerce Department reports that retail sales
increased a sharp 2.1% in May.

June 15   The U.S. Supreme Court reaffirms its 1973 ruling in *Roe
v. Wade*, which gave women unrestricted rights to abor-
tions in the first trimester of pregnancy. The next day
President Reagan criticizes this decision and calls for legislation to "restore legal protection for the unborn."

June 16   The Commerce Department announces that housing
starts climbed 19.1% in May.

General Secretary Andropov is elected president of the
Soviet Union.

June 18   President Reagan announces the reappointment of Paul
Volcker as chairman of the Federal Reserve Board.

Sally Ride becomes the first American woman to travel
in space when the *Challenger* is launched on its second
flight.

June 20   The Commerce Department reports that personal income for all Americans rose 1.2% in May and that consumer spending jumped 1.4%.

June 23   The Supreme Court rules that the "legislative veto" is
unconstitutional.

June 24- Vice-President Bush travels to Europe to firm up allied
July 7   support for U.S. positions on arms talks. His motorcade
is pelted with rocks thrown by persons opposing the

deployment of U.S missiles in Europe, and more than 20,000 demonstrate near his hotel.

June 28	President Reagan announces that his administration is raising its forecast of economic growth from 4.7% to 5.5% for the fourth quarter of 1983.
	The Senate defeats a proposed constitutional amendment that would permit states and Congress to restrict access to all abortions.
July 5	In a visit to the Soviet Union, Chancellor Helmut Kohl of West Germany is warned by Soviet leaders not to permit the planned deployment in his country of U.S. medium-range nuclear missiles.
July 6	The Supreme Court rules that an employer-sponsored retirement plan cannot pay women lower monthly pension benefits than it pays men.
July 8	Unemployment fell to 9.8% in June; however, the black unemployment rate remained at a near record high of 20.6%.
July 12	President Reagan proposes a constitutional amendment to permit prayer in public schools.
July 18	The president announces that he will create a commission, headed by former Secretary of State Henry Kissinger, to recommend long-term U.S. policies in Central America.
July 20	The House of Representatives approves funds for the development of the MX missile, followed by the Senate's approval on July 26.
July 21	The GNP rose at an annual rate of 8.7% during the second quarter of 1983.
	Reagan seeks to give assurances that the military activities in Nicaragua are routine, although they surpass in scale any previous training exercises in the area.
July 28	Congress votes to repeal legislation passed in 1982 that authorized withholding for taxes of 10% on interest and dividend income.
	The United States and the Soviet Union agree on terms for a new five-year grain purchase deal.

July 29   The Commerce Department announces that the index of
                 leading economic indicators rose 1% in June, the tenth
                 straight monthly advance. In addition, the U.S. trade
                 deficit fell in June after reaching a record high in May.

August 1   The White House cancels a tour by delegates to the con-
                 vention of the International Federation of Business and
                 Professional Women. On the following day, the president
                 personally apologizes to the delegates, but some find his
                 remarks to be degrading and inappropriate.

                 President Reagan creates a study group to investigate the
                 situation of 34.4 million Americans (about 15% of the
                 total population) living in poverty, according to data
                 released by the Census Bureau. A family of four with an
                 income of less than $9,862 is defined as below the pov-
                 erty line; the median income for a family in 1982 was
                 $23,430.

August 8   A military coup in Guatemala ousts President Efrain
                 Rios Montt after seventeen months in office.

August 18   Soviet President Andropov announces a unilateral mora-
                 torium on the deployment of antisatellite weapons.

August 19   The Commerce Department reports that corporate prof-
                 its jumped 14.7% in the second quarter of 1983.

August 21   Benigno Aquino, Jr., leader of the political opposition to
                 President Ferdinand Marcos, is shot to death on his
                 arrival in the Philippines from exile in the United States.

                 Barbara Honegger, a special assistant in the Department
                 of Justice, severely criticizes the Reagan administration's
                 record on women's rights.

August 23   Maureen Reagan, the president's daughter, is hired by
                 the Republican National Committee to help improve the
                 president's image among women.

August 27   The twentieth anniversary of the 1983 March on Wash-
                 ington, led by the Rev. Martin Luther King, Jr., is com-
                 memorated by another march in the capital city. More
                 than 250,000 walk for "jobs, peace, and freedom."

August 28   Prime Minister Menachem Begin of Israel announces
                 that he plans to retire.

August 29	President Andropov says that the Soviet Union is prepared to dismantle all missiles it removed from Europe if the Geneva talks on reducing the number of intermediate-range missiles in Europe end successfully.
August 30	The space shuttle *Challenger* is launched on its third mission and carries aloft the first American black astronaut, Air Force Lt. Col. Guion Bluford.
September 1	The Soviet Union shoots down a South Korean KAL airliner. Worldwide indignation, revulsion, and condemnation of the USSR follows news of the deaths of all 269 persons aboard. President Reagan calls the incident a massacre and announces several minor punitive measures against the Soviet Union. U.S.-Soviet relations reached a new low as each nation hurled charges against the other.
September 19	For the first time, two U.S. Navy ships shell Moslem positions in the hills above Beirut.
September 20	Congressional leaders and the Reagan administration agree to a compromise based on the War Powers Resolution that would allow the administration to keep U.S. troops in Lebanon for eighteen months.
September 30	The National Education Association endorses Walter Mondale for president. On the following day, he also is endorsed by the AFL-CIO.
October 3	As unrest in the Philippines continues, President Reagan postpones his scheduled November trip to that nation.
October 4	The three major automobile companies announce that sales increased almost 17% during the 1983 model year.
October 5	Lech Walesa, founder of the Solidarity union movement in Poland, wins the 1983 Nobel Peace Prize.
October 6	An unidentified American official says that the Soviet Union is preparing to deploy a mobile missile in Syria which would be capable of reaching targets in Lebanon, Israel, and the Mediterranean Sea.
October 7	Syrian-backed Palestinian rebels gain the upper hand over PLO leader Yasir Arafat. The rebels are preparing to drive Arafat from his stronghold near Tripoli.
	The unemployment rate declined to 9.3% in September.

October 10	The Dow Jones average reaches another all-time high of 1284.
October 13	President Reagan gives his approval for the formation of a committee to work on behalf of his reelection.
	The Commerce Department announces that retail sales increased 1.6% in September.
October 14	William Clark, President Reagan's national security advisor, is named to replace James Watt as secretary of the interior.
October 21	Huge antimissile protests take place throughout Europe.
October 23	A bomb blast in Beirut kills 241 Marines. This is the second worst disaster in Marine Corps history, second only to losses at Iwo Jima in World War II. Radical Iranian terrorists are believed to be responsible.
October 25	The United States invades Grenada.
November 2	President Reagan signs a bill declaring the birthday of Martin Luther King, Jr., a federal holiday.
November 3	The Rev. Jesse Jackson announces his candidacy for the Democratic presidential nomination.
November 4	The unemployment rate dropped to 8.8% for October.
November 7	A bomb explodes in the Capitol building in Washington, D.C.
November 8	President Reagan leaves for a six-day visit to Japan and South Korea.
November 14	American cruise missiles, the first in Europe, arrive at a U.S. air base west of London and provoke outcries from antinuclear protestors.
November 15	The ERA amendment fails to pass the House of Representatives.
November 20	More than 100 million adults watch the ABC television movie "The Day After," which depicts the nuclear annihilation of Kansas City and the nightmarish aftermath.
November 22	The twentieth anniversary of John F. Kennedy's assassination is marked by remembrances throughout the nation.

| December 2 | The unemployment rate dropped to 8.4% in November, a two-year low. |

December 4 — Targets in Syria are bombed by U.S. planes. Two aircraft are shot down, and an American naval flier, Robert Goodman, is taken prisoner by the Syrians.

Eight Marines are killed in Lebanon.

December 12 — The U.S. embassy in Kuwait is attacked; seven persons are killed and more than sixty are injured.

December 13 — American ships attack Syrian positions near Beirut.

A presidential commission urges twenty-one as the national drinking age.

December 14 — The USS *New Jersey* shells Syrian antiaircraft positions.

December 15 — The Reagan administration agrees to give Israel $1.4 billion in military aid during 1984.

The last American combat troops leave Grenada.

December 17 — Members of the PLO begin evacuation from Tripoli on Italian ships.

December 29 — The United States formally announces its intention to withdraw from the United Nations Educational, Scientific, and Cultural Organization (UNESCO).

Jesse Jackson leaves for Syria to negotiate the release of the captured American flier.

1984

January 3 — The Federal Deposit Insurance Corporation reports that forty-eight federally insured banks failed in 1983, the highest total since 1939.

January 5 — Commerce Department figures show that all but one of the nation's largest retailers gained 10% or more in sales during December 1983, compared with December 1982. Sears, Roebuck and Company, the largest U.S. retailer, reported an increase of 17.5%.

Sales of automobiles in 1983, including imports, increased by 15.1% over 1982.

January 6	The Labor Department announces that the unemployment rate continued downward to 8.1% in December.
January 11	The Kissinger Commission endorses most of the Reagan policies in Central America.
January 12	The United States and China sign agreements on industrial cooperation.
January 13	The Labor Department announces that prices paid by producers for finished goods rose only 0.6% in 1983, the smallest increase since 1964. Credit was given to the sharp decline in energy prices.
	The Federal Reserve Board reports that industrial production averaged 6.5% higher in 1983 than in 1982.
January 16	President Reagan calls for the resumption of arms talks with the Soviet Union.
January 18	The Commerce Department discloses that housing starts in 1983 increased 60.3% from 1982's depressed level.
January 19	Real personal income, adjusted for inflation, rose 3.2% in 1983, while the GNP climbed to an annual rate of 4.5% during the fourth quarter.
	The National Urban League reports that the economic circumstances of black Americans declined in 1983, stating that black unemployment was more than twice as much as white unemployment, that 42% of black families were headed by single mothers, and that one-third of all blacks were living in poverty.
January 29	President Reagan announces that he will seek reelection in 1984 and also asks for the renomination of Vice-President Bush.
February 1	The president submits a $925.5-billion budget to Congress which was $180.4 billion out of balance. The budget for the 1985 fiscal year beginning October 1, 1984, included a proposed 14.5% increase in defense spending.
February 3	The Labor Department reports that the unemployment rate in January fell to 7.9%.

| February 8 | The growing deficit problem is credited to a 10% decline in the Dow Jones average. |

February 8   The growing deficit problem is credited to a 10% decline in the Dow Jones average.

February 9   Soviet President Andropov dies. Konstantin Chernenko succeeds him.

February 17   President Reagan proposes increased American aid to U.S.-supported governments in Central America.

February 21   The president begins to remove Marines from Beirut and to place them on ships offshore. Reagan acted as the position of President Amin Gemayel deteriorated and his army crumbled.

February 28   Senator Hart upsets former Vice-President Mondale in the New Hampshire primary. President Reagan receives 86% of the votes in the Republican primary.

March 9   Unemployment in February declined to 7.7%.

March 13   Senator Hart wins Democratic primaries in Massachusetts, Rhode Island, and Florida, while Mondale wins in Georgia and Alabama. The results force Senator John Glenn and former Senator George McGovern to withdraw from the race. Jackson finishes third in Georgia and Florida, saying he will remain in the race.

March 15   The Senate rejects an amendment to permit silent prayer in public schools.

The Federal Reserve Board states that industrial production rose by 1.2% in February, while housing starts jumped 11.2%.

March 19   The U.S. balance of payments showed a record deficit of $40 billion in 1983.

March 30   President Reagan formally ends U.S. participation in the multi-nation Lebanese peace-keeping force.

April 5   Major banks increase their prime lending rate from 11.5% to 12%, the highest level since October 1982.

The Senate approves additional military aid to El Salvador and for the anti-Sandinista rebels in Nicaragua.

April 6   Unemployment for March was 7.7%, virtually unchanged from recent months.

               Reports surface that the Central Intelligence Agency (CIA) has participated in the mining of Nicaraguan harbors.

April 9   Nicaragua asks the International Court of Justice to order the United States to halt the mining. The Reagan administration says it will not accept the court's jurisdiction on disputes involving Latin America for two years.

April 10   Administration economists estimate that the real GNP will grow by 5% in 1984.

April 11   Reports appear that President Reagan has approved the decision to mine Nicaraguan ports.

April 19   The Commerce Department discloses that the economy grew at an annual rate of 8.3% during the first quarter of 1984, a sharp increase from the 5% rate in the previous quarter.

April 26   President Reagan begins a five-day visit to China.

April 30   With 1,967 votes needed for the Democratic nomination, Mondale has 1,075, Hart 575, Jackson 150; 275 support others or are uncommitted.

May 4   Unemployment held steady at 7.7% in April.

May 7   José Napoleon Duarte, a political moderate, is elected president of El Salvador.

May 8   The Soviet Union announces it will not participate in the summer Olympic Games in Los Angeles.

               Major banks boost their prime lending rate from 12% to 12.5%.

May 17   The Senate supports the Reagan administration's plan to cut federal budget deficits.

May 19   Duarte begins a four-day visit to the United States to meet President Reagan and members of Congress. He appeals for additional military aid, and he pledges to end death squad activities in El Salvador.

May 20   Soviet Defense Minister Dimitri Ustinov announces that the USSR has increased the number of submarines carrying nuclear missiles off the coasts of the United States as a countermeasure to the deployment of U.S. missiles in Europe.

May 28	President Reagan leads a Memorial Day tribute to an unidentified U.S. serviceman killed in the Vietnam War.
May 30	The U.S. trade deficit sets another record in April at $12.2 billion.
June 1	Unemployment fell to 7.4% in April.
June 2	President Reagan visits Ireland.
June 5	Mondale wins the key New Jersey primary and also West Virginia; Hart carries the California, New Mexico, and South Dakota primaries. Mondale claims that he has enough delegates to win a first-ballot victory at the Democratic convention.
June 6	Leaders of eight nations participate in ceremonies commemorating the fortieth anniversary of D-day.
June 15	The Federal Reserve Board reports that industrial production advanced 0.4% in May.
June 25	Major banks raise their prime interest rate from 12.5% to 13%. The U.S. dollar sets or approaches record highs in relation to major foreign currencies.
June 28	Congress approves a plan to bring pressure on the states to raise the legal drinking age to twenty-one.
July 6	Unemployment fell to 7.0% in June.
July 12	Mondale announces that he has asked Representative Geraldine Ferraro to be the Democratic candidate for vice-president. Never before has a major party nominated a woman for such a high office. By announcing his choice before the convention, Mondale broke another precedent.
July 18	The Democratic convention nominates Mondale as its presidential candidate.
July 19	The Democratic convention nominates Ferraro as its candidate for vice-president. Mondale calls for a "new realism" in public life and warns that taxes will have to go up.

July 23   The Commerce Department says that the GNP rose by an impressive 7.5% during the second quarter of 1984.

July 24   President Reagan announces he has no plans to raise taxes.

July 28   The Olympic Games open in Los Angeles.

August 2   The Census Bureau reports that the nation's poverty level edged upward to 15.3% in 1983, the highest level since 1965, and that the number of poor people totaled 35.3 million.

August 3   The unemployment rate for July rose slightly to 7.4%.

                 The stock market concludes the week with the heaviest trading volume ever. The Dow Jones average rose 87.46 points, setting another record.

August 4   President Reagan charges that Mondale, if elected, will raise taxes by $1500 per household. The president proposes no personal tax increases if reelected.

August 8   Congress approves additional economic and military aid for Central America.

August 11   While testing a radio microphone, President Reagan jokes about outlawing the Soviet Union, saying that "bombing will begin in five minutes."

                 The president signs into law an act to prohibit high schools from barring students who wish to assemble for religious or political activities outside school hours.

August 22   Reagan and Bush are renominated by the Republican convention.

September 3   In southern California, President Reagan starts his campaign by saying that, if reelected, America's message to the world would be: "You ain't seen nothing yet."

September 7   The unemployment rate continued at 7.4% in August.

September 10   Mondale unveils his proposals for cutting the federal deficit by increasing taxes.

September 12   The House Ethics Committee votes unanimously to investigate charges that Ferraro has violated congressional standards by claiming an exemption from the requirement that she disclose her spouse's finances.

Reagan declares that Mondale's plan to cut budget deficits will increase taxes for "working families all across America" and adds that, whereas "we see an America where every day is the Fourth of July, they see an America where every day is April 15."

September 17   Mondale says he will make war and peace a major issue and charges that Reagan has made the world more dangerous.

September 20   The Commerce Department announces that the third-quarter GNP rose 3.6%, about one-half the rate for the second quarter.

A suicide bomber drives a station wagon to the front of the U.S. embassy annex in Beirut and detonates 400 pounds of TNT. The explosion kills two Americans and scores of Lebanese.

September 28   For the first time, Reagan meets with a major Soviet leader—Foreign Minister Andrei Gromyko—at the White House. No known progress is made on issues dividing the superpowers.

October 2   Raymond Donovan, secretary of labor, pleads not guilty to a 137-count indictment charging him in an attempt to defraud the New York City Transit Authority.

October 5   The unemployment rate remained at 7.3% for September.

October 7   Reagan and Mondale meet in Louisville, Kentucky, for their first televised debate, consisting of responses to questions posed by journalists.

October 11   Bush and Ferraro debate in Philadelphia.

October 21   With foreign affairs the subject, Reagan and Mondale hold their second debate, this time in Kansas City.

November 6   President Reagan wins a record-breaking reelection victory, carrying forty-nine states and receiving 525 electoral votes. He wins 59% of the popular vote to 41% for Mondale.

November 21   The United States and the Soviet Union agree to send high-level disarmament teams to Geneva in early 1985.

U.S.-Nicaraguan talks aimed at reducing tensions end. No positive results are reported.

November 27   Secretary of the Treasury Donald Regan announces plans for a complete revision of the income tax law, the most encompassing since 1913.

November 28   Senator Robert Dole is elected Senate Majority Leader.

November 29   Secretary of Defense Caspar Weinberger says U.S. military forces will not be drawn gradually into combat in Central America, but, if American forces are committed anywhere, it would be with the clear intention of winning.

December 20   Prices at the consumer level rose two-thirds of 1% during November, the smallest increase since June. With only the December report to come, 1984 is almost certain to be the third consecutive year in which inflation was held to about 4%.

HIGHLIGHTS IN THE LIFE OF RONALD REAGAN

1911   Born on February 6 in Tampico, Illinois, the son of John and Nelle Reagan.

1920   Moved with his family to Dixon, Illinois, ninety miles west of Chicago.

1932   Graduated from Eureka College, Eureka, Illinois, where he was a three-letter man in football and captain of the swimming team. He earned a Bachelor of Arts degree in economics and sociology.

Hired as a $10-per-game, play-by-play baseball announcer at radio station WOC in Davenport, Iowa.

1933   Became a full-time sportscaster at radio station WHO in Des Moines, Iowa.

1937   Went to California to cover the Chicago Cubs spring training and signed an acting contract with Warner Brothers. Reagan made his film debut playing a radio announcer in *Love Is on the Air.*

1940   Married Jane Wyman.

Portrayed George Gipp in *Knute Rockne, All American,* one of the president's favorite movie roles.

1941   Daughter Maureen is born.

1942   Appeared in *King's Row,* the high point of his film career.

1942-1945   Served in the U.S. Army Air Corps, attaining the rank of captain.

1945   Adopted a son, Michael.

1947   Elected to the first of six terms as president of the Screen Actors' Guild.

1948   Marriage to Jane Wyman ends in divorce.

1950   Campaigned for Helen Gahagan Douglas in her unsuccessful Senate race against Richard Nixon.

1952   Married Nancy Davis on March 4.

Daughter Patricia is born.

| 1954- | Served as the host of *General Electric Theater* on television and the |
| 1962 | spokesman for General Electric's personnel-relations program. Reagan spoke at the company's facilities all over the country on the merits of free enterprise versus big government. |

1958   Son Ronald is born.

1962   Switched political affiliation from the Democratic to the Republican party.

1964   Made his final film appearance in *The Killers*.

Co-chaired Californians for Goldwater for President. Reagan gained national attention in October through his televised "A Time to Choose" address on behalf of candidate Barry Goldwater.

1965   Published his autobiography, *Where's the Rest of Me?*.

1966   Elected governor of California.

1968   Made a last-minute run for the Republican presidential nomination but was defeated by Richard Nixon.

1970   Reelected to a second term as governor of California.

1975- / 1979   Formed a political action committee, Citizens for the Republic, in which he helped eighty-six other candidates with their campaigns. He began a radio program and wrote a newspaper column.

1976   Narrowly defeated by President Gerald Ford for the Republican presidential nomination.

1979   Announced his candidacy for president.

1980   Won the Republican nomination for president, with George Bush as his running mate.

Elected president on November 4, defeating incumbent Jimmy Carter.

1981   Sworn in on January 20 as the 40th President of the United States.

Economic Recovery Program

My fellow Americans:

I'd like to take a few minutes of your time to talk about some of the problems we face in this blessed land of ours and what I feel we should do about them. I can't cover all that territory in 5 minutes, so I'll be back every Saturday at this same time, same station, live. I hope you'll tune in.

These aren't easy times for a great many of you. Yesterday we were told that unemployment has gone up another two-tenths of 1 percent—equal to the unemployment rate we had in 1975 as we began to come out of that recession.

We can, however, take some comfort from the fact that 99½ million of our people are employed. Now, I know that's no comfort to those who want to work and can't find a job. And it's no comfort to farmers, independent business people, auto dealers, realtors, and building contractors who see themselves going out of business. These people want answers—and so do you—about what we can do to get our economy back on track.

The last recession before this one came in 1980. And by the time our administration took office, unemployment had almost reached 8 million, the prime rate had reached 21½ percent—the highest in more than a century—and inflation was at 12.4 percent. According to the polls, inflation was the number-one problem in everyone's mind. All of us associated it with the high interest rates, and rightly so. A lender must charge an interest rate high enough to cover inflation as well as give a return on his or her money.

We proposed a program of economic recovery based on the belief that high taxes had deprived people and business of incentive to the point that we'd lost much of our ability to produce. Those high taxes had fueled a rate of increase in government spending that reached 17 percent in 1980 alone. Even high taxes couldn't keep up with that. In the few years between 1976 and 1981, Federal tax revenues increased by $300 billion—but we had $318 billion in deficits.

So, our program also aimed at reducing the rate of increase in government spending. Unfortunately, the interest rate stayed up even though we began to reduce inflation. People couldn't afford to buy automobiles on time. Few could or would take a mortgage to buy or build a home at those rates. Layoffs in the automobile and construction industries increased, and farmers who borrowed to plant and repay at harvest lost money even on bumper crops. By mid-July, we were back in, if we were ever out of, a recession. But for the first time in the many recessions that have taken place over the recent years, we had a plan ready to go.

The Congress had agreed to a budget that cut the rate of increase in spending nearly in half. And it passed a tax-cut program which increased depreciation allowances for business and began a 25-percent cut in income tax rates for individuals, to be phased in over 3 years.

All of this only began last October 1st. Even so, interest rates have been reduced by 20 percent, but that's not nearly enough. They have to come down more, and they should, because our greatest success has been in conquering inflation. It's no longer double digit. For the last 5 months, it's been running at 4½ percent.

By all the rules of the game, interest rates should be down around 9 or 10 percent. Unfortunately, the increase in unemployment increased government costs and reduced revenues. More money had to be spent on unemployment insurance and other benefits. Fewer people working meant fewer people paying taxes. Up went the projected deficit for 1983, and up went the concern in the money market that this would lead to an increase in inflation, as it has in all those past recessions.

The answer to the recession lies in bringing interest rates down. To do that, a signal must be sent that, while the political process always requires some compromise, government this time intends to stay the course; that we're going to make further reductions in spending and hold to a steady, consistent growth in the money supply—in short, that we're going to come out of this recession not with a temporary, quick fix that leads to another recession down the road, but with a solid economic recovery based on increased productivity and jobs for our people.

Now, I know you've been told by some that we should do away with the tax cuts in order to reduce the deficit. That's like trying to pull a game out in the fourth quarter by punting on the third down.

You've also been told our program hasn't worked. Well, of course it hasn't; it hasn't really started yet. Our 5-percent cut in October was almost wiped out by the January increase in the Social Security tax called for in the 1977 tax bill. The reduced budget spending and the 10-percent tax cut in July will be the real beginning of our program.

There's no instant cure, but there is a cure. With your help and your prayers, we'll find it.

I'll be back next Saturday. Thank you, and God bless you.

Note: The President spoke at 12:06 P.M. EST from the Oval Office at the White House.

Caribbean Basin Initiative/Student Loans

April 10, 1982

My fellow Americans:

I'm speaking to you today from Bridgetown, capital of Barbados, the easternmost nation in a chain of beautiful islands in the Caribbean sea that swings south from the tip of Florida in an arc all the way to the shores of South America.

This Caribbean Basin is our third border. Through it come two-thirds of all our imported oil and over half the strategic minerals we need to import for industry and our national defense. As John Adams once said of these islands, "They can neither do without us nor we without them."

I came down here to discuss with some of the leaders of these island nations what we can do about problems we have in common. Wednesday, in Jamaica, I met with Prime Minister Seaga, the Governor General, members of the Cabinet and of Parliament. Day before yesterday, we flew here to Barbados for meetings with Prime Minister Adams, the Governor General, and leaders of five other eastern Caribbean nations. We took yesterday, Good Friday, off. And tomorrow we'll go to church and then fly back to Washington.

On March 17th, I sent the Congress a proposal for a Caribbean Initiative, a plan for trade, aid, and private investment aimed at strengthening the economies of these islands and the countries of Central America bordering on the Caribbean. We're joined in this effort by Mexico, Canada, Venezuela, and Colombia. I believe our plan is sound and in our best interest as well as theirs.

The meetings were worthwhile. And I'm looking forward to hearing from the congressional delegation which has been visiting some of the other islands while we're here.

There are other problems in the Americas. Two of our friends, the United Kingdom and Argentina, confront each other in a complex disagreement which goes back many generations. Because they're both our friends, I've offered our help in an effort to bring the two countries together. Secretary Haig has completed a visit to London and is now in Buenos Aires. We'll do all we can to help bring [*sic*] a peaceful resolution of this matter.

But now I'd like to take a few minutes to talk about a domestic problem. There's obviously a great misconception on the part of many young people with regard to the program of college grants and guaranteed loans and what we're doing with that program in the 1983 budget.

On many campuses, students are being told they may not be able to return to school next year. In some instances, they've even been incited to stage protest demonstrations against what have been called "Draconian cuts" in student aid. One columnist has written, evidently without checking, that

1982   **3**

millions of American youngsters won't go to college next fall because their government is snatching away grants and subsidized loans. Well, a lot of people have simply been misled.

It is true that the amount for guaranteed student loans will decrease from $2.7 billion this year to $2.4 billion in 1983, but not one dime of the money being cut has ever gone directly for loans to students. The actual loans that students receive under this program come from private banks and don't show up in the budget at all. If they did, they'd show the highest level ever—$1.6 billion more in student loan awards in fiscal 1983 than this year.

We haven't cut loans. We've cut the cost to taxpayers of making these loans available. Surely no one can quarrel with the reduction in administrative costs that results in more money for needy students.

About 44 percent of all enrolled college students will receive aid, and undergraduate students who demonstrate need will be eligible for a veritable laundry list of help—up to a $1,600 grant and up to a $2,500 guaranteed loan; work-study support, averaging $700 a year. A parent, regardless of wealth or income, will still be able to borrow up to an additional $3,000 a year. Graduate students will still be able to borrow up to $8,000 a year.

We've taken steps to provide greater aid for students from lower income families. The percentage of students from families earning $12,000 or less, receiving grants, will increase from 64 percent this year to about 75 percent. And the loans outstanding in the Guaranteed Student Loan program, available to future students, will increase by more than $10 billion next year—actually $10.1 billion.

In 1983 more than 4½ million students will receive aid from guaranteed student loans, and that's just one of the programs—a 22-percent increase over this year. All told, there will be 7 million grants and loans for a student population of between 11 and 14 million, if you include even the part-time students.

Well, I'll be back next Saturday. Thank you. And Happy Easter, and God bless you.

Note: The President spoke at 1:06 P.M. (Local) from Casa de Pablo, a private home owned by Paul H. Brandt, president and chairman of the board of A. Brandt Co., Inc., of Fort Worth, Texas, where he stayed during his visit to Barbados.

Nuclear Weapons

April 17, 1982

My fellow Americans:

Throughout our history and particularly in recent years, America's taken on an ever-increasing role as peacemaker—taking the initiative time after time to try to help countries settle their differences peacefully. I don't need to recite the list of diplomatic efforts spanning all administrations in which we've been instrumental in ending war and restoring peace.

Yet, there are some who still ask which nation is the true peacemaker—the United States or the Soviet Union? Well, let us ask them, which country has nearly 100,000 troops trying to occupy the once nonaligned nation of Afghanistan? Which country has tried to crush a spontaneous workers' movement in Poland? And what country has engaged in the most massive arms buildup in history? Or, let's put the question another way. What country helped its World War II enemies back on their feet? What country is employing trade aid and technology to help the developing peoples of the world and actively seeking to bring peace to the Middle East, the South Atlantic, and to southern Africa?

The answer is clear, and it should give us both pride and hope in America. Today, I know there are a great many people who are pointing to the unimaginable horror of nuclear war. I welcome that concern. Those who've governed America throughout the nuclear age and we who govern it today have had to recognize that a nuclear war cannot be won and must never be fought.

So, to those who protest against nuclear war, I can only say, "I'm with you." Like my predecessors, it is now my responsibility to do my utmost to prevent such a war. No one feels more than I the need for peace.

Throughout the first half of my lifetime, the entire world was engaged in war, or in recovering from war, or in preparing for war. Since the end of World War II, there's not been another world conflict. But there have been and are wars going on in various other parts of the world.

This stretch of 37 years since World War II has been the result of our maintaining a balance of power between the United States and the Soviet Union and between the strategic nuclear capabilities of either side. As long as this balance has been maintained, both sides have been given an overwhelming incentive for peace.

In the 1970's, the United States altered that balance by, in effect, unilaterally restraining our own military defenses while the Soviet Union engaged in an unprecedented buildup of both its conventional and nuclear forces.

As a result, the military balance which permitted us to maintain the peace is now threatened. If steps are not taken to modernize our defense, the

United States will progressively lose the ability to deter the Soviet Union from employing force or threats of force against us and against our allies.

It would be wonderful if we could restore our balance with the Soviet Union without increasing our own military power. And ideally, it would be a long step in ensuring peace if we could have significant and verifiable reductions of arms on both sides. But let's not fool ourselves. The Soviet Union will not come to any conference table bearing gifts. Soviet negotiators will not make unilateral concessions. To achieve parity, we must make it plain that we have the will to achieve parity by our own effort.

Many have been attracted to the idea of a nuclear freeze. Now, that would be fine if we were equal in strategic capability. We're not. We cannot accept an agreement which perpetuates current disparities.

The current level of nuclear forces is too high on both sides. It must be the objective of any negotiations on arms control to reduce the numbers of nuclear weapons.

Since World War II, the United States has attempted to get Soviet agreement to such reductions countless times. We began back when we alone had such weapons. We were never able to persuade the Soviet Union to join in such an understanding, even when we proposed turning all nuclear material and information over to an international body and when we were the only nation that had nuclear weapons.

We're preparing a new arms reduction effort with regard to strategic nuclear forces and are already in negotiations in Geneva on intermediate-range missiles threatening Europe. Our objective in these talks is for the elimination of such missiles on the strategic nuclear forces. We will aim on those at substantial reductions on both sides leading to equal and verifiable limits. We'll make every effort to reach an agreement that will reduce the possibility of nuclear war.

If we can do this, perhaps one day we can achieve a relationship with the Soviet Union which doesn't depend upon nuclear deterrents to secure Soviet restraint.

I invite the Soviet Union to take such a step with us. And I ask you, the American people, to support our efforts at negotiating an end to this threat of doomsday which hangs over the world.

Thank you, and God bless you.

Note: The President spoke at 12:06 P.M. EST from Camp David, Maryland.

Taxes, Tuition Tax Credits, and Interest Rates

April 24, 1982

My fellow Americans:

I'd like to talk about three items today, beginning with taxes. About 10 days ago we all kept our rendezvous with the Internal Revenue Service and anted up our income tax. If it'll help ease the pain, let me remind you that in about 2 months, on July 1st, you'll start paying 10 percent less income tax on what you earn.

But that won't mean anything to a growing group of citizens who've already given themselves a tax cut. It's estimated that about $95 billion in income tax is not being paid. That's enough to balance the budget.

Now, if your first reaction was that these are big money operators using tax shelters—and there are some doing that—I'm not talking about them. The $95 billion is tax owed on an estimated $450 billion in, for want of a better word, the underground economy. The people in this economy are, I'm sure, honest people in most of their activities; they just have a double standard where taxes are concerned. They can be the friendly neighborhood fix-it man, a mechanic, craftsman, or a member of the professions. They have one thing in common—they prefer to be paid in cash. The underground economy is a kind of cash-and-carry barter system—no checks, no records or book-keeping, and thus no tax.

As we struggle to trim government spending, it's hard not to think of how close that unpaid tax could come to wiping out the deficit. If I could paraphrase a line from a well-known old poem, "Breathes there a man with soul so dead who never to himself has said: I owe it to my country and my fellow citizens to quit being a freeloader."

Item two: A short time ago, I announced I was asking Congress to pass a bill allowing a tuition tax credit for families sending children to independent or parochial schools. The credit would be for half the tuition up to a ceiling of $500 per child. That ceiling wouldn't apply until 1985. It would be lower to start with and would only apply to families with adjusted gross incomes below $50,000 a year. It would also only be for tuition to elementary and secondary schools. I wish it could be for college, also, but maybe we can do that later when we've solved a few problems.

The public school lobby has protested that this is an attack on the public schools for the benefit of students attending exclusive finishing or prep schools. Well, the overwhelming majority of so-called private schools are church-supported—Catholic, Protestant, and Jewish. The majority of students are from families earning less than $25,000. In some of our large cities, 40 percent of the parochial school students are from minority neighborhoods. Their families pay their full share of taxes to fund the public schools. How high would those taxes go for everyone if those parents decided to send their children to public schools? I think they're entitled to some relief since they're supporting two school systems and only using one.

And now item three: A couple of weeks ago, I told you of how high interest rates were holding back recovery, that a lender must get a return on his money, plus the rate of inflation. For 6 months, inflation has been running at an annualized rate of only 3.2 percent. And, as you know, last month it actually went down three-tenths of 1 percent, the first time in 17 years.

Adding on to that a fair return for a lender, interest rates shouldn't be higher than 10 percent. They are, of course, because the money market, having been burned in past recessions by artificial quick fixes, is afraid that inflation will take off again.

Two industries vital to economic recovery have been especially hard hit by high interest rates—automobiles and housing. But it seems not everyone out there in the marketplace is afraid. The Automobile Dealers Association of Eastern Ohio asked some banks to lower interest rates for new car purchases. The rates were lowered from a 16- to 18-percent level down to 12.9 percent for a 2-week period, March 1st to 13th. The response was so overwhelming they extended the period to March 20th. In the first 3 weeks of February, car dealers of the Youngstown-Warren area had only sold 344 cars and trucks. In those first 20 days in March, they sold 2,200.

In Plainfield, Indiana, whether by coincidence or because he'd heard about this, Mr. Hursel C. Disney, chairman of the First National Bank and Trust, lowered interest rates almost four points for loans to buy cars and trucks, making $2 million available for that purpose. His offer has met with the same overwhelming response. Mr. Disney says the offer is good as long as the $2 million lasts.

I have no way of knowing how far this idea has spread. But one of the major automobile companies which has its own lending operation is now advertising that until May 31st the interest rate on loans for their cars and trucks will be 12.8 percent. And just the other day, the news reported something similar had started in home mortgages.

You know, there really is something magic about the marketplace when it's free to operate. As the song says, "This could be the start of something big."

Thanks for listening, and God bless you.

Note: The President spoke at 12:06 P.M. EST from the Oval Office at the White House.

Economic Recovery Program

May 1, 1982

My fellow Americans:

This broadcast today is coming from the American Pavilion, the World's Fair, that opens in Knoxville, Tennessee, today.

Two nights ago I went on national television asking you to help us get a bipartisan budget passed in this Congress—not just any budget, but a budget that will hold down your taxes and get spending under control so we can reduce deficits, interest rates, and put unemployed Americans back to work. Let me just say, your calls and telegrams really warmed my heart. You came through with the greatest outpouring of support our administration has ever received, and you let us know that, while our program did not in its first 30 weeks solve all the problems that have piled up for more than 30 years, it is beginning to work.

Ernest Key wired us from Georgia: "Gas in Atlanta is 20 cents per gallon cheaper than this time last year. Inflation is almost cut in half. All of this began after October 1st," he wrote. Well, October 1st was the start of our program.

Hazel Quinn from Texas said, "As a senior citizen living on Social Security, your program is working to our benefit. Groceries have remained stable."

John McMullen from Michigan told us that, "The other philosophy of tax and spend has a record of failure. Fight on," he said. Well, we will.

We're seeing signs that the economy is ready to turn up. The record high interest rates we inherited nearly wrecked the housing industry, but as we've begun to bring those rates down, housing starts have increased steadily over the last 5 months. Airline travel, an indicator of future business activity, is up. There'll be an increase in automobile production in the second quarter of 1982.

Another very important sign—Americans are starting to save again. In the 6 months since that first 5-percent phase of our tax cut took effect, the rate of personal savings has risen to 5.7 percent from 5.1 percent for the year before. This means billions more in the capital pool to finance new investments, jobs, and economic growth. It also indicates lower interest rates ahead.

We can do even better if you help us protect the first decent tax incentives for your families—the 10-percent cut in July and the one in 1983—the first since John F. Kennedy's tax cut nearly 20 years ago. Yes, our tax cut is big, and yet it barely offsets the enormous increase in taxes built into the system in 1977. That was the biggest single tax increase in our history, and there are more installments of that yet to come in the next couple of years.

We must be fair to all our people. We're devoting one of the largest shares in the history of the Federal budget to assisting low-income Americans. But let's ask ourselves, where was the fairness in those bankrupt spending policies that gave us double-digit inflation, record interest rates, and a trillion-dollar debt? Where is the fairness now if we make even more painful the highest peacetime tax burden we've ever known? We're not going to do that. With your support, with responsible Republicans and Democrats working together, we can pass a good budget that will help taxpayers more than it hurts them.

Last year with your help we passed a budget bill that lowered the spending increase by more than $30 billion. How big would the projected deficits be if that hadn't been done? Those who fought and voted against those savings are fighting against the additional savings that we've proposed for 1983.

It's extremely difficult for the Congress to withstand the pressures for more spending. That's why I asked Congress to pass, as soon as possible, a constitutional amendment to require balanced Federal budgets, and that's why I'm appealing to all of you at the grass roots. Start putting pressure on the Congress now. Let's find out who's hiding behind the rhetoric of balanced budgets but is unwilling to make the cuts in spending needed to bring them about.

There are now two resolutions pending, one in the House and one in the Senate, that enjoy strong support and that would lead to such a constitutional amendment. They would require the Congress to adopt a balanced statement of taxes and spending each year. But the growth in revenues could not exceed the prior year's growth in national income. In other words, it would contain a limitation so that you couldn't just have a balanced budget by always sending the bill to the taxpayers for whatever the deficit might be. A balanced budget amendment would have to be ratified by three-fourths of the States. The Congress could approve a deficit, but only by a 60-percent vote of the full membership of both the House and Senate.

I'm convinced that most of you do support the need for a constitutional amendment. After my speech night before last, the public response was more than 7 to 1 in favor of the idea.

Government must stay within the limit of its revenues. This is not a political issue between parties. It's an issue simply of sense versus nonsense, of endless red ink versus lasting recovery. With your voices and your support, good sense will prevail.

Thank you, and God bless you.

Note: The President spoke at 12:05 P.M. EDT from the U.S. Pavilion at the Knoxville International Energy Exposition (World's Fair) in Knoxville, Tennessee.

May 8, 1982

My fellow Americans:

It's just possible that you may have heard or read that there's some talk in Washington about a budget. If so, you've also heard a few things that aren't true.

For openers, it's just a plain falsehood to say, as our opponents in Congress and much of the press are saying, that the budget the Senate Budget Committee approved last Wednesday night is going to reduce Social Security payments. It does nothing of the kind. That budget specifically states that the 7.4-percent cost-of-living increase in Social Security benefits due July 1st will be added to the checks beginning July 1st, and that increase will be the only change in those checks.

Those who've rushed to face the TV cameras or get their names in newsprint by frightening our Social Security recipients should be ashamed of themselves. Let me repeat what I've said before. I will protect the benefits of Social Security recipients now and in the future.

The second thing, not quite so urgent, that needs correcting is some misinformation about our original budget proposal, which I submitted in February, and the projected budget deficits for the next 3 years. For some reason or lack of reason, the news media and some Congressmen have repeatedly declared that my February budget proposal contained a $182-billion deficit. Budgets don't contain deficits. Deficits are the difference between expected revenues and proposed spending. A budget either adds to it or reduces it. We plan to do the latter.

Both my February proposal, which the Congress refused to act on, and the one approved by the committee Wednesday night would, if adopted, drastically reduce the deficits. The $182 billion projected for 1983 will be reduced to $106 billion by the Senate budget. The deficits projected for 1984 and '85 will be reduced from $216 billion and $233 billion to $69 billion and in 1985 only $39 billion. That is a $417-billion cut in the deficits over 3 years.

In plain language, the budget which I worked out with the Republican members of the Senate committee reverses an ongoing increase in deficits and sets us on a sure road to a balanced budget in just a very few years.

You remember, of course, the great to-do and the hysteria about our budget a year ago, the talk of budget cuts that would punish the needy and helpless. You're hearing the same thing now about the new budget for 1983 and whether we can afford further budget cuts without doing harm to our social programs. Well, what budget cuts? Where do the cuts come from?

The 1981 budget we inherited was $657.2 billion. Our first budget, the one we had all the fuss about last year, was $728.9 billion. That's an increase of $71.7 billion over the preceding year—hardly what you'd call a cut. Yes, there were reductions of $35.2 billion, but they were reductions only in what had been assumed would be the annual increase in spending. We thought a $71.7-billion increase was enough. Without those $35-billion cuts, the present 1982 budget would be nearly as big as the budget we've proposed for next year.

The 1983 budget, approved by the Senate committee last Wednesday, calls for spending $779 billion. That's an increase over this year of $50.2 billion. Back in 1980 budgets were increasing by 17 percent. When it is passed, the 1983 budget increase will be a little less than 7 percent. This reduction in the rate of government growth, we think, is what you sent us here to do.

Now, I know it's hard hearing all these numbers to keep things straight, but the bottom line is that all the so-called budget cuts have been reductions only in the rate of increase usually in what Congress refers to as the "uncontrollables." Our proposed budget for next year, the one passed by the Senate committee, is $122 billion more than was spent in 1981. Those who've been opposing our budgets—this one and the one last year—would have had an increase of more than $170 billion if they'd have their way.

There've been no cuts in the budgets. There have only been smaller increases than some of our big spenders would have preferred, coupled with what we've done, our tax cuts, to allow you to keep more of what you earn.

Another subject: Yesterday we awoke to the news that unemployment had gone to the highest levels since 1941—9.4 percent. Well, let me just first tell you how I feel about unemployment. This is the problem above all which must be solved.

Maybe those of us who went through the Great Depression have some kind of complex, but to me, as long as there is one single person able and willing to work but unable to find work, that is too high an unemployment rate. I wonder, though, if the news media couldn't serve us better if they would give us more of the statistical information on unemployment provided by the Bureau of Labor Statistics.

Let me explain. The rise in the unemployment rate from 9 to 9.4 percent is in what are called the seasonally adjusted figures. Now, I'm not sure that we live in a seasonally adjusted world. Every month, the Bureau also publishes the unadjusted figures. I feel these latter figures should not be buried or ignored by the press. If they weren't of some importance, the Bureau wouldn't release them along with the seasonally adjusted.

Now, what's this all about? Well, the adjusted figures are given for what should be the rate of unemployment and employment for each month, based on the figures for previous years. Now, I know I'm running the risk of oversimplifying, but I'm also running out of time. The unadjusted figures are simply the actual count of how many are employed and how many are unemployed in a certain month.

Under the seasonally adjusted figures, unemployment, as we know, went up to 9.4 percent in April, higher than the March figure of 9 percent. And that, of course, is bad news. But according to the unadjusted figures, there were 400,000 more people actually working in April than in March and 300,000 fewer unemployed. Likewise, when the figures were announced a month ago, unemployment increased from March over February, according to the adjusted figures. And yet by the actual count, there were 525,000 more people working in March than February and 88,000 fewer unemployed.

Now, I'm sure that next month, when 750,000 or more young people are suddenly out of school, the adjusted figures might look better than the unadjusted. But shouldn't we be allowed to see both?

Regardless, the figures are sad. And something must be done and can be done about unemployment if Congress will get off the dime and adopt the deficit-reducing budget it now has before it. Interest rates will come down when it does, and so will unemployment.

This is no time for politics as usual. There are too many people hurting.

Thanks for listening, and God bless you.

Note: The President spoke at 12:05 P.M. EDT from the Oval Office at the White House.

Armed Forces Day

May 15, 1982

My fellow Americans:

Today marks the United States' 33d observance of Armed Forces Day, a tradition begun by President Truman to honor the men and women who serve our country in uniform. I want to take this occasion to reflect on the job they're doing and what it means to us.

One of the oldest truths in the world is that nothing worth having is cheap. And many times, the greater the good, the higher its cost. Keeping America free has cost us dearly over the centuries. Since 1776 we as a nation have lost thousands of lives and suffered thousands of injuries to guarantee our freedom. Preserving the peace also requires the daily toil of millions of men and women who, without fanfare and glory, serve to protect our freedom and security.

The men and women in our armed services are our final protection against those who wish us ill. The soldier, the sailor, the airman, and the marine in the United States and around the world are the ultimate guardians of our freedom to say what we think, go where we will, choose who we want for our leaders, and pray as we wish.

It is sad that these rights, which should belong to all people, are not fully enjoyed by most of the human family. It is sadder still that some in the world view such freedom as a threat to their right to rule over their fellow citizens, and so long as that's true, we can't afford to take our freedom for granted. It cannot survive without protection. And for their role in protecting our freedoms, we honor the members of our volunteer Armed Forces today.

Their jobs are difficult, requiring judgment, technical know-how, endurance, and in many cases exposure to danger. We ask them to put in long hours under trying conditions. Many serve far from their homes and families, prepared, if need be, to make the ultimate sacrifice for our nation. In short, they give us their all.

So, I would like to thank them today: the Army tank crew member in Germany or Korea, responsible for maintaining a 55-ton machine so that it's ready at a moment's notice; the sailor in the Indian Ocean who's been away from home for 4 months and is working 18 hours a day in a hot engine room or carrying chocks for returning aircraft; the Air Force security policeman guarding our nuclear alert aircraft in the Texas heat or the North Dakota winter; the Marine squad leader on Okinawa working with his men to provide the most efficient combat team in the world. All these people and the rest of their comrades in arms we thank today.

There is another group which deserves special thanks—the wives of our servicemen, wives who take care of the families and raise the children while their husbands are at sea or stationed far away, and wives who have left our shores to be in a faraway land with their husbands.

I had a letter the other day from one young wife describing what life was like where they were stationed. I could read homesickness between the lines, but not one word of complaint—only great pride in what her husband is doing. Their contribution is critical; the separation, the long hours, the hard work, and, up until recently, the low pay—all these have been burdens to them as well. The understanding and encouragement they give our servicemen is something we must all be grateful for.

So, on behalf of all you listening, I want to take these few minutes today to thank our men and women in uniform and their families and to ensure [*sic*] them their government and their fellow citizens are determined to provide them with the equipment, training, and, just as importantly, the respect they have so richly earned. With their help, the United States remains at peace.

Our allies enjoy the same benefit. Our national determination to defend freedom at the borders where it's threatened is fully matched by the quality and spirit of the more than 2 million soldiers, sailors, airmen, and marines who proudly wear the American uniform.

I received another letter from one of our ambassadors in Europe. He wrote that a 19-year-old trooper in our armored cavalry had asked that he send me a message. It was: "Tell the President we're proud to be here, and we ain't scared of nothing."

In James Michener's book, "The Bridges at Toko-Ri," he writes of an officer waiting through the night for the return of planes to a carrier as dawn is coming on. And he asks, "Where do we find such men?" Well, we find them where we've always found them. They are the product of the freest society man has ever known. They make a commitment to the military—make it freely, because the birthright we share as Americans is worth defending. God bless America.

Thanks for tuning in. I'll be with you again next Saturday. Until then, God bless you.

Note: The President spoke at 12:06 P.M. EDT from the Oval Office at the White House.

Federal Budget

May 22, 1982

My fellow Americans:

Let's talk about the budget, the one subject that most directly affects your pocketbooks.

Now, before you say, "This is where I came in," there has been a new development. We're making some progress toward a budget agreement that will hold down your taxes and get government spending under control. This is the one sure way we can keep inflation coming down, bring interest rates down as well as deficit spending, and, most important, get our factories working again.

Washington is a town that loves to spend money—your money. And if that isn't enough, they'll borrow—a trillion dollars so far.

As the French economist Bastiat said a long time ago, public funds seemingly belong to no one; the temptation to bestow them on someone is irresistible.

I've said before, and let me say again, many of the spending proposals are motivated by sincere compassion, compassion we all feel. But pretty soon, if we aren't careful, we find ourselves inventing miracle cures for which there are no known diseases. That's what led to the situation in 1980, when Federal spending was increasing by 17 percent and the inflation rate was 12.4 percent. Interest rates reached a 100-year high of 21½ percent.

Obviously, something had to be done. To continue down the road we were on would have meant disaster. So, when we got here in January of 1981, we changed course.

The 17-percent annual increase in government spending was cut almost in half. That 12.4-percent inflation rate has, for the last 6 months, been 2.8 percent. For the last 3 months, it has only been eight-tenths of 1 percent. Interest rates have come down some, but not enough yet to give the economy the boost it needs.

As you know, we put in place tax incentives to help industry retool and modernize. And we've provided tax reductions for individuals so families could keep more of the money they earn. It's the first broad-based program to help all American taxpayers since President Kennedy's tax cut nearly 20 years ago.

The average family will see its personal withholding rate cut by 20 percent in the next 14 months. There'll be a 10-percent cut July 1st and another in July of 1983.

Even though we've only had the first installment, a 5-percent cut last October, we're seeing some signs of the incentives that a tax cut brings. Personal spending is up, and Americans are saving at a higher rate. Saving is one of the best ways people can help themselves and our country. As the pool of savings expands, interest rates come down and billions of dollars are made available for new investments, mortgages, and jobs.

Yesterday, the United States Senate took another step to get spending under control. It passed a budget resolution that will reduce projected deficits $358 billion over the next 3 years. I'll be honest with you: I would have liked more reductions in spending, but at least it's another step in the right direction—the direction we started to go last year.

In contrast to this responsible action by the Senate leadership, the leadership of the House of Representatives is trying to spend more and to eliminate $150 billion or so of your tax cut. Their idea for reducing the deficit, for example, is to eliminate the third year of the tax cut. They have another idea which somehow doesn't go with their claim of compassion. Once that final income tax cut is in place, we have one further step to go. We permanently index the income tax brackets against inflation. This, too, the spenders would take from you under the phony claim that it only benefits the rich.

During these recent years of inflation, many of you have received cost-of-living pay increases. These don't make you better off. They just keep you even—even, that is, till income tax time. Then you find those added dollars have pushed you into a higher tax bracket where you give the government a greater percentage of your earnings and end up with less purchasing power, not more.

Indexing prevents this from happening. Now, how can indexing hurt the workers and benefit the rich? It can't. And those who say it can are talking through their hats, as usual. The rich and the high income earners are already in the top tax bracket. They also don't get cost-of-living increases. It's the wage earner who needs and, in our program, will get indexing.

Incidentally, to be fair, I must say those same individuals who would take indexing away from you also do want to cut spending—defense spending, and really only defense spending. Eliminating about 73 percent of our planned increase in the defense budget is their goal. Fortunately, some responsible Republicans and Democrats in the House have proposed a better plan, somewhat similar to the one passed by the Senate. It will preserve your tax cuts, reduce spending, and keep America strong. They are calling their plan the bipartisan recovery budget, and it will be voted on the first of this coming week.

If you want interest rates to come down and the economy to get going, it wouldn't hurt if you told your Congressman to vote for the bipartisan recovery budget. But do so right away.

Until next week, thanks for listening, and God bless you.

Note: The President spoke at 12:06 P.M. EDT from the Oval Office at the White House.

Federal Budget / Western Alliance

May 29, 1982

My fellow Americans:

This has been a pretty hectic week and, I'm sorry to say, a bad one for all those Americans who are suffering because of the recession and the high interest rates.

In contrast to the Senate, which passed a responsible budget resolution calling for reductions in the projected deficits for the next 3 years of $358 billion, the majority leadership of the House of Representatives preferred to play politics. In a wild 5 or 6 days, they battled over which of a half a dozen or so budgets we should have, plus 68 amendments, and then came up empty. They will now recess for a vacation and come back to start all over again.

The President is required to submit a budget. Indeed, the budget is referred to as "the President's budget." The one we submitted in February was not one of those the House debated, yet it was a result of 4 months' work by the Office of Management and Budget, the entire Cabinet and their staffs, and the executive staff. The Congress simply ignored it. Nothing in our Federal Government is more in need of an overhaul than the ridiculous procedure we have misnamed "the budget process."

Believing that a budget resolution calling for substantial savings could have an effect on the now unnecessarily high interest rates, I had hoped for cooperation with the Democratic leadership of the House. I thought if we could appear together before the cameras and announce that we had arrived at agreement on a deficit-reducing budget, it would serve notice to the money markets that we were united in an effort to keep inflation and, thus, interest rates down.

A number of responsible Democratic Congressmen did share that hope. And with their help, we'll keep fighting to get a responsible budget which protects your tax cuts and provides for a sound defense program.

Next week, I leave for Europe for the first time as President. Exactly one week from today, while I'm in France, we'll commemorate the 35th anniversary of the Marshall Plan, one of the greatest humanitarian ventures ever undertaken. America helped to rebuild the shattered economies of Western Europe and create a sense of community among Western nations which remains vital today.

We must recognize that, whether in defense, political, or economic affairs, building successful foreign policy begins at home. It's for that reason we put in place an economic recovery program that, at long last, addresses the problems and abuses that have been undermining our economic health for decades.

We're starting to get some encouraging news from those economic statistics that pour out of Washington. Interest rates are heading down—not enough, but it's a start. Inflation is substantially down, and real consumer incomes are rising. And on July 1st, thanks to the second installment of your tax cut, Uncle Sam's bite on your paycheck will be smaller, leaving you more to spend and save as you see fit.

Serious problems remain, such as the need for a sound budget and, above all, unemployment, here and in Europe where it's at record levels. But we're making economic headway, and our common security requires that we continue to work together as friends and allies. That will be my main theme at the seven-nation economic summit in France next week.

But prosperity has little meaning unless we also act to maintain our freedom and protect the peace. The remarkable strength and success of the Western Alliance in preserving the peace for over three decades lies in the fact that we're a voluntary grouping of free peoples, soon to be joined by still another new democracy—Spain. The overriding success of NATO is that, for almost 40 years, Europe has been at peace.

To lay the basis for another generation of peace and prosperity, I'll meet with my 15 NATO colleagues in Bonn, the capital of the Federal Republic of Germany.

Our allies know that America has both the will and the resources to defend itself and to live up to its commitments. Last November 18th, we offered to eliminate all of our Pershing II and ground-launched cruise missiles if the Soviets eliminate their SS-4, -5, and -20 missiles, now targeted on our allies. This offer has the strong support of our NATO allies and has been spelled out in detail at the U.S.-Soviet negotiating table in Geneva.

In my recent speech at Eureka College, I presented a proposal for substantial reductions in strategic arms. We and our allies hope the Soviets will respond positively, and we're prepared to begin START—that's Strategic Arms Reduction Talks—immediately. But arms control can't happen in a vacuum. Over the past decade, the Soviet Union has engaged in a pattern of direct and indirect aggression and suppression in places as varied as Afghanistan, Poland, and Latin America, and that's made it harder for progress in arms control.

We must always remember that, in dealing with the condition in the world today, Western solidarity and defense preparedness are essential to meaningful arms control negotiations. That's the message I'll take with me— the message of a strong, free alliance, working together to protect its freedom and seek meaningful negotiations to build a more peaceful world.

I'm optimistic for the future of our partnerships and the future of freedom. The values for which we and our fellow democracies stand are of enduring and universal worth. Ours is a mission for peace and freedom through Western unity and strength, and with your prayers, it will succeed.

Next Saturday, I'll be talking to you from Europe. Thank you, and God bless you.

Note: The President spoke at 9:06 A.M. PDT from Rancho del Cielo, his ranch near Santa Barbara, California.

Trip to Europe

June 5, 1982

Good day to you all in America:

Maybe I should say "bonjour." I'm speaking to you from the Palace of Versailles right outside Paris, France, and I'm not over here on a vacation. Along with the leaders of the other democratic industrial nations, I'm attending an economic summit, the eighth one in as many years.

Versailles holds significance for the American people beyond its art treasures and architecture. This imposing structure has strong links to our own history. Within these walls Louis XVI and Benjamin Franklin concluded an alliance without which our Revolution's outcome might have been very different. And in 1783 the Treaty of Versailles, which led to the formal recognition of America's independence from England, was signed here.

Now, I don't want to give you a history lesson, but the Versailles Peace Conference, which settled World War I, also greatly affected us as a nation. That conference marked America's emergence as a leader and a world power.

All these historical links between the United States and Versailles involve alliance and friendship—and really, that's what we're doing here again. This time we're discussing economic cooperation. I can assure you our partners are as determined as we are to overcome economic ills and create incentives for employment, investment, and productivity. And they also realize that economic growth is essential to the long-term well-being of the industrial countries.

In our meetings, we are trying to work out ways we can reach those goals together and without stepping on each others' toes. Yes, the countries attending the summit do have economic problems, but look how far we've come.

Over the ruins of the last great wars, we have built thriving democracies, solid friendships, and fundamentally sound economies. We have a right to be proud of our contributions to the economic strength of these industrial democracies. Today is the 35th anniversary of the Marshall Plan, a program that shines as an example of how we've worked for the betterment of our sister democracies. I think it's appropriate that this anniversary occurs here among our friends. Our presence demonstrates America's continuing commitment to the democracies of Europe, Japan, and Canada.

After we leave France we go to the Vatican to call upon His Holiness the Pope and to Rome to visit the government and people of Italy. Italy is a [firm and warm]* friend of the United States, and we couldn't be in the area without stopping by.

And then back on the plane, and we're off to England, a nation whose American ties are as thick as its fog. The next summit we attend is the NATO gathering in Bonn, West Germany. As you know, NATO's origins go back to the North Atlantic Treaty of 1949 which provided for a defensive military alliance of Western Europe and North America, as well as political and economic cooperation. It is this Alliance and its deterrent strength that has kept the peace for the past 33 years. At the NATO summit, we'll work to preserve that peace by strengthening our defenses and demonstrating the Alliance's firm resolve.

---

*White House correction

The happiest event of the meeting will be Spain's addition to the list of NATO members. A democratic country has freely chosen to join other nations in an alliance for their common defense. This has real significance. Did any nation in Eastern Europe freely choose to join the Warsaw Pact? Not one.

Just as it's fitting that the anniversary of the Marshall Plan occurs during the economic summit, it's also meaningful that NATO meets the week of the D-Day anniversary.

One lesson of D-Day is as clear now as it was 38 years ago: Only strength can deter tyranny and aggression. The dawn that rose on the English Channel that June morning revealed a horizon alive with thousands of ships, the largest armada in history. From England, the long-awaited message went around the world. Under the command of General Eisenhower, allied naval forces supported by strong air forces began landing allied armies on the northern coast of France. It was a simple statement, but the operation had been years in the planning.

In the United States, the news came in the middle of the night. But here and there in sleepy towns, lights, nonetheless, came on. President Roosevelt called the people to prayer. "Almighty God, our sons, the pride of our nation, this day have set out upon a mighty endeavor."

Well, it was a mighty endeavor, an endeavor of liberty, sacrifice, and valor. As we honor these men, I pledge to do my utmost to carry out what must have been their wish—that no other generation of young men would ever have to repeat their sacrifice in order to preserve freedom.

This is the last of this series of radio broadcasts, but I'll be back before too long. Until then, thanks for listening, and God bless you all.

Note: The President spoke at 6:05 P.M. (Local) from the Palace of Versailles, Paris, France. His address was broadcast on radio stations in the United States at 12:05 P.M. EDT.

The Economy

August 28, 1982

My fellow Americans:

Hello again. It's great to be back speaking to you over weekly radio. I hope this is the first of many broadcasts to come. I've missed these weekly visits.

Just 12 days ago, I went on television to ask your support for a bipartisan tax reform and spending reduction bill. As you'll recall, I told you I had to swallow hard to support that bill myself. I didn't like the idea of revenue increases and still don't. But to get the spending cuts which I think most of us want and which we must have to reduce deficits, keep interest rates going down, and get the unemployed back to work, we had to accept the increased revenues. But I argued then and I repeat now: Most of the revenue part of that bill was not really a tax increase at all, but a reform of existing tax laws.

The tax cut passed last year remains the biggest tax cut in history. Even with the $99 billion increase, the tax cut over the next 3 years will amount to $335 billion. The savings to the average American family this year is $400; next year it will be $788. Even more important, however, we'll reduce the deficits over these next 3 years by $378.5 billion. If we stay on course and work together, we can look to a day when we can start reducing that trillion-dollar debt. And I think you like that "working together" idea.

I received a letter just the other day from a lady in Florida. I hope she won't mind if I share it with you. Patricia Morgan writes that she sees unity among us again, the kind of unity we had during World War II—we Americans, all pulling together. That's what America is. That is our power. Patricia Morgan, I couldn't agree more. American power is reasserting itself.

The day before yesterday, the Federal Reserve lowered the discount rate to 10 percent—the lowest it has been in 2 years. Double-digit inflation, once 12.4 percent, has been for the last 7 months only 5.4 percent. The prime interest rate, 21.5 percent a year and a half ago, is now 13.5 percent and very probably going lower.

The other day, the Security Savings and Loan of Milwaukee, Wisconsin, made $100 million available for home mortgages at 11.9 percent interest. And we've just seen a week-long breaking of virtually every record on Wall Street for trade in stocks and bonds.

No, we're not out of the woods yet. But we can maintain this momentum, reopen factory gates, rebuild America, and make this country number one again—not overnight, of course, but slowly, surely, we can do it. It all hinges on one question: Do we as a nation have the unshakable determination to get Federal spending under control once and for all? With 20 unbalanced budgets in the last 21 years, the burden of proof is on us.

We need a constitutional check against red-ink spending. Four of five of you support this idea. The Senate recently passed a bill that takes us one step closer to such a constitutional amendment. It is now up to the House leadership to make sure the full House votes on this issue as soon as possible in this session of the Congress. If not, you, the voters, will have an opportunity in November to make your feelings heard about that.

On the subject of spending, though, I can't wait until November. A few days ago a supplemental appropriations bill to fund several programs and agencies for the rest of this fiscal year was sent to me for signature or veto. The legislation contained funding to meet payrolls of the Department of

Defense and other Federal agencies. It also included a vital new program we've sought that is essential to our hemispheric solidarity and security—the Caribbean Basin Initiative. But it also contained funding for several things I've vetoed already as being unnecessary and was almost a billion dollars over budget for domestic programs.

We've gone on record as committed to reduce projected deficits by $380 billion over the next 3 years. I believe that commitment begins with holding the line on a budget that has little more than a month to run. So even though it means delay in getting legislation I believe is vital to our nation's welfare, I have therefore vetoed that supplemental appropriations bill.

Until next week, thanks for listening, and God bless you.

Note: The President spoke at 9:06 A.M. PDT from Rancho del Cielo, near Santa Barbara. As printed above, his address follows the text of the White House press release.

Labor Day

September 4, 1982

My fellow Americans:

I'm glad to join all of you on this final weekend of the summer. Family vacations are now ending, kids are going back to school, and communities all over the Nation are preparing for Labor Day parades. And, by the way, this year marks the 100th anniversary of the first Labor Day parade. It isn't true that I was in that first parade; I've just read about it.

On Monday, we celebrate the dignity and productivity of America's working people. Our country has prospered because we're a nation of workers, and today there are nearly 100 million at work—more than 100 million according to the unadjusted figures and 99.8 million in the seasonally adjusted figures. Now if that confuses you, well, I'm confused, too.

Unfortunately, on this Labor Day, however, too many of our fellow citizens are unemployed. That's a terrible word, "unemployed." It means hardship, uncertainty, frustration, helplessness. Many who are unemployed feel caught up in something they don't understand and over which they have no control. And they're right. It's not the fault of the laid-off fellow in Detroit that he's out of work. It's not his fault the autos aren't rolling down the assembly line. It's not the fault of the unemployed mother in Delaware that the printing plant closed down, throwing her out of a job.

The fact is unemployment has been gaining on us for years. Since 1976 the unemployment rate in this country has averaged over 7 percent—far higher than in earlier postwar years. It was only 2.9 percent in 1953.

I'm convinced that in these last few decades the increased intervention by government in the marketplace, tax policies that took too great a percentage of overall earnings, plus burdensome and unnecessary regulations reduced economic growth and kept us from creating new jobs for newcomers entering the job market.

Today the unemployment rate is 9.8 percent, and still the number of people with jobs is a higher percentage of those of working age than we had in times of full employment—higher than in 1953 when, as I said, unemployment was only 2.9 percent. I guess what I'm trying to point out is that our unemployment problem is due to more than just the present recession. We must not only work our way out of the recession, we must adopt policies that will stimulate economic growth and create new jobs for the increased numbers entering the job market.

This is the goal of our economic recovery program. Yes, it marks a decided turnaround from government tax-and-spend policies of the past four decades—deliberately so. And I believe it'll work. Indeed, the signs are there that it's beginning to work.

Last week I called attention to the decline in interest rates—21½ percent down to 13½ percent; inflation down from 12.4 percent to 5.4 percent since the first of the year. A family of four with a $15,000 income has $1,000 more in purchasing power than it would have if inflation had stayed at 12.4 percent.

Now, I know this is hard to see because prices keep going up. But they aren't going up as fast or as much as they were. What we're all waiting for is that zero rate when they stay where they are or even drop a little. Well, that, too, is what our program is designed to accomplish. And the leading economic indicators by which we know whether the economy is improving or getting worse have climbed for the fourth month in a row. That hasn't happened for a long time.

Clearly, the most important question now before us is whether we have the will and determination to hold our course. The next test will come when the Congress returns to Washington and decides whether to sustain my veto of a supplemental spending bill that would drive up spending once again. I hope we can work together to develop a more responsible bill.

In the meantime, I hope you'll join me this Labor Day weekend in saluting the workers of America. And while we're doing that, perhaps we can spare a moment of prayer for some workers in another country.

Here in America on Labor Day, we hold parades to support the principles of freedom. In Poland a few days ago, the people peacefully gathered to mark the second anniversary of Solidarity—a labor movement which revived our hope that nonviolent change and basic human rights could come to a closed Communist community. Their parade was met with guns, concussion grenades, tear gas, and water cannons.

As we attend our parades and picnics, let us remember how fortunate we are to be a free people. Let us remember the handwritten prayer that was recently found in an alcove of a Polish church. It read, "Thank you, Lord, that into this temple I may bring verses. It's the only place in our homeland where every Pole feels free and where he may evoke his pain. I beg you to give my country the strength to endure."

Well, let us in America be thankful for the strength of our free labor movement. May it long endure.

Thanks for listening, and God bless you. I'll be back next week at this same time.

Note: The President spoke at 9:06 A.M. PDT from Rancho del Cielo, near Santa Barbara.

Crime and Criminal Justice Reform

September 11, 1982

My fellow Americans:

Today I want to talk with you about a subject that's been very much on my mind, even as we've been busy with budgets, interest rates, and legislation. It's a subject I know you've been thinking about, too—crime in our society.

Many of you have written to me how afraid you are to walk the streets alone at night. We must make America safe again, especially for women and the elderly who face so many moments of fear. You have every right to be concerned. We live in the midst of a crime epidemic that took the lives of more than 22,000 people last year and has touched nearly one-third of American households, costing them about $8.8 billion per year in financial losses.

During the past decade alone, violent crime rose by nearly 60 percent. Study after study shows that most serious crimes are the work of a relatively small group of hardened criminals. Let me give you an example—subway crime in New York City. Transit police there estimate that only 500 habitual criminal offenders are responsible for nearly half the crimes in New York's subways last year.

It's time to get these hardened criminals off the street and into jail. The primary responsibility for dealing with these career criminals must, of course, rest with local and State authorities. But I want you to know that this administration, even as it has been battling our economic problems, is taking important action on the Federal level to fight crime.

As Attorney General Smith pointed out recently, an important part of the problem is that Americans are losing faith in our courts and our entire legal system. Nine out of 10 Americans believe that the courts in their home areas aren't tough enough on criminals. Another 8 out of 10 Americans believe that our criminal justice system does not deter crime. And these figures have gone up drastically in the last 10 or 15 years.

We can and must make improvements in the way our courts deal with crime. The administration-backed omnibus anticrime bill, introduced in the Congress last year and given important leadership by men such as Senator Thurmond, would help to achieve this vital goal by cracking down on hardened criminals through important legal reforms. These include revising the bail system so that dangerous offenders, and especially big-time drug pushers, can be kept off our streets.

We also want to stop abuse of the parole system by making jail sentences more certain. And we've been pushing for stronger criminal forfeiture laws, a powerful weapon that would take a lot of the profit out of drug pushing and other forms of organized crime. We've also asked the Congress for tougher Federal penalties for drug trafficking.

Other important legislation would require a judge to take into account the suffering of the victim when it comes time to sentence a criminal, would make it a Federal crime to kill, kidnap, or assault senior Federal officials, and would extend the ability of the Federal Government to transfer property to the States, free of charge, for use as prison facilities.

These are important and imaginative steps. They can strike a real blow against organized crime and professional criminals. Unfortunately, they have yet to be passed by the Congress.

I urge the Congress to act promptly and favorably on these major initiatives against lawlessness in America. Every moment wasted is a moment lost in the war against crime.

The day after tomorrow, Monday, I will send to the Congress another package of major anticrime measures. These will include suggested revisions of the exclusionary rule. Now, this is the rule that can force a judge to throw out of court on the basis of a small technicality an entire case, no matter how guilty the defendant or how heinous the crime. Our bill would stop this grievous miscarriage of justice by allowing evidence to be introduced where the police officer was acting in good faith. This position has already been taken by some enlightened Federal judges, and I'm asking the Congress to make it the law of the land.

The measures I send to the Congress Monday will also include important revisions of Federal procedure that will cut down on interference by

Federal courts in State criminal proceedings and reduce the great number of cases which now overburden our court system and slow the wheels of justice.

And finally, we will press for commonsense revisions of the insanity defense, a defense that has been much misinterpreted and abused.

I wish there was more time to talk with you about these steps and many others we're taking, such as our national strategy for fighting drug abuse. I'll have to save that for some of our future get-togethers. But in the meantime, I hope we can count on your support in our war on crime and our efforts to protect the innocent and put the professional criminals in jail where they belong. Working together, we can make America safe again for all our people.

Till next week, thanks for listening, and God bless you.

Note: The President spoke at 12:06 P.M. EDT from Camp David.

Prayer in Public Schools

September 18, 1982

My fellow Americans:

Today is a special day for our citizens of Jewish faith. It's Rosh Hashanah, the Jewish New Year, marking the beginning of the year 5743 on the Hebrew calendar. So, to all of our friends and neighbors observing this holiday—and speaking for all Americans—I want to wish a happy, peaceful, and prosperous New Year.

Rosh Hashanah also reminds us of the rich and varied religious heritage we Americans are blessed with. More than any other nation, ours draws inspiration from the creeds of many peoples from many parts of the world. They came to our shores from different ports of origin at different times in our history. But all of them—from the men and women who celebrated the first Thanksgiving more than three and a half centuries ago, to the boat people of Southeast Asia—came here with prayers on their lips and faith in their hearts.

It's because of this shared faith that we've become, in the words of the Pledge of Allegiance, "one Nation under God, indivisible, with liberty and justice for all."

At every crucial turning point in our history, Americans have faced and overcome great odds, strengthened by spiritual faith. The Plymouth settlers triumphed over hunger, disease, and a cruel northern wilderness because, in the words of William Bradford, "They knew they were pilgrims. So they committed themselves to the will of God and resolved to proceed."

George Washington knelt in prayer at Valley Forge and in the darkest days of our struggle for independence said that "the fate of unborn millions will now depend, under God, on the courage and conduct of this army."

Thomas Jefferson, perhaps the wisest of our Founding Fathers, had no doubt about the source from which our cause was derived. "The God who gave us life," he declared, "gave us liberty."

And nearly a century later, in the midst of a tragic and at times seemingly hopeless Civil War, Abraham Lincoln vowed "that this nation, under God, shall have a new birth of freedom."

It's said that prayer can move mountains. Well, it's certainly moved the hearts and minds of Americans in their times of trial and helped them to achieve a society that, for all its imperfections, is still the envy of the world and the last, best hope of mankind.

And just as prayer has helped us as a nation, it helps us as individuals. In nearly all our lives, there are moments when our prayers and the prayers of our friends and loved ones help to see us through and keep on the right path. In fact, prayer is one of the few things in this world that hurts no one and sustains the spirit of millions.

The Founding Fathers felt this so strongly that they enshrined the principle of freedom of religion in the first amendment of the Constitution. The purpose of that amendment was to protect religion from the interference of government and to guarantee, in its own words, "the free exercise of religion."

Yet today we're told that, to protect that first amendment, we must suppress prayer and expel God from our children's classrooms. In one case, a court has ruled against the right of children to say grace in their own school cafeteria before they had lunch. A group of children who sought, on their own initiative and with their parents' approval, to begin the school day with a one-minute prayer meditation have been forbidden to do so. And some students who wanted to join in prayer or religious study on school property, even outside of regular class hours, have been banned from doing so.

A few people have even objected to prayers being said in the Congress. That's just plain wrong. The Constitution was never meant to prevent people from praying; its declared purpose was to protect their freedom to pray.

The time has come for this Congress to give a majority of American families what they want for their children—the firm assurance that children can hold voluntary prayers in their schools just as the Congress, itself, begins each of its daily sessions with an opening prayer.

With this in mind, last May I proposed to the Congress a measure that declares once and for all that nothing in the Constitution prohibits prayer in public schools or institutions. It also states that no person shall be required by government to participate in prayer who does not want to. So, everyone's rights—believers and nonbelievers alike—are protected by our voluntary prayer measure.

I'm sorry to say that so far the Congress has failed to vote on the issue of school prayer. Just this week, however, I asked Senate Majority Leader Howard Baker to bring this measure to a floor vote. I'm happy to say he told me he'll do everything he can to accomplish this. However, passage requires a vote by the House of Representatives, as well. So, I call on the House leadership to make an equal effort.

Today, on one of the holiest days of one of our great religious faiths, I urge the Members of the Congress to set aside their differences and act on this simple, fair, and long-overdue measure to help make us "one Nation under God" again.

Thank you. God bless you, and God bless America.

Note: The President spoke at 12:06 P.M. EDT from the Oval Office at the White House.

The Economy

September 25, 1982

My fellow Americans:

I'd like to talk to you today about a piece of news that spells real hope for everyone. I'm talking about the economic war we're waging together and winning against enemy number one—inflation.

Memories fade quickly. Only a short time ago we were told double-digit inflation was here to stay for the rest of this decade. At one point in 1980, inflation was zooming at an annual rate of 18 percent. I'll always remember traveling this country and seeing how many people were frightened that our way of life was slipping away from us. And indeed, between 1978 and 1980 the buying power of the average weekly paycheck declined almost 9 percent. Putting food on the table, keeping families warm and healthy, filling our cars with gas, and, for our elders, preserving the value of pensions—all these things were getting harder and harder to do.

I remember visiting one store in Lima, Ohio, in October 1980. It was Clyde Evans's grocery. I used a survey by Ohio State University and showed how inflation was robbing families of their purchasing power. For a typical family of four, $60 had purchased a week's supply of food in 1976. By 1980 that same $60 only bought, well, at best, a few days' worth. And by 1984, if there was no improvement in inflation, elderly Americans on fixed incomes would literally have gone hungry.

That was the desperate situation we faced when our administration took over in January of 1981, and that's why we've had to make some tough, even unpopular decisions to get runaway spending under control. As I mentioned a moment ago, we're winning the war the experts said was hopeless. In less than 2 years, inflation has been cut more than in half, down to 5.1 percent so far this year.

I know this isn't easy for people to see. You go in to buy, and the price is higher than it was the last time. But it hasn't gone up as much as it did in each of those last few years. That's why, for the first time in quite a while, real after-tax income is increasing; your paycheck buys more than it did.

Some of you are probably thinking, well, what concerns us today is jobs, and I agree. We have a bill in the Congress which will provide job training for a million unemployed people or more per year for permanent jobs in the private sector. This legislation is needed, but it's only a partial remedy.

Let's remember why unemployment has been gaining on us, averaging over 7 percent since 1976. Rising inflation pushed up interest rates in the late 1970's, and together they hit us like a one-two punch, sending shock waves through the economy. It became more difficult for families to get home mortgages, for consumers to carry auto loans, for firms to modernize their machines and keep their product prices competitive. To make matters worse, as high inflation and interest rates were crippling the economy's ability to provide jobs, they were forcing more families to seek a second income. Well, this all came home to roost in 1980, when inflation reached double digits for the second straight year and interest rates soared to 21½ percent—their highest peak in more than a century. Again, that's the mess we inherited.

I don't believe that it follows that those who took us to the edge of economic Armageddon are automatically best qualified to lecture us now on the most fair, effective way to end the crisis. And when those same individuals charge our administration fights inflation by putting people out of work, I say they're exploiting helpless people for their own political gain. It's the most cynical form of demagoguery.

How does making people able to buy more cause some other people to lose their jobs? Creating more jobs requires getting interest rates down further and keeping them down, and that can only come from continued progress against inflation. We've beaten down those 21½-percent interest rates to 13½. And we can—and must—do better. But if the public senses we're giving up the fight against inflation, those who lend money will demand higher interest rates, and we'll be right back in the soup with even higher unemployment.

There's only one major cause of our economic problems: government spending more than it takes in and sending you the bill. There's only one permanent cure: bringing government spending in line with government revenues. We have not had 21 red-ink budgets in 22 years because you, the people, are not taxed enough. The government has run more than $1 trillion into debt because too many politicians spent too much of your money for too long.

Many liberals have made it clear they want to take back the third year of your tax cut and the indexing. This will only give government more money to spend, weaken savings, and hurt those who need help most— lower- and middle-income taxpayers, the backbone of this country. Well, we're not going to let them do it. We need less spending.

So far, I have not received for my signature one appropriations bill for the fiscal year that begins this coming Friday. The leadership in the House is also sitting on an historic measure already approved by the Senate and supported by 80 percent of the public—a constitutional amendment requiring balanced budgets. This amendment offers us our best chance of getting control of runaway spending.

It's tragic at this late date that those who controlled the Congress for so long and spent us to the brink of bankruptcy are still playing politics with these problems and the suffering they caused. Believe me, it's time they realized that much more than an off-year election is at stake.

Till next week, thanks for listening, and God bless you.

Note: The President spoke at 12:06 P.M. EDT from the Oval Office at the White House.

Federal Drug Policy

October 2, 1982

The President. My fellow Americans, those of you who tuned in a few weeks ago may remember that the topic of my broadcast was crime. Well, this week I'd like to narrow that subject down to drugs, an especially vicious virus of crime.

In the last few days, I've had two reports on drugs in America. First, Nancy returned from a trip to Alabama, Mississippi, and Arkansas—one of the many trips she's made, talking to young people and their parents about the drug epidemic. Well, I thought it might be fitting if she told you herself of what she's learned about the drug problem.

So, Nancy.

The First Lady. Thank you.

To everyone at home, I have to tell you that few things in my life have frightened me as much as the drug epidemic among our children. I wish I could tell you all the accounts I've heard—stories of families where lying replaces trust, hate replaces love; stories of children stealing from their mothers' purses; stories of parents not knowing about drugs, and then not believing that the children were on them, and finally not understanding that help was available. I've heard time and again of children with excellent grades, athletic promise, outgoing personalities, but who, because of drugs, became shells of their former selves.

I won't burden you with all the terrifying statistics, but there's one that's especially troubling. While the health of most Americans has been improving, young people between 15 and 24 have a higher death rate than 20 years ago. And alcohol and drugs are one reason for this.

But there are also some very positive signs on the prevention and treatment fronts, especially with the parents' movement. People finally are facing up to drug abuse. They're banding together, and they're making real progress. And I just want to say a heartfelt "thank you" to all those people out there who are working so hard to get drug abuse under control.

The President. Thank you, Nancy.

Now, regarding the other report I mentioned. In the next few days we'll announce the administration's new strategy for the prevention of drug abuse and drug trafficking. This is a bold, confident plan, and I'm elated. For too long the people in Washington took the attitude that the drug problem was so large nothing could be done about it. Well, we don't accept this sit-on-your-hands kind of thinking. We've decided to do more than pay lip service to the problem, and we started where narcotics crime was the worst: south Florida.

This garden spot had turned into a battlefield for competing drug pushers who were terrorizing Florida's citizens. I established a task force under Vice President Bush's leadership to help the citizens of south Florida fight back. As part of a coordinated plan, we beefed up the number of judges, prosecutors, and law enforcement people. We used military radar and intelligence to detect drug traffickers, which, until we changed the law, could not be done. We increased efforts overseas to cut drugs off before they left other countries' borders.

Well, the results of our task force have been dramatic. The Vice President tells me drug-related arrests are up over 40 percent, the amount of marijuana seized is up about 80 percent, and the amount of cocaine seized has more than doubled. The important thing is we're hurting the traffickers. It's true that when we close off one place they can move somewhere else. But one thing is different now: We're going to be waiting for them. To paraphrase Joe Louis, they can run but they can't hide.

The strategy I just received [*sic*] will help us duplicate the south Florida experience for the entire United States. We're undertaking a narcotics policy that might be termed "hot pursuit." We're not just going to let them go somewhere else; we're going to be on their tail.

Now, you probably wonder why I'm so optimistic. Well, for the first time, the actions of the different government agencies and departments dealing with narcotics are being coordinated. There are 9 departments and 33 agencies of government that have some responsibility in the drug area, but until now, the activities of these agencies were not being coordinated. Each was fighting its own separate battle against drugs. Now, for the very first time, the Federal Government is waging a planned, coordinated campaign.

Previous administrations had drug strategies, but they didn't have the structure to carry them out. We now have that structure.

In addition to the enforcement element, our strategy will also focus on international cooperation, education, and prevention—which Nancy's very interested in—detoxification, and treatment and research.

The mood toward drugs is changing in this country, and the momentum is with us. We're making no excuses for drugs—hard, soft, or otherwise. Drugs are bad, and we're going after them. As I've said before, we've taken down the surrender flag and run up the battle flag. And we're going to win the war on drugs.

Till next week, thanks for listening, and God bless you.

Note: The President and Mrs. Reagan spoke at 12:06 P.M. EDT from Camp David.

Solidarity and U.S. Relations with Poland

October 9, 1982

My fellow Americans:

Yesterday the Polish Government, a military dictatorship, took another far-reaching step in their persecution of their own people. They declared Solidarity, the organization of the working men and women of Poland, their free union, illegal.

Yes, I know Poland is a faraway country in Eastern Europe. Still, this action is a matter of profound concern to all the American people and to the free world.

Ever since martial law was brutally imposed last December, Polish authorities have been assuring the world that they're interested in a genuine reconciliation with the Polish people. But the Polish regime's action yesterday reveals the hollowness of its promises. By outlawing Solidarity, a free trade organization to which an overwhelming majority of Polish workers and farmers belong, they have made it clear that they never had any intention of restoring one of the most elemental human rights—the right to belong to a free trade union.

The so-called new trade union legislation under which this contrary and backward step has been taken claims to substitute a structure and framework for the establishment of free trade unions in Poland. But the free world can see this is only a sham. It is clear that such unions, if formed, will be mere extensions of the Polish Communist Party.

The Polish military leaders and their Soviet backers have shown that they will continue to trample upon the hopes and aspirations of the majority of the Polish people. America cannot stand idly by in the face of these latest threats of repression and acts of repression by the Polish Government.

I am, therefore, today directing steps to bring about the suspension of Poland's most-favored-nation tariff status as quickly as possible. This will increase the tariffs on Polish manufactured goods exported to the United States and thus reduce the quantities of these goods which have been imported in the past.

The Polish regime should understand that we're prepared to take further steps as a result of this further repression in Poland. We are also consulting urgently with our allies on steps we might take jointly in response to this latest outrage. While taking these steps, I want to make clear, as I have in the past, that they are not directed against the Polish people. We will continue to provide humanitarian assistance to the people of Poland, through organizations such as Catholic Relief Service and CARE, as we have since the beginning of martial law.

At the same time, I stand by my earlier offer to provide recovery assistance to help the Polish economy back on its feet, once Warsaw restores to the Polish people their human rights.

There are those who will argue that the Polish Government's action marks the death of Solidarity. I don't believe this for a moment. Those who know Poland well understand that as long as the flame of freedom burns as brightly and intensely in the hearts of Polish men and women as it does today, the spirit of Solidarity will remain a vital force in Poland.

Surely, it must be clear to all that until Warsaw's military authorities move to restore Solidarity to its rightful and hard-won place in Polish society, Poland will continue to be plagued by bitterness, alienation, instability, and stagnation.

Someone has said that when anyone is denied freedom, then freedom for everyone is threatened. The struggle in the world today for the hearts and minds of mankind is based on one simple question: Is man born to be free, or slave? In country after country, people have long known the answer to that question. We are free by divine right. We are the masters of our fate, and we create governments for our convenience. Those who would have it otherwise commit a crime and a sin against God and man.

There can only be one path out of the current morass in Poland, and that is for the military regime to stand up to its own statements of principle, even in the face of severe outside pressure from the Soviet Union; to lift martial law; release Lech Walesa and his colleagues now languishing in prison; and begin again the search for social peace through the arduous but real process of dialog and reconciliation with the Church and Solidarity.

I join with my countrymen, including millions of Americans whose roots are in Poland, in praying for an early return to a path of moderation and personal freedom in Poland.

Thanks for listening. I'll be back next week. Let Poland be Poland. God bless you.

Note: The President spoke at 9:06 A.M. PDT from Rancho del Cielo, near Santa Barbara.

The Economy

October 16, 1982

My fellow Americans:

There's an old saying that "no news is good news." Well, I guess that's true sometimes. But still, it's good to be talking with you after a week of good news for the average American family.

This troubled economy of ours isn't out of the woods yet. It takes more than 21 months to undo the piled-up damage of more than 20 years. But with your help, we're getting there.

Last Wednesday night, on television, I tried to paint the big picture, to show where we are, how we got there, and what we're doing to make America well again.

As I pointed out, from day one of this administration, we've been working hard to solve five big economic problems. Problem number one, government was taking too much of your money in high taxes. Number two, government was spending and borrowing too much money, including service on a trillion-dollar debt. This led to number three, backbreaking inflation, which added so much to the burden of millions of Americans trying to make ends meet. And, of course, inflation and government borrowing led to a fourth problem, the high interest rates that made it hard or impossible for people to afford the homes, the cars, the other purchases that keep our economy moving and provide jobs—the final problem.

Well, step by step, we're licking those problems. We fought for and won a tax break that will bring down your income tax rates a total of 25 percent when the final installment goes into effect next July 1st. We've reduced the rate of increases in Federal spending by nearly two-thirds. What we're aiming for is to get the annual increase in spending below the annual increase in revenues which takes place as our economy grows.

We've driven inflation back down into the single digits, from 12.4 percent in 1980 to just 5.1 percent so far this year. This has helped bring down those paralyzing interest rates from a peak of 21½ percent in 1980 to 12 percent today.

And just yesterday, we had another piece of good news. The Producer Price Index went down one-tenth of a percent last month, for an average of only 3.1 percent so far this year. If we can hold that rate steady through December, it will be the best performance in 10 years, and another important step toward the inflation-proof recovery we're all working so hard for.

All of this means new hope, new cause for confidence, not just for the nearly 100 million Americans who are working today, and their families, but for retired citizens and others on fixed incomes who've suffered so much from inflation in recent years.

As for the 11 million Americans still out of work, they will find jobs as the economy continues to heal.

I don't mean to minimize the very real plight of the unemployed. But when we're told over and over again, as we have been in the last few days, that as of September 25th, 682,500 new claims for unemployment insurance were filed, shouldn't we also be told that at the same time 618,000 left the lists?

We're winning the battle on four out of the five problems causing this recession. We've already floored inflation and sent those high interest rates reeling. And as surely as single-digit inflation started the interest rates tumbling, getting those interest rates back down to single digits will drive unemployment back down to single digits, too.

Once we've done that, we'll have delivered a knockout blow to this bitter recession, the latest in a long series of recessions brought about because, until now, our leaders resorted to quick fixes and politics as usual, to treating the symptoms instead of the disease.

Well, as I said last Wednesday, at my age I didn't come to Washington to play politics as usual or sweep problems under the rug where they would only get worse for those who come after. I came here to solve problems, not to add to them. And with your patience, faith, and, yes, courage, we've been able to lay the groundwork for a lasting recovery that will leave America stronger than ever and spare our children and grandchildren some of the things that we've had to endure because of the mistakes of the past.

I don't use that word "courage" lightly. To me, one of the most inspiring things about this job is the chance it's given me to see how bravely Americans from all walks of life have responded to the problems we face. Your courage is one of the most precious gifts as a people, and it's seen us through many a storm. This is not the time to lose that courage—just when it's beginning to pay off.

One man summed it up best nearly 50 years ago, when America faced a far deeper economic crisis than the one we're working our way out of today—the Great Depression of the thirties. "The only thing we have to fear," said Franklin Roosevelt, "is fear itself." He spoke that line in his Inaugural Address in March of 1933. We've been told that line was not intended to be a major point in his address. Still, those were the words more than any others on that March morning that gave back to the American people their courage, their faith in themselves and in this blessed country. It is the best remembered line of his speech.

In times of trouble, fear is a disease of the spirit that can slow recovery and be exploited by those who are more interested in taking advantage of our problems than in helping to solve them. And there are such people. Some are seeking political profit, and others are just naturally given to doom-crying.

Now, I'm not just whistling past the graveyard, nor am I trying to belittle the grief and pain of you, who through no fault of your own, are out of work. I'm saying the downbeat chorus we're being subjected to by so many these days can rob us of our courage. We must not let that happen. Unemployment such as we have now is a terrible thing, but it may not be our number-one problem. Our number-one problem may be fear—fear that we're adrift, that there is no plan, that no one is doing anything to make things better.

Well, that's not true. The improvement in inflation, interest rates, the increase in real wages, in savings, and in retail auto sales, up 8½ percent in September, the surging stock market—all these are the result of a plan, a plan that is working and that offers hope to you who are unemployed. Hang in there. I know from personal experience how tough it can be, but don't give up. And don't listen to those crepe hangers who are howling like a dog sitting on a sharp rock. They howl, but they haven't proposed one thing they'd do to make things better. The truth is, things are being done with no help from them, and things are getting better.

The time for confidence, the time for courage, is now. Thanks to you, we are nearing the end of a long and painful ordeal. With your prayers and support, with your confidence and courage, we can make the difference—not just for ourselves, but for generations of Americans to come.

Until next week, thanks for listening, and God bless you.

Note: The President spoke at 12:06 P.M. EDT from Camp David. The address was broadcast live on nationwide radio and television.

Economic and Budget Issues

October 23, 1982

My fellow Americans:

Over the years, we Americans have faced many hard choices, and, politics being politics, there have been a few who have tried to obscure the issues and exploit them for political gain. But time after time, the common sense of the American voter has outsmarted those who would mislead us. Abraham Lincoln had a simple motto: "Trust the people." I don't think anyone since has improved on that advice. Given the facts, the American people can be counted on to make the right decision.

So today, in the midst of this noisy election year, let's clear the air for a moment and talk facts, not opinions. Specifically, let us expose six big myths that are being spread by people who ought to know better.

Myth number one—and I'm sure you've heard this one again and again—is that increases in defense spending in recent years are one of the main causes of projected Federal deficits. The fact is that the defense share of the Federal budget and the gross national product has been shrinking sharply over the last 20 years. It was 9 percent of the gross national product in 1960. This year, it's only 6 percent.

It's nondefense spending that's been growing. During the last 22 years, while defense spending was shrinking as a part of the gross national product, nondefense spending nearly doubled—from 9 percent of the gross national product to nearly 18 percent. If it weren't for the drastic growth in nondefense spending, we'd actually have a big budget surplus today.

Myth number two is a whopper you've been hearing a lot from the people who'd like to take back your tax cuts. They claim that the other cause of big Federal deficits is the well-deserved tax relief we won for you over the objections of the big spenders in the Congress. That just isn't true.

The reality is that the effect of the tax cuts enacted in 1981 was mainly to hold tax rates even, to keep the hard-pressed American taxpayer from being bled even drier through further hikes and the bracket creep caused by inflation. Between 1980 and '85, taxes, as a share of the gross national product, will drop by less than 1 percentage point. The real culprits for those whopping deficits are the same congressional big spenders who voted down the balanced budget amendment.

Myth number three—and I'm sure you've heard this one, too—is the charge that this administration has slashed Federal social spending and caused a lot of human hardship. Well, that sounds bad. But is it true? The answer is no.

This administration is spending approximately three times as much on nondefense spending as the Kennedy administration spent in 1963, and that's even after you adjust the figures for inflation. Yes, we're doing everything we can to cut waste and root out cheaters. But the budget for the Department of Health and Human Services is greater than at any time in America's history. It amounts to 36.2 percent of the budget. It was only 33.8 percent of the 1980 budget. There are only two budgets in the world larger than our '83 Health and Human Services budget of $274.2 billion—the total budget for the United States and the Soviet Union.

It's easy to see how the myths persist. Not too long ago, a family of six in a Northeastern state was portrayed on television as destitute. That family was eligible for programs totaling $1,159 per month, tax free.

Myth number four is an especially cynical one because it tries to exploit the real suffering many people are feeling and feeds on the kind of fear and despair that I spoke of last week and which can slow the recovery we all want. It claims that the 11 million people who are currently unemployed won't find jobs until after the recession is completely over and we're back to full recovery.

In effect, this myth cruelly condemns millions of our friends, neighbors, and family to a future without hope. The reality is a lot better. Bad as current unemployment is, in most individual cases it's a temporary problem. For example, of all the workers who became unemployed last July, one-third were no longer unemployed within 30 days, and two-thirds were off the unemployment list within 60 days. Now, true, some of those people had withdrawn from the job market. But the majority of them had found new jobs and were helping achieve the economic recovery we're all working so hard for.

Myth number five would have you believe that America's best days are behind us, that we're falling behind our foreign competitors in our standard of living. Well, what's the fact behind the myth? The good old U.S.A. is still the most productive of the world's major industrial countries. In 1980, the last year with reliable information, real per capita income in the United States was 14 percent better than Germany, 20 percent better than France, and a whopping 35 percent ahead of Japan. In the last 2 years, with those countries suffering from the same worldwide recession we're experiencing, the United States is still number one.

And finally, there's the biggest and cruelest myth of all—the doom-peddling argument that there is no end in sight for this bitter recession. The reality behind the myth: We aren't out of the woods yet, but we're getting there. Inflation and interest rates are down. Yesterday a leading bank lowered its prime rate to 11½ percent, and others will follow. Real wages and retail sales are moving up. Housing starts and car sales, so vital to recovery, are both heading up again. And the strong surge of investor confidence we've witnessed in recent weeks means new growth for our economy and more jobs for our people.

It's been a long, hard fight, going on for much more than the last 2 years, and it isn't over yet. But thanks to your patient courage and your ability to see the truth behind the political fairy tales, America is on the road to lasting recovery.

Until next week, thanks for listening, and God bless you.

Note: The President spoke at 12:06 P.M. EDT from Camp David. The address was broadcast live on nationwide radio and television.

Economic Recovery Program

October 30, 1982

My fellow Americans:

I've received a letter declaring that our economic recovery program must be changed before it causes "more economic destruction and human suffering." Well, the writer then went on with further criticisms, as well as proposals for specific actions I should take. Since he's gone public, nationally, on TV and in the press, with much of what was in his message, I am replying to his specific points with an open letter on today's broadcast.

Dear Senator:

I find it hard to understand your unquestioning belief that our economic recovery program is not only responsible for unemployment—which was already serious 2 years ago—but that it threatens "further collapse of the economy."

My feelings of sorrow for those bearing the burden of unemployment are every bit as deep as yours. But you seem to write off or ignore the fact that unemployment was high in 1979 and went higher in 1980. Indeed, in the spring of '80, 1,400,000 workers were laid off or lost their jobs in a period of only a few months. In the last half of 1980, the money supply increased at an all-time high rate of 13 percent. Interest rates went right up with it to a 100-year high of 21½ percent. And, of course, the inflation rate, the basic villain in all this, was in its second straight year of double digits—12.4 percent.

Now, we both know the high interest rates led to layoffs in the automobile industry. And as that industry slowed down, so did steel, rubber, and glass. Those same high interest rates brought down the housing industry as mortgages became too costly, leading to layoffs in lumber, appliances, furniture, and many other related industries.

Now, all of this was taking place before our administration had even taken office. During our first several months in office, the Federal Reserve was below its targeted growth rate in money supply. This had the effect of maintaining the high interest rates well into the summer of '81, when the recession worsened substantially. Our economic recovery program didn't go into effect until October of '81, and then only a part of the program. So, we've only had 13 months of the economic recovery program, and not the entire program at that. And yet, inflation has come down to 4.8 percent so far this year. Interest rates are 11½ and 12 percent, not 21½. The rate of increase in Federal spending per year has been lowered from 17 to 6 percent. And our people have had the first real tax cut since the one John F. Kennedy gave them in the early 1960's.

Is the economy continuing to decline as you said it was? Housing starts and building permits are up. There's been an above-normal increase in home sales for this time of year. Real purchasing power is up. The rate of personal savings is higher than it's been in 6 years. The stock market is some 215 points higher than it was just 10 weeks ago. Now, it's true, there have been a great many bankruptcies and business failures, but the number of new businesses starting up is near a record level.

You suggest that I urge the Chairman of the Federal Reserve to loosen the money supply so as to reduce interest rates. But interest rates have come down almost 50 percent. In 1980, when the money supply was loosened, interest rates skyrocketed. You say, put a moratorium on loans for corporate mergers, but that would be getting into credit control, which was tried and failed a few years ago.

With regard to your proposal to send our special trade representative, Bill Brock, and others to negotiate trade regulations with Japan and our European trading partners—they've been doing that and have had considerable success and intend to continue.

You urge that we embark on a giant public works program funded by government. Isn't that what we tried in all those seven other recessions since World War II? And all we got for that spending was a temporary quick fix, followed by more inflation and then another recession, usually deeper than the one before. Doing this would increase deficits and then repeat the high inflation and deep recession cycle we want to avoid. Make-work jobs would be offset by lost jobs in the private sector.

You mentioned defense spending and two particular construction projects that we could do without. Well, defense spending is providing jobs for hundreds of thousands of American workers, besides providing for our national security.

I appreciate your invitation to come to Michigan to see the unemployed firsthand. When I was in Michigan campaigning in 1980, unemployment in the city of Flint was then 20 percent, and in Detroit it was 18 percent. I saw similar tragic examples in Ohio and other industrial States.

You speak of Americans "searching in vain for jobs that do not exist." Well, certainly that's true. But there also are jobs that do exist and are unfilled because of the lack of workers with the particular training or skill called for in those jobs. Count the pages of help-wanted ads in our metropolitan papers on any given Sunday. Two weeks ago, the Washington Post ran 34 such pages. On the other side of America, the Los Angeles Times on that same day carried 52 pages.

I'm sure that you'll be pleased to know we're starting a job training program in which the Federal Government will work with local officials and businesses and industrial leaders at the community level. The idea will be to train individuals for jobs now available in the communities where they live. Now, since two out of five of today's unemployed are between the ages of 16 and 24, the group with the highest unemployment rate, the program has a great potential.

I think a careful study of the success of our existing policies in laying a groundwork for economic recovery will convince you they deserve more than the 13-month trial they've been given.

End of letter.

Well, I'll be back next Saturday. Till then, God bless you.

Note: The President spoke at 12:06 P.M. EDT from Camp David.

Congressional Agenda/The Economy

November 6, 1982

My fellow Americans:

You may not have been aware, but last Tuesday, when we voted, we were being observed by representatives of countries from five different continents. Officials from Africa, Asia, Europe, and South America joined us here to watch and learn as a part of the international Conference on Free Elections.

Sometimes it's good to stop and think how unique we really are. We accept our right to vote as normal, but it is revolutionary. In the eyes of much of the world, it's a miracle. Last Tuesday, as Americans of every race, creed, and walk of life went to the polls and voted, we demonstrated once again that we are the freest people on Earth.

Now that we've chosen the women and men who will represent us and shape our future, we must get on with the business of the Nation. There are serious problems America must face and genuine opportunities we must seize. You, the people, have sent a workable combination of Republicans and Democrats to Washington, and we must get on with the job.

When the Congress recessed last month for the election campaign, it hadn't finished some of its most important work. So, I've asked them to come back. Our needs are too urgent to wait until next year. We must not fritter away the time while millions of our people are barely hanging on. The economic health of America is at stake.

In this session, as in the next, cooperation will be the key to continue leading America to recovery. Campaign rhetoric and partisan politics must be set aside. Every elected official must bring to his or her work a bipartisan dedication to the good of the Nation. The Congress and the executive branch, Democrats and Republicans, must join together, not to do what's easy, but to do what is right.

In these times of deep unemployment, the Congress must act to bring about growth and new opportunities. First, the Congress must do its part to control government spending. It has not yet lived up to its promise to save $3 in outlays for every $1 already passed in new revenues. Eleven appropriations bills must still be passed, and I will use the veto, if necessary, to keep them within the budget. Second, I urge the Congress to reconsider the constitutional amendment to balance the budget. That bill was among the most important to pass the Senate this year. It was blocked in the House by a minority of big spenders, despite the overwhelming support of the American people. Third, the Congress should act on regulatory reform to help make government and industry more economical and efficient. And fourth, we need the jobs, growth, and opportunities our enterprise zones proposal will stimulate in depressed areas. That has been before the Congress for about a year. And fifth, we need the clean air bill, both to protect the environment and make it possible for industry to rebuild and create more jobs.

These and other pressing needs remain on the congressional agenda. We've had enough talk. Campaign cliches must give way to action. If we're to continue the momentum for recovery, if we're to surmount our problems as I know we can, we must act together, and we must act now.

Just yesterday, the Labor Department announced that the unemployment rate reached 10.4 percent. Now, that's only a cold government statistic, but behind it are real people who are hurting. I'm not going to sugarcoat this news, because I cannot hide my own personal ache. I remember what it's like to be 21 and to feel your future has been mortgaged by the generation before you. That's a terrible tragedy we must never allow to happen again.

In our efforts to revive our economy, jobs must be our most urgent priority, and lasting solutions must be our constant and consistent principle.

How deeply I wish that we could relieve our current situation with some immediate magic method. But there is a new spirit building—of optimism and hope for America's future. The severe problems which have been neglected for years and which caused unemployment to trend steadily higher—problems of runaway spending, taxing, double-digit inflation, and sky-high interest rates—are now being attacked at their roots. Inflation is down to 4.8 percent. Interest rates have dropped by nearly 50 percent, and taxes on the people are being cut.

A woman from California wrote me. "As a homemaker," she said, "I'm the one who shops and budgets for our family. I'm the first one to notice that my dollars are buying more. Little by little, I find I can breathe easier. For the first time in 5 years, I feel I can do some much needed repairs in our home."

Well, her letter reflects the growing confidence in our country. As more and more Americans see daylight ahead, our economy will grow stronger. We're seeing it begin to happen. Last month, new home sales rose by 24 percent, and new orders for capital goods also increased. Personal savings reached a 6-year high, which helped bring down interest rates and fuel the historic advance in our stock and bond markets. This will provide American industry more capital to invest in our future, and that means better productivity and more jobs.

The groundwork is being laid for the rejuvenation of our economy and the return of millions of Americans to our country's work force.

That wonderful Old Testament book of Ecclesiastes teaches us that "to everything there is a season." Well, my fellow citizens, I've never believed more strongly that America is beginning a season of hope, a genuine hope that springs from the vitality of the American spirit. Now we must seize our opportunity and live up to the principles of courage, hard work, and economic responsibility that made our country great in the first place.

I know our people will not fail America. They never have. Our task is to be sure our leaders do not fail the American people.

Thank you for listening, and God bless you.

Note: The President spoke at 12:06 P.M. EST from the Oval Office at the White House.

East-West Trade Relations and the Soviet Pipeline Sanctions

November 13, 1982

My fellow Americans:

During the campaign 2 years ago, I spoke of the need for the United States to restore the balance in our relationship with the Soviet Union. For too many years we had stood still while the Soviets increased their military strength and expanded their influence from Afghanistan to Ethiopia and beyond. I expressed a belief, which you seemed to share, that it was time for the United States to chart a new course. Since then, we've embarked upon a buildup of our defense forces in order to strengthen our security and, in turn, to strengthen the prospects for peace. We still have a long way to go. But the fact that we've started on a new course has enabled us to propose the most comprehensive set of proposals for arms reduction and control in more than a quarter of a century. It's always been my belief that, if the Soviets knew we were serious about maintaining our security, they might be more willing to negotiate seriously at the bargaining table.

In the near future, I will be speaking to you in more detail about this matter of arms control and, more importantly, arms reductions. But right now I have something in the nature of news I'd like to bring you.

The balance between the United States and the Soviet Union cannot be measured in weapons and bombers alone. To a large degree, the strength of each nation is also based on economic strength. Unfortunately, the West's economic relations with the U.S.S.R. have not always served the national security goals of the alliance.

The Soviet Union faces serious economic problems. But we—and I mean all of the nations of the free world—have helped the Soviets avoid some hard economic choices by providing preferential terms of trade, by allowing them to acquire militarily relevant technology, and by providing them a market for their energy resources, even though this creates an excessive dependence on them. By giving such preferential treatment, we've added to our own problems—creating a situation where we have to spend more money on our defense to keep up with Soviet capabilities which we helped create.

Since taking office, I have emphasized to our allies the importance of our economic, as well as our political, relationship with the Soviet Union. In July of 1981 at the economic summit meeting in Ottawa, Canada, I expressed to the heads of state of the other major Western countries and Japan my belief that we could not continue conducting business as we had. I suggested that we forge a new set of rules for economic relations with the Soviet Union which would put our security concerns foremost. I wasn't successful at that time in getting agreement on a common policy.

Then in December of 1981 the Polish Government, at Soviet instigation, imposed martial law on the Polish people and outlawed the Solidarity union. This action showed graphically that our hopes for moderation in Soviet behavior were not likely to be fulfilled.

In response to that action, I imposed an embargo on selected oil and gas equipment to demonstrate our strong opposition to such actions and to penalize this sector of the Soviet economy which relies heavily on high technology, much of it from the United States. In June of this year I extended our embargo to include not only U.S. companies and their products but subsidiaries of U.S. companies abroad and foreign licensees of U.S. companies.

Well, it's no secret that our allies didn't agree with this action. We stepped up our consultations with them in an effort to forge an enduring, realistic, and security-minded economic policy toward the Soviet Union. These consultations have gone on over a period of months.

Well, I'm pleased today to announce that the industrialized democracies have this morning reached substantial agreement on a plan of action. The understanding we've reached demonstrates that the Western alliance is fundamentally united and intends to give consideration to strategic issues when making decisions on trade with the U.S.S.R.

As a result, we have agreed not to engage in trade arrangements which contribute to the military or strategic advantage of the U.S.S.R. or serve to preferentially aid the heavily militarized Soviet economy. In putting these principles into practice, we will give priority attention to trade in high technology products, including those used in oil and gas production. We will also undertake an urgent study of Western energy alternatives, as well as the question of dependence on energy imports from the Soviet Union.

In addition, we've agreed on the following immediate actions. First, each partner has affirmed that no new contracts for the purchase of Soviet natural gas will be signed or approved during the course of our study of alternative Western sources of energy. Second, we and our partners will strengthen existing controls on the transfer of strategic items to the Soviet Union. Third, we will establish without delay procedures for monitoring financial relations with the Soviet Union and will work to harmonize our export credit policies.

The understanding we and our partners have reached and the actions we are taking reflect our mutual determination to overcome differences and strengthen our cohesion. I believe this new agreement is a victory for all the allies. It puts in place a much needed policy in the economic area to complement our policies in the security area.

As I mentioned a moment ago, the United States imposed sanctions against the Soviet Union in order to demonstrate that their policies of oppression would entail substantial costs. Well, now that we've achieved an agreement with our allies which provides for stronger and more effective measures, there is no further need for sanctions, and I am lifting them today.

The process of restoring a proper balance in relations with the Soviet Union is not ended. It will take time to make up for the losses incurred in past years. But acting together, we and our allies are making major progress. And I'm happy to say the prospects for peace are brighter.

I have just returned to the White House from the Soviet Embassy, where I signed the book of condolence for President Brezhnev. New leaders are coming to power in the Soviet Union. If they act in a responsible fashion, they will meet a ready and positive response in the West.

Till next Saturday at this time, good-by, and God bless you.

Note: The President spoke at 12:06 P.M. EST from the Oval Office at the White House.

International Free Trade

November 20, 1982

My fellow Americans:

I've talked to you on a number of occasions about the economic problems and opportunities our nation faces. Well, as you've probably heard on news reports, America's problems are not unique. Other nations face very severe economic difficulties. In fact, both developed and developing countries alike have been in the grip of the longest worldwide recession in postwar history. And that's bad news for all of us. When other countries don't grow, they buy less from us, and we see fewer jobs created at home. When we don't grow, we buy less from them, which weakens their economies and, of course, their ability to buy from us. It's a vicious cycle.

You can understand the danger of worldwide recession when you realize how much is at stake. Exports account for over 5 million jobs in the United States. Two out of every five acres planted by American farmers produce crops for exports. But because of their recessions, other countries are buying fewer American farm products than last year. Our farmers are hurting—and they're just one group.

So, we're trying to turn this situation around. We're reminding the world that, yes, we all have serious problems. But our economic system—based on individual freedom, private initiative, and free trade—has produced more human progress than any other in history. It is in all of our interests to preserve it, protect it, and strengthen it.

We are reminding our trading partners that preserving individual freedom and restoring prosperity also requires free and fair trade in the marketplace. The United States took the lead after World War II in creating an international trading and financial system that limited governments' ability to disrupt free trade across borders. We did this because history had taught us an important lesson: Free trade serves the cause of economic progress, and it serves the cause of world peace.

When governments get too involved in trade, economic costs increase and political disputes multiply. Peace is threatened. In the 1930's, the world experienced an ugly specter—protectionism and trade wars and, eventually, real wars and unprecedented suffering and loss of life.

There are some who seem to believe that we should run up the American flag in defense of our markets. They would embrace protectionism again and insulate our markets from world competition. Well, the last time the United States tried that, there was enormous economic distress in the world. World trade fell by 60 percent, and young Americans soon followed the American flag into World War II.

I'm old enough and, hopefully, wise enough not to forget the lessons of those unhappy years. The world must never live through such a nightmare again. We're in the same boat with our trading partners. If one partner shoots a hole in the boat, does it make sense for the other one to shoot another hole in the boat? Some say yes, and call that getting tough. Well, I call it stupid. We shouldn't be shooting holes; we should be working together to plug them up. We must strengthen the boat of free markets and fair trade so it can lead the world to economic recovery and greater political stability.

And here's how we're working to do that: We insist on sound domestic policies at home that bring down inflation, and we look to others for no less in their own economies. The International Monetary Fund, the institution that deals with world financial issues, seeks to encourage its member countries to follow sound domestic policies and avoid government restrictions on international trade and investment to foster economic development and raise their people's standard of living.

We remind other countries that, as the U.S. helps to lead the world out of this recession, they will benefit as we buy more goods from them. This will enable them to grow and buy more goods from us. And that will mean more jobs all around. That is the way of free markets and free trade. We must resist protectionism because it can only lead to fewer jobs for them and fewer jobs for us.

In just 4 days, the Trade Ministers of virtually all the free world countries will meet in Geneva, Switzerland. They will seek ways to surmount challenges to the integrity of our international economic system. We were instrumental in convening this international meeting because we believe strongly that our trading system is at a crossroads. Either free world countries go forward and sustain the drive toward more open markets, or they risk sliding back toward the mistakes of the 1930's and succumbing to the evils of more and more government intervention. And this is really no choice at all.

The United States will reject protectionist and defeatist proposals. Instead, we will set new goals and lay out a program for limiting government intervention in world markets. We will lead with a clear sense of our own commercial interests and a quiet determination to defend those interests. We will take actions at home and abroad which enhance the ability of United States industries to compete in international trade.

Let no one misunderstand us. We're generous and farsighted in our goals, and we intend to use our full power to achieve these goals. We seek to plug the holes in the boat of free markets and free trade and get it moving again in the direction of prosperity. And no one should mistake our determination to use our full power and influence to prevent others from destroying the boat and sinking us all.

That's how the United States is working in the world on behalf of freedom, economic prosperity, and peace.

I'll be back again next week. Thanks for listening. God bless you.

Note: The President spoke at 12:06 P.M. EST from Camp David.

Highway and Bridge Repair Program

November 27, 1982

My fellow Americans:
This special holiday weekend is a time when we all give thanks for the many things our land is blessed with. It's also a fitting time for us to think about ways in which we can preserve those blessings for future generations.

One of our great material blessings is the outstanding network of roads and highways that spreads across this vast continent. Freedom of travel and the romance of the road are vital parts of our heritage, and they helped to make America great. Four million miles of streets and roads make it possible for the average citizen to drive to virtually every corner of our country—to enjoy America in all its beauty and variety. They also form a vital commercial artery unequaled anywhere else in the world.

Our interstate system has reduced by nearly a day and a half the time it takes to drive coast to coast. And more efficient roads mean lower transportation costs for the many products and goods that make our abundant way of life possible. But let's face it: Lately, driving isn't as much fun as it used to be. Time and wear have taken their toll on America's roads and highways. In some places the bad condition of the pavement does more to control speed than the speed limits.

We simply cannot allow this magnificent system to deteriorate beyond repair. The time has come to preserve what past Americans spent so much time and effort to create, and that means a nationwide conservation effort in the best sense of the word. America can't afford throwaway roads or disposable transit systems. The bridges and highways we fail to repair today will have to be rebuilt tomorrow at many times the cost.

So I'm asking the Congress when it reconvenes next week to approve a new highway program that will enable us to complete construction of the interstate system and at the same time get on with the job of renovating existing highways. The program will not increase the Federal deficit or add to the taxes that you and I pay on April 15th. It'll be paid for by those of us who use the system, and it will cost the average car owner only about $30 a year. That's less than the cost of a couple of shock absorbers. Most important of all, it'll cost far less to act now than it would to delay until further damage is done.

And I should point out, delay is also dangerous as well as costly. And let me give you a few examples.

There's already a section of interstate highway in Illinois that's so far gone the truckers call it the only all-gravel interstate in the country. There are bridges that school bus drivers won't drive across until the children get out of the bus and cross on foot. Little League baseball actually had to be suspended on a field underneath the Queensborough Bridge in New York because of the condition of the bridge. And in one small community in Pennsylvania, a family living beneath a bridge that's part of I-70 has told their children not to play outdoors because rubble from the bridge keeps falling into the yard.

Overall, we have 4,000 miles of interstate highway that need resurfacing and 23,000 bridges that need replacement or repair. Our cities also have vital public transit capital needs for new buses, new or rebuilt rail cars, and track improvements that will total $50 billion over the next 10 years.

Common sense tells us that it'll cost a lot less to keep the system we have in good repair than to let it crumble and then have to start all over again. Good tax policy decrees that wherever possible a fee for a service should be assessed against those who directly benefit from that service. Our highways were built largely with such a user fee—the gasoline tax. I think it makes sense to follow that principle in restoring them to the condition we all want them to be in.

So, what we're proposing is to add the equivalent of 5 cents per gallon to the existing Federal highway user fee, the gas tax. That hasn't been increased for the last 23 years. The cost to the average motorist will be small, but the benefit to our transportation system will be immense. The program will also stimulate 170,000 jobs, not in make-work projects but in real, worthwhile work in the hard-hit construction industries, and an additional 150,000 jobs in related industries. It will improve safety on our highways and will make truck transportation more efficient and productive for years to come.

Perhaps most important, we will be preserving for future generations of Americans a highway system that has long been the envy of the world and that has truly made the average American driver king of the road.

Thanks for listening, and until next time, God bless you.

Note: The President spoke at 9:06 A.M. PST from Rancho del Cielo, near Santa Barbara.

Caribbean Basin Initiative

December 4, 1982

I'm speaking to you today from San José, Costa Rica. Later this evening, I'll return to Washington, having visited six neighboring heads of state. Our delegation has seen firsthand the vitality and potential of our New World neighbors. We've also heard and discussed their needs and aspirations and how they affect our own vital national interests.

United States interests require that we support our fellow Americans with a hemispheric policy which preserves and promotes democratic institutions, advances and encourages free market economies, and provides the security essential for these systems to develop and flourish. In our discussions during these last 4 days, I pledged our continued commitment to work as friends and neighbors with the other nations of this Western Hemisphere. We'll stand firmly with them to achieve the promise of economic progress and political stability that is the legacy of peace in the Americas.

Through cooperation, together we can protect ourselves from counterfeit revolutionaries who seek to destroy growth and impose totalitarianism on people who love freedom. Let us remember something very important: If our neighbors, particularly our nearest neighbors in the Caribbean Basin, are in trouble, their troubles inevitably become ours, unless we work together to solve them.

Right now their difficulties are not entirely of their own making. World prices for their traditional products—sugar, bananas, bauxite, and coffee—have been declining sharply for several years. At the same time, the prices for their essential imports, particularly petroleum, have remained high. This worldwide recession, the longest and most severe in postwar history, has hit their economies with all the fury of the tropical storms they're exposed to each year.

We cannot afford to ignore these difficulties. Our ties with the countries of the Caribbean Basin are very close. One-half of our trade passes through this area. Prolonged social and economic disruption would cause an exodus of desperate people seeking refuge where so many others have already found it—in the United States. The interests of Caribbean Basin countries are our interests; their security is our security.

The difficulties in the Caribbean Basin may seem overwhelming, but just as tropical storms give way to sunshine and calmer seas, economic despair will give way to optimism if people have the prospect to build a better life in freedom. Our support for democratic institutions is already helping. U.S. assistance to help these countries defend themselves from outside-supported subversion is likewise showing signs of progress. Our Caribbean Basin Initiative, designed to provide economic opportunity by stimulating investment and trade, offers the hope of economic progress, which anchors democracy and freedom.

In September the United States Congress approved funds for emergency balance-of-payments assistance as the first step in this initiative. I also attach great importance to the 1983 fiscal year package of foreign assistance. But our goal is not a temporary boost from foreign aid. Our goal is to help our neighbors strengthen democratic institutions and free economies that stand on their own. We need long-term incentives to expand production and create new jobs. The trade and investment portions of our Caribbean Basin Initiative legislation are designed to accomplish this.

I've proposed that we offer our neighbors the opportunity to trade with us freely by eliminating trade barriers for most products for 12 years, and by providing tax incentives for U.S. investment in their economies. With our markets beckoning, the inducement to expand existing enterprises and invest in new ventures will increase. This will create growth and jobs, both for Caribbean countries and for the United States.

Trade is the path to new progress for everyone. All developing countries, including ours, succeeded by expanded [*sic*] free enterprise at home and by increasing their trade with other countries. By helping them, we help ourselves. As their economies grow, we'll have new markets for our exports. The faster their standards of living rise, the more jobs will be created in the United States.

The impact on our own domestic industries of more goods coming from the Caribbean will be minimal, since the quantity of imports from these small countries will not be great. Moreover, our industries and our jobs will have safeguards to protect them from disruption.

Since taking office, I've held numerous discussions with Caribbean Basin leaders. They have assured me that their Caribbean Basin Initiative will provide more fuel for their private economies to be engines for lasting growth. They, too, have faith that private enterprise can flourish with the magic of the marketplace.

This initiative, I'm pleased to say, is only part of a wider undertaking in the Caribbean Basin. Canada, Colombia, Mexico, and Venezuela have joined us with impressive initiatives of their own. I'm asking the Congress only that we in the United States do our part by doing what we can do best—create economic opportunity.

The leaders of the Congress have promised to give the Caribbean Basin Initiative urgent consideration during the current session. The initiative has already received substantial bipartisan support. I urge all Members of the Congress to look carefully at the benefits which the Caribbean Basin Initiative will bring to our neighbors, and to us. Final passage this year is top priority.

I'll be leaving tonight to return to Washington. I can't close without saying how impressed I've been with the leaders I've met here in the nations of South and Central America and the people. I believe we've created bonds which will serve to bring the nations and peoples of the Americas into a closer accord. These two great continents joined by the countries of Central America can be the hope of the world.

Until next week, thanks for listening, and God bless you.

Note: The President spoke at 11:06 A.M. (Local) from the Casa Presidencial in San José, Costa Rica.

Production of the MX Missile

December 11, 1982

A few weeks ago, I talked with you about our quest for peace—for a secure world in which our children and our children's children can grow up without fear, enjoying the blessings of peace and freedom. As President, my first duty is to do everything in my power to achieve these goals.

Two of the keys to preserving the peace are deterrence and arms reduction. One of these keys has worked perfectly for 37 years. Since the end of World War II, we've prevented the outbreak of a new global war by a national policy of deterrence. To do that meant maintaining our defense forces so that any enemy knew in advance that an attack on us or our allies would bring disaster, not victory, to the attacker. Now, when a potential enemy knows that by starting a war he'll lose more than he hopes to gain, he just won't start a war in the first place. That's what deterrence is all about.

A key feature of this policy has been to maintain strong strategic forces. Our triad, as it's called—our three-legged plan of land-based missiles, sea-based missiles, and manned bombers—makes clear to any aggressor that, if he attacks us, we will still have the strength to strike back, the ability to retaliate. That's because no potential attacker has the strength to knock out all three legs of our defense triad at the same time.

If we only had two parts to this force, then preserving the peace would be more difficult. Potential attackers might even come to believe they could launch and win a nuclear war. We must never let this happen. That's why last year I ordered all three legs of our strategic forces to be modernized.

There's no question about the need for modernizing them. Today all three are made up mainly of weapons we developed more than 10 years ago—more than 20 years ago in the case of our bombers. Sooner or later older systems become ineffective and vulnerable. Our most pressing problem today is that the Soviet Union, because of its massive buildup of nuclear weapons, could destroy virtually all of our land-based missiles in a single nuclear attack. If we do nothing to correct that situation, we will have weakened the chances for peace. This is why we need the new MX Peacekeeper missile—to help restore our strategic deterrent and literally to keep the peace.

The Peacekeeper is a modern missile, and it is survivable. I agree with my scientific and military advisers that the closely spaced basing plan we proposed will work. Congress had ordered us to submit a basing proposal for the MX by December 1st, which we did. However, we're prepared to review this matter with the Congress in the new year.

The basing mode is not an issue. There's plenty of time to decide on that. What we need now is a clear, positive vote on the missile itself, to go forward on production of the missile. Why? Because we're negotiating with the Soviet Union at Geneva to reduce substantially nuclear arsenals on both sides—the other key to protecting the peace in the nuclear age. These are tough negotiations, but our team is hanging in there. However, if we just cancel the Peacekeeper, the MX—if we say we won't deploy it—we remove a major incentive for the Soviets to stay at the table and agree to reductions.

Look at it from their perspective. If we're willing to cancel a weapon system without getting something in return, why should they offer to eliminate or reduce weapons that give them an advantage over us?

In 1977 my predecessor sent his Secretary of State to Moscow with a proposal that the Soviets reduce the number of their heavy SS-18 missiles. At the time, we had nothing comparable to the SS-18 and no new missiles to deploy. The result was what you'd expect. The Soviets refused to even consider the proposal. I can't believe the American people want to make that mistake a second time. The stakes are just too high.

Without the Peacekeeper, we weaken our ability to deter war, and we may lose a valuable opportunity to achieve a treaty to reduce nuclear weapons on both sides. With it, we make progress on both paths to peace. On both counts, there's no doubt that we need it.

In the weeks ahead, we'll continue to bring the facts to you, the American people, and your representatives on this vital issue. We've already done it in hearings before the Senate. I only wish the House had given us the opportunity to do the same before it voted last Tuesday to cut funds for the Peacekeeper missile. It's hard to make a good decision before you've heard the facts. And in my opinion, the House of Representatives voted without really considering the facts.

As we present our case for the Peacekeeper missile to you, I hope you'll keep in mind that, by continuing to maintain our ability to deter attack, we make it less likely that the horror of nuclear war will ever occur. And by keeping our defenses credible, we offer the Soviet Union a realistic incentive to reduce tensions and to agree to significant and verifiable arms reductions.

These are vital objectives. But I can't achieve them without the support of the American people and the United States Congress. To protect the peace, we must provide the funds necessary to offset the enormous Soviet military buildup and restore a military balance, particularly in nuclear weapons. And to achieve the arms reductions we want, we must give the Soviets the incentive to negotiate. We must go to the bargaining table in a position of strength, not weakness.

My fellow Americans, with your continued support for a strong defense and for the Peacekeeper missile—but only with your support—we can achieve both of these crucial goals.

Thanks for listening, and God bless you.

Note: The President spoke at 12:06 P.M. EST from Camp David.

Economic Recovery/National Defense

December 18, 1982

My fellow Americans:

For many of us, this holiday season is the most special time of the year—a time when faith, joy, and love lift our spirits and bring new meaning to our lives. It's a time when we can look into the heart of America and know that her heart is good. And this year, especially this year, it's a time when we can look to our future with new hope—1983 will be a better year.

Together, we've launched a great national effort to correct the dangerous, neglected problems that were leading our country toward disaster. The
job hasn't been easy; it's been a long, tough haul. And let's not kid ourselves,
we have much more to do before we can truly say America is well again.

For too many of us, economic recovery is still a faceless stranger in
some cold, distant future, not a warm friend who's come to grace our family
hearth. But despite our frustrations, let's not lose sight of the essential: America is on the mend. To move forward again we had to get rid of what was
holding us back—runaway spending, double-digit inflation, record interest
rates, a tax burden soaring out of sight, and an alarming erosion of our
national defense, which jeopardized our security and undermined our leadership abroad. Progress is always slower than we'd like, but there's no doubt
we're making headway on each of these deep-rooted problems.

Looking to the future, I see an America that will help to lead the world
out of its longest, deepest recession in postwar history; 1983 will witness a
higher level of economic activity and lower unemployment. This view is held
not only by my economic advisers but by the vast majority of private fore-
casters across the country, and the forecasts are being borne out by the facts
and figures. Momentum for recovery is not weakening but building. Sharp
declines in inflation, interest rates, and the first reductions in personal income
tax rates have given consumers more money to spend, more incentives to
save, and more confidence to do both. Workers' real hourly earnings have
registered their first year-to-year improvement since 1978.

One of the most encouraging signs we're seeing is the strong recovery in
a bedrock American industry—housing. More homes built will mean new
demand for big-ticket items like appliances, whose sales have been lagging.
Auto and retail sales are also picking up, and business start-ups are near a
record. All this will stimulate demand for labor, and that means jobs. I think
it's encouraging that the help-wanted advertising index in October—the most
recent month available—rose 4.1 percent after falling for the previous 10
months. Equally encouraging, initial claims for unemployment insurance
have begun to trend lower.

Now, let me say a word about another long-ignored problem we've
begun to correct—the decline of our nation's defenses. The day I took office,
almost 2 years ago, our Armed Forces were in a dismal state of readiness.
Shortages of skilled manpower, faulty equipment, lack of spare parts, insuffi-
cient fuel and ammunition for proper training—all had left the United States
exposed and vulnerable.

Let us always remember we have no higher responsibility than safe-
guarding the security and freedom of our country.

One of my first priorities was to restore the readiness of our Armed
Forces. We've begun to pay our soldiers a decent wage for the risks they

take, and that incentive is bearing fruit. Reenlistment is up significantly, and the educational caliber of enlistees is improving, too.

But we're not just giving our men and women in uniform the better pay they deserve; we're also providing them the training and equipment they weren't getting before. We have increased pilot flying time, extended basic training, and restocked spare parts inventories.

By providing adequate compensation for our soldiers, by giving them the tools they need to do their jobs, we're restoring dignity, honor, and pride to the uniform of the United States of America. And, by strengthening the credibility of our Armed Forces, we increase the probability of reaching a satisfactory arms control agreement with the Soviet Union.

A stronger defense is an investment in peace. It helps ensure that our sons and daughters will not have to pay the price that so many before them had to.

Two years ago, there was growing doubt about America's determination to protect its vital interests and fulfill its obligations as a trustee of freedom, democracy, and peace. Well, I don't think anyone harbors such illusions anymore. With our friends in the Americas, Europe, Africa, and Asia, we're working in a spirit of partnership to stimulate economic progress and to build a more peaceful world.

The United States will redouble its efforts to restore sovereignty to Lebanon and to renew negotiations for an end to turmoil and bloodshed in the Middle East. And we'll strive to strengthen world peace through intensive negotiations with the Soviet Union. I want the Russian people to know the United States is committed to negotiate significant reductions in existing levels of weapons and to foster a more stable relationship between our two nations.

In this season when people all over the world celebrate the birth of Jesus, the one we call the Prince of Peace, let us rededicate ourselves to this sacred mission.

Our country may face enormous challenges, but the great advantage of our democracy is that we do not act from fear or simply respond to threats. We Americans have never been pessimists. We conquer fear with faith, and we overwhelm threats and hardship with courage, work, opportunity, and freedom.

We're a nation built and sustained by hope. And for all of us in America, this is a time for new hope.

Till next week, thanks for listening, and God bless you.

Note: The President spoke at 12:06 P.M. EST from the Oval Office at the White House.

Christmas Day

December 25, 1982

Merry Christmas from the White House. Nancy and I wish we could personally thank the thousands of you who've sent us holiday cards, greetings, and messages. Each one is moving and tells a story of its own—a story of love, hope, prayer, and patriotism. And each one has helped to brighten our Christmas.

Some of the most moving have come from fellow citizens who, unlike most of us, are not spending Christmas day at the family hearth, surrounded by friends and loved ones. I'm thinking of the 12 U.S. marines who sent us a card from Beirut, Lebanon, where they'll spend their Christmas helping to rebuild the shattered hopes for peace in a suffering land. And I'm thinking of the petty officer serving aboard the U.S.S. *Enterprise* who asked that we remember him and his shipmates this holiday season. "Christmas in the Indian Ocean is *no* fun," he writes, "but it's for a very good cause."

Well, that's right, sailor. You're serving a very good cause, indeed. On this, the birthday of the Prince of Peace, you and your comrades serve to protect the peace He taught us. You may be thousands of miles away, but to us here at home, you've never been closer.

One of my favorite pieces of Christmas mail came early this year, a sort of modern American Christmas story that took place not in our country's heartland, but on the troubled waters of the South China Sea last October. To me, it sums up so much of what is best about the Christmas spirit, the American character, and what this beloved land of ours stands for—not only to ourselves but to millions of less fortunate people around the globe.

I want to thank Mr. Gary Kemp of Neenah, Wisconsin, for bringing it to my attention. It's a letter from Ordnance Man, First Class, John Mooney, written to his parents from aboard the aircraft carrier *Midway* on October 15th. But it's a true Christmas story in the best sense.

"Dear Mom and Dad," he wrote, "today we spotted a boat in the water, and we rendered assistance. We picked up 65 Vietnamese refugees. It was about a two-hour job getting everyone aboard, and then they had to get screened by intelligence and checked out by medical and fed and clothed and all that.

"But now they're resting on the hangar deck, and the kids—most of them seem to be kids...are sitting in front of probably the first television set they've ever seen, watching 'Star Wars.' Their boat was sinking as we came alongside. They'd been at sea five days, and had run out of water. All in all, a couple of more days and the kids would have been in pretty bad shape.

"I guess once in awhile," he writes, "we need a jolt like that for us to realize why we do what we do and how important, really, it can be. I mean, it took a lot of guts for those parents to make a choice like that, to go to sea in a leaky boat in hope of finding someone to take them from the sea. So much risk! But apparently they felt it was worth it rather than live in a Communist country.

"For all of our problems, with the price of gas, and not being able to afford a new car or other creature comforts this year...I really don't see a lot of leaky boats heading out of San Diego looking for the Russian ships out there....

"After the refugees were brought aboard, I took some pictures, but as usual I didn't have my camera with me for the REAL picture—the one blazed in my mind....

"As they approached the ship, they were all waving and trying as best they could to say, 'Hello, America sailor! Hello, Freedom man!' It's hard to see a boat full of people like that and not get a lump somewhere between chin and belly button. And it really makes one proud and glad to be an American. People were waving and shouting and choking down lumps and trying not to let other brave men see their wet eyes. A lieutenant next to me said, 'Yeah, I guess it's payday in more ways than one.' (We got paid today.) And I guess no one could say it better than that.

"It reminds us all of what America has always been—a place a man or woman can come to for freedom. I know we're crowded and we have unemployment and we have a real burden with refugees, but I honestly hope and pray we can always find room. We have a unique society, made up of castoffs of all the world's wars and oppressions, and yet we're strong and free. We have one thing in common—no matter where our forefathers came from, we believe in that freedom.

"I hope we always have room for one more person, maybe an Afghan or a Pole or someone else looking for a place...where he doesn't have to worry about his family's starving or a knock on the door in the night..." and where "all men who truly seek freedom and honor and respect and dignity for themselves and their posterity can find a place where they can...finally see their dreams come true and their kids educated and become the next generations of doctors and lawyers and builders and soldiers and sailors.

"Love, John."

Well, I think that letter just about says it all. In spite of everything, we Americans are still uniquely blessed, not only with the rich bounty of our land but by a bounty of the spirit—a kind of year-round Christmas spirit that still makes our country a beacon of hope in a troubled world and that makes this Christmas and every Christmas even more special for all of us who number among our gifts the birthright of being an American.

Until next week, thanks for listening. Merry Christmas, and God bless you.

Note: The President's remarks were recorded on December 23 in the Cabinet Room at the White House for broadcast on December 25.

New Year's Day

January 1, 1983

My fellow Americans:

I've always thought New Year's Day was an especially American tradition, full of the optimism and hope we're famous for in our daily lives—an energy and confidence we call the American spirit.

Perhaps because we know we control our own destiny, we believe deep down inside that, working together, we can make each new year better than the old.

Although last night was one of parties, today is one of resolutions. Reviewing the old year, we try to decide what we can do better in the new. Most of us are with our families, near the warmth of the hearth, watching the parades with our children and football with our friends. Gathered together, we find strength and renewal.

But this special holiday time is tragically marred for too many of us. You may have spotted the reason on the road last night if you had to drive home: the drunk driver.

Each year, approximately 25,000 lives are lost in alcohol-related automobile accidents. An additional 650,000 are seriously injured. The personal pain and heartache caused by these needless tragedies is immeasurable, and billions of dollars are lost in medical costs, wages, and through hours of missed work. This weekend, while millions of Americans are traveling on our highways and streets and while hundreds of millions more are celebrating with their loved ones, let's take a few minutes to think of ways to protect ourselves and our families from the menace of the drunk and drug-influenced driver.

The first step is to realize that a drunk-driver accident is no accident. The motorist who drinks too much and then drives, who uses drugs and then gets behind the wheel of a car, is a disaster waiting to happen. Overall, alcohol is now involved in up to 55 percent of all fatal highway crashes and is a contributing factor in more than 2 million motor vehicle accidents each year. The drunk driver has turned his car into a weapon—a weapon that threatens the lives and safety of the innocent.

Fortunately, there's a brighter side. Today we have one of our best opportunities in years to tackle this tragic problem. Public awareness has never been higher. Citizens' groups, local officials, legislators, judges, police officers—people from all over the country are saying, "Enough is enough. Let's get these killers off our roads and get them off now."

Last April, I appointed a Presidential Commission on Drunk Driving to explore the problem more fully and to work with State and local governments to develop effective programs. Their interim report has already come in and has some useful findings. For example, we've found that people who've had too much to drink are less likely to drive when they know they have a good chance of being caught. The potential drunk driver who understands that prosecution is certain and the penalty swift will be less likely to insist on driving home.

For this deterrent to work, however, State and local law enforcement officials must make it clear that they mean business. Programs are already springing up in some States with good results. In areas where police have made drunk drivers a prime target, traffic deaths have begun to decline. For example, in Maine, alcohol-related crashes have dropped 41 percent since that State's drunk driving program was strengthened. The highway death rate there is the lowest since they started keeping records. Maryland has also intensified its program, and highway deaths there are at a 19-year low.

Since 1980, 11 States have raised the legal drinking age, and many other communities, counties, and States have strengthened their laws, some requiring mandatory jail sentences for first offenders. In New York, for example, the fines and fees levied on those arrested are directed to local alcohol programs. In many areas, citizens' groups are assisting State and local task forces, providing legislative support, and participating in court monitoring and victim assistance. Of course, until we change our attitudes and our laws, our best protection is still to buckle our safety belts.

There's much to be done if we're to rid ourselves of this scourge on our roads, and there's a continuing need for private initiative. We must each make it our personal responsibility. If we band together, we can change the laws that will help make the difference. If we insist long enough and loudly enough, we can save lives. So I thought it appropriate to start the ball rolling on this, the first day of the new year.

Today, we're taking a break from the concerns and the bustle of the work-a-day world. But we're also making a new beginning. As we gather around our dining room tables for the mid-day meal, let us thank God for life and the blessings He's put before us. High among them are our families, our freedom, and the opportunities of a new year.

Let us renew our faith that, as free men and women, we still have the power to better our lives, and let us resolve to face the challenges of the new year holding that conviction firmly in our hearts. That, after all, is our greatest strength and our greatest gift as Americans.

So, till next week, thanks for listening, Happy New Year, and God bless you.

Note: The President's remarks were recorded on December 23 in the Cabinet Room at the White House for broadcast on January 1.

U.S.-Soviet Relations and the Vice-President's Trip to Europe

January 8, 1983

My fellow Americans:

Today I'd like to share with you some thoughts on one of the most important aspects of America's role in the world—our relations with the Soviet Union. Keeping the peace for both countries—for that matter, for all mankind, depends on our wise and steady management of this relationship.

As you know, a new leader has come to power in Moscow. There's been much speculation about whether this change could mean a chance to reduce tensions and solve some of the problems between us. No one hopes more than I do that the future will bring improvement in our relations with the Soviets and an era of genuine stability. What could be more important than reducing the danger of confrontation, increasing the prospects for enduring peace, lowering nuclear arsenals, relieving human suffering in Afghanistan, Kampuchea, and elsewhere?

With your support, this administration has embarked on an effort to restore our nation's strength, credibility, and clarity of purpose in the world. Our aim has been to ensure that America has the will and the means to deter conflict and to defend the interests of freedom. We've done this for one reason and one reason only—because a strong, respected America is the surest way to preserve the peace and prevent conflict.

In this effort, we must learn from history. We all experienced the soaring hopes and then plunging disappointment of the 1970's, when the Soviet response to our unilateral restraint was to accelerate their military buildup, to foment violence in the developing world, to invade neighboring Afghanistan, and to support the repression of Poland.

The lesson is inescapable. If there are to be better mutual relations, they must result from moderation in Soviet conduct, not just our own good intentions. In recent days, some encouraging words have come out of Moscow. Clearly, the Soviets want to appear more responsive and reasonable. But moderate words are convincing only when they're matched by moderate behavior.

Now we must see whether they're genuinely interested in reducing existing tensions. We and our democratic partners eagerly await any serious actions and proposals the Soviets may offer and stand ready to discuss with them serious proposals which can genuinely advance the cause of peace.

We do not insist that the Soviet Union abandon its standing as a superpower or its legitimate national interests. In fact, we hope that the new leadership in Moscow will come to realize that Soviet interests would be improved by ending the bloodshed in Afghanistan, by showing restraint in the Middle East, by permitting reform and thus promoting stability in Poland, by ending their unequaled military buildup, as we have proposed, by reducing the most dangerous nuclear arms to much lower and equal levels.

We stand ready to work toward solutions to all outstanding problems. Now, this doesn't mean that we should neglect our own defenses. That would undercut our ability to maintain peace and jeopardize whatever chance we may have for changing Soviet conduct. But it does mean that we're always ready to sit down with the Soviets to discuss practical steps that could resolve problems and lead to a more durable and genuine improvement in East-West relations.

Next month, Soviet and American negotiators will resume talks in Geneva on strategic and intermediate-range nuclear forces. We've proposed drastic cuts in those threatening intermediate-range forces. The Soviets have responded in both negotiations with proposals of their own. So, a serious foundation for progress has been laid. America will negotiate energetically and in good faith to achieve early agreements providing for reduced and equal levels of forces. The Soviet leadership must understand that the way to reduce the nuclear threat is by negotiating in the same sincere spirit and not by trying to sow division between the American people and our NATO partners. That kind of negative tactic is certain to fail and can only delay real progress.

A cornerstone of our approach to relations with the Soviet Union is close consultation with our allies on common political and security issues. In this spirit, I've asked Vice President Bush to travel to Europe. Beginning at the end of this month, he will visit the Federal Republic of Germany, the Netherlands, Belgium, Switzerland, Italy, France, and Great Britain, and at the Vatican he will meet with Pope John Paul II. In Switzerland the Vice President will meet with the negotiating teams for the Strategic Arms Reduction Talks, which we call START, and the Intermediate-range Nuclear Forces arms control talks we call INF and will attend a meeting of the Committee on Disarmament in Geneva.

The Vice President's visit to these close friends and allies and his discussions at the Vatican and in Geneva underscore our fundamental commitment to peace and security in Europe and to genuine arms reductions.

So, the new year begins with reason for all of us to hope that, if we continue to act firmly and wisely, 1983 can be a time of peaceful progress for America, for our allies, for the people of the U.S.S.R., and for the entire world.

Till next week, thanks for listening, and God bless you.

Note: The President spoke at 12:06 P.M. EST from Camp David.

Dr. Martin Luther King, Jr.

January 15, 1983

My fellow Americans:

A few hours from now in the East Room of the White House, I'll be hosting a reception honoring the memory of a man who played a truly historic role in expanding the freedom we enjoy in America.

Dr. Martin Luther King, Jr., was born into a world where bigotry and racism still held sway. Before he died, he had touched the conscience of a nation and had contributed immeasurably to the human rights of black Americans. He was a man of character and a man of courage.

Early in his life, Martin Luther King learned the meaning of discrimination. He and his father—a distinguished minister in a large Baptist church—went to a shoe store and were told that they would have to go to the back of the store. To his credit, the father took his son and walked out, vowing as he went to fight against such racism and discrimination.

As Martin Luther King grew older, following his father's example, he studied, earned a college degree, and was ordained into the ministry. Racism was still widespread in the world in those days. In this country, which served in so many ways as an example of liberty, racial discrimination remained a tragic taint. Injustice held black Americans in a vice-like [*sic*] grip, making it harder for them to build a better life. Black Americans were forced into separate facilities, as they were bused past nearby schools to be put into segregated and sometimes inferior schools miles away. No matter how qualified for a job, they often knew they need not apply because their skin color, rather than their skills, might determine who filled the position. Roughly one-tenth of our people were forced to endure humiliating and degrading conditions. One such rule in one city required all blacks to sit in the back section of public buses.

But sometimes a single, human act of courage can change the world. In 1955 a brave woman named Rosa Parks refused to give up her seat and move to the back of the bus. She was arrested. When the bus company refused to change the rule, a young minister in a local Baptist church, Martin Luther King, Jr., helped organize a boycott that captured the attention of the country. In 6 months, the courts had ruled the segregation of public transportation to be unconstitutional.

It was the first real test of Dr. King's nonviolent philosophy. He advocated nonviolence because he believed that, with hard work and good will, people's hearts can be touched and progress can be made. Yet, progress is not easy. In his book, "The Strength To Love," Dr King wrote, "Nothing pains some people more than having to think."

Well, during the years following the bus boycott, Dr. King, with tremendous courage and resourcefulness, got a lot of Americans thinking. He was instrumental in getting passage of legislation that provided Federal protection for the crown jewel of American liberty—every American's right to vote. That legacy still lives. Last year I signed into law the longest extension of the Voting Rights Acts since its passage—a measure that will protect the right to vote for many years to come.

In 1964, Dr. King was awarded the Nobel Peace Prize—the youngest man ever to earn that high award. Through his actions, his teachings, and his deep dedication to nonviolence, he opened the eyes of his fellow citizens. Civil rights legislation was passed, but, perhaps even more important, he awakened the moral sense of an entire nation. He appealed to the good that is in our people.

In 1968, Martin Luther King was brutally murdered, shot down by a cowardly assassin. He had remained true to his principles to the end, never succumbing to the hatred that had destroyed the effectiveness of lesser men. On the steps of the Lincoln Memorial, he had held a great and peaceful civil rights rally. He spoke there of a dream—his dream for an America where there would be no place for hatred. His words are now a moving part of our history.

Had he lived, the man we honor on this day would be only 54 years old. He cannot be with us. But today in Atlanta, Vice President Bush is attending a gathering honoring his 83-year-old father who did so much to start his son on the road to achievement and martyrdom.

In honoring them both, we should look to the future as well as the past. Yes, we should be proud of the progress we've made. But we also must face the fact that, 15 years after Martin Luther King's death, traces of bigotry and injustice still remain.

So, let the anniversary of this courageous American's birth be for us both a time of thanksgiving and a time of renewal. Let us be grateful for the providence that sends among us men and women with the courage and vision to stand peacefully but unyieldingly for what is right. But let us also make this a time when we rededicate ourselves, young and old, black and white, to carry on the work of justice and to totally reject the words and actions of hate embodied in groups like the Ku Klux Klan.

Martin Luther King, Jr., showed us how much good a single life, well-led, can accomplish. His death proved how much harm a single hand, intent on evil, can inflict. Let each of us honor his memory by pledging in our own lives to do everything we can to make America a place where his dream of freedom and brotherhood will grow and flourish from sea to shining sea.

If we do this, then his sacrifice will not have been in vain, and we will have helped to make our country the special place we all know in our hearts that it was meant to be.

Thank you for listening. God bless you.

Note: The President spoke at 12:06 P.M. EST from the Oval Office at the White House.

Domestic Social Issues

January 22, 1983

My fellow Americans:

A week ago, Graham Washington Jackson, an ex-Navy musician, died in Atlanta at the age of 79. You probably don't recognize his name, but his face became familiar to millions of Americans when President Roosevelt died in Warm Springs, Georgia, in 1945. There's a very famous, very moving photo of Chief Petty Officer Jackson, tears streaming down his face while he played "Going Home" on his accordion as F.D.R.'s body was borne away by train to Washington.

Mr. Jackson once said that, as he began to play, "It seemed like every nail and every pin in the world just stuck in me." Mr. Jackson symbolized the grief of the Nation back in 1945, and I just wanted his own family to know the Nation hasn't forgotten their personal grief today, 38 years later.

As I'm sure Mr. Jackson's family would tell you, in times of sorrow the warmth and support of a family's ties are especially important. I've spoken a great deal about the strength and virtues of the American family. I'd like to return to that topic today, because the family will again be a top priority as we head into the new year—for the family is still the basic unit of religious and moral values that hold our society together.

In the year ahead we face serious, painful problems, like unemployment. In a few days I'll speak about the economic situation facing us, but I also want you to know we'll not ignore the moral essentials in the coming months. As many of you know, I strongly support an amendment that will permit our children to hold prayer in our schools. The amendment would allow communities to determine for themselves whether voluntary prayer should be permitted in their public schools. We didn't get that amendment through the last Congress, but I'll continue to push for it in the next Congress.

I believe that schoolchildren deserve the same right to pray that's enjoyed by the Congress and chaplains and troops in our armed services. The motto on our coinage reads, "In God We Trust." No one must ever be forced or pressured to take part in any religious exercise, but neither should the Government forbid religious practice. The public expression through prayer of our faith in God is a fundamental part of our American heritage and a privilege which should not be excluded from our schools.

Today, 5 million American kids attend private schools because of the emphasis on religious values and educational standards. The overwhelming majority of these schools are church-supported—Catholic, Protestant, and Jewish. And the majority of students are from families earning less than $25,000. In many parochial schools the majority of students are from minority neighborhoods. In addition to private tuition, these families also pay their full share of taxes to fund the public schools. I think they're entitled to some relief, since they're supporting two school systems and only using one.

Last year, as a matter of tax equity, we introduced legislation to give these families a break. We don't seek to aid the rich, but those lower- and middle-income families who are most strapped by taxes and the recession. In proposing tuition tax credits, we hope to provide greater choice and wider educational opportunity for our children. The Congress failed to pass the measure we proposed, but we're not giving up. In the coming session, we will again work to secure passage of tuition tax credits.

There's another issue closely identified with families, although the issue itself often splits families apart. Ten years ago today, the Supreme Court overturned the State laws protecting the lives of the unborn. Heated debate on abortion has raged ever since. On one hand, there is the argument that a woman should have control over her own person. On the other hand, there is the argument that another life is involved here—the unborn child. That's the belief which has drawn many here to Washington today to march and pray.

I, too, have always believed that God's greatest gift is human life and that we have a duty to protect the life of an unborn child. Until someone can prove the unborn child is not a life, shouldn't we give it the benefit of the doubt and assume it is? That's why I favored legislation to end the practice of abortion on demand and why I will continue to support it in the new Congress.

Now, some of you may be thinking. "Well, he hasn't said a thing that's new." I guess that's true. Some values shouldn't change. But I want you to know there are certain family issues I'll advocate even though it's the budget and the economy that will be getting the headlines, especially in the days ahead.

I realize, though, that to the family with a member unemployed, the economy is a family member. And I'll take that up in my State of the Union address Tuesday night. I hope you'll tune in.

Until next week at this same time, thanks for listening, and God bless you.

Note: The President spoke at 12:06 P.M. EST from Camp David.

Fiscal Year 1984 Budget

January 29, 1983

My fellow Americans:

On Monday, I will send to the Congress my budget message for fiscal year 1984. I wanted to give you a little preview of that message today.

Much of the debate in the weeks and months ahead will focus on the deficit. That's a dirty word which awhile back I'd hoped might be a thing of the past by 1984. But the deficit is going to be large. And I wanted to tell you the whys and wherefores of this deficit dilemma and how our budget seeks to remedy it.

Ironically, the deficit problem has been aggravated by our success in reducing inflation. You know, inflation is actually a form of taxation. During the 1970's, the government slyly got tax increases every year when cost-of-living pay raises pushed people into higher tax brackets.

Well, we've pretty much strangled the inflation tax, and the result is that the government no longer gets a free ride. If the government wants or needs more tax money, it should openly raise taxes, not follow practices that create inflation. Of course, raising taxes isn't as safe politically as letting inflation do it. So, lowering inflation has been quite a shock to the system.

Another reason the deficit is so burdensome is because the long recession has temporarily shrunk the number of people paying taxes. At the same time, the recession has added to the deficit by causing us to pay out more money in unemployment benefits, food stamps, and the like.

The interest on the national debt is also a reason for the deficit. About 12 percent of our budget, $103 billion a year, goes just to pay the interest. Fortunately, inflation and interest rates are down, so we're not financing that debt at the very high interest rates we once were. But it is still a very big chunk. In fact, it's more than the whole Federal budget was just about 20 years ago.

The necessary process of restoring our neglected national defense also has put pressure on our resources, but it's something we had to do. Where peace and freedom are at stake, we can't afford to gamble. And the fact is that the real purchasing power devoted to maintaining our military declined by a startling 20 percent in recent years.

Finally, despite our great strides in reducing the growth in spending over the last 2 years, the vast majority of domestic spending programs are still in place. The result of all this is that deficits have now reached towering levels that cast a pall of uncertainty over the financial markets and threaten to slow and weaken the economic recovery ahead of us. Well, I don't intend to let that happen. As I outlined in my State of the Union message, I'm advocating sweeping changes designed to reduce the mounting Federal deficits that threaten our economic growth. And here's what I propose.

First, I will recommend an overall Federal spending freeze. So far, we've only cut the rate of increase in Federal spending. The government has continued to spend more money each year—just not as much more. We've got to do something about that, so I propose the budget for 1984 will increase no more than the rate of inflation. This will include a 6-month freeze in the cost-of-living adjustments recommended by the bipartisan Social Security Commission and a one-year freeze on Federal employee pay and retirement programs. Now, while this means that defense spending will be up and non-defense spending, in total, will be down, it doesn't mean that all nondefense programs are being cut. In fact, some of them are increasing at even a greater rate than defense.

Second, I propose to adjust our program to restore America's defense by making $55 billion in defense savings over the next 5 years. The Secretary of Defense has assured me these reductions can be achieved without diminishing our ability to negotiate arms reductions or endangering our security.

Third, I'll ask the Congress to adopt specific measures to control the growth of spending for entitlement programs. Now, these are programs that have automatic increases built into them by legislation passed by Congress. When we submit the budget, we have to accept those built-in raises. Well, we are—for the first time—proposing some badly needed structural reforms, tailoring the benefits and eligibility rules to serve those with genuine need. In the food stamp program alone, last year we identified almost $1.1 billion in overpayments. This kind of error and waste takes money from those who really need benefits. We want to put a stop to it. I'm also proposing certain cost controls and incentives for economies in health care and measures to prune back the unaffordable costs of the Federal retirement system.

Fourth, I am proposing a standby tax that wouldn't start until 1986, and wouldn't start at all unless the deficit is greater than 2½ percent of the gross national product. And even then, it won't start unless Congress has first passed our spending cuts. You might call this tax a safety net for the deficit.

This way we can preserve the tax cuts and tax indexing we've already won for the American people and still have a fallback mechanism in place to cap the deficit if need be.

As I said the other night, America is on the mend. The leading economic indicators are up in December for the eighth time in the last 9 months. The auto companies are calling people back to work. General Motors alone is calling back more than 21,000 auto workers over the next 3 months. Construction contracts last month rose to the highest level in 3 years. And housing starts are up.

But in spite of the improving economy, much still needs to be done for the unemployed. In the days ahead, I will submit legislation designed to get at the special problems of the long-term unemployed and young people seeking to enter the job market. I'll propose extending unemployment benefits, including incentives to employers who hire the long-term unemployed. We will also seek more money for the programs benefiting displaced workers in the Jobs [*sic*] Training Partnership Act adopted last year.

Our budget is fair and realistic. It is a budget that will position America to take full advantage of the recovery. I look forward to working in a bipartisan spirit with the Congress in passing this budget.

Till next time, thanks for listening, and God bless you.

Note: The President spoke at 12:06 P.M. EST from the Oval Office at the White House.

Economic Recovery Program

February 5, 1983

My fellow Americans:

I'd like to talk to you about a word. It's a word we've all been hearing a lot lately. The word is "Reaganomics." Somewhere along the line, our economic program got tagged with that label. To tell you the truth, it isn't a name I would have chosen. It sounds like a fad diet or an aerobic exercise. But we seem to be stuck with it. With every anchorman on the evening news, a goodly share of political pundits, and more than a few politicos using it, it has a good chance of becoming standard Americana.

There wouldn't be anything wrong with that, except that it's used as a term for something that's supposed to have failed. So if you don't mind, I'm asking for equal time—well, at least, for about the next 5 minutes.

We are, and have been for some time, in a recession. Unemployment was running at 10.8 percent as the year ended. But we learned yesterday the welcome news that it dropped to 10.4 percent in January. And if you include our men and women in the military as part of the work force, which makes sense, it's down to 10.2 percent.

Still, only about two-thirds of our industrial capacity is being used. Our government is facing large deficits, and interest rates are still too high. And we're told all of this is the result of an economic program put into place by our administration and which, for obvious reasons, is called Reaganomics.

I know some will say I'm being defensive, but I'll risk that, because in the weeks ahead decisions are going to be made here in Washington that will have a bearing on whether unemployment continues to go down and the economy continues to go up. You will help determine some of these decisions because public opinion does influence government. Therefore, you must have a clear fix on the facts, the economic realities.

Thomas Jefferson said, "If the people know the truth, they'll never make a mistake." So, let's start with some dates.

Back in 1979 inflation was rising, unemployment was increasing, and by 1980 we were in a recession. Unemployment had reached such a point in the last half of 1980 that I referred to it as a depression. I was criticized for that by technical-minded people who said it was only a recession. But you'll have to forgive me. I was campaigning in Flint, Michigan, where the unemployment rate was already 20 percent; in Detroit, it was 18 percent, and across the line in Ohio, steel mills were closing. In an Indiana city, unemployment was 23 percent. Inflation was in double digits for 1979 and '80 and reached 14 percent during the 1980 campaign. Interest rates went to 21½ percent, and the housing industry was at a standstill.

Our administration opened up shop on January 20th, 1981. The prime interest was still above 20 percent, inflation was 12.4 percent, and unemployment was 7.3 percent. The 1981 budget had already been put in place by the previous administration and began on October 1st, 1980. Now, there was nothing we could do about that budget—it wasn't ours—although we did manage to squeeze out a few billion dollars through some management changes. For the most part, however, we were engaged in a struggle to get our budget proposals for 1982 adopted and the other part of our economic recovery program—tax cuts for all Americans to help stimulate the economy.

All the time, interest rates stayed high, unemployment kept increasing and, by July, the bottom had fallen out.

About this same time, our economic program, most of it, was passed— major reductions in the growth of spending and a 25-percent cut in income tax rates to be phased in over a 3-year period. But none of this went into effect until October 1, 1981. The first portion of the tax cut was only 5 percent; another 10 percent would take place in July of 1982. Reaganomics, as they would have it, started only 16 months ago. There was another 10-percent cut in the income tax scheduled for this coming July.

Now, what has happened in those 16 months of Reaganomics? Well, with the help of the Federal Reserve Board, inflation has dropped to only 3.9 percent for all of 1982, the lowest it's been in 10 years. Interest rates are about half what they were. The effect of that is a 40-percent increase in housing starts. Automobile sales are up, as are all retail sales. Factory orders have begun to increase. One timber company I know of, which a year ago today was completely shut down, is now on two shifts a day, 5 days a week. Real wages are up for the first time in 3 years. And the rate of personal savings is up, meaning more capital for investment. And, as I've already mentioned, "the lagging indicator," as it's called, unemployment, just took its first drop—10.8 to 10.4. A survey of business establishments shows somewhere around 300,000 more people working. We've a long way to go, but that's a start, at last.

Now, I've seen in the flesh some of these statistics I've quoted. A few days ago, I visited a Chrysler plant in Fenton, Missouri, where 1,700 workers are being called back to a newly modernized plant. Another plant will be calling back an additional 1,500 workers by late summer. In nearby Hazelwood, the Ford plant was adding another entire shift. And General Motors has announced it plans to call back more than 21,000 of the indefinite layoffs over the next few months. For 8 out of the last 9 months, the leading economic indicators have been up.

In the weeks ahead, there'll be debate as to what course we should follow. The choice that will be offered is to turn away from our economic recovery program and go back to what was being done before. May I point out, all of the good things I've mentioned didn't begin until after our program, Reaganomics, if you will, was put in place. Prior to that, everything had been a mess for 3 years or more. I wonder if they'll still use that name when they've found out it works.

Until next time, thanks for listening, and God bless you.

Note: The President spoke at 12:06 P.M. EST from Camp David.

Fiscal Year 1984 Budget

February 12, 1983

My fellow Americans:

Today, all over our land, we remember the birth of one of our greatest sons, Abraham Lincoln—the self-educated backwoodsman who became a lawyer, Congressman, and President. Whoever would understand in their hearts the meaning of America will find it in the life of Abe Lincoln.

I was told once that, if you stand to one side of his statue at the Lincoln Memorial, you can see the profile of a man of strength and wisdom, and by standing on the other side, the profile of a man of compassion. Well, I did that, and it's true. He taught us the true meaning of "We, the people...." He made us understand that no man is good enough to govern another man without that other's consent. And he lived by his words. "I am not bound to win, but am bound to be true."

In the spirit of Lincoln, America has carried forward the dream of democracy, guaranteeing political rights for all her citizens. And as our nation has matured, we have sought to meet more fully the obligations that spring from our national conscience. In the history of mankind, there has never been a people who've strived harder or done more than we Americans to help all who are truly in need.

This administration is committed to carry on that tradition. When the first stage of our economic program was passed a year and a half ago, I said, "America now has an economic plan for her future. We're going forward, and we're not leaving anyone behind." Well, getting our economy back on sound footing has been a long, tough haul, and the job isn't done yet. But evidence grows that the worst of what we inherited is behind us. The economy is improving. Recovery has begun.

What about the second part of our pledge—to make sure no one in America is left behind? Now, I know that some have charged that the social safety net is in shreds. Well, if I may quote Lincoln one more time, "Truth is generally the best vindication against slander."

By and large, our administration is being criticized for our sincere and, I might add, long overdue attempts to target benefits to the truly needy and to reduce benefits for those who should be able to manage for themselves.

Now, let me give you a few figures: Welfare, medical, nutrition, and housing assistance for our most needy citizens, plus compensation for the unemployed, is almost one-fourth, 24 percent, higher in the fiscal [*sic*] 1984 budget than it was in 1981. In our fiscal year 1984 budget we've proposed $93 billion in assistance for the needy and unemployed. Twenty-three years ago, the Federal Government wasn't spending $93 billion on its entire budget.

Look at one specific area—nutrition assistance programs. The doom and gloom criers have been having a lot of fun with the charge that we're increasing hunger. Well, the facts are this administration is committed to providing adequate nutritional assistance to all who need it. And we're fulfilling that commitment. The Federal Government is subsidizing 95 million meals a day. Meal subsidies are now being targeted more heavily than ever toward children from low-income households. Nutrition standards are being maintained. More people are receiving food stamps than ever before, and average benefits per person have grown at a rate faster than food price inflation. Yes, there has been a slight reduction in the number of school lunches, but that's because there's been a reduction in enrollment.

Here's another myth from the misery merchants: They've frightened too many Americans dependent on Social Security into believing our administration would take away their checks. I have pledged repeatedly that we have only one goal—to save a system badly in need of repair. The best thing that could happen to Social Security is to get it out of the news, out of politics, and back into the confidence of the American people. With cooperation from the Congress, we can pass the Social Security Commission's bipartisan plan and start to do just that.

What about their charge that we're slashing spending on social programs to spend more on defense? Well, it's true that we're requesting $1.6 trillion in defense spending over the next 5 years. But I'll bet you haven't heard that, during this same period, spending budgeted for entitlement programs will be over $2 trillion, or $500 billion more than defense. What we propose to spend on defense is a much smaller part of the Federal budget and our total economy than was being spent 10, 20, 30 years ago. Yet the threat to America's freedom is greater than it was in those earlier times.

So, let me repeat, far from trying to destroy what is best in our system of humane, free government, we're doing everything we can to save it by slowing down the destructive rate of growing in taxes and spending and by pruning nonessential programs. This way enough resources will be left to meet the requirements of the truly needy, and we will meet the challenge of fairness. The most unfair situation was the one our people were trapped in before, when record inflation, taxes, and interest rates were slamming shut the gates of prosperity on every American family. We're out of that trap now. If we work together, we can have a healthy and lasting economic recovery.

As Lincoln once said in another turbulent time, "If we do not make common cause to save the good old ship of the Union on this voyage, nobody will have a chance to pilot her on another voyage."

Well, America met her test then. With your help, we'll do it again.

Until next week, thanks for listening, and God bless you.

Note: The President spoke at 12:06 P.M. EST from the Oval Office at the White House.

Defense Spending

February 19, 1983

My fellow Americans:

This Monday will mark the 251st birthday of George Washington, the Father of our Country. Unlike Abraham Lincoln, Franklin Roosevelt, and most other famous Presidents, Washington was not a great orator or man of words. He was, above all, a man of action and character. His courage, firmness, and integrity first led a ragged, outnumbered army to triumph against the mightiest empire of his time and then guided our infant republic to maturity as the first President of the United States.

George Washington didn't say much, but when he did speak, as both a soldier and a statesman, what he said was worth listening to. As President, in his first annual address to the Congress, he offered a wise piece of advice on defense preparedness that is as timely today as it was when he uttered it nearly two centuries ago.

"To be prepared for war," George Washington said, "is the most effectual means of preserving the peace." When I reread this quote a few days ago, it brought to mind the current public debate over this administration's efforts to protect the peace by restoring our country's neglected defenses.

Now, I know that this is a hard time to call for increased defense spending. It isn't easy to ask American families who are already making sacrifices in the recession, or American businesses which are struggling to reinvest for the future, and it isn't easy for someone like me who's dedicated his entire political career to reducing government spending.

On the other hand, it's always very easy and very tempting politically to come up with arguments for neglecting defense spending in time of peace. One of the great tragedies of this century was that it was only after the balance of power was allowed to erode and a ruthless adversary, Adolf Hitler, deliberately weighed the risks and decided to strike that the importance of a strong defense was realized too late. That was what happened in the years leading up to World War II. And especially for those of us who lived through that nightmare, it's a mistake that America and the free world must never make again.

I want you to know that members of my administration and I have agonized over the current defense budget. We've trimmed back our plans for rebuilding defense by more than half. We've hunted for savings in nonessential programs. We've weighed economic risks and economic benefits. The defense budget we finally presented is a minimal budget to protect our country's vital interests and meet our commitments.

For those who wish to cut it back further, I have a simple question. Which interests and which commitments are they ready to abandon? Let me make just a few key points about our defense program.

First, we must develop a responsible and balanced understanding of the danger we face. Over the past 20 years, the Soviet Union has accumulated enormous military might, while we restrained our own efforts to the point where defense spending actually declined, in real terms, over 20 percent in the decade of the seventies.

Today, the Soviets outinvest us by nearly 2-to-1. Even with the defense increases of the past 2 years, they outproduce us substantially in almost every category of weapons. And in actions such as the brutal invasion and occupation of Afghanistan, they have demonstrated their willingness to use these weapons for aggression.

Finally, Soviet military power has spread around the globe, threatening our access to vital resources and our sea lines of communication, undermining our forward line of defense in Europe and Korea, and challenging us even at home, here in our own hemisphere.

We must face the facts. If we continue our past pattern of only rebuilding our defenses in fits and starts, we will never convince the Soviets that it's in their interests to behave with restraint and negotiate genuine arms reductions. We will also burden the American taxpayer time and again with the high cost of crash rearmament. Sooner or later, the bills fall due.

For instance, our land-based missiles were designed in the 1950's and installed in the sixties, and many of the pilots of our B-52 bombers are younger than the planes they fly. The fact is these past fits and starts in a decade of neglecting our defenses have left this administration, this Congress, and the American taxpayer stuck with double duty.

We had to act quickly to increase the basic readiness and staying power of our forces so that they could meet any immediate crisis if one arose. At the same time, we have to make up for lost years of investment by undertaking the research and development and the force modernization needed to meet crises that could arise in the future. We simply cannot afford [avoid]* performing this double duty unless we're willing to gamble with our immediate security and pass on to future generations the legacy of neglect we inherited. That kind of neglect would only weaken peace and stability in the world, both now and in the years ahead.

I have lived through two world wars. I saw the American people rise to meet these crises, and I have faith in their willingness to come to their nation's defense in the future. But it's far better to prevent a crisis than to have to face it unprepared at the last moment. That's why we have an overriding moral obligation to invest now, this year, in this budget, in restoring America's strength to keep the peace and preserve our freedom.

---

*White House correction

Till next week, thanks for listening, and God bless you.

Note: The President spoke at 12:06 P.M. EST from the Oval Office at the White House.

Natural Gas Consumers and Regulatory Reform Legislation

February 26, 1983

My fellow Americans:

Today I'd like to talk to you about a subject that touches on all of us one way or another—in our homes, schools, at workplaces, and in the overall economy. I want to talk about one of our major energy sources—natural gas—and what this administration proposes to do to ensure abundant supplies of it at reasonable prices.

As the situation stands now, the American consumer is being hurt by government regulations that actually contribute to higher gas bills. We want to change that. Now, I know all too well that energy is a subject that some people in public life just can't resist playing politics with. It's unfortunate, but I guess it's a fact of life, or at least a fact of life as we know it in Washington, which can be pretty different from hometown America.

Many of you, I'm sure, recall the howls that went up when we acted to deregulate oil prices 2 years ago. Remember how you were told that deregulation would lead to skyrocketing prices for the gasoline that fuels millions of American cars, or the oil that heats millions of American homes? Well, the evidence is in, and the doomsayers were dead wrong.

You don't have to go any further than the nearest filling station to see that prices have gone down, not up, since decontrol, just as we promised they would. The economic realities of the marketplace have done more to bring down the price of oil than all those years of frenetic government regulating.

I think there's a lesson here for all of us and one that goes a lot deeper than the price of energy. Way back in 1824, Thomas Jefferson wrote about the difference between two kinds of political mentalities. Both of them are still very much with us today. Here's what Jefferson said about them: "Men by their constitutions are naturally divided into two parties—those who fear and distrust the people and wish to draw all powers from them, and those who identify themselves with the people and have confidence in them."

Now, the vast majority of us identify with the second group, the one that believes in trusting the wisdom of the people rather than taking power away from them and concentrating it in the other hands. On a more personal level, anyone who's ever wrestled with a tax form or had to make sense out of a complicated bureaucratic regulation knows how costly and time-consuming government overregulation can be. And that brings me back to regulation; in this case, regulation of natural gas.

I'm convinced—and I believe that the evidence backs me up—that, just as deregulation of oil has led to a better deal for the American consumer, a freer market in natural gas will have the same beneficial effect for you. So, next week I'm sending the Congress a proposal for correcting the problems that have resulted from past excessive regulation of the natural gas market. While I'm taking this step out of the deep belief in the principle involved, there are human reasons as well.

In recent months, thousands of you have written to me, to Members of Congress, and to State and local officials expressing your distress about rapidly rising natural gas bills. Some areas of the country have been especially hard hit, and it's clear that consumers are being poorly and unfairly served by the existing regulatory system. That system prevents natural gas producers and their customers from entering into contracts that respond to market forces, including pressure for lower prices that are now possible due to plentiful gas supplies and declining oil prices.

Today there's a surplus of natural gas, and oil prices are dropping. These factors normally would result in lower natural gas prices. But the regulatory morass has kept the marketplace from achieving lower natural gas prices. In sharp contrast, the Department of Energy estimates that, if our proposal is enacted, natural gas prices will drop by at least 10 to 30 cents per thousand cubic feet in the first year.

The measure I will submit to the Congress is not a partisan plan, and it resorts to no quick political fixes. Instead, our approach is a comprehensive proposal that can, and I believe will, be supported by Congressmen and Senators of both parties and will benefit the consumers they represent.

Basically, our legislative package will allow a freer market for natural gas so that there will be real and long-term incentives to produce and market abundant gas supplies at the lowest possible cost, just as gasoline and home heating oil prices have declined since we deregulated oil. Although we believe free markets not only can but will achieve these results, we aren't asking you, the consumer, to take that on faith.

To assure that consumers are protected, I have insisted on a provision which reverses the present law and provides that, until 1986, there will be a moratorium on the automatic pass-through to consumers of increased gas costs by the gas pipelines, other than those caused by inflation, which, as you know, has been declining steadily.

The key to cheaper, more abundant energy for all Americans is a policy that combines consumer protection, incentives to produce, and efficient, economic use of our resources. That's what our program will do. And I look forward to working closely with Members of both parties in the Congress to obtain its passage without delay.

Until next week, thanks for listening, and God bless you.

Note: The President spoke at 12:06 P.M. EST from the Oval Office at the White House.

Employment Programs

March 5, 1983

My fellow Americans:

Today I'd like to talk about jobs for our people. Now, without sounding too much like I'm giving a lecture, there are two basic types of unemployment—cyclical and structural.

Cyclical unemployment results from changes in the business cycle, the ups and downs of the overall economy. Almost half of our current unemployment program [problem]* is cyclical—the direct result of the recession. The best cure for cyclical unemployment is to get the economy moving again, and our economic program is doing just that.

Recently, the figures for industrial production, housing starts and sales, and new orders for manufactured durable goods have all been good news. Just this week the index of leading economic indicators, a harbinger of what's to come, registered the biggest single jump in 33 years. This improving economy will assist those who suffer from cyclical unemployment as business picks up and workers are called back to stores, factories, offices, and construction sites around the country.

As you know, the unemployment rate dropped in January and then held to that level in February. I've said before, unemployment always lags behind the rest of the recovery. But the rate will be heading downward. The other economic indicators are too encouraging for it to hold out much longer.

We here in Washington can ease the transition for the cyclically unemployed with short-term help. We can move up job opportunities by accelerating certain government projects and aiding those in deep distress. The Congress and I are working out our differences on such legislation right now, and I would hope it could be on my desk for signature within the next week.

Now, the other kind of unemployment is structural. Structural unemployment is not the result of temporary slumps in the economy. It is caused

---

*White House correction

by deep and lasting changes in science, technology, competitiveness, and skills. The structurally unemployed are those who don't have the skills demanded in today's workplace. Generally, we're talking about the long-term unemployed—the displaced workers from declining industries and the young who lack work training and experience.

I know this is pretty dry stuff, but I think it's important to explain because structural unemployment is a problem that will be with us for some time. And, remember, that behind those dry terms are people—black teenagers who desperately want a first job and older workers grappling with the adjustment of losing their life's work.

Up until now, no one has successfully addressed structural unemployment on a national scale. But next week, I will send the Congress a proposal that brings some important new approaches to the problem. We want to provide incentives for businesses to hire the long-term unemployed.

Under our proposal, a worker who's been unemployed for an extended period could convert the unemployment benefits he receives into job vouchers which would entitle his new employer to a tax credit. The overwhelming majority of those who've been unemployed for long periods would gladly trade their benefits for a job, if they could only find one. What they're looking for is an opportunity to become productive again. This voucher system gives them a better chance to do just that.

We also want to increase by about 10-fold to $240 million the funding for that part of the Job Training Partnership Act that helps displaced workers. This program will offer matching grants to the States for retraining, job search, and relocation assistance to displaced workers. And we also propose allowing States to use up to 2 percent of their unemployment insurance tax revenues—that could mean an estimated $374 million of additional funds—for reemployment assistance.

And, of course, I'm asking the Congress for over $3 billion for those programs that last year replaced the ineffective CETA program, where only 18 percent of the money was actually used for training the unskilled.

That old cliché that you can't get a job until you have experience and you can't get experience until you have a job really is true for too many young people, especially our minority young people, among whom the unemployment rate is a staggering 45 percent for black teenagers. One of the main reasons many youngsters have difficulty finding jobs, especially their first job, is the minimum wage. Employers simply aren't willing to pay this set wage rate to youth with no work experience. So, to help young people find jobs, I propose a youth opportunity wage at $2.50 per hour, 25 percent below the regular minimum rate of $3.35.

Young people, of course, don't have to accept this amount, and I know many will be able to command the regular minimum wage. But this new wage will allow youngsters who don't have any experience to make a start in the workplace. What we're trying to do is get them some experience so they can move up the pay scale.

Some people have feared that, as a result of the new youth wage, businesses would replace adults with young people. Well, we've taken precautions so that won't happen. First of all, the youth wage will only be available during the summer months, when kids are out of school. And second, we will add provisions that absolutely prohibit businesses from displacing current workers by hiring young people at a lesser wage.

The American economy is on the mend. And one of the reasons is that we've finally begun to correct some of the past errors of government that brought on inflation, high interest rates, and recession. But as the economy mends, government can only help to ease the painful transition for many of our people. The proposals I've outlined today do this by assisting the unemployed in finding the training, the help, and the jobs they desire and deserve.

Until next week, thanks for listening. God bless you.

Note: The President's remarks were taped at 4:15 P.M. PST in the library of the St. Francis Hotel, San Francisco, California, on March 4 for broadcast at 12:06 P.M. EST on March 5.

Education

March 12, 1983

My fellow Americans:

I'd like to talk to you today about one of the most important issues that touches our lives and shapes our future: the education of America's children. We've always had a love affair with learning in this country. America is a melting pot, and education has been a mainspring for our democracy and freedom, a means of providing gifts of knowledge and opportunity to all citizens, no matter how humble their background, so they could climb higher, help build the American dream, and leave a better life for those who follow.

Broad educational opportunity not only secured our role as the pathbreaker to progress, it also protected and strengthened our freedom. We were wise enough to heed Thomas Jefferson's warning that "any nation which expects to be ignorant and free expects what never was and never will be."

But in recent years, our traditions of opportunity and excellence in education have been under siege. We've witnessed the growth of a huge education bureaucracy. Parents have often been reduced to the role of outsiders.

Government-manufactured inflation made private schools and higher education too expensive for too many families. Even God, source of all knowledge, was expelled from classrooms.

It's time to face the truth. Advocates of more and more government interference in education have had ample time to make their case, and they've failed. Look at the record. Federal spending on education soared eightfold in the last 20 years, rising much faster than inflation. But during the same period, scholastic aptitude test scores went down, down, and down.

The classroom should be an entrance to life, not an escape from it.

As the leader of the free world, the United States must strengthen its defenses, modernize its industries, and move confidently into a new era of high technology. To do this, we need a smart and highly skilled work force. Yet, only one-sixth of our high-school graduates have taken junior and senior level courses in science and math. And many U.S. high schools do not offer sufficient math to prepare graduates for engineering schools.

America can do better. We must move forward again by returning to the sound principles that never failed us when we lived up to them. Can we not begin by welcoming God back in our schools and by setting an example for children by striving to abide by His Ten Commandments and the Golden Rule? We've sent an amendment to the Congress that will permit voluntary prayer in school again.

But better education doesn't mean a bigger Department of Education. In fact, that department should be abolished. Instead, we must do a better job teaching the basics, insisting on discipline and results, encouraging competition and, above all, remembering that education does not begin with Washington officials or even State and local officials. It begins in the home, where it is the right and responsibility of every American.

Parents and teachers have the toughest, sometimes the most thankless, but always the most important jobs in America. They need our help and support.

Our administration has put together an education package that addresses the challenge of restoring opportunity to families and excellence in our schools. It contains several proposals to help parents reestablish control and to assist them in meeting education costs.

First, tuition tax credits, which we've already sent to the Congress, will soften the double payment burden for those paying public school taxes and independent or parochial school tuition. This proposal will help those who need help the most—low- and middle-income families.

Second, we're proposing a voucher system to help parents of disadvantaged children. We want to give States or individual school districts the option of using certain Federal education funds to create vouchers so these parents can choose which school, private or public, they want their children to attend.

Third, we're proposing a system of educational savings accounts to help families save for college education. Parents will be able to save up to $1,000 per year, per child, with no tax on the interest.

These proposals will expand opportunities by allowing parents to keep more of their own money, rather than taxing it away to finance bigger bureaucracies. They will also increase healthy competition among schools. Without a race, there can be no champion, no records broken, no excellence in education or any other walk of life.

We're talking about no less than the future of this nation. Last Monday, I was pleased to meet 40 of America's top high-school math and science students. I told them that science and technology are keys to prosperity, learning, and a better quality of life.

We've already sent legislation to the Congress to stimulate training of more math and science teachers. Another program we've proposed will encourage existing math and science teachers to go back to school themselves to update their own knowledge. And we're also beginning a new program, one I intend to participate in myself, to honor some of America's best science and math teachers. They are a true national resource.

Private sector initiatives can also make great contributions. We're encouraging corporations, community organizations, and neighborhood groups across the country to adopt schools and help them meet their education needs with funds, equipment, and personnel.

Finally, to combat adult illiteracy, we will encourage college students to provide tutoring, either through voluntary community service or as part of our expanded work-study program.

Just as we're now seeing a healthy revival of our national economy, we can improve America's educational system and make it the best in the world again. But we must not delay. I hope we'll have your support and the cooperation of the Congress.

Until next week, thanks for listening, and God bless you.

Note: The President spoke at 12:06 P.M. EST from Camp David.

House of Representatives' Budget Proposal

March 19, 1983

My fellow Americans:

Tomorrow at 11:30 P.M. is the first day of spring, and it coincides with an important change in our economy. A season of hope is giving way to a season of progress. We're seeing proof that our great national struggle to make our economy well again is beginning to pay off. Yes, we have a long way to go, but factories are reopening, workers called back, production in housing, autos, and steel picking up, and new breakthroughs in high technology busting [*sic*] out all over.

America is moving forward. The economy is growing stronger—and stronger than most people, including ourselves, predicted.

The question is no longer will we have recovery, but how long will recovery last? It's been nearly 20 years since the United States enjoyed a long-lasting economic expansion that didn't trigger ruinous inflation and high interest rates. We're trying to build that kind of recovery now. We can have it if we stick to common sense and don't go back to the big spending and taxing addiction that brought this economy to its knees in 1980.

Unfortunately, it's still true that the more things change, the more they stay the same. America is on the mend, but this recovery could be stopped dead in its tracks if big spenders in the Congress have their way. I was greatly encouraged when we had some bipartisan success on a couple of sticky problems. But unfortunately, those who place their faith in big government and heavy spending reverted to type.

Right now, House liberals are pushing a budget—the so-called liberal Democratic budget—that, if implemented, would reverse the progress we've made and wreck our program to rebuild the economy. They want to throw out the window much of the domestic budget savings we've achieved over the last 2 years. And they would go much further, seeking $181 billion in higher domestic spending over the next 5 years, excesses that would send the budget, prices, and interest rates soaring out of control and our economy into a tailspin.

To cite just one example, Medicare would be driven into bankruptcy by the failure of their budget to address its problems. Our proposed budget meets the needs of our people without bankrupting the system.

Now, how do they propose to pay for their reckless binge? Two ways: by compromising America's defense security and by slapping massive new tax increases on every working family. Ignoring the Soviets' tremendous advantage in military forces, the liberals would cripple our efforts to modernize America's defenses. To put it bluntly, their budget gambles with our security and safety. Their proposed $163-billion cut in defense spending over the next 5 years would put the United States right back in the position of military vulnerability we were in after a decade of neglect in the 1970's.

We were shocked to learn when we got here that we had so many ships that couldn't leave port, planes that couldn't take off, and helicopters that couldn't stay aloft—all of this because of our lack of spare parts, sometimes of crew, inability to keep things repaired, or shortage of fuel.

We've begun to do something about that, and we've made real progress with our investment in peace through strength. But passage of the liberal budget would seriously undermine our rebuilding progress. Here are just some of the things that we might have to do if they have their way: deactivate one active and one reserve division; decommission one entire carrier battle group and some two dozen other ships; deactivate three Marine Corps fighter squadrons; deactivate two active and two reserve Air Force tactical fighter wings and six continental U.S. air defense squadrons; terminate major weapons programs from each service; sacrifice hard-won gains in readiness and sustainability by cutting our budgets for major repairs and ammunition by 25 percent and by cutting back on troop exercises and training.

Such cuts would send the worst possible signal to the Kremlin. They would remove Soviet incentives to negotiate arms reductions with us because we'd be telling them, "Stand firm, the United States will disarm itself."

Remember, they would do this on the pretext of reducing the deficit. They would really be doing it so they could increase spending on other things by $181 billion.

The other part of the liberal budget is a huge $315-billion tax increase on wage earners. And here, too, they would pretend to reduce the Federal deficit, but by putting you deeper in the hole. That never works, and nothing could be more unfair or less compassionate. Their unfair tax increases would put a choke hold on Main Street America. They would eliminate the third year of your tax cut, which provides maximum benefit to families earning between $10,000 and $50,000, the very same families they claim we're hurting. But they are the families who will benefit most by the July tax cut.

They also want to eliminate our historic reform of tax indexing. Indexing will protect you from being pushed into a higher tax bracket when you get a cost-of-living raise. Indexing prevents government from stealing a greater percentage of your earnings and leaving you with less purchasing power. And indexing helps low- and medium-income wage earners the most for one simple reason: The rich are immune to bracket creep. They're already in the top tax brackets. Indexing won't help them a bit.

Attempts to take away the third year of your tax cut and indexing are simply gimmicks so they can spend more of your money. A typical median-income family would have to pay $3,550 in higher taxes through 1988.

The people who want to do this are the same ones who left us with 12.4 percent inflation in 1980 and the highest interest rates in more than 100 years.

Well, let me make one thing plain: After all our national struggle to reduce inflation, to begin controlling a government which grew bloated at your expense, to bring down interest rates and make the dollar worth something again; after helping you to increase personal savings, worker productivity, and our industrial and military strength; after winning the fight to lower your taxes so we could restore hope and build new incentives into the economy—after all these hard-won victories earned through the patience and courage of every citizen, I don't want America's recovery and security to be

sacrificed on an altar of discredited hand-me-down theories. And if you'll
help us, they won't be.

Till next week, thanks for listening, and God bless you.

Note: The President spoke at 12:06 P.M. EST from Camp David.

House of Representatives' Budget Proposal

March 26, 1983

My fellow Americans:

As I'm sure you heard, the majority in the House of Representatives
passed its budget resolution this week. Since the vote on that budget was
announced by those who supported it, they've proclaimed it a great victory
over me. You, the people, are treated as mere spectators in the contest. But
you weren't. You were down on the field very much in that game. And if
those proposals ever become law, you'll find you're on the losing team.

Let me remind you what lies at the heart of that liberal budget—a $315
billion tax increase over the next 5 years, falling squarely on the backs of you
who work and earn to support your families and pay the government's bills.
It's not just a coincidence that that $315 billion they want to raise would
require canceling the third year of your tax cut, due in July, and tax indexing. Three-quarters of that tax increase would have to be paid by low- and
middle-income families and many of you who are already living from paycheck to paycheck.

Indexing is an historic reform that'll put an end to bracket creep. The
unfair thing about our present income tax system is that it's based on the
number of dollars you earn, not their value. As you earn a greater number of
dollars, you're pushed into a higher tax bracket, and the government takes a
higher percentage of your paycheck, even though you might only be receiving
a cost-of-living raise to stay even with inflation.

Indexing puts an end to the injustice of bracket creep. Indexing is not a
tax cut per se; it prevents an automatic increase and keeps you from getting
poorer.

How can those who talk so much about fairness and compassion turn
around and take away the third year of your tax cut and the indexing? How
can they justify hitting the median-income family with a $3,550 tax increase
over the next 5 years? How can they pretend to help you cope with your
bills, put money aside for education, and save for your retirement when
they're reaching deeper and deeper into your pockets?

They can't. And they won't, if we don't let them. It's not right for them to overtax you just so they can spend more. And they do want to spend more—a lot more. Their budget would cancel virtually all the savings we've made in the last 2 years. It would turn back the clock to the high inflation, high interest rate nightmare of 1980 by giving a green light to at least 10 brand-new government spending programs. At the same time, it would allow a program of crucial importance to our senior citizens—Medicare—to go bankrupt. It would wipe out our initiatives to reduce food stamp waste, despite documented evidence that food stamp rip-off artists plunder the system and cost taxpayers hundreds of millions of dollars a year.

In all, the liberal alternative budget would approve nearly $200 billion in additional inflationary spending. Make no mistake, this money cannot be retrieved and the deficit reduced, as they claim, by slashing defense spending authority by more than $200 billion. Once you begin reducing personnel in our armed services, closing down aircraft plants, decommissioning ships, fighter squadrons, and one weapons program after another, you not only gamble with America's security, you create a new army of unemployed. And that means the deficit would go up, not down.

It's this simple: If you liked the 21-percent prime interest rate, 18-percent mortgage rates, double-digit inflation, and sky-is-the-limit tax increases of 2 years ago, you'll love their budget, because that's what it would bring back. Those who fought to get this budget passed are the same people who began saying our economic program had failed almost the day it was passed. That was more than a year ago, and much of our tax reduction program is still not in place today. But more and more evidence is coming in that proves America is on the mend and recovery has definitely begun.

Last Monday the Commerce Department estimated that, during these first 3 months of 1983, our economy will grow at an annual rate of 4 percent. And we believe the recovery will pick up strength as the year goes on. The double-digit inflation of 1980, which drove up costs and robbed you of your earnings, has been knocked all the way down to four-tenths of 1 percent in the last 6 months—the lowest 6-month rate in 22 years. This February, consumer prices actually declined for only the second time since 1965. The first time was in December.

Those towering interest rates which closed factory gates and industries like autos and steel, leveled the housing industry, and brought so many small businesses to their knees have now been knocked down themselves. The prime rate was 21½ percent in 1980; today it's down to 10½. I believe interest rates can, should, and will go lower.

As inflation and interest rates come down and our tax cuts come on stream, families have more to spend or save, as you wish. And that is why savings and productivity are growing again. Recently I received a letter from the president of a family-owned lumber company in Minneapolis, one which—like so many other small firms—has been hard hit by the recession. But now this man's mood has turned optimistic. He told me that his sales for the months of December and January were the best for 3 months in his company's 50-year history. And he wrote, "Mr. President, don't get stampeded into some ill-conceived pump-priming scheme that will lead to another round of inflation boom and bust. You were elected to break that cycle. What you've done is working." Well, my answer to that fine gentleman is, "I won't be stampeded. I intend to do everything I can to protect this recovery all of us have worked so hard to achieve."

But this isn't just my struggle; it's yours, too. You're not spectators, and I need your help. Together we still have time to beat back the unfair tax increases, hold the line on spending, and keep America strong. If you can't make the big spenders see the light, you can make them feel the heat. Please tell your Representatives not to turn back the clock and squander America's future. Tell them to work with us to keep America on the upswing. If you do, we can usher in a bright new age of prosperity that outshines any other in our history.

Until next week, thanks for listening, and God bless you.

Note: The President spoke at 12:06 P.M. EST from the Oval Office at the White House.

Easter and Passover

April 2, 1983

My fellow Americans:

This week as American families draw together in worship, we join with millions upon millions of others around the world also celebrating the traditions of their faiths. During these days, at least, regardless of nationality, religion, or race, we are united by faith in God, and the barriers between us seem less significant.

Observing the rites of Passover and Easter, we're linked in time to the ancient origins of our values and to the unborn generations who will still celebrate them long after we're gone. As Paul explained in his Epistle to the Ephesians, "He came and preached peace to you who were far away and peace to those who were near. So then you were no longer strangers and aliens, but you were fellow citizens of God's household."

This is a time of hope and peace, when our spirits are filled and lifted. It's a time when we give thanks for our blessings—chief among them freedom, peace, and the promise of eternal life.

This week Jewish families and friends have been celebrating Passover, a tradition rich in symbolism and meaning. Its observance reminds all of us that the struggle for freedom and the battle against oppression waged by Jews since ancient times is one shared by people everywhere. And Christians have been commemorating the last momentous days leading to the crucifixion of Jesus 1,950 years ago. Tomorrow, as morning spreads around the planet, we'll celebrate the triumph of life over death, the Resurrection of Jesus. Both observances tell of sacrifice and pain but also of hope and triumph.

As we look around us today, we still find human pain and suffering, but we also see it answered with individual courage and spirit, strengthened by faith. For example, the brave Polish people, despite the oppression of a godless tyranny, still cling to their faith and their belief in freedom. Shortly after Palm Sunday Mass this week, Lech Walesa faced a cheering crowd of workers outside a Gdansk church. He held his hand up in a sign of victory and predicted, "The time will come when we will win."

Recently, an East German professor, his wife, and two daughters climbed into a 7-foot rowboat and crossed the freezing, wind-whipped Baltic to escape from tyranny. Arriving in West Germany after a harrowing 7-hour, 31-mile journey past East German border patrols, the man said he and his family had risked everything so that the children would have the chance to grow up in freedom.

In Central America, Communist-inspired revolution still spreads terror and instability, but it's no match for the much greater force of faith that runs so deep among the people. We saw this during Pope John Paul II's recent visit there. As he conducted a Mass in Nicaragua, state police jeered and led organized heckling by Sandinista supporters. But the Pope lifted a crucifix above his head and waved it at the crowd before him, then turned and symbolically held it up before the massive painting of Sandinista soldiers that loomed behind. The symbol of good prevailed. In contrast, everywhere else the Holy Father went in the region, spreading a message that only love can build, he was met by throngs of enthusiastic believers, eager for Papal guidance and blessing.

In this Easter season when so many of our young men and women in the Armed Forces are stationed so very far from their homes, I can't resist recounting at least one example of their sacrifice and heroism. Every day I receive reports that would make you very proud, and today I'd like to share just one with you.

While the San Diego-based U.S.S. *Hoel* was steaming toward Melbourne, Australia, on Ash Wednesday, its crew heard of terrible brush fires sweeping two Australian States. More than 70 people were killed and the destruction was great. Well, the crew of this American ship raised $4,000 from their pockets to help, but they felt that it wasn't enough. So, leaving only a skeleton crew aboard, the 100 American sailors gave up a day's shore leave, rolled up their sleeves, and set to work rebuilding a ruined community on the opposite end of the Earth. Just Americans being Americans, but something for all of us to be proud of.

Stories like these—of men and women around the world who love God and freedom—bear a message of world hope and brotherhood like the rites of Passover and Easter that we celebrate this weekend.

A grade school class in Somerville, Massachusetts, recently wrote me to say, "We studied about countries and found out that each country in our world is beautiful and that we need each other. People may look a little different, but we're still people who need the same things." They said, "We want peace. We want to take care of one another. We want to be able to get along with one another. We want to be able to share. We want freedom and justice. We want to be friends. We want no wars. We want to be able to talk to one another. We want to be able to travel around the world without fear."

And then they asked, "Do you think that we can have these things one day?" Well, I do. I really do. Nearly 2,000 years after the coming of the Prince of Peace, such simple wishes may still seem far from fulfillment. But we can achieve them. We must never stop trying.

The generation of Americans now growing up in schools across the country can make sure the United States will remain a force for good, the champion of peace and freedom, as their parents and grandparents before them have done. And if we live our lives and dedicate our country to truth, to love, and to God, we will be a part of something stronger and much more enduring than any negative power here on Earth. That's why this weekend is a celebration and why there is hope for us all.

Thanks for listening, and God bless you.

Note: The President spoke at 9:06 A.M. PST from Rancho del Cielo, near Santa Barbara.

Federal Income Taxation

April 9, 1983

My fellow Americans:

In just a few days, the date many of us dread more than any other will be upon us—April 15th, deadline for filing income tax returns.

Like Federal employees, taxpayers also work for the government—they just don't have to take a civil service exam. Here in America, land of opportunity, governments at all levels are taxing away 40 percent of our nation's income. We've been creeping closer to socialism, a system that someone once said works only in heaven, where it isn't needed, and in hell, where they've already got it.

We know that the secret of America's success has been our drive to excel, a spirit born and nurtured by our families. With their dreams and hard work, they've built our nation, made her great, and kept her good. Everything we've accomplished began in those bedrock values parents have sought to impart throughout our history—values of faith in God, honesty, caring for others, personal responsibility, thrift, and initiative.

But families cannot prosper and keep America strong if government becomes a Goliath that preys upon their wealth, usurps their rights, and crushes their spirit. For too many years, overgrown government has stood in your way, taking more and more of what you earned, no matter how hard you tried.

Make no mistake, the thousands of small businesses and the workers in steel, autos, and housing who have suffered so badly from the recession didn't lose their jobs by chance. Years of confidence—or excuse me, I should say, well-intentioned but strong-headed policies plundered their earnings and crippled their ability to produce and compete. By 1981 double-digit inflation and excessive regulations had driven up the price of their products. Record interest rates made it too difficult for their firms to borrow money to modernize their equipment, and record tax increases sharply increased the price of their labor in the marketplace.

It's taken us 2 years to reverse that damage, get productivity growing again, and foster a recovery that's starting to bring people back to work. We've done it by reducing inflation from 12.4 percent to only four-tenths of 1 percent for the last 6 months, by chopping in half that towering prime interest rate, and by passing the first comprehensive tax rate reduction for all Americans who earn and save since the Kennedy tax cuts in the 1960's.

On July 1st, you'll receive the final installment of your 25-percent personal income tax rate reduction. It's not as much as we wanted, but it's the most we could get, given the tremendous opposition to any tax reduction by the spending lobbies in Washington.

Here's what it means to you: A median-income family of four, which earned $26,000 in 1981 and has kept pace with inflation, will owe about $700 less in Federal income taxes in 1983 than if our tax program had not been passed. In fact, because of our tax cuts, that family can earn $3,000 more in 1983 than it did in 1981, and it will still owe less in Federal income taxes. That's progress, and that's what we mean by incentives. If you work or save more tomorrow than you did today, your reward will be greater than it was. More of every dollar of your added earnings and interest will be yours to keep. Then, in 1985, our program will index your tax rates so you won't be shoved into higher tax brackets when you receive cost-of-living raises. This will be a protection we never had before.

Many other features of our tax program were designed to help your families. For working wives and mothers, we've reduced the marriage penalty and increased the child-care credit. For family farms and family-owned businesses, we've dramatically reduced the estate tax. For small savers, we've deregulated financial institutions to give you a higher rate of return than you received before. For all of you trying to put money aside for later years, we have introduced strong new incentives for individual retirement accounts, extended IRA's to participants in employer-sponsored pension programs, and doubled maximum Keogh contributions. Further tax breaks for savers will be coming up in 1985, when 15 percent of interest income, up to $450 for single taxpayers and $900 for married couples, can be excluded from taxes.

Taken together, this is the most sweeping program of incentives ever passed to help American families and give them real hope for their future. But just as our program is beginning to mesh and deliver what we promised, with personal savings and spending up, productivity up, auto and steel production and housing construction all recovering, workers being called back, the stock market hitting an all-time high, and consumer confidence surging— just as the recovery is gaining strength—a plan is afoot that would wreck the progress we've made.

For all of you who've worked hard to meet your tax obligations this year, be on guard. The liberal Democrats in the House of Representatives want you to pay more—much more. They want to increase taxes on median-income families by $3,550 over the next 5 years. Nothing could be more unfair. And I promise you this: I will veto any attempt to take away the third year of your tax cut or the indexing which benefits low- and medium-income families the most.

But a recent special report put out by the Democratic study group makes plain they are considering many other options to raise your taxes. You should know that these options include capping mortgage interest deductions, eliminating deductions for State and local taxes—in other words, you'd pay a tax on a tax—limiting charitable contributions for nonitemizers, taxing part of the capital gains on home sales, taxing fringe benefits, and on and on and on.

The liberal Democratic tax policy seems to boil down to this: America makes, government takes. The fallacy of this approach was well understood by a visionary Democrat, President John F. Kennedy, who said in 1963, "The largest single barrier to full employment and to a higher rate of economic growth is the heavy drag of Federal income taxes on private purchasing power, initiative, and incentive." His words are just as true today.

We will not reverse our progress in reducing tax rates. We have only begun. Until next week, thanks for listening, and God bless you.

Note: The President spoke at 12:06 P.M. EST from Camp David.

Withholding Tax on Interest and Dividends

April 16, 1983

My fellow Americans:

Yesterday, April 15th, was tax day, and I know many of you are still recovering. So, I hate to mention taxes again, but there's something I think you should know. It's about misrepresentations surrounding the withholding tax on interest and dividends. People are being badly misled, and that misinformation shouldn't go unanswered.

Americans have been arguing over taxes ever since the Boston Tea Party more than 200 years ago, when an angry band of taxpayers dumped a shipload of tea into Boston Harbor. Well, in the spirit of the Boston Tea Party, I'd like to dump all the misinformation you've been getting on withholding taxes. In fact, I'd almost like to dump overboard some of those who've been spreading this misinformation and scaring people, especially our older citizens, many of whom have written me very frightened.

As you may recall, this whole business started last summer when the Congress passed, and I signed, the law requiring banks and other financial institutions to withhold 10 percent on interest and dividend income.

This withholding, which starts this coming July, is not a new tax. I came to Washington to reduce taxes. And I can tell you, I wouldn't have signed the withholding law if it had been a new tax on our people. It's simply a more effective way of collecting tax money that's already owed, just as employers have been withholding taxes from our paychecks for almost 40 years, a procedure most wage earners accept as both fair and necessary.

What it really gets down to is this: Even in a law-abiding country like ours, there's still a minority of people out there who cheat on their taxes. Last year, Uncle Sam lost billions of dollars in taxes on unreported interest and dividend income. President Kennedy, back in 1961, said, "This is patently unfair to those who must, as a result, bear a larger share of the tax burden." Well, that was true then, and it's true now. I agree with what one editorial writer said about those who cheat: "When they don't pay their taxes, someone else does—you and me."

Withholding 10 percent on interest and dividends will allow the Internal Revenue Service to recover an estimated $18 billion in otherwise lost revenues over the next 5 years—and that's without taxing honest taxpayers a penny more than they now pay.

Past experience has proven that withholding is by far the most effective means of combating those who don't pay their tax bill to the government. The only people who stand to lose under this law are those who haven't been paying their taxes in the first place, and what's wrong with that?

While I'm at it, let me expose a few of the myths which may be bothering some of you. First off, withholding will not place burdens on our older Americans or lower-income individuals. The vast majority of older Americans, 85 percent, are exempted under the law. And to get that exemption, all they have to do is fill out a form no more complicated than a deposit slip. As for low-income individuals, anyone who paid $600 or less in taxes last year, or married couples who paid under $1,000, are exempt as well. In addition, everyone with small savings accounts with interest payments of $150 or less are also exempt. So, for example, most kids' accounts wouldn't have withholding.

All of this raises an obvious question. If withholding is nothing more than a more effective collection method, what's all the controversy about? Well, some of the banking interests seem to think withholding will inconvenience them. But we've taken measures to make sure this changeover isn't burdensome. And as for savers, it will actually be a real convenience for many of them. For example, withholding will free many taxpayers from the chore of preparing quarterly tax payments. It will prevent other citizens from being faced with a substantial accumulated tax bill on April 15th. Most wage earners already prefer to have tax withheld from their paychecks, rather than having to come up with the whole bundle on that annual day of reckoning.

Some of the banks and savings and loans have said withholding will reduce the incentive to save. Well, that just doesn't make sense. Withholding will have a minimal effect on accrued interest. For example, the annual loss on a $1,000 account, earning 9-percent interest, would be less than 50 cents. And such an account would be exempt anyway.

But I think most Americans would forgo the 50 cents if it meant others who are cheating on billions of dollars of unpaid taxes would have to pay their fair share.

The fact of the matter is that those already paying their taxes can get back all of the amount withheld by reducing their estimated tax payments or by adjusting the number of exemptions on their wage withholding.

Thanks to the pressure from a very busy lobby, however, the Congress is now considering repeal of withholding before it's even gone into effect. This would help no one who's doing their fair share, but it would let all those who are not paying their taxes on interest and dividends off the hook. So, I'm not about to let it happen. Rather than asking those who are paying taxes to pay more, I say that those who already owe taxes should pay them. And I'm carrying my veto pen right behind my ear. If the repeal passes the Congress, I'm all set to veto it, just as I am prepared to protect the July tax cut and indexing with a veto if necessary.

Until next week, thanks for listening, and God bless you.

Note: The President spoke at 12:06 P.M. EST from Camp David.

Death of Diplomatic and Military Personnel in Beirut

April 23, 1983

My fellow Americans:

In a few hours I'll undertake one of the saddest journeys of my Presidency. I'll be going to Andrews Air Force Base to meet one of our Air Force planes bringing home 16 Americans who died this week in the terrorist attack on the United States Embassy in Beirut.

I undertake this task in great sadness, but also with a tremendous sense of pride in those who sacrificed their lives in our country's efforts to bring peace to the Middle East and spare others the agony of war. Greater love hath no man. The courage and dedication of these men and women reflect the best tradition of our Foreign Service, our Armed Forces, and the other departments and agencies whose personnel serve our nation overseas, often in situations of great personal danger.

We don't know yet who bears responsibility for this terrible deed. What we do know is that the terrorists who planned and carried out this cynical and cowardly attack have failed in their purpose. They mistakenly believe that, if they're cruel enough and violent enough, they will weaken American resolve and deter us from our effort to help build a lasting and secure peace in the Middle East. Well, if they think that, they don't know too much about America. As a free people, we've never allowed intimidation to stop us from doing what we know to be right. The best way for us to show our love and respect for our fellow countrymen who died in Beirut this week is to carry on their task, to press harder than ever with our peacemaking efforts, and that's exactly what we're doing.

More than ever, we're committed to giving the people of Lebanon the chance they deserve to lead normal lives, free from violence and free from the presence of all unwanted foreign forces on their soil. And we remain committed to the Lebanese Government's recovery of full sovereignty throughout all its territory.

When I spoke after the bombing to Lebanon's President Gemayel, he expressed his people's deepest regret and revulsion over this wanton act of terrorism. I, in turn, assured him that the tragic events of this week had only served to strengthen America's steadfastness as a force for peace in his country and the Middle East. To this end, I've asked Secretary of State George Shultz to leave tomorrow night for the Middle East. Secretary Shultz will now add his personal efforts to continue the magnificent work begun by Ambassadors Phil Habib and Morris Draper, bringing about the earliest possible withdrawal of all foreign forces from Lebanon in a way that will promote peace and security in this troubled region.

The scenes of senseless tragedy in Beirut this week will remain etched in our memories forever. But along with the tragedy, there were inspiring moments of heroism. We will not forget the pictures of Ambassador Dillon and his staff, Lebanese as well as Americans, many of them swathed in bandages, bravely searching the devastated embassy for their colleagues and for other innocent victims.

We will not forget the image of young marines gently draping our nation's flag over the broken body of one of their fallen comrades. We will not forget their courage and compassion, and we will not forget their willingness to sacrifice even their lives for the service of their country and the cause of peace.

Yes, we Americans can be proud of these fine men and women. And we can be even prouder that our country has been playing such a unique and indispensable role in the Middle East, a role no other single nation could play. When the countries of the region want help in bringing peace, we're the ones they've turned to. That's because they trust us, because they know that America is both strong and just, both decent and dedicated. Even in the shadow of this terrible tragedy in Beirut, that is something to remember and draw heart from. It is also something to be true to.

I know I speak for all Americans when I reaffirm our unshakeable commitment to our country's most precious heritage—serving the cause of peace and freedom in the world. What better monument than that could we build for those who gave their all that others might live in peace?

Until next week, thank you, and God bless you.

Note: The President spoke at 12:06 P.M. EST from the Oval Office at the White House.

Education

April 30, 1983

My fellow Americans:

I'd like to talk with you today about a subject of paramount concern to every American family—the education of our children. You may have heard the disturbing report this week by the National Commission on Excellence in Education that I created shortly after taking office. Their study reveals that our education system, once the finest in the world, is in a sorry state of disrepair.

We're a people who believe that each generation will stand upon the shoulders of the one before it, the accomplishments of each ever greater than the last. Our families immigrated here to make a better life not just for themselves, but for their children and their children's children. Education was not simply another part of American society; it was the key that opened the golden door.

Parents who never finished high school scrimp and save so that their children can go to college. Yet today, we're told in a tough report card on our commitment that the educational skills of today's students will not match those of their parents. About 13 percent of our 17-year-olds are functional illiterates and, among minority youth, the rate is closer to 40 percent. More than two-thirds of our high schoolers can't write a decent essay. Our grade is a stark and uncompromising "U" for unsatisfactory. We must act now and with energy if we're to avoid failing an entire generation.

Let me hasten to point out that America's children are just as smart today as they ever were. But most of them do less than an hour of homework a night. Many have abandoned vocational and college prep courses for general ones. When they graduate from high school, they're prepared for neither work nor higher education.

The study indicates the quality of learning in our classrooms has been declining for the last two decades—a fact which won't surprise many parents or the students educated during that period. Those were years when the Federal presence in education grew and grew. Parental control over local schools shrank. Bureaucracy ballooned until accountability seemed lost. Parents were frustrated and didn't know where to turn.

Well, government seemed to forget that education begins in the home, where it's a parental right and responsibility. Both our private and our public schools exist to aid your families in the instruction of your children. For too many years, people here in Washington acted like your families' wishes were only getting in the way. We've seen what that "Washington knows best" attitude has wrought.

Our high standards of literacy and educational diversity have been slipping. Well-intentioned but misguided policymakers have stamped a uniform mediocrity on the rich variety and excellence that had been our heritage.

I think most parents agree it's time to change course. We must move education forward again, with common sense as our guide. We must put the basics back in the schools and the parents back in charge.

The National Commission for [*sic*] Excellence in Education recommends requiring 4 years of English in high school and 3 solid years, each, of math and science. It suggests more and longer school days, higher goals, and tougher standards for matriculation. Our teachers should be better trained and better paid. And, we must no longer make excuses for those who are not qualified to teach.

Parents, please demand these and other reforms in your local schools and hold your local officials accountable. Let our parents once again be the rudder that puts American education back on course towards success through excellence.

There are things the Federal Government can and must do to ensure educational excellence, but bigger budgets are not the answer. Federal spending increased seventeenfold during the same 20 years that marked such a dramatic decline in quality. We will continue our firm commitment to support the education efforts of State and local governments, but the focus of our agenda is, as it must be, to restore parental choice and influence and to increase competition between schools.

We've sent to the Congress a tuition tax credit plan and proposed a voucher system to help low- and middle-income families afford the schools of their choice. We've proposed education savings accounts to help families save for college education. We've sent legislation to the Congress that would create block grants for the training of math and science teachers, and another proposal would encourage those teachers to keep abreast of new developments in their fields. We've also begun an effort to honor some of our finest math and science teachers.

For the sake of all our children, our country, and our future, we must join together in a national campaign to restore excellence in American education. At home, in school, in State government, and at the Federal level, we must make sure we have put our children first and that their education is a top priority.

"Train up a child in the way he should go," Solomon wrote, "and when he is old he will not depart from it." Well, that's the God-given responsibility of each parent and the trust of every child. It is a compact between generations we must be sure to keep.

I would like to close with a special challenge to America's students who may think I just want to pile on more homework. Your generation is coming of age in one of the most challenging and exciting times in our history. High technology is revolutionizing our industries, renewing our economy, and promising new hope and opportunity in the years ahead. But you must earn the rewards of the future with plain hard work. The harder you work today, the greater your rewards will be tomorrow. Make sure you get the training and the skills you need to take advantage of the new opportunities ahead. Get a good education; that's the key to success. It will open your mind and give wings to your spirit. There's a dazzling new world waiting for you. My generation only discovered it. But you, by summoning all the faith, effort, and discipline you can muster, can claim it for America.

Until next week, thanks for listening, and God bless you.

Note: The President taped his radio address in the Roosevelt Room at the White House on April 29 for broadcast on April 30. The transcript of the address was released by the Office of the Press Secretary on April 30.

Mother's Day

May 7, 1983

My fellow Americans:

This is a very special weekend in American life, a time specially set aside to honor our mothers and the mothers of our children. As we do, we acknowledge their role as the heart of our families and reinforce our families as the cornerstone of our society.

In our families, and often from our mothers, we first learn about values and caring and the difference between right and wrong. Those of us blessed with loving families draw our confidence from them and the strength we need to face the world. We also first learn at home, and, again, often from our mothers, about the God who will guide us through life.

The mothers we honor this weekend, young or not so young, partners or alone, well-to-do or sometimes agonizingly poor, are as diverse as our varied population. But they share a commitment to future generations and a yearning to improve the world their children will inherit. They shape the America we know today and are now molding the character of our country tomorrow.

Since men seem to have written most of our history books, the role of women and mothers in our communities and families has not always been given its due. But the truth is the Wild West could never have been tamed, the vast prairies never plowed, nor God and learning brought to the corners of our continent without the strength, bravery, and influence of our grandmothers, great-grandmothers, and the women who came before them.

Living through blizzards, plagues, prairie fires, and floods, these women made homes and started families, organized churches, and built schools. They served as teachers, field hands, physicians, and the center of the family.

I was reading a book recently about Kansas frontier women and came across a passage that seemed to sum it all up. Esther Clark wrote, "Mother has always been the gamest one of us. I can remember her hanging onto the reins of a runaway mule team, her black hair tumbling out of its pins and over her shoulders, her face set and white while one small girl clung with chattering teeth to the sides of the rocking wagon and a baby sister bounced about on the floor in paralyzed wonder.

"I remember, too, the things the men said about Leny's nerve. But I think as much courage as it took to hang onto the reins that day, it took more to live 24 hours at a time, month in and out on the lonely and lovely prairie without giving up to the loneliness."

Of course, Leny's nerve and strength are echoed in modern-day women and mothers who face different but equally trying tests of their courage. There are mothers like Rachel Rossow of Connecticut, for example, and Dorothy DeBolt of California, who with their husbands have adopted between them 25 handicapped boys and girls in addition to their own children.

I had a chance to visit with Rachel and her family last month, and I can tell you I've never seen a happier group. I know the strains on them must be great, emotionally and financially, but not as great as the love they feel for each other.

Of course, many millions of American mothers are quiet, everyday heroes struggling to stretch budgets and too often maintaining their families alone. Many also contribute to society through full-time careers, and others are forced to work just to make ends meet. They're raising children in a fast-paced world where basic values are constantly questioned. Their monumental challenge is to bring their children into adulthood, healthy and whole, nurturing their physical and emotional growth while avoiding the pitfalls of drug abuse and crime.

The lives of American mothers today are far removed from the prairies, and yet they have a nobility about them, too. Government should help, not hinder, parents in this task. And that's why our policies have been designed to restore the family to its rightful place in our society, combat the inflation that stole from family budgets, expand opportunity through a renewed economy, and hasten the return of values and principles that made America both great and good.

On the economic front, I think we've made some solid progress in bringing relief to your financially strapped families. When we took office, inflation was at 12.4 percent, but it's only been one-half of 1 percent for the last 6 months. You can see a difference on the grocery shelves. A loaf of bread, for example, costs only 2 cents more now than it did in 1980. If we'd continued with the old rate of inflation, by now it would have cost 11 cents more. Milk is about 16 cents cheaper than it would have been, hamburger about 18 cents cheaper per pound, and the savings on a dozen eggs are as much as 50 cents. I don't have to tell the people who do the shopping how these savings add up. But for those of you who don't, we estimate that a family of four on a fixed income of $20,000 has $1,700 more in purchasing power this year than they would have had under the old inflation rate.

The progress we're making with the economy, just like the national renewal we're seeing spring up all around us, is the product of our reliance again on good old-fashioned common sense, renewed belief in ourselves, and faith in God.

Now and then I find guidance and direction in the worn brown Bible I used to take the oath of office. It's been the Reagan family Bible and, like many of yours, has its flyleaf filled with important events; its margins are scrawled with insights and passages underlined for emphasis. My mother, Nelle, made all those marks in that book. She used it to instruct her two young sons, and I look to it still.

A passage in Proverbs describes the ideal woman, saying: "Strength and dignity are her clothing, and she smiles at the future. She opens her mouth in wisdom, and the teaching of kindness is on her tongue. Give her the product of her hands, and let her works praise her in the gates."

Well, that passage calls for us to recognize the enormous strengths and contributions of women, wives, and mothers and indicates to me that society always needs a little reminding. Well, let us use this weekend as a symbol that we will always remember, reward, and recognize them and use their examples of love and courage as inspiration to be better than we are.

Till next week, thanks for listening, and God bless you.

Note: The President spoke at 9:06 A.M. PDT from Rancho del Cielo, near Santa Barbara.

Small Business

May 14, 1983

My fellow Americans:

This is the last day of Small Business Week, so I'd like to mark the occasion by speaking about the importance of entrepreneurs and how we're trying to help them.

When you think about it, every week should be Small Business Week, because America *is* small business. Small firms account for nearly half our jobs; they create some 60 percent of new jobs; and they're on the cutting edge of innovation, providing products and ideas for the future. Everything from ballpoint pens to FM radios, automatic transmissions, and helicopters was conceived in the minds of entrepreneurs—men and women who had the spirit to dream impossible dreams, take great risks, and work long hours to make their dreams come true.

In his book, "Wealth and Poverty," George Gilder wrote, "most successful entrepreneurs contribute far more to society than they ever recover. And most of them win no riches at all. They are the heroes of economic life. And those who begrudge them their rewards demonstrate a failure to understand their role and their promise." Well, he's right. Too often, entrepreneurs are forgotten heroes. We rarely hear about them. But look into the heart of America, and you'll see them. They're the owners of that store down the street, the faithful who support our churches, schools, and communities, the brave people everywhere who produce our goods, feed a hungry world, and keep our homes and families warm while they invest in the future to build a better America.

That word "invest" helps explain why entrepreneurs are a special breed. When small business people invest their money, they have no guarantee of a profit. They're motivated by self-interest. But that alone won't do the trick. Success comes when they can anticipate and deliver what you, the consumer, wants, and do it in a way that satisfies you. As Gilder points out, entrepreneurs intuitively understand one of the world's best-kept secrets: Capitalism begins with giving. And capitalism works best and creates the greatest wealth and human progress for all when it follows the teachings of Scripture: "Give and you will be given unto...search and you will find...cast your bread upon the waters and it will return to you manyfold."

In the Parable of the Talents, the man who invests and multiplies his money is praised. But the rich who horde [*sic*] their wealth are rebuked in Scripture. True wealth is not measured in things like money or oil, but in the treasures of the mind and spirit. Oil was worthless until entrepreneurs with ideas and the freedom and faith to take risks managed to locate it, extract it, and put it to work for humanity. We can find more oil and we can develop abundant supplies of new forms of energy if we encourage risk-taking by thousands and thousands of entrepreneurs, not rely on government to horde [*sic*], ration, and control. The whole idea is to trust the people. Countries that don't, like the U.S.S.R. and Cuba, will never prosper.

Entrepreneurs have always been leaders in America. They led the rebellion against excessive taxation and regulation. They and their offspring pushed back the frontier, transforming the wilderness into a land of plenty. Their knowledge and contributions have sustained us in wartime, brought us out of recessions, carried our astronauts to the Moon, and led American industry to new frontiers of high technology.

We came to Washington confident that this small business spirit could make America well and get our economy moving again. Well, it's working. And we want to keep on using that special principle of giving by putting America's destiny back into the people's hands, providing you new incentives to save, invest, and take risks, so more wealth will be created at every level of our society.

We know small business is ready. That group fared better during the recent recession, laid off less workers than big business, and will recover faster. Over the last 2 years, you heard about the high rate of small business failures. You heard about it over and over again. What you didn't hear very often was that in 1981 a record 580,000 new businesses were formed. And 560,000 new enterprises were begun in 1982. They're the seeds of lasting recovery.

I think America's witnessing a renaissance in enterprise, and it's being nurtured by victories we've won—for example, reducing the regulatory burden; knocking down the rate of inflation by more than two-thirds; cutting more than in half the record 21½ percent prime interest rate we inherited; passing a Small Business Innovation Development Act to direct millions of dollars in research funds to high-tech firms; passing the Prompt Payments Act to assure that small businesses dealing with the Federal Government get paid promptly; and, most important, providing solid incentives for new investment and risk-taking by cutting personal tax rates, shortening depreciating schedules, and sharply reducing estate taxes on family-owned businesses and farms.

At least 85 percent of the 13 million small firms in America pay their taxes by personal rates, not by corporate rates. These firms will provide most of the new jobs to bring down unemployment. Any action that tampers with the third year of the tax cut or the indexing provision, which protects you from being pushed by inflation into higher tax brackets, would harm small business and send unemployment up, not down. That's why I must and I will veto any attack on the tax incentives. They belong to you, the people. They're not the government's to take away.

If the Congress wants to help us spur small business growth and jobs in depressed regions, it should pass our enterprise zones proposal. This could provide genuine opportunity for those in need. So, we hope there'll be no further delay.

Governments don't reduce deficits by raising taxes on the people. Governments reduce deficits by controlling spending and stimulating new wealth, wealth from investments of brave people with hope for the future, trust in their fellow man, and faith in God.

Till next week, thanks for listening, and God bless you.

Note: The President spoke at 12:06 P.M. EDT from Camp David.

Armed Forces Day

May 21, 1983

My fellow Americans:

Each year we set aside a special day to pay special tribute to our men and women in uniform. Today is Armed Forces Day and, on behalf of a grateful nation, I would like to offer them our thanks and appreciation.

Their job is unusually difficult not only because it involves hardship and danger, or because it requires long periods away from families and loved ones, or even because it may demand the giving of one's life in defense of our nation. The difficulty of the military profession grows out of all of these, plus the fact that our service men and women are always faced with several of the most fundamental questions we ask as individuals and as a nation—the questions of war and peace and the use of force in the world.

Americans have asked these questions again and again for more than 200 years. They're still debating them today. Perhaps the reason these questions persist is because there are no easy answers. The answers lie in seeming paradoxes, underlying truths that may appear contradictory on the surface.

The most fundamental paradox is that, if we're never to use force, we must be prepared to use it and to use it successfully. We Americans don't want war and we don't start fights. We don't maintain a strong military force to conquer or coerce others. The purpose of our military is simple and straightforward: We want to prevent war by deterring others from the aggression that causes war. If our efforts are successful, we will have peace and never be forced into battle. There will never be a need to fire a single shot. That's the paradox of deterrence.

The men and women in our Armed Forces also live with a second paradox. They spend their entire time in service training to fight and preparing for a war which we and they pray will never come. As individuals, these men and women want peace as much as we do as a nation. In fact, they want it even more, because they understand that war is not the romantic heroism we read about in novels or see in the movies, but the stark truth of suffering and sacrifice and the slain promise of youth.

Our service men and women know firsthand the horrors of war and the blessings of peace, but they also know that just wanting peace is not enough to guarantee that peace will be sustained. As George Washington said, "To be prepared for war is one of the most effectual ways of preserving peace."

Today, Americans are again asking important questions about war and peace. Many have been debating two very important questions: How could we prevent nuclear war, and how could we reduce American and Soviet nuclear arsenals?

The answers to these questions are not found in simple slogans, but again, in paradoxes. To prevent nuclear war, we must have the capability to deter nuclear war. This means we must keep our strategic forces strong enough to balance those of the Soviet Union.

It must be absolutely clear to the Soviets that they would have no conceivable advantage in threatening or starting a nuclear war. In seeking to reduce American and Soviet nuclear arsenals, we must convince the Soviet Union that it is in our mutual interest to agree to significant, mutual arms reductions. And to do that, we cannot allow the current nuclear imbalance to continue. We must show the Soviets that we're determined to spend what it takes to deter war. Once they understand that, we have a real chance of successfully reaching arms reduction agreements.

Last month I sent to the Congress a proposal to modernize our intercontinental ballistic missile force. By building the MX Peacekeeper and small, single-warhead missiles, we will not only preserve our ability to protect the peace, we will also demonstrate that any Soviet quest for nuclear superiority will not work, that it is in everyone's interest to end the arms race and to agree to mutual arms reductions.

There's a direct relationship between modernization programs, like the MX Peacekeeper, and the twin objectives of deterrence and arms control. The MX and other modernization measures will help us to achieve our fundamental goal, and that is to strengthen the peace by seeking arms reduction agreements that make for more security and stability by reducing overall force levels while permitting the modernization of our forces needed for a credible deterrent.

I know that the paradox of peace through a credible military posture may be difficult for some people to accept. Some even argue that, if we really wanted to reduce nuclear weapons, we should simply stop building them ourselves. That argument makes about as much sense as saying that the way to prevent fires is to close down the fire department. It ignores one of the most basic lessons of history, a lesson that was learned by bitter experience and passed down to us by previous generations.

Tyrants are tempted by weakness, and peace and freedom can only be preserved by strength. So, let us resolve today, as we honor the brave men and women who serve in our Armed Forces, to give them the support they need to protect our cherished liberties and preserve the peace for ourselves and our children.

Till next week, thanks for listening, and God bless you.

Note: The President taped his radio address in the Diplomatic Reception Room at the White House on May 20 for broadcast on May 21. The transcript of the address was released by the Office of the Press Secretary on May 21.

Williamsburg Economic Summit

May 28, 1983

My fellow Americans:

Over this Memorial Day weekend, while most of us turn our thoughts to picnics and family outings, an annual summit meeting is taking place in Williamsburg, Virginia, one that's important to our future. It takes place at an appropriate time. A bipartisan majority in the Congress has just demonstrated its support for the recommendations of the Scowcroft Commission to modernize our strategic forces and carry us forward on the road to genuine arms reduction.

This is a reassuring signal to our friends and allies meeting in Williamsburg. Here in this old colonial capital, the cradle of so much early American history, the leaders of the major free industrial nations are meeting to discuss the problems, the challenges, and the opportunities that our countries and our peoples share.

Since the last summit in France a year ago, we've made important progress. Today, America is leading the world into an economic recovery that's already being felt in many of the other countries represented here.

Another encouraging development is that, more so than any other time in the recent past, the economic policies of the individual summit countries are converging around low inflation and improved incentives for investment, a good sign for a sustained worldwide recovery.

We still have our differences. Friends always will. But they're fewer and less critical today than in a long time. I think most of us are agreed on not only where things stand today but what we must do in the weeks and months ahead. All of us seek the same goal—a healthy, sustained economic recovery that will revive troubled economies in North America, Europe, and the rest of the world. That means more and better jobs. And the way to achieve this is to ensure that the new recovery does not rekindle inflation. We're doing this. And we're seeking trade between our countries that is open and free of protectionist restraints, so that both industrial and developing nations can profit from an expanding, rather than a contracting, market.

We're also encouraging responsible domestic economic policies in all of our countries which will make for greater productivity and more stable exchange rates.

Here at home, our economy is already strongly on the mend. The rising tide of recovery is also beginning to reach to many of our friends and allies. But to keep it going, and to extend its benefits to others still in the grip of the worldwide recession, we must all stick to anti-inflationary, high-productivity policies that adapt new technology, retrain workers, and increase efficiency. The worst thing that could happen now, and one that could stall or at least slow the recovery that's currently under way, would be a political resort to "quick fixes" that could trigger a new round of worldwide inflation and rising interest rates.

Now, I know that all of this sounds like economic shoptalk—a little remote, perhaps, from the everyday concerns of the average American. But while this is an economic summit, the topics it is considering have an impact on almost every phase of our lives—jobs, low inflation, and the opportunity for a better future for ourselves and our families. For when you get right down to it, freedom is at the base of the enormous productivity of the industrial West, a freedom that has spawned more progress, more individual rights, and more security and opportunity than are enjoyed by any other people living under any other system.

And it's our shared belief in freedom that is the strongest bond uniting each of the seven nations meeting here in Williamsburg this weekend. Each of our nations recognizes the rights and dignity of its citizens. We all believe, in the words of our Founding Fathers, "that all men are created equal, that they are endowed by their Creator with certain unalienable rights." That's a simple enough phrase, but it represents an incredible leap forward from the tyranny and injustice that still haunts too many other parts of the globe.

And because we, the nations meeting at the summit, are united in our love of personal and economic freedom, our common commitment to maintain peace and defend liberty is that much stronger. There's been a lot of speculation about what will come out of this weekend's summit. I'll leave the detailed analysis to the Monday-morning quarterbacks, though for this one they'll have to wait till Tuesday morning. But I'm confident that we and our friends and allies will leave this meeting more, not less, united, that we'll leave it with fewer, not more, differences, and that while it would have been a good session, much will remain to be done.

For the issues we address here in this beautiful and historic setting in the spring of 1983 will still be with us for many years to come. The Williamsburg summit is not the end of our work, but it marks the beginning of a new, more stable period of the free developed world learning to work together, devising long-term strategies to meet the problems we face, and handing over a better world to the successor generation, the young people born in the postwar era who must carry and protect the torch of freedom as America approaches the 21st century.

Until next week, thanks for listening, and God bless you.

Note: The President taped his radio address in the Map Room at the White House on May 26 for broadcast on May 28. The transcript of the address was released by the Office of the Press Secretary on May 28.

American Red Cross/Williamsburg Economic Summit

June 4, 1983

My fellow Americans:

Normally I discuss only one topic on these weekly broadcasts, but this week will be an exception. I want to speak to you about the economic summit we just concluded at Williamsburg, Virginia. Before I do, however, I must draw your attention to a very serious situation facing thousands of our fellow citizens and an institution we love and need very much—the American Red Cross.

As you know, 10 months of bad weather have ravaged many sections of the country. Tornadoes, floods in the South, savage storms along the Pacific coast, an earthquake in California, and now, mudslides in Nevada and Utah have inflicted terrible destruction on lives and property.

The Red Cross is doing everything it can to help, as it always does. But its budget has been exhausted by its huge relief operations during this relentless spell of bad weather. The Red Cross has no additional disaster funds to meet these new catastrophes.

There will be other disasters, no doubt. And the Red Cross must be ready for them. All of us would want to be able to count on this vital, charitable institution if and when our families ever need help. So, let's make sure the Red Cross has what it needs to continue giving assistance to other disaster victims. We can do that through our own personal contributions. The Red Cross has launched an appeal to replenish its disaster funds. I urge you and your family: please help and give today through your local Red Cross chapter.

Now, a few words about our deliberations at the economic summit at Williamsburg. I was very pleased that the leaders of the great democracies could meet in that beautiful colonial city so rich in history and culture. It was a perfect place to renew ties and pledge our best efforts to achieve stronger prosperity and security by living up to those cherished values that bind us—democracy, individual freedom, moral purpose, human dignity, and personal development.

Perhaps you're thinking, "That sounds fine. But how does it affect me?" Well, Williamsburg was meaningful and constructive in several ways. The leaders of the seven free industrialized nations met in a private, informal setting—one that encouraged some of the best talks among the allies in recent years. We were determined, as sincere and well-intentioned individuals, to talk through our problems, to rise above bickering and discord so, together, we could forge a common strategy for growth and jobs to ensure the better future our people deserve.

I think we succeeded. Our meetings produced a shared spirit of confidence, optimism, and cooperation—confidence that an economic recovery is beginning, optimism that it can spread to all countries and that it will last, if our countries cooperate to keep inflation down, reduce interest rates further, and put a stop to protectionism.

Williamsburg also demonstrated, to the chagrin of the Soviets, that the spirit of unity in the West for peace through strength is alive and well. Every Western leader who attended agreed that we must resist Soviet efforts to drive a wedge between us. And we all committed ourselves to maintain our security while seeking real arms reductions and working for the cause of peace.

The Williamsburg summit was a positive gain that sent a message of hope to the world. That makes it all the more important for each country to follow up with sound, commonsense policies that carry us forward toward greater progress.

This coming week I'll meet with the bipartisan leadership of the Congress to discuss concrete ways we can follow up on the summit. Here at home, we must not jeopardize what we've worked so hard to build—a strong recovery from a terrible recession caused by years of economic mismanagement. In 2½ years, inflation has been knocked all the way down from an annual rate of 12.4 percent to 3.9 percent and, for the last 6 months, only eight-tenths of 1 percent.

The prime interest rate has been cut more than in half—from a killing 21½ percent to 10½ percent today. Industries like autos, housing, and steel, which had been brought to their knees by those terrible inflation and interest rates, are now regaining strength and calling back workers.

Since we took office, thanks to the incentives provided by tax cuts, among other things, more than 1.1 million new businesses have started up.

That's an American record. These are the seeds for millions of new jobs and new technologies for the future. Yes, unemployment is too high. But it fell slightly again in May, and it will fall further. Nearly 800,000 jobs have been created since December. Last month there were 375,000 more people on the payrolls than the month before.

So, let me repeat: We must keep going forward and not undo the progress we've made. I sincerely hope the Congress will work with us. But let there be no misunderstanding about my position. Hardworking families are already overtaxed, and you know I'm not just whistling in the dark. The United States did not succumb to a decade of difficulties because you, the people, are not taxed enough. We got ourselves in difficulty because government spends too much. We don't need tax increases; we need spending restraint. And that's why the Williamsburg communiqué makes an explicit call, one I'm prepared to defend with Presidential vetoes.

We will tackle budget deficits, and we must do it by limiting the growth of government expenditures. In the spirit of the summit, I will also continue to oppose quick fixes of protectionism—legislation like the local content rule, which would force domestic manufacturers of cars to build them with a rising share of U.S. labor and parts. Well, it's a cruel hoax. New cars would be more expensive, more jobs would be destroyed than protected. We would buy less from our trading partners, they would buy less from us, and the world economic pie would shrink. Recrimination and retaliation would increase.

We left Williamsburg confident that we can build lasting prosperity, but only with hard work, discipline, incentives, cooperation, and competition. And we can build a safer, more peaceful world, but only if our free nations stand together and remain strong. It's not easy, but nothing worth having ever is.

Till next week, thanks for listening, and God bless you.

Note: The President spoke at 12:06 P.M. EDT from Camp David.

Environmental and Natural Resources Management

June 11, 1983

My fellow Americans:

I think it's time to clear the air and straighten out the record on where my administration stands on environmental and natural resources management matters. I know you've heard and read a million words about where others think we stand. Now, how about 5 minutes of the truth?

A few weeks ago, when Bill Ruckelshaus was sworn in as Director of the Environmental Protection Agency, he very graciously pointed out that when his Agency was created 13 years ago, with him as its first Director, California was the environmental leader of the Nation. Having been Governor of California at that time, I was, and am, very grateful to Bill for those kind words.

Let me just say, I feel now as I felt then about environmental matters. I believe in a sound, strong environmental policy that protects the health of our people and a wise stewardship of our nation's natural resources. But that's enough about me.

The Secretary of the Interior, Jim Watt, is the prime target for those who claim that this administration is out to level the forests and cover the country with blacktops. Someone in the press the other day said if Jim discovered a cure for cancer, there are those who would attack him for being pro-life.

Let's go back a little first and set the stage. Jim rides herd on all the national parks and most of the 80 million acres of national wilderness. There are other things, like wildlife refuges, which up the total considerably. In fact, the Federal Government owns one-third of all the land of the United States.

When he came to Washington 2½ years ago, Jim found that visitor facilities in our national parks had been allowed to deteriorate to the point that many failed to meet standards for health and safety. It's being corrected. The National Park Service has made a major effort to improve maintenance at the parks that so many Americans love and love to visit. And today, they provide a wider, more beautiful variety of outdoor splendor than you can find anywhere else in the world.

Not too long ago, however, a new firestorm was raised about our wilderness lands. The perception was created that Secretary Watt was turning some of these lands loose from wilderness classification and government ownership. I should point out that wilderness lands are areas of such wild beauty that they're totally preserved in their natural state. No roads violate them, and no structures of any kind are allowed, and there are now almost 80 million acres of such land.

So, what was the firestorm all about? Well, hang on, and follow me closely. As a result of legislation passed several years ago, a study was made of some 174 million acres of land to see if any or all of it should be declared wilderness and added to the present 80 million acres. Conditions were imposed in the review procedures to ensure that wilderness standards would be met.

If, for example, there were roads on the land, it was ineligible. It was ineligible if there was any dual ownership by other levels of government or if title to mineral rights was held by individuals or governments. Also, with limited exceptions, any package had to contain no less than 5,000 acres to be eligible. The study had been going on under the previous administration, and some 150 million of the designated 174 million acres had already been turned down by previous administrations as being ineligible for wilderness classification.

Now, think hard now. Do you recall hearing one word about this or any attack being made on anyone at the time? I don't. When we arrived, there were still about 25 million acres to be studied. A few months ago, another 800,000 acres—that's a fraction of what the previous administration rejected—were disqualified as not meeting wilderness qualifications. Yet, the reaction this time was instantaneous, volcanic in size, and nationwide in effect: "Jim Watt was giving away wilderness land. Our children and grandchildren would be deprived of ever seeing America as it once was."

Well, nobody bothered to mention that our administration has proposed to the Congress addition of another 57 wilderness areas encompassing 2.7 million acres. That's more than three times as much land as was disqualified. Nor did anyone mention that I've already signed legislation designating sites in Indiana, Missouri, Alabama, and West Virginia as new wilderness areas.

The truth is that our National Park System alone has grown to 74 million acres, and almost 7,000 miles of river are included in our National Wild and Scenic River System. We have 413 wildlife refuges totaling some 86.7 million acres. This record is unmatched by any other country in the world.

Our environmental programs also are the strongest in the world. Last year, expenditures by business and government to comply with environmental laws and regulations were estimated at over $55 billion, or $245 per man, woman, and child in the United States.

We have made a commitment to protect the health of our citizens and to conserve our nation's natural beauty and resources. We have even provided financial and technical support to other nations and international organizations to protect global resources. Thanks to these efforts, our country remains "America the Beautiful." Indeed, it's growing more healthy and more beautiful each year. I hope this helps set the record straight, because it's one we can all be proud of.

Till next week, thanks for listening, and God bless you.

Note: The President spoke at 12:06 P.M. EDT from Camp David.

Federal Reserve Board Chairman/Space Shuttle Flight and Science Education

June 18, 1983

My fellow Americans:

As the saying goes, we interrupt this program for a news flash. Some years ago, a favorite movie theme was the crusading reporter. In every such picture, the reporter—hat on the back of his head, clutching the phone— would yell, "Give me the city desk. I've got a story that'll crack this town wide open!" I've read that line a few times myself. Well, I'm not wearing a hat or clutching a phone, but before getting into today's broadcast, I'd like to make an important announcement.

The term of the Federal Reserve Board Chairman expires August 5th. I have today asked Chairman Paul Volcker to accept reappointment for another term. He's agreed to do so, and I couldn't be more pleased. Paul Volcker is a man of unquestioned independence, integrity, and ability. He is as dedicated as I am to continuing the fight against inflation. And with him as Chairman of the Fed, I know we'll win that fight. End of news flash.

Today marked the launching of the seventh space shuttle flight. This particular shuttle flight is unique in several respects. It's the first space flight of an American woman—Dr. Sally Ride, another example of the great strides women have made in our country. Women are working as hard and contributing as much as men, and their work is finally receiving the recognition it deserves. I know I speak for all of us when I wish Dr. Ride and her fellow crew members the best of luck in their bold journey. Nancy and I look forward to being on hand to greet them when they land next Friday.

This particular shuttle flight also represents another first. Aboard that space shuttle will not only be communications satellites and NASA experiments but also a small colony of ants. This experiment is designed to look at the effect of prolonged weightlessness on the ant colony's social structure. While this particular experiment is interesting, the story behind it is even more fascinating.

About 5 years ago, some folks in two high schools in Camden, New Jersey, got together and launched a project for students to send up an experiment in a space shuttle flight. Community leaders and local education officials saw this as a fresh opportunity for students to develop an interest in science and engineering. Now, this may not sound all that original. After all, there are lots of high schools with strong science preparatory programs. But the people backing this project didn't go out hunting for an exceptional high school or exceptional scholars.

This project started in two inner-city high schools in Camden, New Jersey. Camden High School is about 85 percent black and 15 percent Hispanic. Woodrow Wilson High School is about 51 percent black and 44 percent

1983 **113**

Hispanic. Many of the students are from poor families. Before this project, interest in science was not very strong. One Camden High student said, "When it came to taking science, a lot of students didn't want to do it. They didn't want to try." But that good old American volunteer spirit found a way.

RCA, Camden's largest private employer, offered to pay the cost of launching an experiment on the shuttle if the students could come up with an idea for a project and actually design and build it. The administration and faculty at the high schools took up RCA's offer and started space science courses and encouraged student participation.

Dozens of local companies, universities, and individuals helped out by contributing money, materials, or manpower. And most importantly, the students themselves studied computers and designed computer programs to help run the experiment. They build the canister in which the experiment would take place. They raised funds for the project by selling T-shirts.

Not only were they interested in the project itself, they developed a broader interest in science and engineering in general. Elective science classes now have many more students than they had before the project. One of the schools installed a planetarium because of the interest in space.

Billy Joyce, a 17-year-old student, said, "Before this experiment with the ants, I wasn't really into this science class. But when it got started, I got interested. Just the idea of getting these ants aboard the shuttle and into space made this class something to look forward to. And it got me interested in doing things I've never done before."

This whole project illustrates some very important lessons in the area of education. It shows the part local community involvement plays in stimulating intellectual curiosity and educational excellence. Local businesses, school teachers, and administrators and, most importantly, the students themselves, developed ideas and turned those ideas into real educational opportunities.

These students didn't become fascinated with science because of some Federal bureaucracy in Washington, though NASA played a positive role, but mainly because of interest developed at the grassroots level. Regardless of whether or not this experiment in the space shuttle flight succeeds, these high school students in Camden, New Jersey, have gained a new-found interest in learning and in the wonders of science that will serve them well all their lives.

There's a lesson here for all of us who believe that individual effort and initiative count and that we can make America's education system what it should be—the best in the world.

Till next week, thanks for listening, and God bless you.

Note: The President spoke at 12:06 P.M. EDT from Camp David.

June 23, 1983

My fellow Americans:

Ever since our Commission on Excellence in Education came forth with its findings, you, the taxpaying citizens of this country, have been treated to a noisy debate about what to do.

First, the Commission report made the point that, on the average, educational quality has deteriorated in recent years. Now, make sure you remember that term "on the average." Admittedly, there are schools, school districts, and even some parts of individual schools that have managed to maintain a high level of quality.

Then, the Commission pointed out a number of remedies which, if employed, would bring the average level up to the standard our children are entitled to. Many of the remedies would call for no increase in spending; some, admittedly, would shift funding from less important things to things of greater educational value, and here and there, there might be a need for more money. Basically, however, the Commission's thrust was one of making better use of resources we already have.

All of what I've just pointed out was lost, however, in an explosion of voices. There were special interest voices that saw a chance to get more money for their particular cause. There were political voices that saw a campaign horse to ride. And there was demagoguery to help raise the noise level.

In making the report public and discussing the matter of education costs, I was accused of being "grotesquely inaccurate and outrageous." This seems to have been prompted by a statement that more was being spent on education than on national defense.

I can only explain their hysteria by assuming that they were comparing Federal spending on education to Federal spending on defense. That, of course, is ridiculous. The Federal Government bears overwhelming responsibility for national defense, but it provides less than 10 percent of all education costs, which are and always have been a responsibility of the State and local governments.

Since this hassle won't die down in 15 [*sic*] minutes, I thought you might like some real figures from the U.S. Department of Education. In the '82-'83 school year, government at all levels spent $215.3 billion on education. The 1983 defense spending is $214.8 billion. Actually, the $215 billion for education doesn't include Department of Defense spending for remedial education or private corporation spending on employee education, all of which is estimated to be about $30 billion or more. Nor does it include what parents spend on books, etc.

One of the noisemakers wants the Federal Government to add $11 billion to Federal education spending. Another demands $14 billion. And most of them accuse us of whacking the budget down to a starvation level.

The facts are, the Federal budget for education in 1980 was $14.1 billion. In 1981, which was still not our budget, it was $14.8. Our first appropriation, the one for 1982, held the level for education at $14.8 billion, the same as in 1981. This year we'll spend about $15.3 billion.

Now, these are a lot of figures to absorb when you can only hear them and not see them. Let me see if I can simplify things. The cost per pupil has nearly doubled, up 183.2 percent in 10 years. In the same 10 years, the number of pupils has dropped by 14 percent.

Some distinguished Members of Congress—I'll be kind and not name them—took me on for pointing out that the decline in educational quality seems to have begun shortly after the Federal Government started providing that less than 10 percent of the funding. What I had in mind was that the Federal Government began regulating and kibitzing a lot more than 10 percent, and maybe that contributed to the decline.

Now hang on, I have to resort to some numbers again. The Federal funding boom began in 1960. The teacher-pupil ratio went from one teacher to 26 pupils, then to one teacher to 19 pupils in 1980. But the Scholastic Aptitude Test scores of college-bound high-school graduates dropped in that same period from 975 to 890. Maybe it's just a coincidence, but at least it raises a question as to whether more money is the—well, dare I use the term?—"quick fix" for poor quality education.

Already a great many educators and school boards and Governors and State legislators who've read the Commission's report are enthusiastically moving to implement it.

The Commission urged that we return to basics as requirements for a high-school diploma: 4 years of required English; increase the number of years of required mathematics and science; eliminate some of the frill, the "snap," courses so tempting to students when there are few, if any, compulsory courses; make history a required course, and the same for languages for the college-bound; require more homework. These were a few of the Commission's recommendations.

Yes, they talked of something that could translate into more money—better pay for better teachers to attract the brightest and the best to choose teaching as a career. Do what is done in every other profession and business—offer merit pay raises for those who earn and deserve them.

The Commission gave us a course to follow. It leads to better education for our sons and daughters. Let's ignore the noisemakers and set sail.

Thanks for listening, and God bless you.

Note: The President spoke at 12:06 P.M. EDT from the Oval Office at the White House.

Independence Day

July 2, 1983

My fellow Americans:

On Monday, America will celebrate her 207th birthday. I love the Fourth of July. I enjoy picnics and fireworks and long summer days, and I get excited with the thought that millions of our people all across our great country will, on this Fourth of July weekend, join together in thinking about freedom and the men and women who sacrificed to make it our inheritance.

It's easy to forget just what a Revolution these Americans made. It's easy to forget how they amazed the world and how many hopes they raised. President George Washington, in the very first Inaugural Address, warned Americans that they had a new responsibility. He said, "the preservation of the sacred fire of liberty and the destiny of the republican model of government are justly considered, perhaps, as *deeply,* as *finally,* staked on the experiment entrusted to the hands of the American people."

Now, you may not think of yourself or our democracy as an experiment, but look around. All over the world, millions and millions of people still live under tyranny. Their leaders claim that they're the wave of the future, that history is on their side. And yet, their people look to us for hope. Their people look to America as the cradle of freedom, the place where the great civilized ideas of individual liberty, representative government, and the rule of law under God are realities.

Yes, these people see America as the experiment that works. And democracy works because of the physical and moral courage of individuals—some famous, others deserving of recognition.

I think of a group of women we honored in Washington this past April, an honor long overdue. They were nurses who'd been captured in the Philippines during World War II and then spent nearly 3 years in prison camps. Lieutenant Colonel Madeline Ullom, who was captured at Corregidor, has described tending wounded soldiers during the long months of siege: "Our atmosphere was one of dusty pall, ever present, in which we moved, worked, tried to eat, tried to breathe in an endless nightmare," she said.

In Santa Tomas Prison Camp, Colonel Ullom and her fellow nurses quickly organized into shifts and began to care for other prisoners. They fought against diseases and starvation. They lacked medicine and equipment and food. But miraculously, every one of the 81 American women POW's had survived.

These women would not describe themselves as extraordinary Americans; they simply volunteered to serve their country, and they chose to serve it with courage and hope. Their patriotism, as they gathered in Washington 40 years after their capture and imprisonment, remained strong and vibrant.

Of course, we're accustomed to thinking of courage during a time of war, but democracy requires political courage as well. In 1954, when he was convalescing from a painful back operation, Senator John F. Kennedy had time to think about political courage. The result was a book entitled "Profiles in Courage," in which he wrote, "In the days ahead, only the very courageous will be able to take the hard and unpopular decisions necessary for our survival in the struggle with a powerful enemy. And only the very courageous will be able to keep alive the spirit of individualism and dissent which gave birth to this nation, nourished it as an infant, and carried it through its severest tests upon the attainment of its maturity."

We've seen a great example of this kind of political courage just recently when a majority, made up of both Republicans and Democrats in the Congress, set aside narrow political considerations and embraced a bipartisan program for enhancing America's security and stability through meaningful arms reductions and modernization of our defenses.

It was not easy for many of these men and women to vote for the MX missile. Some have been harshly criticized by other Members in their own party. Indeed, they faced considerable pressure and corresponding political risks. While accepting such risks, the only benefit they've received is the knowledge that they placed foremost their hopes for successful arms reductions and greater security of their nation.

Together with the Congress, we're doing everything possible to achieve genuine arms reductions. Our negotiators have been given instructions that provide greater flexibility in our negotiations with the Soviet Union. The proposals are fair, realistic, and would bring a much greater degree of stability for all the peoples of the world. There's absolutely no doubt that the prospects for success in our negotiations have been significantly improved because of the political courage shown by the Congress.

The task now is to be patient and to sustain our resolve. On this Fourth of July weekend, I salute those Members of the Congress who are putting the interests of America first. They're part of a long American tradition of proving democracy's critics wrong—of showing that we have the courage to stand up for what is right and what is necessary.

Our democratic experiment is alive and well at year 207. And with the help of the kind of political leadership and vision that we've seen in recent weeks, we can count on many happy returns.

Until next week, God bless you, and God bless America.

Note: The President spoke at 9:06 A.M. PDT from Rancho del Cielo, near Santa Barbara.

Economic and Fair Housing Issues

July 9, 1983

My fellow Americans:

In recent weeks, even the gloomiest critics have had trouble denying that things are getting better for you and your families. The number of people working is up 1.1 million from last December. Unemployment remains too high, but it's coming down—9.8 percent in June, as announced yesterday.

We're seeing strong economic growth, and we're seeing it while inflation is at its lowest level in a decade—3½ percent over the last year. This sharply lower inflation and the first decent tax cut since the 1960's are allowing families to keep more of their own earnings to spend or save.

Contrary to propaganda blasts you hear, America is heading in a better direction today than before. For example, thanks to the tax cuts and our progress against inflation, a medium-income family earning $25,000 has nearly $600 more in purchasing power today than in 1980. Low-income families are being helped, too. Nothing was more cruel for them than those back-to-back years of double-digit inflation—before we got here, I hasten to add. If your family was on a fixed income of $10,000 at the start of 1979, that income was worth less than $8,000 by the end of 1980. In other words, inflation, which for years had been part of deliberate government economic planning, robbed you of $2,000. Now, that's not my idea of fairness, and I doubt if it's yours. If you tried to save a dollar at your bank during that same period, it would have lost 20 cents in value.

Well, we haven't abolished inflation or high taxes, but we're gaining on them. Your after-tax purchasing power helps determine your economic well-being, But this fact is ignored by the big spenders who claim to carry the banner of fairness and compassion. According to them, the whole issue of fairness revolves around government spending programs. And even on government spending, some of them have been misleading you. You've been led to believe that any budget savings in these programs would hurt the needy, and that's not true.

The problem we set out to solve back when we inherited those record inflation and interest rates was not government doing too much for the needy, but government doing too much for the non-needy. Before our budget reforms were passed, surveys indicated that 2 out of every 5 dollars in benefits went to those with total incomes and benefits well above the poverty line. Also, some of the programs to help the poor had the effect of keeping them poor and dependent, robbing them of their self-respect.

America is a wealthy nation, but our wealth is not unlimited. So we've tried to face up to the reality too many have ignored. Unless we prune nonessential programs, unless we end benefits for those who should not be subsidized by their fellow taxpayers, we won't have enough resources to meet the requirements of those who must have our help. And helping those who truly need assistance is what fairness in government spending should be all about. We're trying to do this. Let me give you one statistic I doubt you've ever heard.

Our budget request for 1984 would have the Federal Government spend, after inflation, two-and-a-half times what it spent in 1970 on assistance to the poor. So while, yes, there have been some cuts, they've been nowhere near as draconian as critics charge. Why haven't you had this information? Well, maybe one reason is the drumbeat of gloom and doom from misery merchants in some of the media.

One major newspaper recently ran an editorial entitled, "Poorer, Hungrier." In 1979, according to this editorial, a team of doctors declared Federal food programs had eliminated most of the malnutrition in America. The editorial asked, "What would they find today?" Their answer, of course, was to say that under this administration things had worsened.

The truth is low-income Americans are receiving more food assistance in 1983 than ever before in history. During our administration, food assistance has grown by 34 percent. More people are being served, and the grants for the neediest have been increased. We subsidize in whole or in part 95 million meals a day.

The average food stamp benefit, per person, has grown faster than the increase in food prices through inflation. The infant mortality rate has continued to decline. A greater percentage of school-lunch-program dollars are dedicated to providing meals for children of low-income families. Subsidies for meals served to children from low-income families have also increased in this administration.

Our administration is also distributing surplus cheese, butter, powdered milk, rice, flour, honey, and cornmeal to the needy and elderly. This is in addition to commodities regularly provided to schools and charitable institutions. The total comes to $1.7 billion so far.

Those budget reductions you've heard so much about have been achieved by improving efficiency, reducing dependency, cutting waste and abuse, and targeting on the neediest families. And that's as it should be. We're committed to fairness, and we'll continue to take actions needed to bring it about throughout our society.

Next week we'll be taking a new initiative to keep a pledge I made in my State of the Union address—the pledge to strengthen enforcement of fair housing laws for all Americans. We believe in the bold promise that no person in the United States should be denied full freedom of choice in the selection of housing because of race, color, religion, sex, or national origin. We're proposing a series of amendments that will put real teeth into the Fair Housing Act.

For example, the Justice Department can now act on complaints only when there's reason to believe there exists a practice of discrimination. Under our proposal, if conciliation fails, Secretary Pierce at HUD could forward individual complaints to the Attorney General for litigation. We're also proposing to extend the current law to prohibit discrimination on the basis of handicap or size of family. And our proposal will create substantial civil penalties for landlords and others found violating the law. This will include stiff fines up to $50,000 for a first offense and $100,000 for a second offense.

We believe this is an important step for civil rights. For a family deprived of its freedom of choice in choosing a home, our proposal will mean swift action and strong civil penalties to prevent discrimination in the first place. As I said, we're committed to fairness and we're committed to use the full power of the Federal Government whenever and wherever even one person's constitutional rights are being unjustly denied.

Till next week, thanks for listening, and God bless you.

Note: The President spoke at 12:06 P.M. EDT from Camp David.

Arms Control and Reduction

July 16, 1983

My fellow Americans:

Today I want to talk to you about peace. Back in June of 1963, President John F. Kennedy delivered an arms control speech that is still remembered for its eloquence and vision. He told the graduating seniors at American University: "I speak of peace, therefore, as the necessary, rational end of rational men. I realize that the pursuit of peace is not as dramatic as the pursuit of war and, frequently, the words of the pursuer fall on deaf ears. But we have no more urgent task."

Twenty years have passed since those words were spoken, and they've been a troubled era, overshadowed by the dangers of nuclear weapons. We've seen the world's inventory of nuclear weapons steadily expand. Despite many sincere attempts to control the growth of nuclear arsenals, those arsenals have continued to grow. That's the bad news.

The good news is that now, at last, there is hope that we can finally begin to reverse this trend. Americans have joined together—Republicans and Democrats, liberals and conservatives—to face the greatest challenge of our time: the urgent task of pursuing a lasting peace in the nuclear era. Our political process has forged a consensus, a bipartisan consensus that has united us in our common search for ways to protect our country, reduce the risk of war and, ultimately, dramatically reduce the level of nuclear weapons—the foundation we need for successful negotiations.

Remember, our MX Peacekeeper missile program calls for the deployment of 100 missiles. The level ultimately deployed, however, will clearly be influenced by the outcome in Geneva. If an agreement is reached which calls for deep reductions—which is, of course, our goal—the number of missiles could certainly be adjusted downward.

As the Scowcroft Commission rightly pointed out, the MX Peacekeeper missile is an essential part of a comprehensive modernization and arms control program to ensure deterrence today and in the future. We're building the MX Peacekeeper to strengthen deterrence. But it also provides vital negotiating incentives and leverage in Geneva.

Andrei Sakharov, the distinguished Soviet physicist and Nobel Prize laureate, recently published an eloquent article which forcefully makes the same point. He notes that, given the Soviet advantage in land-based, strategic missiles, talks about limitation and reduction of these systems could become easier if the United States were to have MX missiles, albeit only potentially. Andrei Sakharov is a hard man for anyone to ignore.

When the Congress reaffirms its support for this program and authorizes the funds to modernize our strategic deterrent, our agenda for peace will be strengthened even further. In NATO, as in our other alliances, there's a renewed feeling of solidarity. Last May at Williamsburg, the leaders of the major industrialized nations demonstrated their commitment to vigorously pursue the twin objectives of arms reductions and deterrence in the Williamsburg communiqué. This solidarity is a source of much strength.

For the graduates of June 1983, this is a time of opportunity and hope—a hope that they and their children will enjoy a safer, more secure world. That's why we must sustain our consensus. And that's why I've spent hundreds of hours meeting with members of this administration, with the bipartisan commission on strategic forces, with our arms negotiators, with Members of the Congress, and with concerned citizens.

My message to them and to you is that we have no higher priority than reducing and ultimately removing the threat of nuclear war and seeking the stability necessary for true peace. To achieve that objective, we must reduce the nuclear arsenals of both the United States and the Soviet Union. We must achieve greater stability; that is, we must be sure that we obtain genuine arms reductions, not merely agreements that permit a growth in nuclear arsenals or agreements that proclaim good intentions without the teeth necessary to verify and enforce compliance.

Our current goal must be the reduction of nuclear arsenals. And I for one believe we must never depart from the ultimate goal of banning them from the face of the Earth. That's why we presented ambitious but realistic proposals, and that's why I have been and continue to be willing to consider any serious Soviet counteroffer. And that's why I've made our original proposal more flexible and why I continue to seek new ideas for achieving an arms reduction breakthrough.

Indeed, the draft treaty our negotiators recently introduced in Geneva documents our flexibility. As opportunities permit, the U.S. position will continue to evolve. The United States will negotiate patiently but urgently and always in good faith.

But we cannot and we must not settle for less than genuine, mutual, and verifiable arms reductions. America's postwar generation has preserved world peace in its lifetime, but it's been an uneasy peace. Today's young Americans—indeed, all members of the human family—desire more and deserve more. And you deserve to know that your government is doing everything possible to meet your expectations.

Time and again our nation has proved that there are no limits to what we Americans can achieve when we work together. Well, today we are working together to do what is right. And as a result, we can look forward to a more secure tomorrow.

Till next week, thanks for listening, and God bless you.

Note: The President spoke at 12:06 P.M. EDT from Camp David.

International Monetary Fund/Organ Donorship

July 23, 1983

My fellow Americans:

Before I get to the heart of my remarks today, I want to mention some important legislation currently before the Congress. I'm sure you're all aware of the difficulties some countries are having in meeting payments on their debts. Their problem touches all of us in a very real way and, indeed, poses a threat to the stability of the world financial order. For that reason, something called the International Monetary Fund was created some years ago. It's better known as the IMF, and that's how I'll refer to it.

Nations, including our own, contribute to IMF, and countries with temporary balance-of-payment problems borrow from it on a short-term basis. In order to get a loan, they have to agree to terms the Fund managers lay down with regard to correcting the practices and policies that contribute to their financial difficulties.

I've asked the Congress to approve an $8½ billion contribution to the Fund. Some in the Congress and a great many citizens think this is a giveaway which will increase our deficit. The IMF is not foreign aid, and the $8½ billion is not being given away. We will have additional drawing rights in that amount from the IMF. In fact, in its entire history, the two countries that have borrowed the greatest amounts from the Fund have been the United Kingdom and the United States. The sum we're asking Congress to approve does not increase our budget and is returned with interest as loans are repaid.

In addition, it creates jobs, because it keeps the wheels of world commerce turning. Exports account for one out of five manufacturing jobs in the United States. The IMF and its programs help keep Americans at work. This is important legislation for international economic stability, and I hope you'll support it.

But today, I want to speak only of—or not speak, I should say, of great national issues. Instead, I'm taking to the airwaves in hopes we can save one little 11-month-old girl from Texas and many others like her. The young girl from Texas is Ashley Bailey, and all 11 pounds of her are in critical condition at the University of Minnesota Hospital in Minneapolis. She is now fed intravenously and has but 2 or 3 weeks to live unless she receives a liver transplant.

Back in May, Congressman Charlie Stenholm of Texas wrote me of the plight of this baby girl who must receive a transplant to survive. The surgery was estimated to cost $140,000. The Congressman said there'd been a tremendous outpouring of community and business support in the Abilene, Texas, area, and about $75,000 already had been raised. A week or so after I received the letter, the Texas and Federal Medicaid programs contributed $82,000 toward the operation, and medical expenses were no longer a problem for little Ashley. What she needed then, and needs now, is a donor. Time is running out. I'm issuing a plea to the Nation to find Ashley a donor.

Once one is found, an Air Force jet is standing ready in case immediate commercial transportation is not available. Have a pencil ready; I'll give you a phone number in just a few seconds.

Right now, somewhere in America, there might be a pair of stunned and grief-stricken parents whose own baby has died in an accident or is sadly near death. I know if these parents were aware their baby could make it possible for Ashley to live, they would have no hesitation in saying, "Save that little girl."

I urge any of you who know of a possible liver donor for Ashley to call The Living Bank in Houston. The number is 800-528-2971. I'll repeat the number: 800-528-2971. Please call.

There are many other children like Ashley. We're looking for donors for them, as well. Right here in the White House we have an electrician, Stuart Thomas, whose daughter Candi—another 11-month-old girl—is waiting for a transplant. The helicopter squadron at Andrews Air Force Base is alerted to transport Candi and her mother to Pittsburgh as soon as a suitable liver is found.

In the last few days we lost little Courtney Davis from Beaumont, Texas, and Michelle Heckard from Shenandoah Heights, Pennsylvania, because we couldn't find livers to save their lives.

Nancy and I receive so many requests from families in need of organ donors that I directed the Surgeon General to conduct a conference on organ transplants. The major recommendation was to develop a public awareness program on organ donorship. This is under way, and I hope my broadcast today adds to the momentum. The project will stress education for doctors, State highway police, hospital officials, and others on the need to consider organ donorship when accidental death occurs.

America has faced shortages in the past of everything from nylons during World War II to oil in the 1970's. But modern medical science has provided us with a new shortage—a shortage of living organs—livers, hearts, lungs, eyes, kidneys. I urge all Americans to fill out donor cards, little cards you carry in your wallet or purse that, in the event of your death, offer the hope of life to others. You can obtain these cards by simply calling your local kidney, heart, or lung associations.

Americans are giving people. In many of the cases where these very expensive operations are essential, local citizens have raised money to help the families in need. I've already mentioned the community support given to Ashley. Well, not far from Washington, Morningside, Maryland, raised over $100,000 for the Goode family, whose little Nicky needs a transplant.

That kind of caring should make us all proud to be American. We can save more of our children and adults through organ donorship. Organ donors offer the greatest gift of all—the gift of life. Right now Ashley Bailey, as well as other desperately ill children, are waiting for that gift. Please help us find donors for these children.

Until next week, thanks for listening, and God bless you.

Note: The President's address was taped at 10:30 A.M. at the White House for broadcast at 12:06 P.M. EDT.

July 30, 1983

My fellow Americans:

Last Saturday, I told you about little Ashley Bailey and her desperate need for a liver transplant. I expressed the hope that someone listening might know of a possible donor who could assure 11-month-old Ashley of a chance to live. I listed several others who, like Ashley, are waiting for transplants if donors can only be found. I gave a phone number where possible donors could respond. Well, God bless you all, the response was overwhelming. Over 5,000 calls were received from people in 47 states. Many callers asked for donor cards so they could help others even after they're gone. Six liver transplants have already taken place. Six children, including Candi Thomas, one of the little girls I mentioned last week, have been given a new lease on life. And two people have received cornea transplants. They were given the gift of sight by one of our neighbors who heard about a chance to help.

I'm sorry to say, Ashley's situation remains the same. None of the available livers was suitable. She still needs a transplant soon, in order to live. Time is short. But your response has been so generous, I have to believe there will be a donor found. I'm going to keep on praying. One thing I know: We live in a country where people truly care for one another.

Today, I'd like to take you behind the headlines and talk about an issue that affects every U.S. taxpayer—efficient management of the Federal Government. Government has grown like a patchwork quilt. Whenever a new need was identified, a new program was patched on regardless of what it cost. The door was wide open for fraud, waste, and abuse. Is it any wonder that we hear so many infuriating stories about government throwing money away, about food stamp rings that illegally obtain aid meant for the poor and needy, or about illegal aliens receiving government loans?

Already, we've cut the volume of new Federal regulations by one-quarter, reducing paperwork on the American people by 300 million hours a year. We've reduced the rapid rate of growth in government spending. And the Inspector General program has helped save or put to better use over $22 billion that was being improperly spent.

In the Defense Department alone, our efforts have saved or put to better use $16.1 billion. And the Department's 18,000 auditors and investigators have my full backing in their continuing fight against the fraud and waste typified by the recent $916 plastic cap purchase. Would you pay that much for a plastic cap? Well, the government shouldn't, either. And Secretary Weinberger is cracking down, seeing to it that negligent employees will be fired and irresponsible government contractors taken to court. Those horror stories you've been seeing and hearing about scandalous prices that we're paying for spare parts are the result of our own investigations and represent the findings of more than a score of Defense Department Inspector Generals.

We've saved $50 million in government-wide travel costs by using airline discount fares. We've also discontinued one out of every five government publications, eliminating 73 million copies of such vital reports as "A Moment in the Life of a Lizard" and "Growing Ornamental Bamboo." And we're ahead of schedule in our efforts to reduce Federal civilian employment by the equivalent of 75,000 full-time workers.

This coming week I'll bring my senior appointees together at the White House to continue an ambitious program to upgrade management of the Federal Government. Our long-range goal is to overhaul the entire administrative system. I call this effort Reform 88. It's a big job. Our government has over 2.8 million civilian and 2 million active military personnel in over 22,000 buildings, using 19,000 computers, 330 differing financial systems, and 200 payroll systems, and there's never been an effective effort to manage this growing administrative monster.

Each year we've fallen behind the private sector in management techniques. Well, we're bringing this to an end now. Reform 88 is geared to get results. Over a 6-year period, it'll save the taxpayers, or result in a better use of, tens of billions of dollars that could mean as much as the equivalent of nearly $2,000 for the average American family. And these savings won't be obtained by cutting help to the deserving but by eliminating waste and inefficiency.

For example, in debt collection, where the government is owed over $280 billion, we'll be using modern methods to ensure that Federal loans are paid back. You may have heard about the individual who obtained 10 Housing and Urban Development loans and defaulted on all 10. Well, in the future, deadbeats like that will be headed off at the pass. We'll do it by using credit bureaus and prescreening to determine the credit worthiness of applicants for loans and grants. And to help reduce the $40 billion in delinquent debt, we'll be automating our collection techniques just like private industry.

It's about time the notion that government is the servant, not the master, came back into fashion. One of our highest priorities is to restore to the American people a government well managed and responsive to your needs and respectful of your tax dollars. The greatest nation in the world deserves the best government, and with your support, we'll have it.

Until next week, thanks for listening, and God bless you.

Note: The President spoke at 12:06 P.M. EDT from Camp David.

International Trade

August 6, 1983

My fellow Americans:

I'd like to talk to you today about trade—a powerful force for progress and peace, as you well know. The winds and waters of commerce carry opportunities that help nations grow and bring citizens of the world closer together. Put simply, increased trade spells more jobs, higher earnings, better products, less inflation, and cooperation over confrontation. The freer the flow of world trade, the stronger the tides for economic progress and peace among nations.

I've seen in my lifetime what happens when leaders forget these timeless principles. They seek to protect industries and jobs, but they end up doing the opposite. One economic lesson of the 1930's is protectionism increases international tensions. We bought less from our trading partners, but then they bought less from us. Economic growth dried up. World trade contracted by over 60 percent, and we had the Great Depression. Young Americans soon followed the American flag into World War II.

No one wants to relive that nightmare, and we don't have to. The 1980's can be a time when our economies grow together, and more jobs will be created for all. This was the spirit of the Williamsburg summit in May. The leaders of the industrialized countries pledged to continue working for a more open trading system. But sometimes that's easier said than done.

Take the case of our own economy. Things are looking up for America. Inflation has been knocked down to 2.6 percent. Economic growth in the second quarter reached 8.7 percent, and 1,700,000 Americans have been hired since last December. Yesterday we learned that total unemployment has dropped to 9.3 percent. Nearly 500,000 of our fellow citizens found jobs in July. More Americans are working than any time in this nation's history. This good news restores confidence in our economy and our currency.

Some people dislike our strong dollar and blame it on our interest rates. Well, we do not want disorderly currency markets, and we've intervened to bring back order to otherwise disorderly markets. But let's remember something. Other countries have higher interest rates than we do, yet their currencies have fallen in relation to ours. One good reason is inflation. It's not the interest you earn from holding a currency that matters most; it's the confidence you have that the value of your money won't depreciate from higher inflation.

America's inflation rate has declined dramatically. Now a strong dollar makes our purchases from abroad less expensive, and that's good.

Winning the war against inflation is probably the best economic legacy we could leave to the next generation. Remember what life was like only a

few years ago when the value of the dollar was being talked down and inflation was going through the roof?

But a strong dollar also brings problems. It makes the goods our exporters are trying to sell more expensive. Still, we're tough competitors. Some
$200 billion worth of goods were sold by Americans last year. So, do we
listen to those who would go back to dead-end protectionism and to sabotag-
ing the value of our currency, or do we go forward, keeping our faith in the
American people who made this nation the greatest success story the world
has ever known?

I believe our challenge is to marshal the power of this country's best
minds and create the technology that will restore America's economic leadership. I have appointed a Presidential Commission on Industrial Competitiveness, asking distinguished leaders from business, labor, and academia to
advise us on how best to strengthen our ability to compete in world markets.

We believe the U.S. trade position would be strengthened by uniting
many of this government's trade responsibilities under one roof, so we proposed legislation to create a department of international trade and industry.
We're also taking action to create opportunities for trade.

Ten days ago, our negotiators reached a new, long-term grain agreement
with the Soviet Union. Since 1981 we've ended the unfair embargo that had
been slapped on American farmers. And now we have an agreement that
obligates the Soviets to increase their minimum purchase of wheat—or grain,
I should say—by 50 percent.

This, along with the likelihood of substantial purchases from China,
represents a major step forward for our farmers. It symbolizes our determination to help them regain the markets they lost. It also proves that, while we
oppose Soviet aggression, we seek to promote progress and peace between
our peoples.

Yesterday I signed legislation to stimulate more trade and opportunity—
the Caribbean Basin Initiative. This package of incentives will establish new
commercial relationships between the people of the Caribbean and the United States. Stimulating trade will mean new jobs for their citizens as well as
ours. It underscores our belief that economic development based on free
market principles is the key to helping our neighbors build a future of freedom, democracy, and peace.

Finally, let me mention an important agreement on textiles we've just
reached with the People's Republic of China. No free market currently exists
in textiles, and only what is called the multifiber arrangement, signed by 46
countries. We're a party to that arrangement, but China is not, and our
bilateral agreement with them expired last December. To prevent a flood of
imports from harming our struggling textile industry, we imposed unilateral
quotas on China's products. They responded with large reductions in their
purchases of American farm products.

We faced three options: option 1, end our restrictions on Chinese textiles, which would help our farmers but risk further damage to our textile workers; option 2, cut back Chinese exports even further, which would cost our farmers billions more in lost sales; or option 3, negotiate a tough but fair 5-year agreement with China to permit controlled, moderate growth of Chinese exports. We chose option 3.

Our textile producers can be assured there will be no flood of imports, and they can get on with the task of modernizing their industry, which is the best long-term assurance of jobs for our own people. This new agreement will mean more business for our farmers, and it promises China the opportunity to sell its products here. That's important for good relations between our two countries.

Bit by bit, we're restoring America's reputation as a reliable supplier and as a supporter of free and fair trade for progress and for peace.

Till next week, thanks for listening, and God bless you.

Note: The President spoke at 12:06 P.M. EDT from Camp David.

Situation in Central America

August 13, 1983

My fellow Americans:

I'm speaking to you from El Paso, Texas. Tomorrow, I'll be in Mexico, meeting with President de la Madrid.

Earlier this week I met with the new national, bipartisan Commission on Central America. This Commission will look at long-range issues and recommend a truly national approach to them.

One thing especially impressed me. The Commission members are all distinguished, well-educated people, but they've made their first task a concentrated study of Central America. Professor Kissinger has promised to make their learning program a tough one. I mention this because the polls say many Americans are confused about what we're supporting in Central America and about why that region, so close to home and to our strategic trading arteries, is important to us.

The mail I receive tells the same story. Well, my staff recently put together a composite letter that combines the most widespread misconceptions. It goes like this:

"Dear Mr. President: The United States has not learned any lessons from history. We refuse to understand the root causes of violence and revolution. El Salvador proves that we continue to support ruthless dictators who oppose change and abuse human freedom. And by refusing to deal decently with the Sandinista government in Nicaragua, we have forced it into the arms of Cuba and the Soviet Union. Military measures will just make things worse. Anyway, democracy can't work in Central America." End of composite letter.

Sound familiar? I'm sure you've heard it all before. But let's look at what is really happening.

We have learned from history. Years of poverty and injustice in Central America are a root cause of the violence. That's why our economic assistance there is greater, three times greater than our military aid.

We are on the side of peaceful, democratic change in Central America, and our actions prove it daily. But we aren't the only ones interested in Central America. The Soviet Union and Cuba are intervening there, because they believe they can exploit the problems so as to install ruthless Communist dictatorships, such as we see in Cuba.

We are not supporting dictators either of the far right or the far left. We're working hard with Costa Rica and Honduras, which are true democracies, and we're helping El Salvador to become one. Only democracy can guarantee that a government will not turn against its own people, because in a democracy, people are the masters of government, not the servants.

Now, it's true that some members of El Salvador's security forces still misuse their public trust. You can't instantly erase something that's been going on for a century or more. But we deplore even passive acceptance of such actions, and I can assure you great progress is being made. Can anyone really believe that the situation would improve if our influence for moderation were removed?

Commitment to human rights means working at problems, not walking away from them. And there are many brave Central Americans who, at great personal risk, are working to end these abuses. President Magaña of El Salvador is such a man.

That brings me to Nicaragua. We have dealt decently with Nicaragua, more decently than the Sandinista government there has treated its own citizens and neighbors. The Sandinistas were not elected. They seized power through a revolution that, true enough, overthrew a dictatorship, but then the Sandinistas betrayed their repeated promises of democracy and free elections. They betrayed many who fought beside them in the revolution, and they've set up a Communist dictatorship. Having seized power, the Sandinista bosses revealed they had chosen sides with Cuba and the Soviet Union a long time ago. We did not push them into that camp.

Unfortunately, there have been such distortions about U.S. policy in Central America that the great majority of Americans don't know which side we're on. No wonder a great many sincere people write angrily that we should support regional dialog, emphasize economic assistance, or take any number of other actions, all of which we're already doing and have been doing for more than 2 years.

Well, it's time to get away from fairy tales and get back to reality. We support the elected government of El Salvador against Communist-backed guerrillas who would take over the country by force. And we oppose the unelected government of Nicaragua, which supports those guerrillas with weapons and ammunition. Now, that, of course, puts us in sympathy with those Nicaraguans who are trying to restore the democratic promises made during the revolution, the so-called *contras.*

Our neighbors in the Americas are important to us, and they need our help. We're working hard to provide economic and political support for development so that ballots will replace bullets in that troubled region. That's the reason for the Caribbean Basin Initiative and all our economic assistance. At the same time, we're helping our neighbors create a defensive shield to protect themselves from Communist intervention while they go forward with economic reform. We do this by providing training, assistance, and firm demonstrations of our resolve to deter Communist aggression. And that's the reason for the bipartisan commission, which has now begun its work.

If we all look calmly at the facts, we can unite to protect our national interests and give our neighbors the help they need without spooking ourselves in the process.

Till next week, thanks for listening, and God bless you.

Note: The President spoke at 10:06 A.M. MDT from the Marriott Hotel in El Paso, Texas.

Federal Civilian Employment

August 20, 1983

My fellow Americans:

Before getting into the main subject of today's broadcast, I have what I think is a newsworthy item.

Just about a year ago the Security [*sic*] and Loan Association of Milwaukee, Wisconsin, made a sizable sum—millions of dollars—available for home mortgage loans at an 11.9-percent interest rate. The going rate at the time was about 16 percent. I'm happy to say a number of banks throughout the country followed suit. I'm even happier to say that Milwaukee Security Savings and Loan has done it again. One hundred million dollars has been made available for home mortgages at a 9.9-percent interest rate. The president of the savings and loan says it's their way of trying to help the economic recovery that is now under way. Well, they deserve a big "thank you" from all of us.

Last month, on one of these talks, I told you about a few of the things we've been doing to cut down on waste and fraud, unnecessary paperwork, red tape, and on abuses of Federal loan programs, all adding up to current and future savings to you, the taxpayer, of billions of dollars. Well, I didn't have any illusions about making the front page with that information, and we didn't. But I thought you had a right to know we've been making progress in restoring government to its rightful role as the servant of the people.

Today, I'd like to share with you some of the other things we're doing to protect your tax dollars and make government more efficient and responsive to your needs.

One important area in which we've made real progress is the employment figure for nondefense Federal agencies. There are a number of vital functions that the Federal Government has to perform, as we all know. But the Federal Government should perform those functions in an efficient, economical manner. It shouldn't cost you, the taxpayer, a penny more than is needed to get the job done.

With that in mind, we made a department-by-department, agency-by-agency review of government operations, looking for needless fat. As a result, by last January, there were 112,000 fewer people working in nondefense Federal agencies. Fifteen departments, agencies, and commissions have been able to reduce their payroll numbers by 20 percent or more. And we've accomplished 90 percent of these savings not by layoffs, but by just not replacing those who retired or left government service. And guess what? The government is actually doing things more efficiently than it was before.

We're still providing the needed services, and we're doing it with fewer people. The savings to the taxpayer is nearly a billion and a half dollars a year in salaries alone. As you know, most civilian government jobs are not particularly hazardous. Yet we found that one out of every four retirements from government service was a disability retirement. The government didn't require much evidence of disability and this led to considerable abuse of the system.

Today, just by requiring adequate evidence before allowing that kind of retirement, the figure is down nearly 40 percent since 1979 with a savings to the taxpayer of more than a billion dollars by 1985. And to help prevent accidents and disabilities, we have initiated a new health and safety program for Federal employees to reduce the number of injury claims by 3 percent per year over the next 5 years.

The Civil Service Retirement System is one of the most generous in the world. And, of course, we all want dedicated government employees to be rewarded for their efforts, just as the overwhelming majority of Americans who work in the private sector deserve to be. But sometimes civil servants have received preferred treatment.

When we came to office, the Civil Service Retirement System was indexing benefits to inflation twice a year, an advantage enjoyed by virtually no one in the private sector. By going to a once-a-year cost-of-living adjustment for Federal retirees and by making other fair adjustments, we have continued to protect them from inflation while saving the taxpayer some $2½ billion by 1985.

In recent weeks, there's been a lot of talk about my call for merit pay to reward outstanding teachers in America's schools. Well, I think the same principle should apply to the Federal Government itself. Earlier this year, we announced a proposal to require Federal employees to earn, not just automatically inherit, their pay raises. We're still working with Members of the Congress to refine this merit plan to reward good work and good workers so that you, the people, are better served by your government.

Finally, there's something I'd like to get off my chest. It deals with all those headlines about the Pentagon paying $100 for a 4-cent diode or $900 for a plastic cap. What is missing or buried in all those stories about waste is who provided those figures for all the horror stories. This administration exposed those abuses—abuses that had been going on for years. It was Defense Secretary Cap Weinberger's people, his auditors and inspectors, who ordered the audits in the first place, conducted the investigations, and formed a special unit to prosecute defense-related fraud. In just an 18-month period, the Defense Department has obtained 650 convictions, and we're going to keep on exposing these abuses where we find them. I thought you deserved to know that.

Well, till next week, thanks for listening. God bless you.

Note: The President spoke at 9:06 A.M. PDT from Rancho del Cielo, near Santa Barbara.

Situation in the Middle East

August 27, 1983

My fellow Americans:

Last June, the 19th of June to be exact, a well-known TV network producer was the commencement speaker at the high school where he had graduated on that same day, June 19th, 43 years ago. In speaking to this year's graduates, he pointed out some things that should be of concern to them regarding the state of the world. They were items taken from the front page of a June 19th issue of the New York Times, their graduation day.

He said, "In Washington, the administration is asking for more money, not to fight cancer or educate young people, but more money to build some of the most destructive weapons the world has ever seen." Not very reassuring for a high-school graduate hoping to live to an old age, and not very reassuring, either, to have a President who is called a warmonger.

He went on to say, "In Latin America, the Times tells us, the United States is prepared to go to war to keep unfriendly powers out of this hemisphere. If push comes to shove, a young high-school graduate could end up fighting there."

"In Europe," he told them, "a people not much different from you is being crushed in what the Times reports is being called an uncompromising and unrelenting fashion. And in Detroit, the Japanese threat, among other things, is forcing the Ford Motor Company out of the car business."

He pointed out that it didn't seem like much of a world to look forward to, but there it was on page one, graduation day, June 19th. Yes, *his* graduation day, June 19th, 1940. And, as he went on to say, "We're all still here," although he wouldn't have bet on it back in 1940.

The President being called a warmonger was Franklin Delano Roosevelt, who kept increasing the defense budget. The Japanese threat was military, not economic, and Ford was going into the fighter plane business. And, oh, yes, the European country that was being crushed was France, not Poland.

Well, here it is 43 years later, and as he told the class of '83, "A good case can be made that the world is better, not worse." And the class of 1940 had something to do with that, just as the class of '83 can have a hand in making things better for graduating classes yet to be, even a class 43 years from now.

Young Americans are already doing their share to build a better world. Today our servicemen are participating in multinational peacekeeping forces in Lebanon and the Sinai Peninsula.

In the agreement between Lebanon and Israel, Israel agreed to withdraw its military forces totally. The responsibility now rests on others to negotiate in good faith on their own arrangements for withdrawal. Until this happens, Lebanon will remain a potential trouble spot.

But our current efforts in Lebanon are only a small part of our search for peace in the Middle East, including a compassionate, fair, and practical resolution to the Palestinian problem.

The Middle East peace initiative which we announced almost a year ago is definitely alive and available to those parties willing to sit down together and talk peace. We remain committed to the positions we set forth, and we stand ready to pursue them in the context of the Camp David accords. Those positions are in the best long-term interest of all parties. Most importantly, they're the only realistic basis for a solution that has thus far been presented.

The United States continues to support UN Security Council Resolutions 338 and 242.

The establishment of new Israeli settlements in the occupied territories is an obstacle to peace, and we're concerned over the negative effect that this activity has on Arab confidence in Israel's willingness to return territory in exchange for security and a freely and fairly negotiated peace treaty.

The future of these settlements can only be dealt with through direct negotiations between the parties to the conflict. The sooner these negotiations begin, the greater the chance for a solution.

This administration, like those before it, is firmly committed to the security of the State of Israel. We will help Israel defend itself against external aggression. At the same time, the United States believes, as it has always believed, that permanent security for the people of Israel and all the peoples of the region can only come with the achievement of a just and lasting peace, not by sole reliance on increasingly expensive military forces.

Unfortunately, the opportunities afforded by our initiative have yet to be grasped by the parties involved. We know the issues are complex, the risks for all concerned high, and much courageous statesman—statesmanship, excuse me—will be required. Nevertheless, those complex issues can be resolved by creative and persistent diplomacy. Those risks can be overcome by people who want to end this bitter and tragic conflict. And in the process, the United States will be a full partner, doing everything we can to help create a just and lasting peace.

Until next week, thanks for listening, and God bless you.

Note: The President spoke at 9:06 A.M. PDT from Rancho del Cielo, near Santa Barbara.

Soviet Attack on Korean Civilian Airliner/Labor Day

September 3, 1983

My fellow Americans:

This weekend marks the 89th observance of Labor Day, a special day for all Americans. Before I get to that topic, however, I'm going to speak to you briefly about the recent act of brutality that continues to horrify us all. I'm referring to the outrageous Soviet attack against the 269 people aboard the unarmed Korean passenger plane.

This murder of innocent civilians is a serious international issue between the Soviet Union and civilized people everywhere who cherish individual rights and value human life. It is up to all of us, leaders and citizens of the world, to deal with the Soviets in a calm, controlled, but absolutely firm manner. We have joined in this call for an urgent U.N. Security Council meeting.

The evidence is clear; it leaves no doubt; it is time for the Soviets to account. The Soviet Union owes the world a fullest possible explanation and apology for their inexcusable act of brutality. So far, they've flunked the test. Even now, they continue to distort and deny the truth.

People everywhere can draw only one conclusion from their violent behavior: There is a glaring gap between Soviet words and deeds. They speak endlessly about their love of brotherhood, disarmament, and peace, but they reserve the right to disregard aviation safety and to sacrifice human lives.

Make no mistake on this last point. This is not the first time the Soviets have shot at and hit a civilian airliner when it flew over Soviet territory. Our government does not shoot down foreign aircraft over U.S. territory, even though commercial aircraft from the Soviet Union and Cuba have overflown sensitive U.S. military facilities. We and other civilized countries follow procedures to prevent a tragedy, rather than to provoke one. But while the Soviets accuse others of wanting to return to the Cold War, it's they who have never left it behind.

I met with the National Security Council last night. Tomorrow I will meet with congressional leaders of both parties to discuss this issue, as well as the situation in Lebanon, on which the National Security Council met today. We're determined to move forward and to act in concert both with the Congress and other members of the international community. We must make sure that the fundamental rules of safety of travel are respected by all nations, even the Soviet Union.

Now, let me turn to another subject that's also very much on our minds this weekend—Labor Day. More than any other country in the world, ours was built not by some small, privileged elite, but by the physical, mental, and moral strength of free working men and women, people who asked for nothing but the chance to build a better future in a climate of fairness and freedom. As one of the founding fathers of the American labor movement, Samuel Gompers, put it, our society is based on the right of working people "to be full sharers in the abundance which is the result of their brain and brawn and the civilization of which they are the founders and the mainstay."

Those words have meant a lot to me over the years. I've always believed that America can only be true to itself when its promise is shared by all our people. One of the best ways to make sure that happens is to build a healthy, growing economy that opens up more and more opportunity to our people. We've been working at that for more than 2½ years now. With your help and the help of a bipartisan group in the Congress, our efforts are showing good results.

Just this week, Commerce Secretary Baldrige announced that in July inventories registered their biggest advance in 20 months. That means the economic recovery has boosted the confidence of manufacturers and encouraged business firms to restock. It adds up to more work for people in a wide range of industries and trades and means this recovery will continue to be strong.

Meanwhile, the civilian unemployment rate has dropped by 1.3 percentage points since last December. The number of unemployed has declined by more than 1.3 million, and a healthy, growing economy has added almost 2½ million people to the Nation's payrolls.

Another good way of testing progress is to measure how well the American family, the average family, is going today. An American family earning $25,000 has $600 more today in purchasing power than it would if inflation were still raging at its 1980 rate. And then there are your tax savings. The typical American family will pay $700 less in Federal income taxes than if the old 1980 rates were still in effect.

Now, I know that, for many Americans on this Labor Day, life is still tough. None of us can be fully satisfied until many more of our people find work. And we won't be satisfied until we cut inflation all the way back to zero. But every week, our economy is gaining fresh strength, and that's good news for us all.

Finally, let me say that on this weekend, I hope you'll take a moment to celebrate not only the working people of this nation but something that makes it all possible—our freedom. As I mentioned at the outset, we've watched with horror these past few days as totalitarianism has shown its ghastly face once again. That's why here in America we must remain a bastion of free men and women working together toward a brighter future.

Till next week, thanks for listening, and God bless you.

Note: The President spoke at 12:06 P.M. EDT from the Oval Office at the White House.

American International Broadcasting

September 10, 1983

My fellow Americans:

During my first press conference 9 days after being sworn in as your President, I was asked a question having to do with Soviet intentions. In my answer I cited their own words—that they have openly and publicly declared the only morality they recognize is what will further world communism; that they reserve unto themselves the right to commit any crime, to lie, to cheat, in order to attain that. And I pointed out that we should keep this in mind when we deal with them.

I was charged with being too harsh in my language. I tried to point out I was only quoting their own words. Well, I hope the Soviets' recent behavior will dispel any lingering doubt about what kind of regime we're dealing with and what our responsibilities are as trustees of freedom and peace. Isn't it time for all of us to see the Soviet rulers as they are, rather than as we would like them to be?

Rather than tell the truth about the Korean Air Lines massacre, rather than immediately and publicly investigate the crash, explain to the world how it happened, punish those guilty of the crime, cooperate in efforts to find the wreckage, recover the bodies, apologize and offer compensation to the families, and work to prevent a repetition, they have done the opposite. They've stonewalled the world, mobilizing their entire government behind a massive cover-up, then brazenly threatening to kill more men, women, and children should another civilian airliner make the same mistake as KAL 007.

The Soviets are terrified of the truth. They understand well and they dread the meaning of St. John's words: "You will know the truth, and the truth will set you free." The truth is mankind's best hope for a better world. That's why, in times like this, few assets are more important than the Voice of America and Radio Liberty, our primary means of getting the truth to the Russian people.

Within minutes of the report of the Soviet destruction of the Korean jet, the Voice of America aired the story in its news programs around the globe. We made sure people in Africa, Asia, the Middle East, Europe and, most important, the people in the Soviet bloc itself knew the truth. That includes every Soviet misstatement, from their initial denials through all the tortured changes and contradictions in their story, including their U.N. representative still denying they shot down the plane even as his own government was finally admitting they did.

Accurate news like this is about as welcome as the plague among the Soviet elite. Censorship is as natural and necessary to the survival of their dictatorship as free speech is to our democracy. That's why they devote such enormous resources to block our broadcasts inside Soviet-controlled countries. The Soviets spend more to block Western broadcasts coming into those countries than the entire worldwide budget of the Voice of America.

To get the news across to the Russian people about the Korean Air Lines massacre, the Voice of America added new frequencies and new broadcast times. But within minutes of these changes, new Soviet jamming began.

Luckily, jamming is more like a sieve than a wall. International radio broadcasts can still get through to many people with the news. But we still face enormous difficulties.

One of the Voice of America's listeners in the Middle East wrote, "If you do not strengthen your broadcasting frequencies, no one can get anything from your program." Our radio equipment is just plain old, some of it World War II vintage. I don't mind people getting older; it's just not so good for machines.

More than 35 percent of the Voice of America's transmitters are over 30 years old. We have a similar problem at Radio Free Europe and Radio Liberty. We have 6 antiquated 500-kilowatt shortwave transmitters. The Soviets have 37, and theirs are neither old nor outdated. We regularly receive complaints that Soviet broadcasts are clearer than ours. One person wrote and asked why it's not possible for a nation that can send ships into space to have its own voice heard here on Earth.

The answer is simple. We're as far behind the Soviets and their allies in international broadcasting today as we were in space when they launched Sputnik in 1957.

We've repeatedly urged the Congress to support our long-term modernization program and our proposal for a new radio station, Radio Marti, for broadcasting to Cuba. The sums involved are modest, but for whatever reason this critical program has not been enacted.

Today I'm appealing to the Congress: Help us get the truth through. Help us strengthen our international broadcasting effort by supporting increased funding for the Voice of America, Radio Free Europe, Radio Liberty, and by authorizing the establishment of Radio Marti.

And I appeal to you, especially those of you who came from Eastern Europe, Russia, and Soviet-dominated countries, who understand how crucial this issue is, let your Representatives hear from you. Tell them you want Soviet rulers held accountable for their actions even by their own people. The truth is still our strongest weapon; we just have to use it.

Finally, let us come together as a nation tomorrow in a National Day of Mourning to share the sorrow of the families and let us resolve that this crime against humanity will never be forgotten anywhere in the world.

Until next week, thank you for listening, and God bless you.

Note: The President spoke at 12:06 P.M. EDT from the Oval Office at the White House.

Soviet Attack on Korean Civilian Airliner

September 17, 1983

My fellow Americans:

Five days after the Soviets shot down KAL 007, I went on nationwide television to urge that all of us in the civilized world make sure such an atrocity never happens again. And I pledged to you that night, we would cooperate with other countries to improve the safety of civil aviation, asking them to join us in not accepting the Soviet airline Aeroflot as a normal member of the international civil air community—not, that is, until the Soviets satisfy the cries of humanity for justice.

On Thursday, an American delegation led by Lynn Helms, who heads up the Federal Aviation Administration, went to Montreal for an emergency session of the ICAO, the International Civil Aviation Organization. This meeting was called at the request of the Republic of Korea, and 32 countries are attending. The group immediately went to work on a resolution to call for an international investigation, to deplore this atrocity, and to review procedures to prevent civilian aircraft from ever being attacked again. Yesterday, the resolution passed by an overwhelming majority.

The Soviets have not budged. Apparently, their contempt for the truth and for the opinion of the civilized world is equaled only by their disdain for helpless people like the passengers aboard KAL Flight 007. They reserve for themselves the right to live by one set of rules, insisting everyone else live by another. They're supremely confident their crime and cover-up will soon be forgotten, and we'll all be back to business as usual. Well, I believe they're badly mistaken. This case is far from closed. The Soviets' aggression has provoked a fundamental and long-overdue reappraisal in countries all over the globe. The Soviet Union stands virtually alone against the world.

Good and decent people everywhere are coming together, and the world's outrage has not diminished. Repercussions such as that emergency ICAO meeting in Montreal are just beginning. Take the example of aviation. Canada suspended Aeroflot landing rights for 60 days and froze the signing of an agreement for Aeroflot refueling at Gander. The Canadian Air Traffic Controllers Association has withdrawn from a long-standing exchange agreement with its Soviet counterpart organization.

The IFALPA—that's the International Federation of Air Line Pilot Associations—declared the U.S.S.R. an offending state. It called for its member associations to ban all flights to Moscow for 60 days, and it called on related international unions and professional associations to take similar actions. It demanded Soviet guarantees that similar attacks will never be repeated, and, what is most encouraging because it underscores this reappraisal I mentioned, the IFALPA promised to consider further actions against the Soviets if no such guarantees are given.

1983   **141**

Scandinavian Airlines has suspended flights within Soviet airspace for 60 days. Norwegian pilots and air traffic controllers are boycotting all air service between Norway and the Soviet Union. With the exception of France, Greece, and Turkey, all the NATO nations and Japan have temporarily suspended civil air traffic between their respective nations and the Soviet Union. Even neutral Switzerland and pilots in Finland have joined the general boycott. Australia and New Zealand are also taking strong measures in the area of civil aviation.

In the United Nations, the Security Council voted a resolution deploring the Soviet attack, forcing the Soviets to cast their veto to block its adoption. Here, too, we're seeing evidence that a fundamental reappraisal is in the works. Most countries rebuke the Kremlin. Only a few of Moscow's dependables stood up for its defense. Nonaligned nations are looking to the United States for leadership. I've instructed our Ambassador to the U.N., Jeane Kirkpatrick, to sit down with them to seek out new areas of cooperation.

In the Congress, both the House and the Senate mobilized overwhelming bipartisan support for a resolution of condemnation. Some would have us lash out in another way by canceling our grain shipments. But that would punish American farmers, not the Soviet aggressors. The most effective, lasting action against their violence and intimidation—and it's the one action the Soviets would welcome least—will be to go forward with America's program to remain strong.

I'm confident that, if enough of you at the grass roots make your voices heard, we can and will do just that. We may not be able to change the Soviets' ways, but we can change our attitude toward them. We can stop pretending they share the same dreams and aspirations we do. We can start preparing ourselves for what John F. Kennedy called a long twilight struggle. It won't be quick, it won't make headlines, and it sure won't be easy, but it's what we must do to keep America strong, keep her free, and yes, preserve the peace for our children and for our children's children.

This is the most enduring lesson of the Korean Air Lines massacre. If we grasp it, then history will say this tragedy was a major turning point, because this time the world did not go back to business as usual.

Until next week, thanks for listening, and God bless you.

Note: The President spoke at 12:06 P.M. EDT from Camp David.

Peace

September 24, 1983

My fellow Americans and fellow citizens of the world:

This is Ronald Reagan, President of the United States, speaking to you live from the broadcast studios of the Voice of America in Washington, D.C.

In 2 days I will be going to the United Nations General Assembly to speak for a cause that people everywhere carry close to their hearts—the cause of peace. This subject is so important I wanted to share our message with a larger audience than I usually address each Saturday afternoon in the United States. So today I'm speaking directly to people everywhere, from Los Angeles to New Delhi, Cairo, Bangkok, and I'm attempting to speak directly to the people of the Soviet Union. I'd like to talk about ideas and feelings all of us share which I intend to communicate to the United Nations on Monday.

Let me begin by bringing you greetings from the American people and our heartfelt wishes for peace. In these times of stress, I believe that the people of the world must know and understand how each other feel, their fears as well as their dreams. We Americans are a peace-loving people. We seek friendship not only with our traditional allies but with our adversaries, too. We've had serious differences with the Soviet Government, but we should remember that our sons and daughters have never fought each other in war and, if we Americans have our way, we never will.

People don't make wars; governments do. And too many Soviet and American citizens have already shed too much blood because of violence by governments. The American people want less confrontation and more communication and cooperation, more opportunity to correspond, to speak freely with all people over our respective radio and television programs and, most important, to visit each other in our homes so we could better understand your countries and you could know the truth about America.

The treasure we Americans cherish most is our freedom—freedom to lead our lives the way we choose, freedom to worship God, to think for ourselves, and freedom to speak our minds even to the point of criticizing our own government. We do not believe in censorship. When another government criticizes us, we know about it. And if they ever say something good, you can bet we'll know that, too. The trouble is, we don't always have that same freedom to speak to others, especially those who live in the Soviet Union. And one-way communication prevents us from better understanding each other.

For example, the Soviet Government has taken extraordinary steps to justify its firing on a Korean civilian airliner, killing 269 helpless people from

14 countries. But I ask those who have been told the United States is responsible: If you're hearing the truth, why has the outcry been so intense from members of the United Nations, the International Civil Aviation Organization, and why are pilots all over the world boycotting flights to Moscow? We have no quarrel with you, the Soviet people. But please understand, the world believes no government has a right to shoot civilian airliners out of the sky. Your airline, Aeroflot, has violated sensitive U.S. airspace scores of times, yet we would never fire on your planes and risk killing one of your friends or your loved ones.

Now, I guess the picture painted of me by the officials in some countries is pretty grim. May I just say—and I speak not only as the President of the United States but also as a husband, a father, a grandfather, and as a person who loves God and whose heart yearns deeply for a better future—my dream is for our peoples to come together in a spirit of faith and friendship, to help build and leave behind a far safer world. But dreams for the future cannot be realized by words alone. Words must be matched by deeds, by an honest, tireless effort to reduce the risks of war and the loss of life. In this era of nuclear weapons, no achievement could be more meaningful than a verifiable agreement that would dramatically reduce the level of nuclear armaments.

American negotiators in Geneva are offering fair-minded, equitable proposals in the interests of both our countries. In the strategic arms reduction talks, we propose deep cuts in both the number of warheads carried by intercontinental ballistic missiles and in the number of missiles themselves. This proposal offered cuts to far below current United States levels. The Soviet Government declined to consider them. We tried again. Last June we proposed a more flexible approach. Then, during the last round of talks in Geneva, we presented a draft treaty responding to concerns expressed by the Soviet Government.

Also, from the outset of the intermediate-range nuclear force talks 2 years ago, I made clear that the United States was ready to join with the Soviet Union in the total elimination of an entire class of intermediate-range, land-based nuclear missiles. That offer still stands. I regret that the Soviet Government continues to reject this proposal. What could possibly be better than to rid the world of an entire class of nuclear weapons?

But in the effort to move the negotiations forward, we proposed an interim solution—some number on both sides below current levels. Again, the Soviet Government refused. I'm deeply aware of people's feelings and frustrations. I share them. And I intend to keep trying. On Monday, I will go to the United Nations to propose another package of steps designed to advance the negotiations. All we seek are agreements to reduce substantially the number and destructive power of nuclear forces.

Yes, we insist on balanced agreements that protect our security, that provide greater stability, and that are truly verifiable, but these requirements are the essence of fairness. They would provide greater security for all nations.

We, the American people, deeply yearn for peace. If our dreams and hopes are to mean anything, we must sit down together and in good faith let honest negotiations bring us a safer world. But I must speak plainly. Just as government censorship is a barrier to understanding, the inflexibility of the Soviet Government on arms control is holding back successful negotiations.

I have said to my own people, you have the right to expect a better world and to demand that your government work for it. This Monday I will have the honor to carry that message to the 38th General Session of the United Nations. It will be a commitment from the heart and one that I know all people share. For the sake of our children and our children's children, I pray that the Soviet Government will not censor my words but will let their people listen to them and then negotiate with us in good faith.

Thank you for listening, and God bless you.

Note: The President spoke at 12:06 P.M. EDT from the broadcast studios of the Voice of America in Washington, D.C. The address was broadcast over the VOA's worldwide network and carried live, with simultaneous translation in Russian, Ukrainian, Romanian, Lithuanian, Urdu, Bengali, and Hausa. It was rebroadcast to Europe one hour later when VOA's English service to Europe began its regular broadcast cycle. VOA's 34 other language services broadcast the address as they began their programs throughout the rest of the day.

Economic Recovery and Employment

October 1, 1983

My fellow Americans:

With autumn here, schools reopened, and people back at work, a question is on everyone's mind: Will the economic recovery last and the job market continue to improve? Well, I believe the answer is yes. I'm bullish on America. I've been called an optimist. But I'm not like the fellow who notices a car has a flat tire and says, "It's all right; the tire's only flat on the bottom." My optimism springs from solid evidence that America has turned the corner toward long-term economic expansion. If all of us act responsibly we can enjoy a renaissance of growth, progress, and opportunities, free from the ruinous inflation and record interest rates of old.

America's job picture will improve during the next 3 months, and it's likely to get even better after April. That's the good news from a nationwide survey of 11,400 employers in 354 cities, conducted by Manpower, Incorporated. Other recent surveys reflect increases in help-wanted ads across the country. Some of the biggest increases were in the areas that need jobs the most—industrial Midwest States like Ohio, Michigan, Illinois, Indiana, and Wisconsin. Georgia, Maryland, Florida, Virginia, North Carolina, Alabama, Tennessee, and Kentucky also saw increases above the national average.

Growth creates more growth. As workers are called back and start receiving paychecks, the economy expands, increasing the need for still more workers. Since last December the number of unemployed has declined by 1.3 million, and economic growth has added nearly 2½ million people to America's work force. But we must not rest till every American who wants a job can find a job. We need the strength of every back and the power of every mind. Still, let's not be swayed by downbeats who never admit anything's right, never acknowledge the huge problems we inherited, and never admit the progress we've made reducing inflation, interest rates, and, yes, creating new jobs.

The truth is more Americans are working now than at any time in this nation's history. The rising tide of employment is reaching across America into communities large and small, farms and factories, and it's helping people from all walks of life. Sixty percent of the jobs lost in the construction industry during the last recession have been recovered; add to that 70 percent of the jobs in furniture and fixtures, 90 percent in rubber and plastics, 90 percent in automobiles, and 125 percent in lumber and wood products.

One of the most encouraging trends we're seeing is higher employment for women: 2.3 million more women are working now than before we took office. And the jobs are better, too. Women filled more than half of all new jobs in managerial, professional, and technical fields between 1980 and 1982. Also, did you know that self-employed women are the fastest growing part of our business community—growing, in fact, five times faster than the number of self-employed men? It puzzles me why we hear so little about this progress, this proof that opportunities for all Americans are expanding.

Now, many of the people who remain jobless are part of a category economists call "structural unemployment." They may live in economically depressed areas where firms and factories have become outmoded, or they may lack the skills and training needed to seize opportunities in the new service industries and areas of high technology. One of the most serious problems we still face is youth unemployment. Nearly 40 percent of the unemployed in America are less than 25 years old, and nearly half of that group are teenagers.

But there's hope. To strengthen the skills of young Americans, to provide new opportunities for prospective workers of all ages, we've charted a new approach that looks to the future rather than the past. Beginning today, October 1st, an historic and bold program—the Job Training Partnership

Act—will train and retrain more than a million people a year for productive, lasting jobs in the private economy. At the core of my philosophy is the belief that progress begins with trusting people. You at the grass roots can spend your tax dollars far more wisely and productively than any collection of bureaucrats in the Federal Government. That's why this Job Training Partnership Act will be a major step forward from past programs.

Unlike the old CETA program, run primarily by government officials and which either didn't provide enough training or else trained people for jobs that didn't exist, this program will be planned by business and labor people in your own communities—those who know best what training is needed for existing jobs. They'll be receiving the block grants that the Federal Government sends to their own State governments. This time, private enterprise will be participating in a very meaningful way. The business and labor people will be working together in organizations called "PICs"—Private Industry Councils—designed to provide training skills needed right on Main Street America. At least 70 cents of every Job Training Partnership Act dollar must go to training.

On Monday, the Indianapolis Private Industry Council will start sponsoring training at ITT to place low-income youth and adults in existing jobs. In Wilmington, welfare women will be trained for skilled, entry-level jobs. These are just two examples among many of hope being reborn across America. No civilization can survive and grow if it does not learn the lessons of its own history. The Job Training Partnership Act is an important reform that demonstrates we're not only correcting mistakes from our past, we're moving with wisdom and confidence to shape a brighter future. The outlook for America is good and getting better.

Till next week, thanks for listening, and God bless you.

Note: The President spoke at 12:06 P.M. EDT from the Oval Office at the White House.

Situation in Lebanon

October 8, 1983

My fellow Americans:

I'm sure you're all aware of the debate during recent days and weeks with regard to our marines in Lebanon. Congress, on a strong bipartisan basis, has passed a resolution approving their presence there for 18 months if need be. But in the debate, many questions were raised as to what they were doing there and whether their presence there was in our national interest. In the midst of all this debate, I received a letter from the father of a young marine corporal stationed in Beirut, Lebanon.

Justly proud of his son, he enclosed a clipping from his hometown paper. It was a letter to the editor written by his son. And here's what the young corporal had to say about the marines and whether or not there was a reason for their presence in Lebanon. His family had been sending him the hometown paper, and he'd noticed "editorials and opinions denouncing American involvement in the various trouble spots of the world, particularly Central America and the Middle East."

He went on to say, "I've been keeping up with what's happening in Central America, and I have firsthand knowledge of what is happening in the Middle East. In the case of Central America, the general American consensus is to stay out, that we're getting into another Vietnam. Whenever American military forces go abroad, the average American believes that we should keep to ourselves and mind our own business. I'm not an advocate of war," he says, "as I've seen the ravages of war here in Lebanon. War is a very terrible thing. Yet when diplomatic methods fail, we must be prepared to defend and, if necessary, to die for what we believe in, for the American way of life. I do not enjoy being here in Beirut. My fellow marines and I miss the simple yet wonderful aspects of life back home that so many take for granted. Yet, we realize we'll be going home in a few months. But the people of, say, El Salvador or Lebanon are home. For them, there is no escape. It is our duty as Americans to stop the cancerous spread of Soviet influence wherever it may be, because someday we or some future generation will wake up and find the U.S.A. to be the only free state left, with communism upon our doorstep. And then it will be too late."

A young marine corporal writing from Beirut, Lebanon, to his hometown paper—there's no doubt in his mind about the need for us to have a presence there. But many of us are not that sure. Many believe we are involving ourselves needlessly in someone else's quarrel and should bring our young men home and mind our own business. The corporal may not have spelled out the specifics as to why it was in our best interest to be there, but he was certainly correct in his conclusion that it is our business.

Can the United States or the free world stand by and see the Middle East incorporated into the Soviet bloc? What of Western Europe and Japan's dependence on Middle East oil for the energy to fuel their industry? Do we remember the oil embargo and the lines at our own gas stations? And didn't we assume a moral obligation to the continued existence of Israel as a nation back in 1948? I've never heard anyone in this country ever suggest that we should abandon that obligation.

A little over a year ago, I proposed a peace initiative for the entire Middle East. It was based on the Camp David accords and the United Nations Resolutions 242 and 338. We offered our help in bringing the Arab

States and Israel together in negotiations to settle the long-standing disputes that had kept that entire area in turmoil for many years. We sought more peace treaties like the one between Egypt and Israel.

Lebanon, the site of refugee camps for a great many Palestinians, had been torn by strife for several years. There were factions, each with its own militia, fighting each other. Terrorists in Lebanon violated Israel's northern border, killing innocent civilians. Syrian forces occupied the eastern part of Lebanon. Israeli military finally invaded from the south to force the PLO attackers away from the border. There could be no implementation of our peace initiative until this situation was resolved.

With our allies—England, France, and Italy—we proposed a withdrawal of all foreign forces from Lebanon and formed a multinational force to help maintain order and stability in the Beirut area while a new Lebanese Government and army undertook to restore sovereignty throughout Lebanon.

Over the course of several months, Lebanon and Israel negotiated a friendly agreement for security of the border between the two. We stand by this as a good agreement. But Syria, which had earlier agreed to withdraw if Israel did, changed its mind, and today has some 5,000 Soviet advisers and technicians and a massive amount of new Soviet equipment in its country, including a new generation of surface-to-surface missiles—the SS-21. We have to wonder aloud about Syrian protestations of their peaceful intentions.

For a year, we've continued diplomatic negotiations leading to the present cease-fire. President Gemayel is committed to a process of national reconciliation as the means to end factional fighting. The presence of our marines as part of the multinational force demonstrates that Lebanon does not stand alone. Peace for the Middle East and a fair settlement of the Palestinian problem is truly in our national interest.

Until next week, thanks for listening, and God bless you.

Note: The President spoke at 12:06 P.M. EDT from Camp David.

Quality of Life in America

October 15, 1983

My fellow Americans:

I know I court trouble when I dispute experts who specialize in spotting storm clouds and preaching doom and gloom. But at the risk of being the skunk that invades their garden party, I must warn them: Some very good news is sneaking up on you. The quality of American life is improving again. "Quality of life"—that's a term often used but seldom defined. Certainly our standard of living is part of it, and one good measure of that is purchasing power.

Just a few years ago, double-digit inflation was bleeding our purchasing power. Record price increases, interest rates, and taxation punished the thrifty, impoverished the needy, and discouraged entrepreneurs. When an economy goes haywire, confidence is destroyed. Well, today the tables have been turned. Double-digit inflation is gone, and confidence is coming back.

In 1980 the U.S. ranked only 10th among 20 industrial nations in per capita income. By the end of 1982, we'd climbed all the way up to third place. Our stronger dollar has increased purchasing power. Real wages are up. And inflation is down to 2.6 percent.

Sometimes when we shop we don't realize how much inflation has dropped, because prices are still going up. But they're going up much more slowly than before. If food prices had kept rising as fast the last 2 years as the 2 years before we took office, a loaf of bread would cost 7 cents more than it does today, a half gallon of milk 18 cents more, a pound of hamburger 60 cents more, and a gallon of gas 97 cents more.

The prime interest rate has been cut nearly in half, so costs of business, mortgage, education, and car loans have dropped. The Federal income tax on a typical working family is $700 less than if our tax program had not been passed. With parents, students, entrepreneurs, workers, and consumers feeling more secure, opportunities for jobs are expanding. Our work force in September rose by nearly 400,000 to 101.9 million—the highest level in American history. And the trend will continue.

Quality of life is not just more jobs, it's also better jobs. And we're seeing better opportunities opening up for all Americans. Women, for example, filled more than half of all the new jobs in managerial, professional, and technical fields between 1980 and 1982. The number of women-owned businesses is growing five times faster than men's. The future looks brighter. To get a peek at what tomorrow's jobs and products may be, look at the venture capital industry. This is where high-powered capital is invested and much of the technological revolution is taking place.

During the first 9 months of 1983, the venture industry raised about $2½ billion—nearly three times more than in all of 1980. The General Accounting Office has already estimated that previous venture investments of some $209 million in the sample of 72 companies directly generated 130,000 jobs during the decade of the seventies. Well, if $209 million of venture capital generated 130,000 jobs in 10 years, imagine how many jobs $2½ billion will create during the next year. And like interest that compounds, growth and opportunities create more growth and more opportunities.

Capital spending by business, a key source of higher productivity and new jobs, helped propel the economy forward in the third quarter. Much of the increase in spending went for products of high technology like computers and word processors.

We're witnessing an industrial renaissance, and this is only act one. It's being nourished by incentives from lower tax rates, starting with the 1978 capital gains tax reduction, passed, incidentally, over the objections of the last administration, and followed by our own more sweeping tax-cut program in 1981.

Our program to create opportunity and bring big government under control, the subsequent decline in inflation and interest rates, and prospects for robust growth have all led to another basic change: Americans' confidence in their institutions is turning up after nearly two decades of decline. A 1982 survey by the University of Michigan found people more likely to say they trusted the government to do what is right.

Looking beyond the economy, we see more evidence that the quality of life is improving. Life expectancy reached a record high last year, climbing to 74.5 years. Infant mortality declined to an all-time low with only 11.2 deaths per 1,000 live births. And the number of divorces dropped for the first time since 1962. Serious crime dropped 3 percent, the first measurable decline since 1977. Quality education, an American tradition—but one neglected for years—will be restored, thanks to leadership in Washington and vigorous action by your families at the grass roots.

Good things are happening in America. Confidence is returning. Our quality of life is improving because your voices, voices of common sense, are finally getting through. Believe me, it wasn't Washington experts who said government is too big, taxes are too high, criminals are coddled, education's basics are neglected, and values of family and faith are being undermined. That was your message; you made reforms possible.

With your help, we'll make even more progress, because I'll be the first to admit much more progress needs to be made. We're on a new road for America, a far better road, filled with hope and opportunities. Our critics may never be satisfied with anything we do, but I can only say those who created the worst economic mess in postwar history should be the last people crying wolf 1,000 days into this administration, when so many trends that were headed the wrong way are headed back in the right direction.

Thanks for listening, and God bless you.

Note: The President spoke at 12:06 P.M. EDT from Camp David.

Arms Control and Reduction

October 22, 1983

My fellow Americans:

I'd like to talk to you today about the deep desire we share to reduce nuclear weapons and to make our world more safe. Just as important, I want you to know why, despite all our good faith efforts, we are being frustrated in our goal to negotiate an arms reduction agreement.

No issue concerns me more and has taken up more of my time—not just in meetings with advisers but in deliberations with Members of the Congress and close and constant consultations with our allies—than this quest for a breakthrough on arms reductions. And believe me, I do so willingly, because as your President and also as a husband, father, and grandfather, I know what's at stake for everyone.

The trouble is, the obstacle to that agreement we want so dearly is not Washington, and it never has been; it's Moscow. And that's been the case in all our current arms reduction negotiations with the Soviet Union.

But today I'd like to focus on the longer range INF missile negotiations now under way in Geneva. Some have asked, "If we do want an agreement, why are we, the United States, planning to base new missiles in Europe?" Well, the question reflects some basic misunderstandings. It's been the Soviet Union who's been deploying such forces for a number of years, while the West watched and worried.

In 1977 the Soviets had in place 600 warheads on their longer range INF missiles. More significantly, they began adding the SS-20, a new, highly accurate mobile missile with three warheads, which could reach in minutes every city in Europe and many cities in the Middle East, Africa, and Asia. NATO had no comparable weapons.

In October 1979, Soviet leader Brezhnev announced a balance now exists: The Soviet Union—800 warheads; NATO—zero. Some balance. It was only at this point at the end of 1979 that the NATO alliance, not the United States alone, decided the Soviets' large and growing advantage in both nuclear and conventional forces would threaten our safety. So the alliance made what was called "the dual-track decision." We would redress the imbalance by deploying comparable weapons, while seeking an agreement at the negotiating table that would eliminate the need for deployment.

Nothing more dramatically illustrates our sincere desire for peace than our willingness not to deploy if the Soviets would stop threatening Europe with their missiles. How did the Soviets respond? By adding one new missile every week. They now have 1,300 warheads or more, and that number is growing. NATO still has zero.

All along we've been negotiating in good faith. We asked the Soviets to consider the total elimination of these missiles. It took them less than 24 hours to answer, "Nyet." So we proposed an interim solution, some equal but lower number, and the lower the better. With knee-jerk speed, the same answer came back again, "Nyet." And it's remained the same for all our new proposals, because the Soviets insist on a monopoly of longer range INF missiles. They offer what can only be called "a half-zero option"—zero for us, hundreds of warheads for them. As I told the members of the United Nations, that's where things stand today. We will continue our efforts to make the Soviets heed the will of the world, stop stonewalling, and start negotiating in good faith.

But that wish should not become father to the thought. We must look at Soviet words and deeds with a clear head and ask some long-overdue questions. Why does a regime which says it seeks peace repeatedly reject equitable proposals that would preserve peace? What are we to think of Soviet threats against NATO countries: warning Turkey it could become "a nuclear cemetery"; telling Scandinavian countries they are "a bridgehead for aggression"; and advising West Germany if new missiles are deployed, the military threat to it will grow manifold?

These are not words of a peacemaker but of a nation bent on intimidation. It is inconceivable that any Western leader would make such crude and provocative threats.

Finally, what is the credibility of a regime which exploits peace demonstrations in the West but brutally puts down any demonstration for reduced weaponry in its own country? As President Mitterrand of France recently observed, "Pacifism is in the West, and Euro-missiles are in the East. I consider that an unequal relationship."

My fellow Americans, the values of Western civilization and the beliefs that bind free people together are being tested. The Soviets are engaged in a campaign to intimidate the West, but it will not work. At home, bipartisan support in the Congress remains strong. And the unity of our NATO alliance will not break. Just this week, Prime Minister Craxi of Italy visited the White House and assured me of Italy's continued staunch support. Earlier this year, at the Williamsburg summit, the leaders of the industrialized nations agreed the policy is correct, fair, and should go forward. The spirit of Williamsburg is as strong as ever.

There is simply no sensible alternative to the parallel goal of deterrence and arms reduction. We will remain at the negotiating table just as long as it takes to reach a breakthrough. But the Soviets must understand: NATO's mission is to defend Europe and preserve peace, which it has done for 34 years. And NATO will continue to meet its responsibilities. Our countries will remain united, strong, and we will protect the safety of our people.

Until next week, thanks for listening, and God bless you.

Note: The President recorded his address on October 21 in the Map Room at the White House for broadcast at 12:06 P.M. EDT on October 22.

NATO Nuclear Weapons

October 29, 1983

My fellow Americans:

Before getting into today's subject, I would just like to say a heartfelt word of thanks to all of you for the thousands of wires and calls that have come in, supportive of the actions of these last few days and, particularly, supportive and grateful to those young men in uniform who are performing so magnificently.

Now today, I'd like to talk about a very important decision that was made Thursday by the Defense Ministers of the North Atlantic Treaty Organization, or NATO, as it's commonly called. This decision has great importance for us and for the NATO alliance as a whole, because it addresses the future size and composition of our shorter range nuclear forces in Europe.

As you know, we're negotiating with the Soviets in Geneva on the longer range missiles. The current imbalance on those systems is over 350 to 0 in their favor. But with regard to the shorter range missiles, the tactical missiles, I think you'll be very pleased with today's news. But first, a little background.

The nuclear forces in Europe are fundamental to our overall strategy of deterrence and to protecting our allies and ourselves. The weapons strengthen NATO and protect the peace because they show that the alliance is committed to sharing the risks and the benefits of mutual defense. Just by being there, these weapons deter others from aggression and, thereby, serve the cause of peace. Unfortunately, we must keep them there until we can convince the Soviets and others that the best thing would be a world in which there is no further need for nuclear weapons at all.

The alliance's goal, as General Rogers, NATO's Supreme Allied Commander for Europe, has so often said, is to maintain no more military forces than are absolutely necessary for deterrence and defense.

In December of 1979, NATO reached a decision to reduce immediately the number of shorter range nuclear weapons stationed in Europe. In 1980 we carried out that decision by removing 1,000 of these weapons. The same decision also committed the alliance to a further review of the remaining systems of this category, and that brings us to our decision of Thursday.

Drawing on the recommendation put forward by a special, high-level study group, the NATO Defense Ministers decided that, in addition to the 1,000 nuclear weapons which we withdrew in 1980, the overall size of the NATO nuclear stockpile could be reduced by an additional 1,400 weapons.

When these 2,400 weapons have been withdrawn, the United States will have reduced its nuclear weapons in Europe by over one-third from 1979 levels, and NATO will have the lowest number of nuclear weapons in 20 years. What this means is that the alliance will have removed at least five nuclear weapons for every new missile warhead we will deploy if the negotiations in Geneva don't lead to an agreement.

This step, taken by the alliance as a whole, stands in stark contrast to the actions of the Soviet Union. The Soviet leaders have so far refused to negotiate in good faith at the Geneva talks. Since our 1979 decision to reduce nuclear forces, the Soviet Union has added over 600 SS-20 warheads to their arsenal. Coupled with this, they offer threats and the acceleration of previous plans, which they now call countermeasures, if NATO carries through with its deployment plan intended to restore the balance.

The comparison of Soviet actions with NATO's reductions and restraint clearly illustrates once again that the so-called arms race has only one participant—the Soviet Union.

On Thursday NATO took a dramatic and far-reaching decision, a decision that puts us a giant step along the path toward increased stability in Europe and around the world. As we reduce our nuclear warheads in Europe and, of equal importance, take the necessary actions to maintain the effectiveness of the resulting force, we will continue in the future what we've accomplished so well in the past—to deter Soviet aggression. We seek peace and we seek security, and the NATO decision serves both.

Now, let me bring you up to date on the negotiations in Geneva. Progress toward an equitable, verifiable agreement on the reduction of intermediate-range nuclear missiles has been slow to come. Most recently, I proposed three initiatives which go a long way toward meeting important concerns expressed by the Soviet Union. By our actions on the talks we have ensured that all of the elements of a mutually advantageous agreement are on the table. The Soviet Union has now advanced some additional proposals of its own. We'll study these proposals, and we'll address them in the talks in Geneva.

Unfortunately, the Soviet proposals permit them to retain SS-20 missiles while not allowing NATO to deploy its own. The proposals are also coupled with an explicit threat to break off the Geneva talks. I hope that the Soviet Union is truly interested in achieving an agreement. The test will be whether the Soviets, having advanced their latest proposals, decide finally to negotiate seriously in Geneva.

For our part, we continue to seek an equitable and verifiable agreement as quickly as possible. We will stay at the negotiating table for as long as necessary to achieve such an agreement.

Thank you for listening, and God bless you.

Note: The President spoke at 12:06 P.M. EDT from Camp David.

America's Veterans

November 5, 1983

My fellow Americans:

Next Friday, November 11th, we'll celebrate Veterans Day—the day America sets aside to honor millions of our finest heroes. They are the men and women who defend our country and preserve our peace and freedom. This Veterans Day offers more reason than ever to think about what these special people mean to America.

Our most recent heroes—those still serving and those who have just come back from Beirut and Grenada—carried on with the same dedication and valor as their colleagues before them. If we remember that their dedicated service is in defense of our freedom and if we understand that they put their lives on the line so we might enjoy justice and liberty, then their sacrifices will not be in vain. This is our obligation. And this has been the spirit of Veterans Day from the beginning.

Veterans Day was originally called Armistice Day. It was first celebrated in 1919, the year we commemorated the armistice ending a war that was to have ended all wars. Two years later, a solemn ceremony was held in Châlons-sur-Marne, a town in northeastern France. The ceremony would have deep meaning for America. The remains of four unknown American soldiers had been brought to the town square from four American military cemeteries in France. An American sergeant, Edward F. Younger, placed a bouquet of white roses on one of the caskets. The American Unknown Soldier of World War I had been designated. After transport across the Atlantic aboard Admiral Dewey's flagship, the cruiser *Olympia,* our nation laid this hero to rest in Arlington National Cemetery on Armistice Day, November 11, 1921.

Sixty-two years have now passed. Millions of people from every corner of the world have come to the Tomb of the Unknown Soldier to pay their respects to America's fallen heroes. The First World War did not end all wars. The assault on freedom and human dignity did not end. Our nation had laid to rest too many other heroes. From Guadalcanal and Omaha Beach to MIG Alley and Pork Chop Hill, from Khe Sanh and the A Shau Valley to Beirut, America's best continue to give of themselves for us and for freedom-loving people everywhere. Yes, veterans have given their best for all of us, and we must continue to do our best by them.

Today, I reaffirm my determination to obtain the fullest possible accounting for our Americans missing in Southeast Asia. The sacrifices they made and may still be making and the uncertainty their families still endure deeply trouble us all. We must not rest until we know their fate.

Our hearts turn also to our disabled veterans. Their sacrifices and hardship endure every day of the year. A compassionate government will show them that we do remember and honor them. We will meet their special needs. In particular, there is no substitute for caring, quality health care, and that care will be provided.

Yesterday, I had the opportunity to visit Camp Lejeune, North Carolina. I went there to pay tribute to the many who gave their [*sic*] last full measure of their devotion. They kept faith with us and, indeed, they were heroes. Where do we get such brave young Americans? And where do we get those that came to their aid—the marines in Beirut who witnessed an unspeakable tragedy and returned to their posts with the same dedication and even greater resolve; the air crews working around the clock; the Army doctors performing medical miracles; and the sailors helping in countless ways? Such men and women can only come from a nation that remains true to the ideals of our Founding Fathers.

I also met with families and friends of those who lost their lives. I share their sorrow, and they have my prayers, as I know they have yours. These brave men protected our heritage of liberty. We must carry on. I believe we can and will. The spirit and patriotism that made America great is alive and well.

There was a brief ceremony in a hospital ward of Fort Bragg, North Carolina, last week that showed what I'm talking about. News photographers were taking pictures of soldiers who had just been awarded Purple Hearts and other decorations for valor. One wounded soldier, Private First Class Timothy Romick of the First Battalion, 75th Rangers, wearing a Purple Heart and a Combat Infantry Badge on his pajamas, interrupted the photographers. He said, "Wait a minute." And he pulled out a small American flag. This young Army ranger put the flag above his decorations. And then he said, "Okay. You can take your pictures now, because this is what I'm proudest of."

Each time our nation has called upon our citizens to serve, the best have come forward. Words cannot express our gratitude and admiration. But we can and should take the opportunity on this Veterans Day to remember their gift to us. When you see one of our young men and women in uniform on the street or someplace, how about a smiling "hello" and, maybe, a "thank you."

Veterans know better than anyone else the price of freedom, for they've suffered the scars of war. We can offer them no better tribute than to protect what they have won for us. That is our duty. They have never let America down. We will not let them down.

Until next week, thanks for listening, and God bless you.

Note: The President spoke at 12:06 P.M. EST from Camp David.

Trip to Japan and the Republic of Korea

November 12, 1983

My fellow Americans:

I'm sure you've heard Nancy and I have been traveling far from home this week. We're visiting two of America's most valued friends in the Pacific, Japan and the Republic of Korea.

The great energy and vitality of these free people is most impressive, and we're enchanted by the treasures of their past. We visited the revered and lovely Meiji Shrine in Tokyo. While there, we watched an exhibition of Yabusame, a spectacular equestrian sport dating hundreds of years, where riders gallop at full gait shooting arrows at three separate targets. On Friday I had the honor of being the first American President to address the Japanese Diet, their national parliament.

Today we're in South Korea, a staunch ally recently struck by great tragedy—the downing of Korean Air Lines Flight 007, followed by the assassination of key members of the Korean Cabinet. This has brought grief and bitterness to this part of the world, but it has also brought new determination. Free people, no matter where they live, must stand together against terrorism. We stand united with the people of Japan and Korea.

I will underline our commitment on Sunday when I visit our GI's along the demilitarized zone at the 38th Parallel. Our soldiers are serving with our Korean allies to deter aggression from the Communist North. Working with our partners to make tomorrow more prosperous and more secure is what our trip is all about.

America is a Pacific nation with good reason to strengthen our ties in this region. Mike Mansfield, our Ambassador to Japan, likes to say, "The next century will be the century of the Pacific." The citizens of our lands may live 5,000 miles apart; we may be different in customs, language, and traditions; and yes, we are often competitors in the world's markets. But what unites us is more important—our love of freedom and our optimism for the future.

Japan, Korea, the United States, and our many other friends in the Pacific region are building a better tomorrow. Individual opportunity coupled with hard work and reward produces astonishing results. When an entire society pursues these goals, miracles occur. Japan and Korea are classic examples of nations rising from the ashes of war to set standards of economic prosperity that dazzle the world.

There's much talk in the Congress of protecting American jobs, but protectionism is defensive and dangerous. Erecting barriers always invites retaliation, and retaliation is a threat to the one out of every eight American jobs dependent on our exports. At the end of this vicious cycle are higher costs for consumers and lost American jobs, the exact opposite of what we all want.

Let's recognize Japanese and Korean efficiency for what it is. If their products are better made and less expensive, then Americans who buy them benefit by receiving quality and value. And that's what the magic of the marketplace is all about.

The best course for us to take is to take the offensive and create new jobs through trade, lasting jobs tied to the products and technology of tomorrow. I'm confident American products can compete in world markets if they can enter foreign markets as easily as foreign products can enter ours. Currently they can't. Restrictions and tariffs limit U.S. imports into Japan and Korea. In our meetings I've insisted that reciprocity and open markets are vital to our mutual prosperity.

Prime Minister Nakasone and I have agreed on an agenda for progress to reduce and gradually eliminate these barriers. My goal is to help our farmers bring Japanese consumers lower prices for beef, citrus, and other agricultural goods; help our mining, coal, and gas industries export energy resources to a resource-poor Japan; and help our communications industries find new markets for their satellites and other products.

I also encouraged the Prime Minister to open his capital markets to more foreign investment. This will increase demand for Japanese yen, helping its price rise in relation to the dollar, thereby making it easier for the Japanese to buy our products and making our products better able to compete in other markets.

Economic issues are important, but as I noted, freedom and peace exist in an uneasy climate here. We need to remember that Japan and Korea are key allies. They know what living in the shadow of communism is like. It was a Japanese communications center that tracked the cold, calculating words of that Soviet pilot who gunned down the Korean airliner and 269 innocent victims.

Japan contributes about $20,000 for every U.S. soldier stationed here. Both Korea and Japan are committed to help us defend peace, and both are carrying an important share of the military burden. They and we share the same hopes and dreams for our loved ones. We're civilized nations believing in the same virtues of freedom and democracy.

The Williamsburg summit this summer brought together representatives of the Atlantic alliance and Japan in a common strategy for economic growth and military security. It demonstrated that our free world, spread across oceans, can join together to protect peace and freedom.

On this trip, we and our Pacific friends are taking another important step forward together. We've made our partnership stronger, and that means tomorrow can be better for us, our children, and people everywhere.

Until next week, thanks for listening, and God bless you.

Note: The President recorded his address on November 11 while in Tokyo, Japan, for broadcast at 12:06 P.M. EST on November 12 in the United States.

First Session of the 98th Congress

November 19, 1983

My fellow Americans:

Like many of you coming home for Thanksgiving, the Members of Congress adjourned yesterday to return to their districts. They can take some satisfaction from a change in the public's attitude about their performance. According to a Harris survey, confidence in the Congress—as well as in other major American institutions—has increased over the past year. There are some good reasons for that, and one of the most important can be summed up in two words: economic growth. Even the most committed pessimists are reluctantly concluding America is enjoying one humdinger of an economic recovery.

Pretty soon people will stop talking about economic recovery and begin discussing a new phenomenon we haven't seen since the 1960's—a powerful, long-lasting economic expansion. Because whether we're looking at industrial production—which has registered the biggest 12-month increase in 7 years—or factory use—now at a 2-year high—or the drop in unemployment—which has been faster than in the past six recoveries—or inflation—which remains below 3 percent, the best performance since 1967—we're looking at an economy whose engines are humming with open track ahead.

From autos to housing and from construction to high technology, growth is strong, confidence is building, and progress is being made. The Congress deserves its share of the credit both for helping us pass some key reforms and for bravely resisting attempts by some to return us to the old days of tax and tax and spend and spend.

As most of you know, our bipartisan Commission on Social Security recommended, and the Congress adopted, a landmark bill setting the Social Security system on a sound financial footing. At the same time, the Congress granted our request for the first major overhaul of the Medicare program which provides health insurance protection for retired and disabled Americans.

Before our returns [reforms],* the Medicare laws required that we pay hospitals on a cost-plus basis, footing the bill for whatever cost they wound up incurring in treating Medicare patients. So, hospitals had little incentive to hold down costs. Under our new reforms, hospitals will be paid a fixed price to care for each illness. If they control costs, they'll retain sufficient funds to upgrade the quality of their care. We estimate these reforms will save taxpayers over $20 billion in the next 5 years, and the savings can be realized without taking benefits away from anyone.

The Congress helped ensure a responsible continuation of revenue sharing, which supports vital economic activities in local communities. I was also pleased to sign into law several key appropriations bills. The spending levels were not as low as we requested, but they were lower than liberal Members wanted, and that would have meant higher deficits.

Perhaps the greatest contribution of the Congress was not what it did for us, but what it didn't do to us. The big spenders are still alive and well. And these people spared no effort to take away the third year of your tax cut, to delay indexing—the historic reform that'll protect you from being pushed by inflation into higher tax brackets—and to hit you with huge new tax increases. Well, with the help of responsible Republicans and Democrats, we fought them back and won. And with your help, we'll keep fighting and winning.

The record on the domestic side, however, was not all roses. The single, greatest failure of the Congress continues to be its inability to pass a responsible budget to help bring down deficits. By "responsible," I don't mean a budget that raises taxes to accommodate higher spending; I mean a budget that reduces spending to match revenues. You, the people, should not be forced to subsidize their extravagance. They should force themselves to spend within your means. Handcuffing big spenders and stopping them from taxing more of your earnings will be our first order of business come January.

---

*White House correction

I was also distressed that the Senate voted down—and the House refused to consider—our bill to provide tuition tax credits to deserving families. It was charged that this bill would have favored the rich. Well, that's a false charge. Those in high tax brackets were not eligible for the tax credits. The bill would have benefited those low- and middle-income people who bear the burden of tuition to send their children to parochial or independent schools and, at the same time, pay their full share of taxes to support the public school system. There would be no loss of revenue to public education, but there would be healthy competition among schools, which would improve the quality of education in both systems. Tuition tax credits and other unfinished business Americans want and need, like prayer in school and enterprise zones, will be pushed again by us as soon as the Congress returns.

I believe we're seeing another positive change that's making us feel more confident about our country—a return to bipartisanship in foreign policy. Our administration's highest goal is to help build a safer, more secure, and peaceful world. That mission rests upon the twin pillars of deterrence and dialog, upon a military balance together with serious negotiations to resolve differences peacefully. Thanks to bipartisan support, we're doing both. We're restoring America's military strength, and we're pursuing large reductions in nuclear weapons through genuine arms control. Last week I told the Diet, the Japanese legislature, our goal must be the eventual elimination of all such weapons.

We've had bipartisan support for our rescue mission in Grenada and for our continued peacekeeping role in Lebanon. And this same spirit of putting country before party helped pass the Caribbean Basin Initiative to stimulate trade, cooperation, and progress with our Caribbean neighbors and a bill to start up Radio Marti, the voice of truth to the imprisoned people of Cuba. I've said it before and I'll say it again, I don't believe for one minute America's best days are behind her. And judging by their confidence, neither do the American people.

Until next week, thanks for listening, and God bless you.

Note: The President spoke at 12:06 P.M. EST from the Oval Office at the White House.

James G. Watt

November 26, 1983

My fellow Americans:

There's a change of management over at the Department of the Interior. James Watt has resigned, and Judge William Clark has taken his place.

When Jim became Secretary of the Interior he told me of the things that needed doing, the things that had to be set straight. He also told me that if and when he did them, he'd probably have to resign in 18 months. Sometimes the one who straightens out a situation uses up so many Brownie points he or she is no longer the best one to carry out the duties of day-to-day management. Jim understood this. But he also realized what had to be done, and he did it for more than 30 months, not 18.

Now, with the change in management, it's time to take inventory. The Federal Government owns some 730 million acres—about one-third of the total land area of the United States. The Department of the Interior has jurisdiction over most of that, including our national parks, wildlife refuges, wilderness lands, wetlands, and coastal barriers. Not included in those 730 million acres are our offshore coastal waters, the Outer Continental Shelf, which is also Interior's responsibility. And I've asked Bill Clark to review policy, personnel, and process at the Department of the Interior.

Our national parks are the envy of the world, but in 1981 they were a little frayed at the edges. Since 1978 funds for upkeep and restoration had been cut in half. Jim Watt directed a billion-dollar improvement and restoration program. This 5-year effort is the largest commitment to restoration and improvement of the park system that has ever been made.

You, of course, are aware of the economic crunch we've been facing. Yet, even so, Secretary Watt set out to increase protection for fragile and important conservation lands. In 1982 he proposed that 188 areas along our Gulf and Atlantic coasts be designated as undeveloped coastal areas. And that proposal became the basis for the historic Coastal Barrier Resources Act. This act covers dunes, marshes, and other coastal formations from Maine to Texas—lands that provide irreplaceable feeding and nesting grounds for hundreds of species of waterfowl and fish. And, under Secretary Watt, we've added substantial acreage to our parks and wildlife refuges and some 15,000 acres to our wilderness areas.

Interior is also in charge of preserving historic sites and structures. In the economic recovery program we launched in 1981, we gave a 25-percent tax credit for private-sector restoration of historic structures. The result has been private investment in historic preservation five times as great as in the preceding 4 years. Secretary Watt has explored other ways to involve the private sector in historic preservation. And one of the efforts we're all proudest of is the campaign to restore Ellis Island and that grand lady in New York Harbor, the Statue of Liberty. This campaign is being led by Lee Iacocca, the chairman of Chrysler, and is being financed almost entirely by private contributions.

Preservation of endangered species is also a responsibility of the Department, and the approval and review of plans to bring about recovery of endangered plant and animal species has nearly tripled in the 30 months of Secretary Jim Watt. From the very first, Jim pledged to the Governors of our 50 States that the Department would be a good neighbor, that they would be included in land planning, and that small tracts of isolated Federal lands would be made available to communities needing land for hospitals, schools, parks, or housing. He also stated that isolated small tracts would be sold to farmers and ranchers.

An example of what I'm talking about is a strip of land 1 mile long and only 2 to 20 feet wide that was recently sold. I think you can imagine how these efforts must have erased some problems private landowners had with clouded title to their property.

Of course, all this was distorted and led to protests that he was selling national parks and wilderness. What he actually did was sell, in 1982, 55 tracts that totaled only 1,300 acres, and this year, 228 tracts totaling a little over 10,000 acres. The largest parcel was 640 acres; that's one square mile. None of it was park, wildlife refuge, wilderness, or Indian trust lands. They are not for sale. And not one acre of national parkland was leased for oil drilling or mining, contrary to what you may have read or heard.

When territories were becoming States, they were promised title to Federal lands within their borders, some lands to be used for public education. But as more and more Western States joined the Union, there began to be a delay; in fact, a permanent delay in turning over these lands. Jim Watt promised the Governors that if they'd identify lands they had a right to claim under their statehood acts, we'd make the Federal Government honest. The Governors responded and, as a result, by the end of this year more land will have been delivered to the States to support their school systems than at any time since 1969.

Changes have been made in the management of forest lands which are eligible for multiple use. Those lands will provide lumber on a sustained-yield basis. This will benefit Americans who cherish the dream of owning their own home.

We've made giant strides in implementing a national water policy which recognizes State primacy in managing water resources. People must be a part of our planning, and people need a reliable, safe drinking water supply, water for generating power, and water for irrigation.

Since I've mentioned energy, let me touch on that for a minute. It's estimated that 85 percent of the fuel we need to keep the wheels of industry turning is on Federal-owned property, including the Outer Continental Shelf. Efforts to increase the supply of energy have been carried out in full compliance with environmental stipulations. We can and will have an increased energy supply with an enhanced environment.

James G. Watt has served this nation well. And I'm sure William Clark will do the same.

Till next week, thanks for listening, and God bless you.

Note: The President spoke at 9:06 A.M. PST from Rancho del Cielo, near Santa Barbara.

The American Family

December 3, 1983

My fellow Americans:

This is a very special time of year for us, a time for family reunions and for celebrating together the blessings of God and the promises He has given us. From Thanksgiving to Hanukkah, which our Jewish community is now celebrating, to Christmas in 3 weeks' time, this is a season of hope and of love.

Certainly one of the greatest blessings for people everywhere is the family itself. The American Family Institute recently dedicated its book of essays, "The Family in the Modern World," to Maria Victoria Walesa, daughter of Danuta and Lech Walesa, to whose christening came 7,000 Poles expressing their belief that the family remains the foundation of freedom. And, of course, they're right. It's in the family where we learn to think for ourselves, care for others, and acquire the values of self-reliance, integrity, responsibility, and compassion.

Families stand at the center of society, so building our future must begin by preserving family values. Tragically, too many in Washington have been asking us to swallow a whopper: namely, that bigger government is the greatest force for fairness and progress. But this so-called solution has given most of us a bad case of financial indigestion. How can families survive when big government's powers to tax, inflate, and regulate absorb their wealth, usurp their rights, and crush their spirit? Was there compassion for a working family in 21½-percent interest rates, 12½-percent inflation, and taxes soaring out of sight? Consider the cost of childrearing. It now takes $85,000 to raise a child to age 18, and family incomes haven't kept up. During the 1970's, real wages actually declined over 2 percent. Consider taxes. In 1948 the tax on the average two-child family was just $9. Today it is $2,900.

As economic and social pressures have increased, the bonds that bind families together have come under strain. For example, three times as many

1983   165

families are headed by single parents today as in 1960. Many single parents make heroic sacrifices and deserve all our support. But there is no question that many well-intentioned Great Society-type programs contributed to family breakups, welfare dependency, and a large increase in births out of wedlock. In the 1970's the number of single mothers rose from 8 to 13 percent among whites and from 31 to a tragic 47 percent among blacks. Too often their children grow up poor, malnourished, and lacking in motivation. It's a path to social and health problems, low school performance, unemployment, and delinquency.

If we strengthen families, we'll help reduce poverty and the whole range of other social problems.

We can begin by reducing the economic burdens of inflation and taxes, and we're doing this. Since 1980 inflation has been chopped by three-fourths. Taxes have been cut for every family that earns a living, and we've increased the tax credit for child care. Yesterday we learned that our growing economy reduced unemployment to 8.2 percent last month. The payroll employment figure went up by 370,000 jobs.

At the same time, new policies are helping our neediest families move from dependence to independence. Our new job-training law will train over a million needy and unemployed Americans each year for productive jobs. I should add that our enterprise zones proposal would stimulate new businesses, bringing jobs and hope to some of the most destitute areas of the country. The Senate has adopted this proposal. But after 2 years of delay, the House Democratic leadership only recently agreed to hold its first hearing on the legislation. This is a jobs bill America needs. And come January, we expect action.

We're moving forward on many other fronts. We've made prevention of drug abuse among youth a top priority. We'll soon announce a national missing children's center to help find and rescue children who've been abducted and exploited. We're working with States and local communities to increase the adoption of special-needs children. More children with permanent homes mean fewer children with permanent problems.

We're also stiffening the enforcement of child support from absent parents. And we're trying hard to improve education through more discipline, a return to the basics, and through reforms like tuition tax credits to help hard-working parents.

In coming months, we'll propose new ways to help families stay together, remain independent, and cope with the pressures of modern life. A cornerstone of our efforts must be assisting families to support themselves. As Franklin Roosevelt said almost 50 years ago, "Self-help and self-control are the essence of the American tradition."

In Washington everyone looks out for special interests groups. Well, I think families are pretty special. And with your help, we'll continue looking out for their interests.

Till next week, thanks for listening, and God bless you.

Note: The President spoke at 12:06 P.M. EST from Camp David.

Situation in Lebanon

December 10, 1983

My fellow Americans:

I'd like to talk to you today about the deep desire we all share to bring peace to Lebanon.

These past several weeks have brought bitter tragedy and sorrow to all of us. The loss of even one of our splendid young Americans is an enormous price to pay. The number of dead and wounded is a terrible burden of grief for all Americans. It's unimaginably more so for the families who have lost a father, husband, a son, or a brother. Their deaths are testimony to the savage hatreds and greedy ambitions which have claimed so many innocent Lebanese lives.

The human toll in Lebanon is staggering. Lebanon's losses since 1975 would be comparable to the United States losing 10 million of its citizens. What conceivable reason can there be for this wanton death and destruction?

Lebanon's suffering began long before a single marine arrived. In the early 1970's many thousands of Palestinians entered Lebanon. Lebanon's fragile political consensus collapsed, and a savage civil war broke out.

The Palestinians also had a military, the armed PLO. Trained in terrorist tactics by Soviet-bloc nations and Libya, the PLO joined the civil war and attacked Israeli targets, villages and schools across the border between Lebanon and Israel.

In the midst of all this, Syria was asked to intervene and stop the civil war. In the process, it occupied a large part of Lebanon. However, Syria did nothing to control terrorism against Israel's northern border. Israel decided to neutralize the PLO and, in June 1982, mounted a full-scale invasion across the border. This resulted in another major round of fighting between Syria, the PLO, and Israel. Shelling and bombing pounded Beirut. Thousands more died.

We negotiated a cease-fire and then joined the multinational force at the request of the Lebanese Government to make possible the peaceful separation of the forces. This is the second time in 25 years that we have come to support the Lebanese Government in restoring peace.

In 1958 President Eisenhower used a bipartisan congressional resolution to send 8,000 American soldiers and marines to Lebanon. When order was restored, our military came home. But in 1958 there were no occupying foreign armies, and there was no Soviet presence in Syria. Today, there are more than 7,000 Soviet military advisers and technicians.

In September 1982 I offered a plan to bring peace to the region. It called for a just solution to the Palestinian problem as well as a reasonable settlement of issues between the Arab States and Israel.

Success in Lebanon is central to sustaining the broader peace process. We have vital interests in the Middle East which depend on peace and stability in that region. Indeed, the entire world has vital interests there. The region is central to the economic vitality of the Western World. If we fail in Lebanon, what happens to the prospects for peace, not just in Lebanon but between Israel and her neighbors and in the entire Middle East?

Once internal stability is established and withdrawal of all foreign forces is assured, the marines will leave. But because we care about human values for ourselves, so must we be concerned when freedom, justice, and liberty are abused elsewhere. That's the moral basis which brought our marines to Lebanon.

We have acted with great restraint despite repeated provocations and murderous attacks. Our reconnaissance flights have only one purpose, and the Syrians know it: to give the greatest possible protection to our troops. We will continue to do whatever is needed to ensure the safety of our forces and our reconnaissance flights.

The peace process is slow and painful, but there is progress which would not have been possible without the multinational force. Last May with our help the Governments of Lebanon and Israel negotiated an agreement providing for the withdrawal of Israeli forces. In September when the Israelis pulled back their forces from the Shuf Mountains near Beirut, Lebanese attempts to extend their authority into this area were met by violent opposition from forces supported by Syria. We will redouble our diplomatic efforts to promote reconciliation and achieve withdrawal of all foreign forces.

At a recent meeting in Geneva all the Lebanese parties agreed to recognize the present government as the legitimate representative of the Lebanese people. Talks have begun to broaden the base of the government and to satisfy the legitimate grievances of all the people.

My special envoy, Ambassador Don Rumsfeld, has returned to the region and will continue trying to move the peace process forward on all fronts. Lebanon's agony must end.

Today is the 35th anniversary of the United Nations Universal Declaration of Human Rights. The Lebanese people are struggling for their human rights. We call upon everyone involved to give that birthright back to the Lebanese.

Until next week, thanks for listening, and God bless you.

Note: The President spoke at 12:06 P.M. EST from Camp David.

Drunk Driving

December 17, 1983

My fellow Americans:

This is the season when we appreciate our families and friends and spend time looking for just the right gifts for them. We arrange our homes with decorations and make an effort to prepare for special moments. Yet, during these holiday festivities our loved ones are in danger. That's why I want to ask you today for your help.

Unless all of us unite to take action, thousands of our citizens, perhaps a member of your own family, will suffer terrible deaths. I wish I were overstating the case, but I'm not. And there are tens of thousands of parents who have lost children. Their heartaches and tears are testament to the magnitude of the threat that hangs over us.

If I were alerting you about a foreign power brutally murdering tens of thousands of our fellow citizens, a cry for bold action would sweep our country. Well, I'm not referring to a foreign enemy; I'm talking about drunk drivers.

Due to the irresponsible use of alcohol, 25,000 Americans—men, women, and children—are killed each year. The statistics are overwhelming. We've lost more than a quarter of a million of our countrymen to drunk drivers in the last 10 years. That's 500 every week, 70 every day, one every 20 minutes.

Every year, nearly 700,000 people are injured in alcohol-related crashes. Every one of these casualties is someone's son or daughter, husband or wife, mother, father, or friend. The personal tragedies behind the statistics are enough to break your heart.

A few days ago, Mr. and Mrs. Gerald Price of Johnson City, Tennessee, joined me at the White House to proclaim this week National Drunk and Drugged Driving Awareness Week. It was fitting they be here. About 2½ years ago, their son Timothy was killed by a drunk driver. Then, just a year ago, their daughter Elizabeth was killed when a drunk driver veered onto her side of the road.

All of us can share the grief of these parents who lost two of their children in separate incidents. But now is not just the time for sympathy; now is the time to act. The Prices were at the White House when I officially received the report of our Commission on Drunk Driving.

Commission Chairman John Volpe and the other members took their jobs seriously, and they've made some suggestions you ought to know about. Right off the bat, we should understand there are no magic solutions. It'll take a long-term commitment, coming at the problem from different directions.

The first step, according to the Commission, is making sure that our friends and neighbors—as well as the people in the city halls and in the State legislatures—fully comprehend what we're facing.

Secretary of Transportation Elizabeth Dole has been speaking tirelessly around the country on this issue. Just this week, the Licensed Beverage Information Council, the Outdoor Advertising Association of America, and Secretary Dole joined in unveiling this year's Friends Don't Let Friends Drive Drunk campaign to enlist all of us to protect our friends from themselves. This is an excellent example of the private sector and government working together to attack a serious problem.

We must change the lax attitude about driving when there's even a question about sobriety. We'll need to be stern at times, but putting our foot down can save someone's life.

The Commission found out that some of our laws and law enforcement are lax, as well. Some drunks have been arrested more than once, but they're still out there on the highways. What greater travesty could there be than knowing your loved one was killed by an individual already convicted of drunk driving?

We must make it harder on the first-timers. And we must make sure that repeat offenders are taken off the road. The Commission made numerous, specific recommendations, and we're moving forward on them. But in a free society such as ours, with the separation of powers between Federal, State, and local governments, it will take all of us working together.

Much of the credit for focusing public attention goes to the grass-roots campaign of organizations like MADD, Mothers Against Drunk Drivers, and RID, Remove Intoxicated Drivers. The activists in these organizations, many of whom have lost loved ones to drunk drivers, have helped strengthen laws and law enforcement at the State and local level. And in those States that have toughened their laws and their enforcement, lives have been saved.

The automobile has always been close to the hearts of Americans. We've valued our mobility as a precious freedom, and individual ownership of a car has provided greater mobility to more people than ever before. If there's one lesson we've learned in the last 200 years, it is that with freedom must come responsibility.

Some of our citizens have been acting irresponsibly. Drinking and driving has caused the death of many innocent people. It is up to us to put a stop to it, not in a spirit of vengeance but in the spirit of love.

I pray that each of you will have a safe and happy holiday. Until next week, thanks for listening, and God bless you.

Note: The President spoke at 12:06 P.M. EST from the Oval Office at the White House.

Christmas

December 24, 1983

My fellow Americans:

Like so many of your homes, the White House is brimming with greens, colorful decorations, and a tree trimmed and ready for Christmas day. And when Nancy and I look out from our upstairs windows, we can see the National Christmas Tree standing in majestic beauty. Its lights fill the air with a spirit of love, hope, and joy from the heart of America.

I shared that spirit recently when a young girl named Amy Benham helped me light our national tree. Amy had said that the tree that lights up our country must be seen all the way to heaven. And she said that her wish was to help me turn on its lights. Well, Amy's wish came true. But the greatest gift was mine, because I saw her eyes light up with hope and joy just as brightly as the lights on our national tree. And I'm sure they were both seen all the way to heaven, and they made the angels sing.

Christmas is a time for children, and rightly so. We celebrate the birthday of the Prince of Peace who came as a babe in a manger. Some celebrate Christmas as the birthday of a great teacher and philosopher. But to other millions of us, Jesus is much more. He is divine, living assurance that God so loved the world He gave us His only begotten Son so that by believing in Him and learning to love each other we could one day be together in paradise.

It's been said that all the kings who ever reigned, that all the parliaments that ever sat have not done as much to advance the cause of peace on Earth and goodwill to men as the man from Galilee, Jesus of Nazareth.

Christmas is also a time to remember the treasures of our own history. We remember one Christmas in particular, 1776, our first year as a nation. The Revolutionary War had been going badly. But George Washington's faith, courage, and leadership would turn the tide of history our way. On Christmas night he led a band of ragged soldiers across the Delaware River through driving snow to a victory that saved the cause of independence. It's said that their route of march was stained by bloody footprints, but their spirit never faltered and their will could not be crushed.

The image of George Washington kneeling in prayer in the snow is one of the most famous in American history. He personified a people who knew it was not enough to depend on their own courage and goodness; they must also seek help from God, their Father and Preserver.

In a few hours, families and friends across America will join together in caroling parties and Christmas Eve services. Together, we'll renew that spirit of faith, peace, and giving which has always marked the character of our people. In our moments of quiet reflection I know we will remember our fellow citizens who may be lonely and in need tonight.

"Is the Christmas spirit still alive?" some ask. Well, you bet it is. Being Americans, we open our hearts to neighbors less fortunate. We try to protect them from hunger and cold. And we reach out in so many ways—from toys-for-tots drives across the country, to goodwill by the Salvation Army, to American Red Cross efforts which provide food, shelter, and Christmas cheer from Atlanta to Seattle.

Churches are so generous it's impossible to keep track. One example: Reverend Bill Singles' Presbyterian Meeting House in nearby Alexandria, Virginia, is simultaneously sponsoring hot meals-on-wheels programs, making and delivering hundreds of sandwiches and box loads of clothes, while visiting local hospitals and sending postcards to shut-ins and religious dissidents abroad.

Let us remember the families who maintain a watch for their missing in action. And, yes, let us remember all those who are persecuted inside the Soviet bloc—not because they commit a crime, but because they love God in their hearts and want the freedom to celebrate Hanukkah or worship the Christ Child.

And because faith for us is not an empty word, we invoke the power of prayer to spread the spirit of peace. We ask protection for our soldiers who are guarding peace tonight—from frigid outposts in Alaska and the Korean demilitarized zone to the shores of Lebanon. One Lebanese mother told us that her little girl had only attended school 2 of the last 8 years. Now, she said, because of our presence there her daughter can live a normal life.

With patience and firmness we can help bring peace to that strife-torn region and make our own lives more secure. The Christmas spirit of peace, hope, and love is the spirit Americans carry with them all year round, everywhere we go. As long as we do, we need never be afraid, because trusting in God is the one sure answer to all the problems we face.

Till next week, thanks for listening, God bless you, and Merry Christmas.

Note: The President spoke at 12:06 P.M. EST from the Oval Office at the White House.

New Year's Eve

December 31, 1983

My fellow Americans:

New Year's Eve is a time for looking back on the year past, and in a moment, I want to talk about all that 1983 meant to America. But first I want to mention the topic of my radio talk 2 weeks ago—drunk driving.

A drunk or drugged person at the wheel of a car isn't a driver, that person is a machine of destruction. So let's enjoy all the wonderful celebrations that go with New Year's Eve, but, please, when we drive, let's drive sober.

Nineteen eighty-three was the 207th year for our Grand Old Republic. Though the year had its measure of hardship and even tragedy, it was a time when we Americans acted with courage, self-confidence, and vigor.

We had reason to feel glad. America was on the mend. And as our economy regained strength, we watched the progress of a sparkling recovery—one of the strongest recoveries in 20 years. I said from the beginning it would take time for our economic program to work. You can't cure 25 years of failed economic policies overnight. And, yes, we had some hard months at first. But 1983 saw our patience pay off as our program took hold.

On this New Year's Eve, the prime interest rate is 11 percent, about half of what it was when we took office. Inflation for 1983 is running at only 3.2 percent, about a quarter of what it was just 3 years ago. Housing starts are running 60 percent higher than on this day last year.

Nineteen eighty-three saw the stock market reach new highs as it pumped vast new funds into the economy and raised the value of pension funds where millions of working Americans have their savings. During 1982, American manufacturers sold 5.8 million new cars. This year, they've sold 6.7 million.

As our basic industries and agriculture gain new strength, American ingenuity and enterprise are creating whole new industries—industries like robotics and bioengineering. Just a few years ago, home computers were unheard of. By the end of 1982, American companies had sold some 2½ million home computers. This year, the figure is expected to climb to 7½ million.

This is one of the seasons when we Americans fly the most, to visit family and friends, because there's nothing like being home for the holidays. Well, the deregulation of the airline industry has increased competition and helped push fares down. And deregulation of banking is helping millions.

In 1983, for the first time, everyday savers and small businesses received marked interest rates, earning $3½ billion in additional income. The best news of all: On New Year's Eve 1982, 100.8 million Americans had jobs. But today, the figure has climbed by 3.6 million, an all-time high for our nation.

All this means that in 1983 it was easier to pay bills, put children through college, buy homes, or borrow the money to start a new business than it had been in many years. Once again, the American economy has begun to reward fresh ideas and good, hard work.

Just as 1983 saw our economy recovering, it saw a new sense of purpose in our Armed Forces and foreign policy. In the military, morale has soared. Some pundits used to claim we could only attract recruits when our economy was weak. But now, even with a strong economy and growing opportunities in civilian life, our Armed Forces are attracting more and better qualified recruits than ever. There's one statistic that shows just how dramatic the turnaround has been. If 1979 Air Force retention rates had continued, three out of four pilots would have left the service after their first tours. In 1983, better than three out of four stayed in.

Morale has improved partly because we've given our men and women in uniform better pay and better equipment. But I just have to believe the courage of our soldiers and marines in Lebanon and Grenada has a lot to do with it. And, as we celebrate the New Year, I wonder whether you would all join Nancy and me in setting aside a moment to remember those who, in 1983, gave their lives in the cause of freedom and to pray for those brave young men spending this day so far from home.

In foreign policy, this year we've given firm support to democratic leadership in Central America. In Grenada we set a nation free. In Asia, our trip to Japan and Korea further strengthened our partnership with those nations. In Europe, 1983 saw the NATO Alliance pass through harsh trials, but the Alliance has emerged more firmly united than ever—more ardent in the cause of freedom and peace, more dedicated to the paths of deterrence and dialog.

In Lebanon, the road to peace has proven long and hard, but there has been progress that would have been impossible without our marines and the other troops in the multinational peacekeeping force. Representatives of all Lebanese factions agreed in Geneva to recognize the government of President Amin Gemayel. And talks have begun that will broaden the government's base. It isn't easy. Progress is painfully slow, but progress is being made.

Nineteen eighty-three was a good year for America. If all of us keep pulling together, we can make 1984 even better. Happy New Year and, until next week, thanks for listening, and God bless you all.

Note: The President recorded his address on December 28 at the Century Plaza Hotel in Los Angeles, California, for broadcast on December 31.

School Discipline

January 7, 1984

My fellow Americans:

This is my first radio talk in 1984, so Happy New Year.

My prayer for you this new year is that you and your families will prosper in health and happiness. When I spoke to you last Saturday on New Year's Eve, I made one request to everyone: when we drive, let's drive sober. Well, I was delighted to hear some very heartening news from Transportation Secretary Elizabeth Dole. Last New Year's weekend was the safest on our highways in 35 years. Our efforts to keep drunk, violent drivers off the road are beginning to show progress.

Today I want to talk about a subject which also deals with violence and is on our minds as the holidays end and our children go back to school: the problem of classroom discipline. The sad truth is, many classrooms across the country are not temples of learning, teaching the lessons of goodwill, civility, and wisdom important to the whole fabric of American life. Many schools are filled with rude, unruly behavior and even violence.

According to a 1978 report by the National Institute of Education, each month three million secondary school children were victims of in-school crime. I don't mean ordinary high jinks. I mean crime. Each month some two and a half million students were the victims of robberies and thefts, and more than 250,000 students suffered physical attacks. In large cities, the problem was so bad that almost 8 percent of urban junior and senior high-school students missed at least one day in the classroom per month because they were afraid to go to school.

Now maybe you're thinking: that was back in 1978. Well, a study released in 1983 indicates this 1978 report probably understates the problem today.

Just as school violence affects our sons and daughters, it also affects their teachers. That 1978 National Institute of Education study found that each month some 6,000 teachers were robbed, about 125,000 a month were threatened with physical harm, and at least 1,000 teachers each month were assaulted with violence so severe they required medical care. One psychiatrist who treats teachers says many of them suffer symptoms identical to those of World War I shell-shock victims. It's that bad.

Today, American children need good education more than ever. But we can't get learning back into our schools until we get the crime and violence out. It's not a question of anyone asking for a police state. It's just that—as Albert Shanker of the American Federation of Teachers put it—"We're not going to get people interested in English or mathematics or social studies and languages, unless we solve discipline problems and take out of our schools those students who prevent teachers from teaching."

Today, I'm asking Americans to renew our commitment to school discipline. Here at the national level, we're directing the Federal Government to do all it can to help parents, teachers, and administrators restore order to their classroom.

The Department of Education will study ways to prevent school violence, publicize examples of effective school discipline, and continue its joint project with the National Institute of Justice [*sic*] to find better ways for localities to use their resources to prevent school crime.

The Department of Justice will establish a National School Safety Center. This Center will publish handbooks informing teachers and other officials of their legal rights in dealing with disruptive students and put together a computerized national clearinghouse for school safety resources.

I've also directed the Justice Department to file court briefs to help school administrators enforce school discipline.

But, despite the importance of these efforts, we can't make progress without help from superintendents and principals, teachers, parents, and students themselves.

I wish I could tell you all the stories I've heard of schools that have been turned around by determined local efforts. At Southwestern High in Detroit, once one of the city's most violent schools, firm discipline has raised the attendance rate from 53 to almost 87 percent.

In my home State of California at Sacramento's El Camino High, a discipline compact between parents and the school has helped achievement levels soar. And in the Watts section of Los Angeles, George Washington Preparatory High School recently established a policy of strict discipline with impressive results. Just five years ago, only 43 percent of the school's seniors expressed an interest in going to college. Well, last year, 80 percent of the seniors did go to college.

So please—if you have discipline problems at your school—find out what you can do to help. By working together, we can restore good order to

America's classrooms and give our sons and daughters the education they deserve.

Until next week, thanks for listening. And God bless you.

Note: The President spoke at 12:06 P.M. EST from Camp David.

National Bipartisan Commission on Central America

January 14, 1984

My fellow Americans:

Last April I addressed a joint session of the Congress and asked for bipartisan cooperation on behalf of our policies to protect liberty and democracy in Central America. Shortly after that speech, the late Senator Henry Jackson encouraged the appointment of a blue-ribbon commission to chart a course for democracy, economic improvement, and peace in Central America.

I appointed twelve distinguished Americans to the National Bipartisan Commission on Central America and asked former Secretary of State Henry Kissinger to serve as its Chairman. This week the members of that group delivered to me their report on the crisis confronting our Latin neighbors.

I believe the Commission has rendered an important service to all Americans—all of us from pole to pole in this Western Hemisphere. The members of this Commission represented both political parties and a wide cross section of our country. They reached agreement on some very key points. They agreed that the crisis is serious and our response must include support for democratic development, improved living conditions, and security assistance.

They agreed that the United States has a vital interest in preventing a Communist Central America because if our own borders are threatened, then our ability to meet our commitments to protect peace elsewhere in the world—in Europe, the Middle East, and Asia—would be significantly weakened.

The members also agreed that Nicaragua's regime has violated its promise to restore democracy. And they warned that Nicaragua's export of subversion could undermine the stability of neighboring countries, producing waves of refugees—perhaps millions of them—many of whom would seek entry into the United States.

The Commission concluded, "The crisis is on our doorstep." The report of this distinguished body presents no quick fix to ease the pain and suffering of tomorrow. There is none. Nor can we alone bring peace to this or any other part of the world. As the report notes, solutions to Central American problems must primarily be the work of Central Americans. But we can and must help because it is in our interest to do so and because it's morally the right thing to do.

The Commission did present us positive recommendations to support democratic development, improve human rights, and bring the long-sought-for peace to this troubled region so close to home. The recommendations reinforce the spirit of the administration's policies that help to our neighbors should be primarily economic and humanitarian. And since this report does present a bipartisan consensus, I will send to the Congress when it reconvenes a comprehensive plan for achieving the objectives set forth by the Commission. I urge the Members of Congress to respond with the same bipartisan spirit that guided the Commission in its work.

This Central American democracy, peace, and recovery initiative, which I call the Jackson Plan, will be designed to bring democracy, peace, and prosperity to Central America. It won't be easy. But it can be done. I believe peace is worth the price.

There may be an argument for doing much, and perhaps an argument for doing nothing. But there is no valid argument for doing too little. Well, I opt for doing enough: enough to protect our own security and enough to improve the lives of our neighbors so that they can vote with ballots instead of bullets.

The government of Nicaragua must also understand this. They cannot threaten their peaceful neighbors, export subversion, and deny basic human freedom to their own people as the Commission has so rightly observed.

Now, you may have heard that there's a controversy between the administration and the Congress over human rights and military aid to beleaguered El Salvador. Well, I agree completely with the objective of improving prospects for democracy and human rights in El Salvador. I am also committed to preventing Cuban- and Nicaraguan-supported guerrillas from violently overthrowing El Salvador's elected government and others in the region. So is the bipartisan Commission. So too, I believe, is our Congress.

Our administration will continue to work closely with the Congress in achieving these common goals. As we move to implement the recommendations of the bipartisan Commission, we will be offering the promise of a better tomorrow in Central America. But we must oppose those who do not abide by the norms of civilized behavior, whether they be of the extreme right or extreme left. Senator Henry Jackson would have had it so.

Until next week, thanks for listening, and God bless you.

Note: The President spoke at 12:06 P.M. EST from Camp David.

Economic Recovery Program

January 21, 1984

My fellow Americans:

It's that time again when we are deluged by a blizzard of economic facts, figures, and predictions.

I hope you'll keep in mind that economic forecasting is far from a perfect science. If recent history's any guide, the experts have some explaining to do about what they told us had to happen but never did.

When our economic program first began in late 1981, many of the doom criers had warned it would push inflation and interest rates through the roof. It hasn't quite worked out that way. We inherited 12.4-percent inflation in 1980. Today it's 3.2. And the prime interest rate has dropped from over 21 percent to 11 percent.

Last year, those pessimists were back again. They told us bad times would go on and on and on. One forecaster said we were on the brink of a major collapse. Another one of Wall Street's favorites made headlines when he said the recovery would be "one of the weakest on record."

I'm not trying to belabor a point, but these predictions just aren't panning out. Far from being weak, this recovery has been one of the strongest since the 1960's. More people are on the job than ever before in our history. From solid growth in housing to new frontiers in high technology, from a healthy recovery in real wages to a big improvement in productivity, and from record increases in venture capital to new highs in the stock market, America is moving forward, getting stronger, and confounding everyone who said it can't be done. Well, like the Little Engine That Could, it is being done.

I only wish this would convince the naysayers to let up a little. But they don't seem willing. This year we're hearing a new variation of their gloomy refrain, not about inflation or interest rates taking off, not about the recovery that won't happen, but about the recovery that can't last. Government deficits, we're told, will kill the recovery by draining capital needed by business to keep the economy expanding.

Well, I happen to believe that those who underestimated the strength of this recovery may be wrong about the size of future deficits, too. But let's be clear, the deficits do matter. The problem is, they were created by a pattern of overspending that began 50 years ago and that's been hard to break. We must bring deficits down and work toward a balanced budget. The question is: How? By spending cuts and economic growth or by tax increases? I don't think you need to be an economist to understand the evidence. We don't face large deficits because you're not taxed enough. We face those deficits because government spends too much.

Even with our tax reductions now in place, families are still being taxed at near record peacetime levels. Yet, as fast as taxes have gone up, spending has gone up even faster. In the past, raising taxes simply encouraged government to spend more. And since people had less money in their pockets to spend or save, economic growth was hurt. So, fewer people were employed and able to pay taxes. Deficits went up, not down.

The World Bank has released a study showing that countries with lower tax burdens have consistently enjoyed higher growth rates. Japan, where I recently visited, has had the lowest tax burden and the highest growth rates of all the developed nations.

We must try harder to reduce spending. Back in 1967 as Governor of California, I asked a group of business executives to survey the State bureaucracy and identify potential savings. They made about 2,000 recommendations. And we implemented most of them. Their work helped return fiscal integrity to a State that had been spending a million dollars a day it didn't have.

Now we're trying the same approach in Washington, because, believe me, there's plenty of fat to cut. The Grace Commission, comprised of nearly 2,000 leaders of private industry, has just presented us a blueprint for reducing wasteful spending.

The Commission recommended that the Federal Government upgrade its computer systems. This could save $4 billion. Tracking certain incorrect pension payments could save $4 billion. These are but two of some 2,500 examples that could save taxpayers billions and billions of dollars. And, as the late Senator Everett Dirksen said, "A billion here, a billion there—pretty soon you're talking about real money."

We should prepare for strong protests from Washington-based representatives of the many special interests groups. They will fear that implementing such management reforms means cuts for their favorite programs.

What we're really talking about is doing things more efficiently without hurting people in need, and without compromising America's security. Yes, we have a deficit problem. But let's be sensible about it. When warnings about deficits seem to be hysterical, just remember the lessons of recent history. Predictions are often wrong. Some may be using predictions to mask their favorite pastime: raising your taxes.

Others may underestimate our ability to cut government down to size over time. Like death and taxes, the doom criers will always be with us. And, they'll always be wrong about America until they realize progress begins with trusting the people.

With your support, we'll make this year's batch of pessimists as wrong as last year's.

Until next week, thanks for listening. And God bless you.

Note: The President spoke at 12:06 P.M. EST from Camp David.

Goals for Space

January 28, 1984

My fellow Americans:

Three days ago in my State of the Union message, I spoke to you about taking on the challenge of America's next frontier, space, as one of four great goals for the '80's. But today I'd like to tell you more about that challenge, about how we can advance America's leadership in space through the end of this century and well into the next. And how, by reaching for exciting goals in space, we'll serve the cause of peace and create a better life for all of us here on earth.

For a quarter of a century, we've moved steadily forward in the exploration and utilization of space, extending our knowledge of our solar system, our galaxy, and our universe. The space shuttle, our most recent advance in space technology, gives us routine access to space.

Just as the Yankee clipper ships of the last century symbolized American vitality, our space shuttles today capture the optimistic spirit of our times.

Our many achievements have proven that we can do much in space and that there's much more we must do to ensure that America lives up to her description, a land of hope and opportunity.

Our space goals will chart a path of progress toward creating a better life for all people who seek freedom, prosperity, and security.

Our approach to space has three elements. Let me discuss each of them briefly. The first is a commitment to build a permanently manned space station to be in orbit around the Earth within a decade. It will be a base for many kinds of scientific, commercial, and industrial activities, and a stepping-stone for further goals.

Scientists from NASA, universities, and private industry will do research in and around the space station—research that's only possible in a zero-gravity and vacuum of space. As needed, private industry will fund expansions of the NASA facility where companies can manufacture new products and provide new services.

But most importantly, like every step forward, a space station will not be an end in itself but a doorway to even greater progress in the future. In this case, a space station will open up new opportunities for expanding human commerce and learning, and provide a base for further exploration of that magnificent and endless frontier of space.

International cooperation, the second element of our plan, has long been a guiding principle of the United States space program. The tricentennial of the first German immigration to America was celebrated last year with a joint space effort. Just as our friends were asked to join us in the shuttle program, our friends and allies will be invited to join with us in the space station project.

The third goal of our space strategy will be to encourage American industry to move quickly and decisively into space. Obstacles to private sector space activities will be removed, and we'll take appropriate steps to spur private enterprise in space.

We expect space-related investments to grow quickly in future years, creating many new jobs and greater prosperity for all Americans. Companies interested in putting payloads into space, for example, should have ready access to private sector launch services.

Transportation Secretary Elizabeth Dole will work to stimulate the private sector investment in commercial, unmanned space boosters. We need a thriving, commercial launch industry. NASA, along with other departments and agencies, will be taking a number of initiatives to promote private sector investment to ensure our lead over current and potential foreign competitors. So, we're going to bring into play America's greatest asset: the vitality of our free enterprise system.

We've always prided ourselves on the pioneer spirit that built America. Well, that spirit is a key to our future as well as our past. Once again, we're on a frontier. Our willingness to accept this challenge will reflect whether America's men and women today have the same bold vision, the same courage and indomitable spirit that made us a great nation.

The peaceful use of space promises great benefits to all mankind. It opens vast new opportunities for our industry and ingenuity. The only limits we have are those of our own courage and imagination. When President John Kennedy challenged America to go to the moon, he said it would not be one person going, but an entire nation putting him there.

Our space program has done so much to bring us together, because it gives us the opportunity to be the kind of nation we want to be—the kind of nation we must always be—dreaming, daring, and creating.

Until next week, thanks for listening. And God bless you.

Note: The President spoke at 12:06 P.M. EST from the Oval Office at the White House.

Budget Deficits/Peace in Central America and Lebanon

February 4, 1984

My fellow Americans:

As you know, last Sunday I announced my candidacy for re-election to this office. I asked for your support to help finish what we began three years ago—getting government spending firmly under control, encouraging growth in our economy, and strengthening peace so we can provide opportunities for the liberty and happiness of our citizens today and for millions still unborn.

I wasn't surprised that my announcement set off some pretty sharp rhetoric from the other side, but I'd like to think that, with some goodwill and common sense, Republicans and Democrats could rise above election-year politics for the good of our country. Certainly, there are important areas, and three come immediately to mind, where we could and should be working together.

For example, I believe there's basis for agreement on a downpayment on projected budget deficits. I think we could reduce projected deficits by at least $100 billion over the next three years. So, frankly, I was a bit puzzled why those new converts to concern about looming deficits held back on joining a bipartisan working group.

Now, I understand they will be prepared to meet next week. I urge them to approach the negotiations in the same spirit as we will. Let's try to put the partisan issues aside. I repeat that all issues can [*sic*] be on the table for discussion. But, obviously, we cannot compromise the principles of our tax program without compromising our economic recovery and America's future.

I simply can't agree to increase taxes on families already pinching pennies to pay their bills. We want to reduce the deficit, not the recovery. And it would be foolhardy, indeed, to compromise America's defense rebuilding program just as we're beginning to restore the credibility that was so recklessly squandered.

Yet, this does not mean that there aren't areas in which to find bipartisan agreement. We could focus on the less contentious spending cuts still pending before the Congress. These could be combined with measures to close certain tax loopholes that the Treasury Department has indicated it believes worthy of support.

If we focus on what we might agree on, we can get something done for the people. And the Grace Commission has come up with some 2,500 recommendations for reducing wasteful government spending. We should examine them together.

Uniting to promote democracy, peace, and prosperity in the troubled region of Central America is a second area where Republicans and Democrats should work together. Last July, I appointed 12 distinguished Americans to the National Bipartisan Commission on Central America and asked former Secretary of State Henry Kissinger to serve as its Chairman. Three weeks ago, the members of that Commission delivered to me their report on the crisis confronting our Latin neighbors. Their recommendations are the basis of legislation that I will soon present to the Congress.

I should point out that the late Senator Henry Jackson first proposed the idea of the Bipartisan Commission on Central America, and he served until his death as one of its senior counselors. All his life, "Scoop" said what he believed and stuck to it. He believed in freedom, dignity for the individual, and a strong America. And he believed Republicans and Democrats should leave politics at the water's edge on important questions of national security. Senator Jackson's wisdom is the guiding spirit of our legislation. It offers a balance of political, economic, diplomatic, and security initiatives that can bring stability and a better life to our neighbors and ultimately greater security to our own country. This plan deserves the bipartisan support of the Congress. We have a responsibility to act.

Continued support for the peace process in the Middle East is a third critical area where Republicans and Democrats must rise above politics. We're working closely with Lebanon's President Gemayel to find a political solution. Support for his government is broadening among the different groups. And just as important, our efforts to strengthen the Lebanese Army and its ability to keep the peace are making sure and steady progress.

Yes, the situation in Lebanon is difficult, frustrating, and dangerous. But that is no reason to turn our backs on friends and to cut and run. If we do, we'll be sending one signal to terrorists everywhere: They can gain by waging war against innocent people.

The men and women who patrol our streets here at home also face great dangers every day. But the greatest danger of all would be to yank those police officers off the streets and to leave our neighborhoods and families at the mercy of criminals. If we're to be secure in our homes and in the world, we must stand together against those who threaten us. This is a time for unity, not partisan politics.

Until next week, thanks for listening, and God bless you.

Note: The President spoke at 12:06 P.M. EST from Camp David.

U.S.-Soviet Relations

February 11, 1984

My fellow Americans:

I'd like to speak to you about a subject always on the minds of Americans, but of particular interest today in view of the death of Soviet leader Yuri Andropov: our relations with the Soviet Union.

Changes of leadership have not happened often in the Soviet Union. Yuri Andropov was only the sixth Communist party leader in the 66 years since the Russian Revolution. In recent months, he'd been totally absent from public view, so his death did not come as a shock to the world. Nevertheless, the importance of the U.S.-Soviet relationship makes his passing away a time for reflection on where that relationship is heading.

The changes in Moscow are an opportunity for both nations to examine closely the current state of our relations and to think about the future. We know that our relationship is not what we would like it to be. We've made no secret of our views as to the reasons why. What is needed now is for both sides to sit down and find ways of solving some of the problems that divide us.

In expressing my condolences to Mr. Andropov's family and to the Soviet Government, I emphasized once again America's desire for genuine cooperation between our two countries. Together we can help make the world a better, more peaceful place. This was also the message for the Soviet people in my address on Soviet-American relations last month. In that speech, as in my private communications with the late Chairman Andropov, I stressed our commitment to a serious and intensive dialog with the Soviet Union, one aimed at building a more constructive U.S.-Soviet relationship.

This commitment remains firm, and Vice President Bush will lead our delegation to Moscow for Mr. Andropov's funeral. He will be accompanied by Senate Majority Leader Howard Baker, and our Ambassador in Moscow, Arthur Hartman. I hope there will be an opportunity for the Vice President to meet with the new General Secretary. As we engage in discussions with Soviet leaders, we recognize the fundamental differences in our values and in our perspectives on many international issues. We must be realistic and not expect that these differences can be wished away. But realism should also remind us that our two peoples share common bonds and interests. We are both relatively young nations with rich ethnic traditions and a pioneer philosophy. We have both experienced the terrible trauma of war. We have fought side by side in the victory over Nazi Germany. And, while our governments have very different views, our sons and daughters have never fought each other. We must make sure they never do.

Avoiding war and reducing arms is a starting point in our relationship with the Soviet Union.

But we seek to accomplish more. With a good faith effort on both sides, I believe the United States and the Soviet Union could begin rising above the mistrust and ill will that cloud our relations. We could establish a basis for greater mutual understanding and constructive cooperation, and there's no better time to make that good faith effort than now.

At this time of transition in the Soviet Union, our two nations should look to the future. We should find ways to work together to meet the challenge of preserving peace. Living in this nuclear age makes it imperative that we talk to each other, discuss our differences, and seek solutions to the many problems that divide us.

America is ready. We would welcome negotiations. And I repeat today what I have said before: We're prepared to meet the Soviets halfway in the search for mutually acceptable agreements. I hope the leaders of the Soviet Union will work with us in that same spirit. I invite them to take advantage of the opportunities at hand to establish a more stable and constructive relationship. If the Soviet Government wants peace, then there will be peace.

In recent days, millions of citizens inside the Soviet Union, the United States, and countries throughout the world have been brought together by one great event, the Winter Olympics. The competition is fierce and we cheer for the men and women on our respective teams. But we can, and should, celebrate the triumphs of all athletes who compete in the true spirit of sportsmanship and give the very best of themselves.

And when each race or event is done and our teams come together in friendship, we will remember that we are meant to be one family of nations.

We who are leaders in government have an obligation to strive for cooperation every bit as hard as our athletes who reach within for the greatest efforts of their lives. If the Soviet Government would join us in this spirit, then together we could build a safer and far better world for the human family, not just for today, but for generations to come.

Until next week, thanks for listening. God bless you.

Note: The President spoke at 9:06 A.M. PST from Rancho del Cielo, near Santa Barbara.

Crime and Criminal Justice Reform

February 18, 1984

My fellow Americans:

Shouldn't we have the right as citizens of this great country to walk our streets without being afraid and to go to bed without worrying the next sound might be a burglar or a rapist? Of course, we should.

But in reality we don't. The sad fact is too many of our friends and loved ones live in fear of crime. And there's no mystery as to why. For too many years, the scales of criminal justice were tilted toward protecting rights of criminals. Those in charge forgot or just plain didn't care about protecting your rights—the rights of law-abiding citizens.

We came to Washington determined to change that by restoring the proper balance to our criminal justice system and by assisting all of you who, through Neighborhood Watch-type programs, are trying to protect life, property, and security in your communities.

Common sense is beginning to pay off. In 1982, the crime rate dropped by 4.3 percent—the biggest decline since 1972. But we still face a tremendous challenge, and meeting that challenge is what I want to talk to you about today.

Since drugs are related to an enormous amount of violent crime, drug trafficking and organized crime are among our major targets. For the first time in this nation's history, we've thrown the resources of the F.B.I. into drug enforcement. A new border interdiction program is under way. Task forces aimed at drug gangs cover the nation, and they've indicted more than 1,300 persons in the last year.

In fact, since our administration came into office, the number of drug-related convictions has increased 33 percent. Since 1981, the number of enforcement agents, prosecutors, and the amount of funding and Federal cooperation with State and local agencies have all greatly increased.

Even the military is providing assistance in the fight against drug traffickers. But we still need to do more. We need new laws to stop drug traffickers from harming our people, especially our young people. And we need tougher laws to fight other forms of crime so we can make the lives of all Americans more secure.

This issue should never turn into a prolonged partisan struggle, but it has. The Senate recently passed overwhelmingly our Comprehensive Crime Control Act. The House has done nothing and continues to wait. But wait for what? Bottling up long-overdue reforms that would provide you, the people, greater protection against dangerous criminals is a serious mistake you should not tolerate.

Let me give you some examples of what's at stake here. One of our bill's reforms would create tougher laws permitting Federal prosecutors to seize the profits and assets of organized crime and drug traffickers. This would be a severe blow to the crime czars. Why should any right-minded person oppose it?

Another reform, involving the so-called "exclusionary rule," would allow evidence obtained reasonably and in good faith to be used in a criminal trial. How many times have we seen law enforcement officers handcuffed by the maze of technicalities that make collection and presentation of evidence so difficult?

Our bill also makes sentencing more uniform and certain. There's nothing complicated about this. The sentence imposed should be the sentence served, with no parole. Too many sentences today are inadequate and the time served too short.

Another important reform concerns bail. It's hard to imagine the present system being any worse. Except in capital cases, Federal courts cannot consider the danger a defendant may pose to others if released. The judge can only consider whether it's likely the defendant will appear for trial if granted bail. Recently, a man charged with armed robbery and suspected of four others was given a low bond and quickly released. Four days later, he and a companion robbed a bank and, in the course of the robbery, a policeman was shot. This kind of outrage happens again and again, and it must be stopped. So we want to permit judges to deny bail and lock up defendants who the government has shown pose a grave danger to their communities.

Our bill would also cut back on the misuse of insanity as a defense, strengthen child pornography laws, and provide greater financial assistance to State law enforcement programs. Independently of our crime package, we're mounting a major effort to combat crime such as sexual assault and family violence. We're also working hard to improve the justice system treatment of our fellow citizens who were the innocent victims of crime.

These reforms make good sense, and there's no excuse for not passing them. The liberal approach of coddling criminals didn't work and never will. Nothing in our Constitution gives dangerous criminals a right to prey on innocent, law-abiding people. I would hope the members of the House could remember this and bring up our bill for consideration without further delay. This is the most comprehensive anticrime legislation in more than a decade. In the interest of true justice and in recognition of this past week, National Crime Prevention Week, it deserves full debate and a vote. Perhaps you might inquire from your Representative if he or she is ready to act and, if not, why not.

Until next week, thanks for listening, and God bless you.

Note: The President spoke at 12:06 P.M. EST from the Oval Office at the White House.

Prayer in Public Schools

February 25, 1984

My fellow Americans:

From the early days of the colonies, prayer in school was practiced and revered as an important tradition. Indeed, for nearly 200 years of our Nation's history it was considered a natural expression of our religious freedom. But in 1962, the Supreme Court handed down a controversial decision prohibiting prayer in public schools.

Sometimes I can't help but feel the First Amendment is being turned on its head. Because, ask yourselves: Can it really be true that the First Amendment can permit Nazis and Ku Klux Klansmen to march on public property, advocate the extermination of people of the Jewish faith and the subjugation of blacks, while the same amendment forbids our children from saying a prayer in school?

When a group of students at the Guilderland High School in Albany, New York, sought to use an empty classroom for voluntary prayer meetings, the 2nd Circuit Court of Appeals said no. The Court thought it might be dangerous, because students might be coerced into praying if they saw the football captain or student body president participating in prayer meetings.

Then there was the case of the kindergarten class reciting a verse before their milk and cookies. They said, "We thank you for the flowers so sweet. We thank you for the food we eat. We thank you for the birds that sing. We thank you, God, for everything." But a Federal Court of Appeals ordered them to stop. They were supposedly violating the Constitution of the United States.

Teddy Roosevelt told us, "The American people are slow to wrath, but when their wrath is once kindled it burns like a consuming flame." Up to 80 percent of the American people support voluntary prayer. They understand what the Founding Fathers intended. The First Amendment of the Constitution was not written to protect the people from religion. That amendment was written to protect religion from government tyranny.

The amendment says, "Congress shall make no law respecting an establishment of religion or prohibiting the free exercise thereof." What could be more clear?

The act that established our public school system called for public education to see that our children learned about religion and morality. References to God can be found in the Mayflower Compact of 1620, the Declaration of Independence, the Pledge of Allegiance, and the National Anthem. Our legal tender states, "In God We Trust."

When the Constitution was being debated at the Constitutional Convention, Benjamin Franklin rose to say, "The longer I live, the more convincing proofs I see that God governs in the affairs of men. Without His concurring aid, we shall succeed in this political building no better than the builders of Babel." He asked: Have we now forgotten this powerful friend or do we imagine we no longer need His assistance? Franklin then asked the Convention to begin its daily deliberations by asking for the assistance of Almighty God.

George Washington believed that religion was an essential pillar of a strong society. In his Farewell Address, he said, "Reason and experience both forbid us to expect that national morality can prevail in exclusion of religious principle."

And when John Jay, the first Chief Justice of the United States Supreme Court, was asked in his dying hour if he had any farewell counsels to leave his children, Jay answered, "They have the Book."

But now we're told our children have no right to pray in school. Nonsense. The pendulum has swung too far toward intolerance against genuine religious freedom. It's time to redress the balance.

Former Supreme Court Justice Potter Stewart noted, if religious exercises are held to be an impermissible activity in schools, religion is placed in an artificial and State-created disadvantage. Permission for such exercises for those who want them is necessary if the schools are truly to be neutral in the matter of religion. And a refusal to permit them is seen not as the realization of State neutrality, but rather as the establishment of a religion of secularism.

The Senate will soon vote on a Constitutional amendment to permit voluntary vocal prayer in public schools. If two-thirds of the Senate approve, then we must convince the House leadership to permit a vote on the issue. I am confident that, if the Congress passes our amendment this year, then the State legislatures will do likewise and we'll be able to celebrate a great victory for our children.

Our amendment would ensure that no child be forced to recite a prayer. Indeed, it explicitly states this. Nor would the state be allowed to compose the words of any prayer. But the courts could not forbid our children from voluntary vocal prayer in their schools. And by reasserting their liberty of free religious expression, we will be helping our children understand the diversity of America's religious beliefs and practices.

If ever there was a time for you, the good people of this country, to make your voices heard, to make the mighty power of your will the decisive force in the halls of Congress, that time is now.

Until next week, thanks for listening, and God bless you.

Note: The President spoke at 12:06 P.M. EST from Camp David.

Budget Deficits

March 3, 1984

My fellow Americans:

If you had to choose between shrinking the size of government or shrinking the size of your paycheck, which would it be? Chances are you think you're paying enough taxes already. And I agree with you.

The trouble is, your opinions don't always count for much in Washington, D.C. It seems to be taken for granted here that the Federal Government has an automatic right to grow at your expense. Listening to people talk, you'd almost think government owns your earnings. So, please be a little skeptical when you hear the moaning from Washington's born-again deficit fighters. The truth is, these are the same people who brought us big and bloated government in the first place. And they haven't changed a bit.

The Democrats use foggy language like "recovering revenue" or "stopping the revenue drain," but you don't need a Ph.D. in bureaucracy to know what they're offering: a choice between a tax increase, a tax increase, or a tax increase.

In the downpayment deficit reduction talks at the White House, suggestions were made on behalf of liberal House Democrats—suggestions for making you pay more taxes. They added up to $100 billion or more. Some examples: liberal Democrats want very badly to eliminate indexing—that's the historic reform that will tie your tax brackets to the rate of inflation. Starting next year, you will no longer be pushed into a higher tax bracket just because you're receiving a cost-of-living raise. Keep in mind that indexing doesn't help the wealthy; they're already in the highest tax brackets. Indexing helps those who need help, but it deprives government of the automatic increase in its allowance, so the spenders want to get rid of it. And I don't intend to let them.

Another suggestion of theirs is a three-year postponement in additional estate tax reductions. This would be a cruel blow to surviving spouses of family-owned farms and businesses. Hasn't the farm community suffered enough with the last administration's grain embargo? And the liberals would raise personal tax rates on millions of families and small businesses. These tax increases are neither wise nor compassionate. And they wouldn't reduce the deficit, they'd just reduce the recovery. And none of us should want that.

Yes, deficits are a problem. I've been saying so for more than a quarter of a century now. But the problem is not the size of the deficit. It's the size of government's claim on our economy. Whether government borrows or increases taxes, it will be taking the same amount of money from the private economy. So, if we raise taxes before cutting spending, the money will just be spent; the deficit won't be reduced, and government will grow bigger.

Now, that's what the House Democrats tried to do last year. Their budget resolution would have raised your taxes, then squandered that money on new programs. Well, we have a better way to cut deficits—cut the growth of government by cutting out the waste. This will reduce government's claim on the people's earnings, leaving more money for you to borrow, spend, invest, and to help our economy grow.

Don't let anyone tell you it can't be done. We've already cut spending by more than $300 billion on a five-year basis. Contrary to what you've heard, we haven't done this by hurting the needy. Total spending on social programs has increased by $71 billion during these last three years.

To cite two examples frequently misrepresented, Social Security and Medicare benefits to America's senior citizens are higher than ever before, even after adjusting for inflation. We've been cutting the growth of government by eliminating waste. My Inspectors General have identified nearly $31 billion in agency fraud, waste, and abuse, and we're going after it.

For example, we've almost stopped the growth of delinquencies on amounts owed the Federal Government. And we boosted collections by $12.5 billion last year. As part of its new "get tough" policy, the Department of Education is cracking down on people who defaulted on their student loans, and they're recovering $390,000 a day. And believe me, there's plenty more waste to cut.

Those $300 billion in budget savings I mentioned are barely half of what we asked for from the Congress. And the Grace Commission made some 2,500 recommendations for reducing billions of dollars in wasteful government spending and subsidies.

I'll be speaking out on this topic in future radio talks, but one thing is clear: raising taxes is a cop-out; cutting waste in government is the right way to go. And this is what we're doing and what we'll continue to do. With your support, we can shrink government and stop the spendthrifts from shrinking your paychecks.

Until next week, thanks for listening, and God bless you.

Note: The President spoke at 12:06 P.M. EST from the Oval Office at the White House.

Economic Recovery

March 10, 1984

My fellow Americans:

During the last two years, the United States has risen from the depths of recession to one of the strongest recoveries in decades, from dark days of despair to a bright new dawn of promise and a hope for all Americans.

I remember saying back when things looked the worst that too much pessimism could be deadly. Well, some people criticized me for trying to sugarcoat bad news. I merely wanted us to remember that there's a psychological factor in recession, and too much hammering at it makes recession worse.

What pulled us through that ordeal, I'm convinced, was our determination to stick to our program, believe in ourselves, and trust in our values of faith, freedom, and hard work, values that have never failed us when we've lived up to them.

And now we're seeing the payoff. 1983 was a banner year for America, notwithstanding voices of pessimism which always found the single dark cloud in every blue sky. Those voices come from many different areas of our society. Recently The Wall Street Journal reported on a survey of one of them: the television networks' nightly news coverage of the economy during the last half of 1983. During that entire period, there were four to fifteen economic statistic stories a month telling us whether inflation, unemployment, interest rates, retail sales, or housing starts were up or down for a given month. The survey found nearly 95 percent of these reports were positive. However, of the 104 lengthy economic news stories in which the networks gave us their interpretation of what was happening, 86 percent were primarily negative. The survey found the economic news in the second half of 1983 was good. But the coverage on network television was still in recession.

Now, please don't get me wrong, every administration must be held accountable. None of us can be excluded from the fury of a free press whenever that's right and proper. But true balance implies consistently showing all faces of America, including hope, optimism, and progress.

Our economy is stronger than practically anyone predicted. The Index of Leading Economic Indicators has been up 16 of the last 17 months. Industrial production has risen 14 straight months. Housing starts climbed 60 percent in 1983 to the highest level in four years. Retail sales surged. Auto sales registered their best year since 1979. And, we had the steepest drop in the unemployment rate in more than thirty years. And yesterday, we learned that unemployment for all workers in February dropped to 7.7 percent. More Americans are now at work than ever before in this nation's history.

Here's one example that sums up the difference between yesterday's policies of depending on government and our approach that begins with trusting people. Last year, we were asked to raise taxes and appropriate money for a $3.5 billion program to put 300,000 people in make-work jobs over a year. We said no, because incentives produce economic recovery and strong, steady growth puts more people back to work than any government program. And it has.

Recovery has put as many people back to work each month as their program would in a year. We've added an average of 300,000 jobs every single month for the past 15 months, and almost 400,000 last month alone. That's 4.9 million additional workers working and paying taxes. Our economic recovery has become economic expansion. And the potential for new jobs and economic growth in the future is beyond our imagination.

The revolution in science and high technology is only beginning. Each time our knowledge expands, each time we push back frontiers of medicine, agriculture, and space, we will be creating entire new industries, modernizing older ones, and raising our standard of living.

The issue before America in 1984 is clear. Which direction will we go now—forward with optimism, faith, and confidence, continuing to build an opportunity society for all our people, or backward in pessimism and fear, surrendering to politicians who would dismantle our program because their agenda is to make government grow big and fat at your expense?

To serve that agenda, they need to dwell on bad news. So when good news comes, they're either dumbstruck or they pretend they didn't hear. Well, with your support, we'll keep our economy moving forward, and we'll keep America's rendezvous with an optimistic future.

Until next week, thanks for listening, and God bless you.

Note: The President spoke at 12:06 P.M. EST from Camp David.

St. Patrick's Day

March 17, 1984

My fellow Americans:

Happy St. Patrick's Day to all of you. You know, this is a day when those of us of Irish descent have an opportunity to boast a little, and, like good Irishmen, celebrate a lot. Because of the Irish, America today is a richer, brighter, freer, and, yes, a bit noisier land than it otherwise would have been.

But today all Americans can take pride in the rich diversity of America's ethnic heritage—especially the Irish-American contribution to that heritage. It's one reason why Nancy and I were delighted to host a lunch here at the White House yesterday for Prime Minister FitzGerald of Ireland. We all had a roaring good time, but there was some important business done as well.

The Prime Minister and I urged all Americans not to give support of any kind to the terrorist IRA element in Northern Ireland. Believe me, it was a call heartily endorsed by all the Irish-American political leaders who were present.

And second, the Prime Minister brought us a message of hope about peace and reconciliation of the problem of Northern Ireland. After all the tragedy of Northern Ireland, it was cheering to hear about groups who are working toward mutual tolerance, and peaceful and democratic solutions.

Here at home, as we prepare to greet the first days of spring, there is also reason for confidence and cheer. Good economic news is bursting out all over, and America's economy seems to be saying, "This is celebration time." Optimism is being bolstered by vigorous new growth, continued low inflation, and better prospects for reducing budget deficits.

Just yesterday we learned that the Producer Price Index rose only four tenths of 1 percent in February, a smaller rise than in January, and a solid sign that inflation remains in check. We're determined to keep the nightmare of runaway inflation from ever coming back. Housing starts reached 2.2 million units in February—the highest level in nearly 6 years. That's an 11-percent increase from the January level, which was revised up to 1.9 million units. And building permits, a signal of builders' intentions, also registered a strong increase, so that means continued housing strength in the months to come.

Combine these signs of economic confidence with a strong recovery in one industry after another—15 consecutive monthly increases in industrial production—business investments stronger than expected, growing research in science and technology, and a welcome rebirth of productivity growth, and we can understand how the United States' economy created nearly 5 million jobs in the last 15 months and has become the engine [*sic*] for a new era of worldwide economic expansion.

We're also making progress toward reducing projected budget deficits. For one thing, the sheer strength of America's economic growth, as measured by all those new jobs created in the last 15 months, means more people are supporting themselves and paying taxes and fewer people need government assistance. As I've said again and again, strong and steady economic growth is the best way to reduce deficits.

And, as you may have heard, I've just reached agreement with the Republican leadership in the Congress on a deficit-reduction package totaling some $150 billion over the next years. Just Thursday night, shortly after we reached agreement, the Senate Finance Committee concluded its work on a major portion of our package. I'm hopeful the entire package will be passed promptly by the Senate.

This $150-billion downpayment deserves strong bipartisan support in the House because it will reduce the deficit in a way that's effective, responsible, and fair by targeting $43 billion of savings in nondefense spending, $57 billion in defense authority reductions, and by raising some $48 billion in revenues, primarily from closing certain tax loopholes of questionable fairness.

Now, make no mistake. The defense cuts will slow our defense buildup somewhat, but not to a point of unacceptable risk. There will be no increase in tax rates on American families and no tax increases that would threaten the economic recovery. Continued strong growth with the prospect of deficits coming down and without renewed inflation spells a brighter future for America's economy, provided the Congress will just stick with our program.

Some might attribute our success to the "luck o' the Irish." Well, maybe we have enjoyed a bit of luck, but, believe me, the real reason is an economic recovery program based on common sense.

Until next week, thanks for listening, and God bless you.

Note: The President spoke at 12:06 P.M. EST from Camp David.

Elections in El Salvador

March 24, 1984

My fellow Americans:

Tomorrow is an historic [*sic*] for the beleaguered nation of El Salvador. Scores of international observers will watch as the people of El Salvador risk their lives to exercise a right we take for granted, the right to vote for their President.

This right of choice is not something that's in common—is common—in all of South or Central America. It contrasts sharply, for example, with Nicaragua where the Sandinistas staged a revolution in 1979 promising free elections, freedom of the press, freedom of religion. Despite these promises, the Sandinistas have consistently broken their word, and the elections that they've announced for November seemed designed only to consolidate their control.

Unlike El Salvador, the Nicaraguans don't want international oversight of their campaign and elections. When the members of the National Bipartisan Commission on Central America visited Nicaragua, the Sandinista dictators briefed them with Soviet intelligence and said the U.S. is the source of all evil.

In El Salvador, the members heard appreciation for our country's efforts to promote peace, democracy, and development. El Salvador is an emerging democracy plagued by a Communist insurgency and human rights abuses which must stop, but a nation which is strongly pro-American and struggling to make self-government succeed.

Nicaragua is a Communist dictatorship armed to the teeth, tied to Cuba and the Soviet Union, which oppresses its people and threatens its neighbors.

The stability of our Latin friends, indeed, the security of our own borders depends upon which type of society prevails—the imperfect democracy seeking to improve, or the Communist dictatorship seeking to expand.

The Bipartisan Commission warned that new Communist regimes could be expected to fall into the same pattern as Nicaragua, namely, expand their armed forces, bring in large numbers of Cubans and Soviet bloc advisors, and increase the repression of their own people and the subversion of their neighbors.

And the Commission warned that a rising tide of communism would likely produce refugees, perhaps millions of them, many of whom would flee to the United States.

Now, these tragic events are not written in stone; but they will happen if we do nothing or even too little. Based on the recommendations of the Commission, I sent the Congress in February a proposal to encourage democratic institutions, improve living conditions, and help our friends in Central America resist Communist threats. Three-fourths of our request is for economic and humanitarian assistance.

And that brings me to an important point: The people who argue that the root of violence and instability is poverty, not communism, are ignoring the obvious. But all the economic aid in the world won't be worth a dime if Communist guerrillas are determined and have the freedom to terrorize and to burn, bomb, and destroy everything from bridges and industries to power and transportation systems.

So, in addition to economic and humanitarian assistance, we must also provide adequate levels of security assistance to permit our friends to protect themselves from Cuban- and Soviet-supported subversion.

Military assistance is crucial right now to El Salvador. The Salvadoran people repudiated the guerrillas when they last voted in 1982, but continued Soviet, Cuban, and Nicaraguan support for the guerrillas, combined with the failure of our Congress to provide the level of military aid I've requested, have put El Salvador in an extremely vulnerable position. The guerrillas have been seizing the identification cards that allow citizens to vote. One of El Salvador's principal guerrilla commanders has pledged an all-out effort to disrupt the elections. And, should there be a need for an election run-off in late April or May, these same guerrillas, who have already assassinated elected Congressmen in El Salvador, will do everything they can to disrupt that election as well.

We're looking at an emergency situation. So I've asked Congress to provide immediate security assistance for El Salvador while the comprehensive bipartisan legislation makes its way through the Congress over the next several months.

This is the moment of truth. There is no time to lose. If the Congress acts responsibly, while the cost is still not great, then democracy in Central America will have a chance. If the Congress refuses to act, the cost will be far greater. The enemies of democracy will intensify their violence, more lives will be lost, and real danger will come closer and closer to our shores. This is no time for partisan politics.

Until next week, thanks for listening. God bless you.

Note: The President spoke at 12:06 P.M. EST from the Oval Office at the White House.

Opportunities for Women

March 31, 1984

My fellow Americans:

A few weeks ago, George Gallup, who regularly surveys the pulse of America, released a poll with very upbeat news. Gallup said the current mood of the American people is the brightest in five years. Our citizens still feel the burdens of everyday problems, but there's a feeling among us that we've finally turned the corner. Real progress is being made, and America is moving forward again.

Better days for America may be bad news for some, but even the most committed gloom-mongers can't deny the truth forever. Our economy is strong, prices are stable, jobs are increasing, and our nation is at peace. We're building a true opportunity society, and this is especially true for today's women.

Women in the eighties are a diverse majority with varied interests and futures. Some seek to pursue their own careers. Some run for political office, others focus on the home and family. Some seek to do all these things. They are members of a growing group called "working mothers," and sometimes their days resemble a script from "Mission Impossible."

Well, no role is superior to another. What's important is that every woman have the right and opportunity to choose the role she wishes, or, perhaps, try to fill them all. And whether the choice be homemaking, career, or both—our administration is trying to help in many different ways.

We've increased training opportunities through the Job Training Partnership Act so women can secure permanent, productive employment. For those whose former spouses are delinquent in child-support payments, we've strengthened the Federal child-support enforcement system, and we have additional proposals pending before the Congress.

For all women we've provided several forms of tax relief—relief, by the way, which could and should have been passed long ago by those in Washington who had a monopoly on power, and who still claim a monopoly on compassion.

We've reduced personal income tax rates by 25 percent. We've greatly reduced the marriage tax penalty. We've almost doubled the maximum child-care tax credit for working mothers. We've expanded IRA accounts, benefiting women whether they work at home or in paid jobs. And, we're moving to bring even greater equity to those accounts, and we've eliminated the widow's tax—the estate taxes levied on a surviving spouse. This will help women who've been hardworking partners on family farms and small businesses.

We're also working with the Congress on historic legislation that reforms inequities in private pension plans. This legislation has passed the Senate, and we're waiting for final action in the House. I hope it will come soon. The reforms would lower the age employees can participate in company pension plans, protect spouses from losing death benefits without their knowledge, permit a break in service of up to five years without loss of pension credit, coordinate State and Federal laws so divorced spouses can collect court-awarded pension benefits more easily, and require private pension plans to survivor's benefits—offer survivor's benefits, I should say, protection to workers after they're 45.

I've always believed the greatest contribution we can make is to get our economy moving and keep it moving. Economic growth will provide more opportunities for women than if all the promises ever made in Washington, D.C., were enacted into law.

Well, economic growth is very strong. And job opportunities for women are popping like springtime tulips. Three million more women are working today in our economy than in January 1981. One exciting area of growth is that of women-owned businesses. The number of businesses owned by women is increasing four times faster than those owned by men.

Yesterday, I met some of the people whose dreams, intelligence, and hard work are making America in 1984 the most forward-looking and successful nation in the world. I had lunch at the White House with the members of my Advisory Committee on Women's Business Ownership— twelve women and three men, all successful in the professional world. They're working with the Small Business Administration on conferences across the country to help women acquire skills to own businesses and compete effectively. They're also trying to identify problems business owners and potential business owners are meeting.

Now, if you've had any, please write to me at the White House, and I'll share your thoughts with the Advisory Committee. Next Thursday, I'll be traveling to New York to attend one of these conferences to meet with and to address women business owners of that great city.

All over this country the entrepreneur is changing the face and brightening the future of America, and she's just getting started.

Until next week, thanks for listening, and God bless you.

Note: The President spoke at 12:06 P.M. EST from Camp David.

Foreign Policy Challenges

April 7, 1984

My fellow Americans:

Yesterday I spoke here in Washington about America's foreign policy challenges and what we're doing to meet them. Well, I'd like to continue talking about those challenges today.

All Americans long for a safer world in which individual rights are respected and precious values flourish. But we're also realistic. We know we live in a troubled world and that we have global responsibilities. Our industries depend on energy and minerals from distant lands. Our prosperity requires a sound financial system and markets open to our goods. And our security is linked with the security of our allies and trading partners.

When I took office, we faced the greatest foreign policy challenges since World War II. Challenge number one was reducing the risk of nuclear war. Second, we had to try to help bring greater stability to regions riddled by terrorism and revolutionary violence that threatened our interests and, ultimately, our security. Third, we had to deal with an international economy that was crippled by soaring inflation rates, low growth, and predictions of an imminent global depression. Finally, we had to restore bipartisan support for a foreign policy that would meet our responsibilities.

How is America meeting her foreign policy challenges today? Well, much better. We've regained our strength and confidence. We're a leader again for peace and progress.

Reducing the risk of nuclear war means maintaining a secure military balance and pursuing every opportunity to reduce weapons by agreement. Today, America is safer because our defenses are stronger. We're offering the most sweeping arms control proposals in history, from reducing nuclear arms to banning chemical weapons.

Does the new Soviet leadership truly want to reach agreements that can make the world safer? They'll never convince the world they're sincere with harsh rhetoric and walk-outs. We do know they respect strength and, in time, we should expect that they will return to the negotiating table where all of us hope and pray that a safer world can be secured.

Our second challenge, peacemaking in troubled regions, has demanded a new direction. We're trying to bring all our strengths to bear. Economic aid alone won't stop Soviet-sponsored guerrillas, and individual rights aren't secure without peace. We need all the tools we have: diplomatic mediation, economic help, security assistance, and promotion of democratic reforms to address complex regional problems. The recent Presidential elections in El Salvador probably couldn't have been held if we'd followed any other approach. And for democracy to have a chance in the future, the Congress must pass the plan we've proposed, which follows the recommendations made by the National Bipartisan Commission on Central America.

Our third challenge, expanding opportunities for economic development and personal freedom, is also being met. America's powerful expansion is pulling the international economy forward. As we buy more from our friends, they buy more from us. Jobs, income, and opportunities increase for all. We've developed creative initiatives to spark private enterprise in the Caribbean. We're expanding our economic relationships with the growing nations of the Pacific Basin. And we're shoring up the international financial system.

You hear about the economic upturn. You don't hear enough about the democratic upturn. Ten years ago, fewer than half the people of Latin America and the Caribbean lived in democracies or countries embarked on a democratic transition. Today, 90 percent of the people do. The tide of the future is a freedom tide.

Finally, our fourth challenge, restoring bipartisan consensus to our foreign policy, is urgently needed. The Congress has given itself many new powers in foreign policy. Over 100 separate restrictions on executive authority were enacted in the 1970's. But the Congress hasn't yet accepted an equal sense of responsibility. We've had some successes in bipartisanship. The Scowcroft Commission helped create a consensus on arms control policy. And the bipartisan Kissinger Commission gave us a comprehensive set of recommendations on Central America. But we must go beyond recommendations to action. I applaud the Senate's approval this week of emergency security assistance to El Salvador, and I hope the House will give its approval.

When we develop a problem-solving plan to help build a safer world and a better world, there must be no Republicans or Democrats, just Americans pulling together.

Until next week, thanks for listening, and God bless you.

Note: The President spoke at 12:06 P.M. EST from the Oval Office at the White House.

Situation in Central America

April 14, 1984

My fellow Americans:

Much has been made of late regarding our proper role in Central America and, in particular, toward Nicaragua. Unfortunately, much of the debate has ignored the most relevant facts. Central America has become the stage for a bold attempt by the Soviet Union, Cuba, and Nicaragua to install communism, by force, throughout this hemisphere.

The struggling democracies of Costa Rica, Honduras, and El Salvador are being threatened by a Soviet bloc and Cuban-supported Sandinista army and security force in Nicaragua that has grown from about 10,000, under the previous government, to more than 100,000 in less than five years.

Last year alone the Soviet bloc delivered over $100 million in military hardware. The Sandinistas have established a powerful force of artillery, multiple rocket-launchers, and tanks in an arsenal that exceeds that of all the other countries in the region put together.

More than 40 new military bases and support facilities have been constructed in Nicaragua—all with Soviet bloc and Cuban support—and an investment of over $300 million. In addition to money and guns, there are now more than 2,500 Cuban and Soviet military personnel in Nicaragua, another 5,000 so-called "civilian advisors," as well as PLO, East German [East-bloc],* and Libyan assistance to the Sandinistas.

And that's not all. Our friends in the region must also face the export of subversion across their borders that undermines democratic development, polarizes institutions, and wrecks their economies. This terrorist violence has been felt by all of Nicaragua's neighbors, not just El Salvador. There have been bombings in peaceful Costa Rica, and numerous attempts to penetrate Honduras—most recently last summer, when the Sandinistas infiltrated an entire guerrilla colony [column]* which had been trained and equipped in Cuba and Nicaragua.

El Salvador, struggling to hold democratic elections and improve the conditions of its people, has been the main target of Nicaragua's covert aggression. Despite promises to stop, the Sandinistas still train and direct terrorists in El Salvador and provide weapons and ammunition they use against the Salvadoran people. If it weren't for Nicaragua, El Salvador's problems would be manageable, and we could concentrate on economic and social improvements.

Much of the Sandinista terror has been aimed at the Nicaraguan people themselves. The Sandinistas who govern Nicaragua have savagely murdered, imprisoned, and driven from their homeland tens of thousands of Miskito, Rama, and Suma Indians. Religious persecution against Christians has increased, and the Jewish community has fled the country. The press is censored, and activities of labor and business are restricted.

The Sandinistas have announced elections for November, but don't hold your breath. Will new parties be permitted? Will they have full access to the press, TV, and radio? Will there be unbiased observers? Will every adult

---

*White House corrections

Nicaraguan be allowed to vote? Given their record of repression, we should not wonder that the opposition, denied other means of expression, has taken up arms.

We've maintained a consistent policy toward the Sandinista regime, hoping they can be brought back from the brink peacefully through negotiations. We're working through the Contadora process for a verifiable multilateral agreement, one that insures [*sic*] the Sandinistas terminate their export of subversion, reduce the size of their military forces, implement their democratic commitments to the Organization of American States, and remove Soviet-bloc and Cuban military personnel.

But the Sandinistas, uncomfortable with the scrutiny and concern of their neighbors, have gone shopping for a more sympathetic hearing. They took their case to the United Nations and now to the International Court of Justice. This does little to advance a negotiated solution. But it makes sense if you're trying to evade the spotlight of responsibility.

What I've said today is not pleasant to hear. But it's important that you know Central America is vital to our interests and to our security. It not only contains the Panama Canal, it sits astride some of the most important sea-lanes in the world. Sea-lanes in which a Soviet-Cuban naval force held combat maneuvers just this week.

The region also contains millions of people who want and deserve to be free. We cannot turn our backs on this crisis at our doorstep. Nearly 23 years ago, President Kennedy warned against the threat of Communist penetration in our hemisphere. He said, "I want it clearly understood that this government will not hesitate in meeting its primary obligations which are to the security of our nation." We can do no less today.

I have, therefore, after consultation with the Congress, decided to use one of my legal authorities to provide money to help the government of El Salvador defend itself.

Until next week, thanks for listening. God bless you.

Note: The President spoke at 12:06 P.M. EST from the Oval Office at the White House.

Federal Income Taxation

April 21, 1984

My fellow Americans:

As a boy growing up in Illinois, swimming was an important part of my life. Pools weren't very common or affordable in those days, so my swimming was done in the Rock River.

I soon learned that swimming with the current downstream was a lot easier than swimming upstream. Nevertheless, today, I'm going to swim against the current. The current I'm talking about is a riptide of criticism that claims this administration's economic policies impoverish the poor and bestow benefits on the rich. This distorted view was created by special-interest demagoguery and political-year oratory dutifully reported by a goodly portion of the press.

A week or so ago, there was a report complete with impressive figures showing that our economic policy has punished people at the poverty level. The report was accurate that, in 1978, an income of $6,662 was the poverty level. It is also accurate that inflation has now pushed the poverty level up to $10,180. In other words, it takes that much to buy what $6,662 would buy in 1978. Critics have concluded on the basis of this report that, because of our economic program, those at that level were much poorer than they had been in 1978. Well, they're right that those at the poverty level have not kept up, but wrong as to what is to blame. It certainly isn't our tax cut, which is helping low-income earners keep more of their hard-earned dollars.

Part of it was caused by the biggest single tax increase in history, which had been passed back in 1977, calling for several successive increases in the Social Security payroll tax to take place between 1977 and 1990. During that same period, by the way, there will be increases in the amount of earnings subject to the tax up to more than $52,800.

But this is only part of the reason those people at the poverty level are having trouble keeping up, and it hasn't anything to do with our across-the-board 25-percent cut in the income tax. The simple truth is, the income tax does not take into account the value of your dollars. It's based on the number of dollars you earn. So even though $10,180 is only worth as much in purchasing power as $6,662 was a few years ago, you have to pay income tax on those $3,500 additional dollars just as if you gained that much in purchasing power.

Now, let's take a look at that other drumbeat—that our tax cut is designed to help the rich get richer and either does nothing for the low- or middle-income earners, or even worse, adds to their burden, and how they arrive at that conclusion. Well, it's true that if your tax burden is $100, your tax cut is only $25. But if your tax is $1,000, your saving is $250, ten times as much. But the ratio stays the same. If your tax burden was ten times as much before, you're still paying ten times as much tax.

There's a better test of whether one group benefits more than another. Did the tax cut increase or decrease the share of the total tax paid by the earners at various levels? In 1982, the last year for which we have complete figures, all those with incomes below $20,000 a year paid 10-percent smaller share of total income tax revenue than they did in 1981. From $20,000 to

$50,000, the share only dropped by 1 percent. From $50,000 up, the share of total tax increased by 7 percent. And if you break that group down to those earning $500,000 and up, their share of the total income tax burden increased by 43 percent.

This, then, is the best-kept secret about our tax cut. The wealthiest Americans are carrying a higher share of the total tax burden after our tax cut than they were before.

Next year, another part of our tax program will go into effect. It's called indexing, and will begin on January 1st. Very simply, it means you will no longer pay an income tax on inflation, which you've done every time a raise or cost-of-living increase pushed you into a higher tax bracket. The greatest beneficiaries of indexing will be those in the lower- and middle-income tax brackets. It will do little for the so-called rich because they're already in top tax brackets.

Many of those who were the loudest in declaring our tax program unfair want to cancel indexing before it goes into effect. Cancelling indexing would increase the tax burden for lower- and middle-income earners by three times as large a percentage as it would for the rich.

And one last point—perhaps the most important. Our program is stimulating strong economic growth, creating more jobs and opportunity than ever before.

Well, so much for swimming upstream. Until next week, thanks for listening. God bless you.

Note: The President spoke at 9:06 A.M. PST from Rancho del Cielo, near Santa Barbara.

Trip to China

April 28, 1984

My fellow Americans:

I'm sure you've heard that Nancy and I are traveling a long way from home this week. We've already flown more than 9,000 miles, stopping off in the beautiful islands of Hawaii to visit the citizens of our 50th state; and then across the International Dateline to Guam where the rays of each sunrise first touch the Stars and Stripes; and then on to our primary destination, China, one of the world's oldest civilizations and a country of great importance in today's Pacific community of nations.

This is our second trip to Asia in the last six months. It demonstrates our awareness of America's responsibility as a Pacific leader in the search for regional security and economic well-being. The stability and prosperity of this region are of crucial importance to the United States. The nations comprising the Pacific Basin represent our fastest growing trading markets. Many say that the 21st century will be the century of the Pacific.

Our relations with China have continued to develop through the last four administrations, ever since President Nixon made his historic journey here in 1972. In 1978, the Chinese leadership decided to chart a new course for their country, permitting more economic freedom for the people in an effort to modernize their economy. Not surprisingly, the results have been positive.

Today, China's efforts to modernize, foster the spirit of enterprise, open its doors to the West, and expand areas of mutual cooperation while opposing Soviet aggression make it a nation of increasing importance to America and to prospects for peace and prosperity in the Pacific.

When Nancy and I arrived in Beijing, we were touched by the friendly hospitality of the Chinese people, and we've been delighted to see the sweeping vistas, the bustling activity, and the many hallmarks of history in this great, old city.

In Beijing, narrow residential streets, traditional one-story houses, and treasures like the Forbidden City, a former Imperial Palace, first erected in 1420, are interspersed with modern high-rises and wide avenues. The streets are normally filled with people riding bicycles. All of you who like bike riding would love Beijing.

From the first moment, our schedule has been fully packed. I've already had extensive meetings with the Chinese leaders—President Li, Prime Minister Zhao, General Secretary Hu, and Chairman Deng. I had the honor of addressing a large group of Chinese and American leaders in science and industry in the Great Hall of the People, and I've spoken to the people of China over Chinese television.

We've also squeezed in some side trips—first, to the magnificent Great Wall, built by the Chinese more than 2,000 years ago to protect their country from outside invaders; and tomorrow, to the ancient city of Xi'an, an archaeological treasure considered the cradle of Chinese civilization and located in a fertile plain near the Yellow River.

In all of our meetings and appearances, I've stressed one overriding point—different as to our two forms of government—different as they may be, the common interests that bind our two peoples are even greater. Namely, our determination to build a better life and to resist aggressors who violate the rights of law-abiding nations and endanger world peace.

When people have the opportunity to communicate, cooperate, and engage in commerce, they can often produce astonishing results. We've already agreed to cooperate more closely in the areas of trade, technology, investment, and exchange of scientific and managerial expertise. And we've reached an important agreement on the peaceful uses of nuclear energy for economic development.

Our last stop in China will be Shanghai, a center of culture and commerce. We plan to visit the Shanghai Foxboro Company, where Americans and Chinese are making high-technology equipment to help advance China's industries. And I'll also visit with the students at Fudan University and speak to them about the meaning of America, the challenges our people face, and the dreams we share.

We can learn much from the rich history of China and from the wisdom and character of her people. And I've told the Chinese that Americans are people of peace, filled with the spirit of innovation and a passion for progress to make tomorrow better than today.

Our two nations are poised to take an historic step forward on the path of peaceful cooperation and economic development. I'm confident that our trip will be a significant success, resulting in a stronger U.S.-China relationship than before. For Americans, this will mean more jobs and a better chance for a peaceful world.

Until next week, thanks for listening, and God bless you.

Note: The President spoke at 9:02 A.M. (Local) from the Diaoyutai Guest House, Beijing, People's Republic of China. His address was broadcast on radio stations in the United States at 12:06 P.M. EST.

Defaults on Student Loans/Reducing Waste in Government

May 5, 1984

My fellow Americans:

When I spoke to you a week ago we were in China working to strengthen cooperation between our two countries, increase opportunities for jobs and a better life for our people, and improve the prospects for a more peaceful world.

As I told the citizens of Alaska when we arrived back in the States, I feel we made significant progress.

Today, I'd like to speak about our efforts toward another goal, one that might not get the headlines of a trip to China, but that nonetheless has an important impact on our lives. I'm talking about reducing waste, fraud, abuse, and mismanagement in government—problems that for too long were permitted to grow and spread like an unchecked cancer, plundering your pocketbooks and hindering government's ability to provide essential public services in an efficient and timely manner.

Our administration is determined to reverse the years of neglect and get this monster under control so we can have a government of, by, and for the people again, not the other way around.

That's why we're pushing comprehensive measures like Reform 88, which involves over 1,000 different projects to upgrade the management of the Federal Government; and why we're moving to implement recommendations of the Grace Commission which I established, and which has identified billions of dollars in wasteful government spending.

Let me give you some specific ways in which we've begun to make progress in improving government's management practices—doing what others said couldn't be done.

First, debt collection: For too long Washington seemed only to care about handing money out, not collecting debts owed. In fact, collection practices were so bad, the Federal Government didn't even know how much was owed and how much was overdue. We inherited a delinquency rate that was growing at the shocking rate of almost 30 percent a year. In the $8-billion guaranteed student loan program, one student out of ten defaults on his or her loan. These defaults each year equaled enough money to give loans to about 700,000 eligible students.

Well, with support from the Congress, we're taking a tough new stance on collections. We're not singling out any individuals or groups, but we can, we must, and we will go after the cheaters who profit from the system at the expense of honest citizens like yourselves who live by the rules.

For instance, one military surgeon in Hawaii refused to pay his student debt, even though he made over $50,000 a year and owned seven pieces of real estate. After being threatened with litigation, he paid in one lump sum the $11,500 that he owed.

Tens of thousands of Federal employees have been reneging on their student loans. They will get one last chance to pay up before finding their July paychecks smaller. Call it enforced repayment through cuts in take-home pay.

Justice Department officials are now aggressively pursuing those who default on loans by putting new emphasis on collection of debts and fines. Our U.S. attorneys collected $201 million last year—a return of $24 for every dollar invested.

The second area—waste, fraud, and abuse—is the by-product of mismanagement. Our management improvements, together with the tremendous accomplishments of our Inspectors General, are a one-two punch taking steam out of the waste and fraud that was eroding faith in our government.

Not only have billions in waste and fraud been rooted out, but preventive actions are nipping problems in the bud before they occur. We're making a very determined effort to crack down on white-collar crime—those who abuse positions of power for their own benefit. Both the Department of

Transportation and the Environmental Protection Agency are pushing nationwide investigations of bid rigging in the awarding of contracts for Federal highway and waste-water treatment facility construction.

The Justice Department has already initiated 270 criminal prosecutions in highway bid rigging involving 255 corporations and 256 individuals in 20 States.

You've all heard of the problems at the Pentagon with spare parts suppliers charging outrageous prices. Well, what you haven't heard is that this waste was actually uncovered by Department of Defense auditors working for the Inspector General I appointed. We are the first administration which has faced up to these abuses and taken action to correct them. The progress we've made is a good start, but it's little more than a ripple in the river of waste, fraud, and abuse that's been rising for years. That's why it's clear the way to reduce the deficit is by strong economic growth and by reducing wasteful, bloated government, not by raising taxes on you, the people.

Until next week, thanks for listening, and God bless you.

Note: The President spoke at 12:06 P.M. EDT from Camp David.

Education

May 12, 1984

My fellow Americans:

I want to talk to you today about a wonderful thing that's happening in our country. It began a year ago, so it's only just begun. But already it's changing our country, and I think it may change it forever. I'm talking about the recent progress in America's schools

You may remember the day a year ago when the National Commission on Excellence in Education came out with its report on what was wrong with the nation's schools. The Commission documented 20 solid years of decline, decline in academic standards and discipline, decline in authority and scholastic results. The Commission said a rising tide of mediocrity was wiping out America's reputation for the best education system in the world. That report was electrifying, and its current swept the country.

Parents and teachers got together, marshaled their resources, and began to turn the situation around. So now, one year later, we can report that together we have met the rising tide of mediocrity with a tidal wave of school reforms.

Those reforms reflect the Commission's advice: get back to basics, tighten standards, heighten academic requirements, and remember discipline in the classroom is vital. In short, make sure that Johnny and Mary can read and write, and make sure their school is allowed the peace without [*sic*] no student can learn and no teacher can instruct.

I want you to listen to some of the things that have happened since the Commission made its recommendations. Thirty-five States have raised high-school graduation requirements. Twenty-one States are reviewing steps to make textbooks more challenging. Eight States have lengthened the school day. Seven have lengthened the school year. And every State in the Union has put together a task force to improve its educational system. School districts across the country are moving toward requiring four years of English in high school and three solid years each of math and science. Many legislatures are currently developing workable and fair merit pay plans. Many States have increased teachers' salaries.

The private sector, too, is playing a big part in the reforms. Local businesses are adopting local schools, sending in their executives and employees to work with students and teachers to make education more exciting and more pertinent to the 1980's.

We're seeing a willingness to reconsider what our schools should be teaching. In the State of Maryland, a commission concluded students aren't being taught enough about American traditions of freedom and liberty. A bipartisan panel came up with a plan to teach students the most basic of democratic arts, the art of citizenship.

In New Jersey, Governor Tom Kane [*sic*] had another creative idea—give scientists and mathematicians in private industry a form of teaching accreditation so that they can go into the schools and teach what they know.

Last year, as part of our program to encourage academic excellence, we began the President's Academic Fitness Awards, a scholastic version of the Physical Fitness Awards. Well, participation in the program exceeded our estimates by 400 percent.

This month, 220,000 high-school seniors, who had maintained high marks and achieved high scores on scholastic aptitude tests, won the Academic Fitness Awards. And yesterday, on the South Lawn of the White House, I personally gave the awards to 60 students from around the country. Just seeing their proud faces spoke a world of words about the importance of education to our country's future and the spirit of renewal that's under way.

This entire reform movement proves how wrong the people are who always insist money is the only answer to the problems of our schools. Well, leaving aside the fact that the 20 years they kept shoveling money in was [*sic*] the same 20 years in which the schools deteriorated, I think it's fair to say they missed the essential point: Money was never the problem. Leadership was. Leadership in getting the schools back to basic values, basic traditions, and basic good sense.

With the leadership of plain American citizens, we're getting back on track. Much remains to be done. Our administration will go forward with our efforts to control school crime, pass tuition tax credits and school vouchers as well. And, once again, I'll continue working for the restoration of voluntary school prayer. For nothing is as basic as acknowledging the God from whom all knowledge springs.

But we can be proud of the progress we're making. And I think this is only the first chapter of a marvelous story about how the people of America came together to recreate a school system that was once the envy of the world.

Let's all write the next chapter together.

Until next week, thanks for listening, and God bless you.

Note: The President spoke at 12:06 P.M. EDT from Camp David.

Summer Jobs for Youth

May 19, 1984

My fellow Americans:

I want to talk to you today about our young people and what we can do to provide them an all-important opportunity—a summer job. This is a crucial time for young jobseekers, May being the month many firms make their summer hiring decisions.

Why are summer jobs so important for teenagers? Well, because when young people are exposed to the world of work, they can reap a wealth of benefits that often remain with them for a lifetime—values of personal initiative, self-reliance, and hard work; practical experience which teaches skills that impart confidence in the ability to compete in the permanent job market; the beginning of work history and references, which are vital to successful careers; and, of course, earnings, which can make the difference between going on to college and greater educational achievements or not.

I'll always remember my first job. I was 14 at the time, and I wound up finding work with a construction company that was remodeling homes. By summer's end, I was laying hardwood floors, shingling roofs, and painting houses.

I recognize that a lot of rules and regulations have changed since then. Fourteen-year-olds can't receive those kinds of opportunities today. But what of those who receive no opportunity to work at all?

That is a crushing disappointment, not just for those individuals who may lose motivation and, eventually, self-respect, but also for our economy, because we're literally throwing away America's most precious resource—our next generation.

The problem of teenage unemployment is most severe among our black and other minority youth. For some time now, the unemployment rate among black youth has been more than twice as high as that for all youth. And while the current economic expansion has brought the overall unemployment rate down with record speed, the drop in black teenage unemployment has been far less dramatic.

As of April, the unemployment rate for all youth, 16 through 19 years of age, was 19.4 percent. Among black teenagers, that rate was 44.8 percent. If a 19.4-percentage unemployment rate is unacceptable, and it is, then a 44.8-percent unemployment rate is a national tragedy. And neither must be allowed to persist.

Our administration has been working hard on this problem, and we're beginning to make headway. But we want and intend to do much more. Clearly, if the dream of America is to be preserved, we must not waste the genius of one mind, the strength of one body, or the spirit of one soul. We must use every asset we have. And our greatest progress will come by mobilizing the power of private enterprise.

We're supporting an extension of the Targeted Jobs Tax Credit program, providing major incentives for employers to hire more disadvantaged youth. Employers can receive tax credits of as much as 85 percent on the first $3,000 in wages they pay. Last year almost 300,000 young Americans were hired out of this program.

The Job Training Partnership Act is another important initiative. The act grants $1.9 billion to States, of which 40 percent must be earmarked for training youth for private-sector jobs. Many private firms are cooperating in this program, and I hope many more will do so in coming weeks.

But one of the barriers to more jobs for youth is the single minimum wage system, because the cruel truth is, while everyone must be assured a fair wage, there's no compassion in mandating $3.35 an hour for start-up jobs that simply aren't worth that much in the marketplace. All that does is guarantee that fewer jobs for teenagers will be created and fewer young people will be hired.

So, we're proposing youth employment opportunity wage legislation that can create more than 400,000 new summer jobs for youth. Our bill would allow employers to hire young people at a lower minimum wage during the summer months. And our legislation would do this without displacing adults. The bill explicitly prohibits employers from displacing adults in order to hire youth at the summer wage.

I'm delighted this concept has been endorsed by the National Conference of Black Mayors. Thanks to the strength of the economy, some 8½ million young people are likely to be employed this summer, an increase over last year.

But America can do better, and must do better, if we're to bring those teenage unemployment rates down further. I'm asking the Congress to pass our youth employment opportunity wage legislation. But I also want to request that all employers review their operations with the aim of creating more summer jobs. You, the business leaders of America, can make a great difference, and the time to act is now.

Until next week, thanks for listening, and God bless you.

Note: The President spoke at 12:06 P.M. EDT from Camp David.

Economic Recovery/National Defense

May 26, 1984

My fellow Americans:

I want to talk to you today about a few elements of America's progress. First: The economy. We've seen some increases in interest rates in recent weeks, and, of course, we don't like that. But we're not about to panic or be buffaloed by the pessimists who ignore the great progress we've made during these last three and a half years.

In 1980, double-digit inflation was a silent thief of every paycheck. Today, it's been cut by nearly two-thirds. For the last two years, it's been under 4 percent.

I mentioned interest rates. Recently, the prime rate climbed from 10.5 percent to 12.5 percent, and that means mortgage rates have also risen. These increases must be laid to fear that inflation is coming back. Well, we're determined to see that it doesn't.

Tax rates have also dropped by nearly 25 percent. If our tax program had not been passed, a median-income family would be paying over $900 a year more in taxes than it does today. And next year, your tax rates will be indexed. From then on, a cost-of-living raise won't bump you into a higher tax bracket.

For years, government has used inflation as a silent partner to raise your taxes without having to pass a tax increase and take the heat for doing so. With indexing, you'll be protected against that kind of theft.

So, with inflation down, interest rates still down significantly, and taxes no longer rising, America is moving forward with impressive power. By virtually any yardstick, our economy is coming back. America is coming back. And for the first time in a long time, hope for the future is coming back.

The strength of the economy continues to defy the experts. Gross National Product—the sum total of what our economy produces—rose 3.4 percent in 1983 and a healthy 8.8 percent in the first quarter of 1984. Back in 1980, Gross National Product went down by three-tenths of 1 percent.

Jobs are coming back. Nearly 5.5 million Americans found work during the last 17 months—the fastest drop in unemployment in over 30 years. Today, some 106 million of us are working, more than ever before in our history. And last year, some 100,000 new businesses started up. That's a five-year high that means more jobs for the future.

Housing is coming back. Three years ago, even the smallest house seemed completely out of reach. The median monthly mortgage payment shot up from $333 in 1977 to $688 in 1981. During that time, the median price for a home went up by $23,000. Since then, monthly mortgage payments have risen only $10. Today, more Americans can afford homes, and more of us are buying homes—some 10,000 each day.

The auto industry is recovering. Domestic car sales dropped by almost 3 million units between 1977 and 1981. Since then, they've increased by 1 million, and they're selling at the fastest rate in five years.

Past recoveries from recession were snuffed out by a rekindling of inflation. Well, this time, inflation is staying down, and we mean to keep it down. In the last 12 months, the Producer Price Index for finished goods—one indicator of future inflation—has risen less than 3 percent. If inflation stays down, interest rates will come down, too, and our economy will keep expanding.

There's another area where America was weak, but is now regaining strength—national defense. Our ability to deter war and protect our security declined dangerously during the 1970's. By 1979 defense spending, as a percent of our total economy, had reached its lowest level in 20 years. Since 1981 we've begun to rebuild America's security and restore the morale, training, and readiness of our Armed Forces.

Our precious freedoms are more secure today than they were 3 years ago. A stronger economy and greater security are good news, but we still face great challenges. We must eliminate billions of dollars in wasteful government spending. We must make our tax system simple and fair, so we can bring your personal income tax rates down further and keep our economy growing. And, we must keep our defenses strong, so the Soviets will decide it's time to return to the negotiating table and work with us to reduce armaments and assure a more peaceful world.

We've made a new beginning. Americans feel prouder and stronger that things are getting better, and rightly so.

Until next week, thanks for listening, and God bless you.

Note: The President spoke at 12:06 P.M. EDT from Camp David.

Trip to Ireland/D-Day Anniversary

June 2, 1984

My fellow Americans:

Top o' the morning to you. I'm speaking from a small town named
Cong in western Ireland, first stop in a ten-day trip that will also take Nancy
and me to France and England. We're in an area of spectacular beauty over-
looking a large lake filled with islands, bays, and coves. And those of you
who, like me, can claim the good fortune of Irish roots may appreciate the
tug I felt yesterday in my heart when we saw the Emerald Isle from Air
Force One.

I thought of words from a poem about Ireland:

> A place as kind as it is green,
> The greenest place I've ever seen.

I told our welcoming hosts that to stand with them on the soil of my
ancestors was, for this great-grandson of Ireland, a very special moment. It
was a moment of joy.

Earlier today we were in Galway, a coastal city celebrating its 500th
anniversary. Legend has it Columbus prayed at a church there on his way to
the New World. For a thousand years, Ireland was considered the western
edge of civilization, and a place that continued to revere learning during a
time of darkness on the continent of Europe.

That reverence earned Ireland its reputation as "The Island of Saints
and Scholars." I was pleased to address representatives of University College
in Galway, to speak to them of Ireland's many contributions to America, and
to give thanks for those great, great forces of faith and love for liberty and
justice that bind our people.

The President of that institution, Dr. O'Heocha, also chaired a group
called the New Ireland Forum which has sought to foster a spirit of tolerance
and reconciliation in Northern Ireland. So, the spiral of violence that has cast
so many innocent lives there, or cost so many, I should say, finally can be
ended.

Ireland is a beautiful, proud, and independent land with a young and
talented population. But they have an employment problem. By the strength
of our economy, and by the presence of some 300 U.S. firms here, Americans
can, and will, help our Irish cousins create jobs and greater opportunities.
And, of course, what helps them will help us, too.

Tomorrow, Nancy and I will travel to Ballyporeen for a nostalgic visit to
the original home of the Reagan clan. On Monday, we'll be in Dublin where
I'll have the honor of addressing a Joint Session of the Irish Parliament, as
John Kennedy did here 21 years ago.

When we leave Ireland, we'll be participating in two events that mark America's determination to help build a safer, more prosperous world.

On June 6th, I'll join former U.S. Army Rangers at the historic battlefield of Pointe du Hoc and later President Mitterrand and other American veterans at Omaha Beach and Utah Beach on the Normandy coast of France. Together, we'll commemorate the 40th anniversary of D-Day, the great Allied invasion that set Europe on the course toward liberty, democracy, and peace.

That great battle and the war it helped bring to an end mark the beginning of nearly 40 years of peace in Europe—a peace preserved not by goodwill alone but by the strength and moral courage of the NATO Alliance. On June 6th, I will reaffirm America's faithful commitment to NATO. If NATO remains strong and unified, Europe and America will remain free. If NATO can continue to deter war, Europe and America can continue to enjoy peace—40 more years of peace.

And let me make one thing very plain. A strong NATO is no threat to the Soviet Union. NATO is the world's greatest peace movement. It never threatens; it defends. And we will continue trying to promote a better dialog with the Soviet Union. The Soviets could gain much by helping us make the world safer, particularly through arms reductions. That would free them to devote more resources to their people and economy.

Growth and prosperity will occupy our attention when we return to London for the annual Economic Summit of the major industrialized countries. And we'll be marking another important anniversary: Fifty years ago, America's leaders had the vision to enact legislation known as the Reciprocal Trade Agreements Act of 1934. It helped bring an end to a terrible era of protectionism that nearly destroyed the world's economies.

We'll talk about how best to maintain the recent progress that has lifted hopes for a worldwide recovery for our common prosperity. You can be proud that the strength of the United States economy has led the way. I believe continued progress lies with freer trade and more open markets. Less protectionism and [*sic*] will mean more progress, more growth, more jobs, a bigger slice of the pie for everyone.

As we meet in Normandy and London, we'll have much to be thankful for, much to be optimistic about, but still much to do.

Until next week, thanks for listening, and God bless you.

Note: The President spoke at 5:11 P.M. (Local) from Galway, Ireland. His address was broadcast on radio stations in the United States at 12:06 P.M. EDT.

Trip to London/Economic Summit

June 9, 1984

My fellow Americans:

Greetings from London. As you probably know, Nancy and I have been in Europe for eight days, visiting Ireland, commemorating the 40th anniversary of D-Day at Normandy, and now meeting with the leaders of the major industrialized countries at the Economic Summit to strengthen the basis for freedom, prosperity, and peace.

Change comes neither easily nor quickly in foreign affairs. Finding solutions to critical global problems requires lengthy and sustained efforts, the kind we've been making ever since my first Economic Summit in Ottawa in 1981. Those efforts are now paying off as we reap the benefits of sound policies. Think back four years—America was weak at home and abroad. Remember double-digit inflation, 20-percent interest rates, zero growth, and those never-ending excuses that such misery would be part of our lives for years to come. And remember how our foreign policy invited Soviet aggression and expansion in Afghanistan, Central America, and Africa. Entire countries were lost. Doubt spread about America's leadership in defense of freedom and peace. And so, freedom and peace became less secure.

Well, a lot has changed. Today, America stands taller in the world. At home we've made a fundamental change in direction—away from bigger and bigger government, toward more power and incentives for people; away from confusion and failure, toward progress through commitment to the enduring values of Western civilization; away from weakness and instability, toward peace through strength and a willingness to negotiate.

Together, with our allies, we've tried to adopt a similar strategy for progress abroad—guided by realism, by common values and interests, and by confidence that we will not remain prisoners of fear and a disappointing past. We can and will move forward to better days.

Last year, the United States hosted the Williamsburg Summit. It had been an active year for allied relations as we grappled with economic and security problems, but we didn't dwell on differences. We joined in a peace and security statement and a blueprint for world economic recovery. Williamsburg was an unprecedented endorsement of Western values. Our Alliance merged stronger and more united than ever. Peace and prosperity were made more secure.

Later in the year, I traveled to Japan and Korea to emphasize the importance we attached to the dynamic Pacific region. Here, too, we faced tough problems, particularly in trade with Japan. But Prime Minister Nakasone is a man of vision and strength, who has worked hard with me to iron out our differences, and we've made progress. Japan has opened up its trading and financial markets and moved to increase its defense expenditures, so vital to preserving peace and freedom in the Pacific Basin. This will mean more U.S. jobs and greater security for both our nations.

In April, I returned to the Pacific region to visit China. Our relations have steadily improved, and our visit capped important agreements that will stimulate U.S. exports to China as we cooperate with them to modernize their economy.

Now, here in London, at this year's Economic Summit, it's clear we've made impressive gains. In 1981, our economies had an average growth of only 1.8 percent and 8.5-percent inflation. Today, our average growth has risen to 4 percent, while inflation has been cut in half. Stronger growth means more jobs, with the U.S. economy leading the way. We've created more than six million jobs in the last 18 months, and we're venturing into new, promising areas. We've offered our Summit partners the opportunity to participate with us in the development of our manned space station—an international space station will stimulate technological development, strengthen our economies, and improve the quality of life into the next century.

I've stress [*sic*] in London that continued progress will require new determination to carry out our common strategy for prosperity and peace. We must summon courage. We must continue with action to curve [*sic*] inflation by reducing unnecessary spending, spur greater growth by reducing regulation, trade barriers, and personal income tax rates. And, yes, we must be prepared for peace by strengthening NATO's ability to deter war, while making clear we're prepared to reduce nuclear weapons dramatically as soon as the Soviets are ready to work with us on this all-important goal.

This has been a year of progress; a year when we and our friends in Europe and the Pacific set aside differences and united as great democracies should be with shared vision and values. That progress, stretching beyond America from the Pacific Basin to a strengthened Atlantic Alliance, is a source of hope for a more prosperous and safer world.

Until next week, thanks for listening, and God bless you.

Note: The President spoke at 5:06 P.M. (Local) from Winfield House, London, England. His address was broadcast on radio stations in the United States at 12:06 P.M. EDT.

Father's Day/Outlook for Families

June 16, 1984

My fellow Americans:

Tomorrow is Father's Day, so naturally our thoughts turn to them and to the well-being of family life in America. Families have always stood at the center of our society, preserving good and worthy traditions from our past, entrusting those traditions to our children, our greatest hope for the future.

Family life has changed much down through the years. The days when we could expect to live in only one home and hold only one job are probably gone forever. Perhaps we will not go back to the old family ways, but I think we can and should preserve family values—values of faith, honesty, responsibility, tolerance, kindness, and love.

And we'll keep on trying to do better, trying to create a better life for those who follow. This hasn't been easy to do in the last decade. It's become more difficult to raise children than it once was.

For example, the dependency exemption on your income tax: The money you can deduct for raising a child or caring for an elderly relative was $600 in the late '40's. That's been increased to $1000 now. But if that deduction had been indexed to keep pace with inflation, today you would be deducting more than $3000 for every one of your children.

Housing became harder to afford. And the cost of private education also became too expensive for millions of middle-income families. By 1980, American families felt the full shock of runaway taxes, inflation, record interest rates, and soaring prices for housing, education, food, and other necessities of life.

They saw the golden promise of the American dream disappearing behind storm clouds of economic misery. Liberals urged huge government subsidies, paying parents for expenses they used to handle themselves. But big government becoming "Big Brother," pushing parents aside, interfering with one parental responsibility after another, is no solution. It only makes bad situations worse, raising prices and taxes for everyone.

We came to Washington with a better idea—help working parents to better provide for themselves and their children by enabling them to keep more of their earnings and help them by making government do its job so the terrifying specter of runaway price increases never returns.

Our tax rate reductions have helped parents, reducing the tax bill that would have been owed by a typical family by over $900 a year. And we've helped parents by reducing the inflation rate by nearly two-thirds since 1980 and by creating more than six million new jobs. Things are getting better for American families, but much remains to be done.

That's why the Treasury Department is making greater tax fairness and greater tax incentives for families a central consideration in the tax reform proposals they're developing. We're trying hard to help fathers and mothers in other ways, too.

Many innocent children are exploited by those who traffic in the gutter of drugs, child pornography, and prostitution. Last month, I signed the Child Protection Act of 1984, a key part of our determination to crack down hard on the smut merchants. And this past week, we opened a National Center for Missing and Exploited Children to help educate parents and authorities on how to protect their loved ones.

We've just launched a nationwide citizen effort to encourage volunteer, court-appointed special advocates in legal cases of neglect and child abuse. Soon, we'll start up a sophisticated detective program to help law enforcement officers identify and capture the so-called serial killers who prey upon women and children.

And we've urged the Congress to pass a law that will strengthen and improve child support from absent parents. Children should not be financially abandoned just because they're separated from one of their parents.

We're trying hard to make two other changes. We want to see fewer abandoned, handicapped, or underprivileged children left in perpetual foster care. And we want to see the unborn child given his or her chance to live and to know the joys of life. Adoption is often the best option. Too often, it's been the forgotten option.

We're seeing hopeful signs that our policies are paying off. Family income is improving; infant mortality rates continue to drop. And the crime rate has taken a steep dive. The outlook for families in America is better today than in 1980. And we're determined to make it better still.

Happy Father's Day. Until next week, thanks for listening, and God bless you.

Note: The President spoke at 12:06 P.M. EDT from Camp David.

Economic Recovery

June 23, 1984

My fellow Americans:

This week, we had some more good economic news: the economy grew by a revised 9.7 percent in real terms for the first quarter and an estimated 5.7 percent for this quarter. Both figures are better than had been predicted.

The strength of our expansion continues to surprise experts and outperform past recoveries. The curious thing is that some experts treat this good news, strong economic growth, as a cause for worry. Well, the common-sense reaction is right—good news is not bad, it's good.

In some key ways this expansion is both different and more durable than those in the past. Stronger growth has enabled more people to find work and bring home paychecks, and it's improved the job outlook for the future. More people are working in America today than ever before. And the United States is creating more jobs at a faster rate than any other major industrialized country in the world, well over six million jobs in the last eighteen months. In fact, we created more jobs in the month of May alone than all the Common Market countries created in the last ten years.

I remember back in 1983 when a bill was introduced in Congress aimed at creating 300,000 jobs a year by spending $3.5 billion of your tax money. Now, I said, no. The private economy will do the job better. And it has done better, much better. Since the recovery began, our economy has been creating, on average, more jobs every month than that government program promised to create in 12 months. And the jobs are benefiting everyone. Nearly three million women, a million blacks, and 650,000 Hispanics have found new jobs.

Recently, the National Federation of Independent Business said that, among its small business membership, the percentage planning to hire new workers is the highest in four years. Since most new jobs are created by firms with a hundred employees or less, that small business survey bodes well for continued job gains in the future. So, economic growth is stronger than before, stronger than anyone expected, and jobs are being created at record rates.

But something else makes this expansion different. Inflation is staying down, and we mean to keep it down. It was up only .2 percent in May and only 4.2 percent over the last 12 months. Barely a third of 1980's 12.4-percent rate. We've reduced inflationary pressures by reducing government spending growth, by promoting greater production through lower tax rates, and by spurring greater competition through the deregulation of key industries. Nor do we see signs that runaway price increases will reappear. This is the first time since the 1960's that we'll be able to enjoy strong and steady growth without high inflation.

Another characteristic of this expansion gives it extra power while helping us fight inflation. Investment by U.S. businesses in new plants and equipment, so crucial to helping workers be more productive and to helping our industries better compete in world markets, has been rising at the fastest rate since 1949. We're witnessing an historic surge of innovation, risk taking, technological development, and productivity growth. American economic leadership is back.

Now, the question is why, and why here in America to a greater degree than anywhere else? Well, America began a fundamental change in direction in 1981; a change from a policy of government promises, a change from taxing you more no matter how hard you tried, to rewarding you for working harder and producing more than before. Personal incentives are changing America, restoring our spirit, strengthening our economy, giving us the opportunity and confidence to shape our future and make it work for us.

And that's why I'm determined to finish the job we've begun by simplifying our tax system and broadening the base so we can bring personal income tax rates down further. If we can do that while keeping Federal spending under control, there'll be no stopping the United States.

We all have a job to do to protect this expansion and keep the lid on inflation, which is the best guarantee against rising interest rates. The Congress must cooperate and restrain spending by passing the downpayment deficit-reduction package. The Federal Reserve must assure enough liquidity to finance the expansion without raising expectations of new inflation. And we must all work to make government live within its means.

If we meet these responsibilities, today's good news will be here to stay, and America's best days will lie ahead.

Until next week, thanks for listening. God bless you.

Note: The President spoke at 12:06 P.M. EDT from Camp David.

Budget Deficits/Drug Abuse

June 30, 1984

The President. My fellow Americans, this week the Congress passed and I will soon sign a series of measures to reduce budget deficits by about $63 billion over the next three fiscal years. My approval of these measures should not by any means be considered the final action on deficits this year. The Congress still has much work to do to achieve spending restraint and help our economic expansion continue.

I stand ready to use my veto to make sure it fulfills that responsibility. Spending restraint and personal incentives for growth are the two greatest deficit-reduction weapons we have. That's why the ultimate solution to budget deficits must be a mandatory restriction on the Congress' [*sic*] ability to spend and a simplification of the entire tax system, enabling us to broaden the tax base and lower personal income tax rates for all of you who work and earn. We're bound and determined to do this.

But today, I don't intend to go on talking about the economy. I have a special guest. Nancy is here with me, and she'd like to speak to you about the problem of drugs and what, together, all of us can do about the problem.

The First Lady. Thank you, Ronnie.

During the past two years, I've traveled throughout our country, and what I've seen happening to our children is terribly frightening. In fact, sometimes it seems as if we could lose a whole next generation to drug abuse. Cocaine, PCP, marijuana, alcohol, speed, these are the enemies of our children. They're cunning and treacherous and, oh, so very patient. As one former teenage alcoholic put it, "Alcohol will wait forever. It's always going to be there." And that child was right. Which is why we must be there as well.

And this enemy shows no mercy. It still sends a chill through me to recall a visit I made some time ago to an elementary school in Atlanta. I asked the class of third-graders how many had been offered drugs, and almost every hand went up.

Many people still seem to think that substance abuse is something that happens to other families. There's a wall of denial that must be broken down. The truth is, drugs and alcohol are everywhere available and everywhere abused. And now people are waking up to that fact.

A 16-year-old girl, who described herself as a recovering drug addict, wrote me to say that she was one of the lucky ones. "I'm doing fine now," she said, "but last Christmas I was in the hospital weighing 87 pounds and not caring whether I lived or died. I only took drugs for a year, but I'm sure I had a problem as soon as I started. I dropped a lot of my old friends because I only wanted to be friends with kids who could get drugs for me. When I collapsed in a public park from malnutrition and exhaustion due to cocaine, my new friends didn't lift a finger to help me. If it hadn't been for my parents who came looking for me, I wouldn't be alive today."

Her letter isn't unusual. Other children have talked frankly to me about how young they were when they began to experiment with drugs and how school became little more than a place to buy dope and get high.

Most parents were completely in the dark. They just didn't believe it could happen to their kids. Again, the wall of denial. But there may be a light at the end of the tunnel—something that fills me with hope about our children's future and about our country's future. We're finally becoming aware of the terrible problem of drugs. Three years ago, there were only 1,000 volunteer parents' groups organized to fight drug abuse. Today, there are more than 4,000, and the number keeps growing. Yes, there is reason for hope.

These are parents who've learned—some the hard way—that the most effective answer to the tragedy of drugs is involvement and knowledge. And, too, now they know that discipline is something you do for a child, not to him.

I'm asked so often what I think is the answer. And I always stress self-confidence, family communication, and active supervision. As a mother of a girl who was experimenting with LSD during the day and finishing a bottle of bourbon every night put it, "It's time for parents to take over and be parents again."

Ronnie, I know you join me in the belief that we [*sic*], if we all work together, become more involved in our children's lives and more knowledge-able, we can help save a generation and help preserve its promise and hope.

The President. Well, I sure do know that, Nancy. And I can't imagine anything that could do more to brighten the skies of America's future.

Until next week, thanks for listening, and God bless you.

Note: The President and Mrs. Reagan spoke at 12:06 P.M. EDT from Camp David.

Anti-Crime Legislation

July 7, 1984

My fellow Americans:

I'd like to talk with you today about a subject that's been a priority since this administration's first day in office—fighting crime in America.

When we came to office, crime was taking the lives of over 23,000 Americans a year. It touched a third of American homes and resulted in about $10 billion a year in financial losses. Yet, just as America has regained her economic strength and international prestige in the last few years, so, too, the crime problem in America has shown improvement for the first time in many years.

In recent speeches in Hartford, Connecticut, and San Antonio, Texas, I've pointed out that the 7-percent decrease in crime reported for last year is the sharpest decrease in the history of the crime statistics; and it marks the first time the serious crime index has shown a decline two years in a row.

Of course we still have a long way to go; but this statistic does demonstrate that our efforts and those of State and local government are finally having an impact on crime.

At the State level, for example, numerous legislatures have passed tough new sentencing laws. And here at the Federal level, we've taken several critically important steps.

First, from our first day in office, the Attorney General and I have emphasized the importance of appointing to the Federal bench, including the Supreme Court, judges determined to uphold the rights of society and the innocent victims as well as the rights of the accused.

Second, we've launched an all-out assault on the illicit drug trade—that fever swamp of career criminals in America—taking our cue from the success of our South Florida Task Force, we've brought aboard more than 1,200 new investigators and prosecutors and established 12 regional task forces throughout the United States to crack down on the big-money drug traffickers.

The results of that effort have been encouraging. The drug task forces have initiated 620 cases; they've indicted more than 2,600 individuals; and 143 of these indictments have been under the Drug Kingpin Law, which carries a maximum penalty of life imprisonment without the possibility of parole.

Third, we've launched a full-scale offensive on the home ground of career criminals—organized crime itself. Organized crime arrests have nearly tripled, and confiscation of their assets is also sharply up. Our new Commission on Organized Crime has brought much-needed public attention to this problem; and, as soon as it receives subpoena power, it will do even more.

Believe me, we in the administration have been trying to speak up for you, the millions of Americans who are fed up with crime, fed up with fear in our streets and neighborhoods, fed up with lenient judges, fed up with a criminal justice system that too often treats criminals better than it does their victims.

Too many Americans have had to suffer the effects of crime while too many of our leaders have stuck to the old, discredited, liberal illusions about crime—illusions that refuse to hold criminals responsible for their actions.

For example, I wonder how many of you know that the major part of our legislative initiative against crime remains right where it's remained for the last three years, dead in the water in the House of Representatives. Now, our crime package includes bills calling for bail reform, tougher sentencing, justice assistance to States and localities, improvement in the exclusionary rule and the insanity defense, and major reforms effecting [*sic*] drug trafficking, prison crowding, capital punishment, and forfeiture. All of these reforms are badly needed and constitutionally sound. In fact, our core crime package has already passed the Senate once by a vote of 91 to 1. But in the House of Representatives, the liberal leadership keeps it bottled up in committee.

I told a group of Texas lawyers yesterday, we're not about to quit on our crime bill. We're going to do what we've done in the past. We're going out to the heartland, and we're taking our case to you, the people.

And so, I'm asking for your help today. Please send a message to the House leadership. Tell them to stop kowtowing to the special interests and start listening to you, the American people.

Americans want this anti-crime legislation, and they want it now. And if those of you listening will lend a hand, we can get it now. Please tell your elected representatives you expect full and fair representation, and that means getting this bill out of committee on to the floor of the House for a vote.

We've made real progress against crime in the last few years. Together, we can keep up the good work.

Until next week, thanks for listening, and God bless you.

Note: The President spoke at 12:06 P.M. EDT from Camp David.

Environmental and Natural Resources Management

July 14, 1984

My fellow Americans:

I'd like to talk to you today about our environment. But, as I mentioned earlier this week, in doing so I might be letting you in on a little secret—as a matter of fact, one of the best-kept secrets in Washington.

More than 15 years ago, the State of California decided that we needed to take action to combat the smog that was choking the beautiful cities of my home State. Out of that concern was born the first serious program to require manufacturers to build cleaner cars and help control air pollution. The auto industry had to build two kinds of cars—one that would be for sale in the other 49 States and one that would meet the stiff anti-pollution standards required in California.

We had other concerns in California, such as protecting our magnificent and unique coastline. And we took the lead in that area as well. It took the rest of the Nation a few years to catch on, but in 1970 the Congress followed California's lead and enacted the Clean Air Act. Other laws to protect and clean up the Nation's lakes and rivers were passed, and America got on with the job of protecting the environment.

Part of the secret I mentioned is that I happen to have been Governor of California back when much of this was being done. Now, obviously, neither the problems in California nor those nationally have been solved, but I'm proud of having been one of the first to recognize that States and the Federal Government have a duty to protect our natural resources from the damaging effects of pollution that can accompany industrial development.

The other part of the well-kept secret has to do with the environmental record of our administration which is one of achievement in parks, wilderness land, and wildlife refuges. According to studies by the Environmental Protection Agency, the quality of our air and water has continued to improve during our administration. In many big cities, the number of days on which pollution alerts are declared has gone down. And, if you live near a river, you may have noticed that the signs have been coming down that used to warn people not to fish or swim.

We came to Washington committed to respect the great bounty and beauty of God's creation. We believe very strongly in the concept of stewardship, caring for the resources we have so they can be shared and used productively for generations to come. And we've put that philosophy to work, correcting deficiencies of past policies and advancing long-overdue initiatives.

Let me give you some facts that our critics never seem to remember. When we took office in 1980, we faced a dusty shelf of reports which pointed out our predecessors had been so busy spending money on new lands for parks that they seriously neglected basic upkeep of the magnificent parks we had. So, we temporarily put off acquiring new parkland, and started a new billion-dollar, five-year program to repair and modernize facilities at our national parks and wildlife refuges. If you've been to just about any national park lately, you've probably seen the results.

We've nearly finished repairing the damage from years of neglect, and I've asked the Congress for almost $160 million to resume buying lands to round out our national park and refuges system.

We also took the lead in developing a new approach to protecting some 700 miles of undeveloped coastal areas—the dunes, beaches, and barrier islands that are some of our most beautiful and productive natural resources.

Now, there are some who want you to believe that commitment to protecting the environment can be measured by comparing the budgets of EPA under the previous administration with those proposed and approved by the Congress under my administration. But they deliberately ignore that the major Federal environmental laws are designed to be carried out by the States in partnership with EPA.

By the time the clean air, clean water, and other big programs put in place in the early 1970's moved into their second decade, the States had largely taken over the job formerly performed by the Federal Government. With the successful delegation to the States, EPA, under the leadership of Bill Ruckelshaus, has been freed to move on to the challenges of the 1980's— such as cleaning up abandoned toxic-waste dumps.

Under our administration, funding for the Superfund clean-up program would have increased from just over $100 million in 1981, to $620 million in 1985. By the end of this year, EPA expects to have undertaken more than 400 emergency actions to remove and contain public health hazards. And, because we recognize that we need to do more clean-up work than the current law provides, I'm committed to seeking an extension of the Superfund program.

As I said, our progress on protecting the environment is one of the best-kept secrets in Washington. But it's not, by far, the only secret. And I'll have more on that in the months ahead.

Until next week, thanks for listening. And God bless you.

Note: The President spoke at 12:06 P.M. EDT from Camp David.

Private Enterprise in Space

July 21, 1984

My fellow Americans:

Yesterday we marked the 15th anniversary of the first manned landing on the moon. We all remember that great moment when Neil Armstrong said, "Tranquility Base here. The Eagle has landed."

But that wasn't our last great moment in space. In fact, it's become increasingly clear that most of our great moments are ahead of us.

For 25 years, we approached space with a certain amount of daring-do [*sic*]. It was the last frontier, and we would be its first pioneers. Space seemed like a vast black desert. But now we're ready to make the desert bloom.

I'm talking about opening space up to business, to private enterprise; opening space up to commerce and experimentation and development. Why? To improve the quality of life on earth. We've learned in the past few years that in the zero gravity of space it's possible to manufacture drugs and pharmaceuticals of a purity much greater than is possible on earth—and in much greater quantities.

The zero gravity of space is allowing us in the space shuttle and soon in a manned space station to experiment with new drugs and new cures for diseases. Do you have a friend or relative with diabetes? Some scientists believe that in space it's possible they may be able to produce a cure for diabetes within the next decade.

In space we also find new opportunities for important breakthroughs in cancer research. Now, cancer research is one of these phrases that to some people means we're still thinking and getting nowhere. But a number of scientists now believe that a cure for some types of cancer might be produced in space sometime in the not-too-distant future. That's not all.

In space we can manufacture crystals that have many times the yield and purity of those made on earth. These will help maintain America's leadership in the computer industry. We can also develop new metals that are lighter and stronger than any we've ever known.

So, the promise and the potential are there. And private industry, private research groups, medical groups, and all sorts of businesses want to get up into space and invest. But it's very costly. It'll involve long-term investment, commitment, and imagination.

For the past year now, our administration has been studying ways to encourage private investment and development. And we've come up with a number of new initiatives to achieve that goal. These initiatives don't involve a special-interest treatment of any sort. What they come down to is a policy designed to do away with laws that inadvertently discriminate against companies that do business in space rather than on the ground.

We also want to make sure these companies are not stymied by needless regulation. For example, the way the law is written now, products made in space might be subject to import tariffs because they weren't made in America. Well, we're going to change that. Another example: Businesses which operate at home receive various kinds of tax incentives. But, again, as the laws are written now, space products companies would not receive those incentives. We'll be looking at that, too.

Also, to encourage research and development, we've been working in partnership with industry and academia to expand basic research opportunities, achieve new breakthroughs, and give U.S. companies making space-age products a boost on the way to the marketplace.

As our country moves into high-tech industries, space will be a big part of the future. As space-related businesses take off, the economy will benefit. Ultimately, it could well mean tens of thousands of jobs, billions of dollars in new foreign trade, and tens of billions of dollars added to the gross national product.

Some of our new initiatives will be accomplished through Executive Order. Others will require congressional action. We're confident that these measures will win considerable support.

I'm proud of our work in this area, of our ability to recognize what private companies have recognized, that we have cultivated space for the past 25 years and now is the harvest time. Now is the time to reap the practical fruits of all that daring.

You know, we've been hearing a lot lately from politicians who keep talking about how dark the future is. Well, I think the narrowness of their vision stems from a kind of blindness to the adventure that technology continues to offer us. Those folks have such a strangled sense of possibilities. But in space, the possibilities are endless. It's good news for all mankind and for our country.

Until next week, thanks for listening, and God bless you.

Note: The President spoke at 12:06 P.M. EDT from Camp David.

U.S. Olympic Team

July 28, 1984

Well, thank you, Bill Simon. This is a genuine pleasure for me and for Nancy. We've been avid sports fans, and I have been all my life. And to be with you here, the men and women who will be wearing our colors in the

23rd Olympiad of the modern Games, is a memory I know we're going to cherish.

I'm certain that you'll remember these Games as the highlight of your life as well. And not just the Games. You've been preparing for this competition for many years. You know better than most it isn't just the will to win that counts, it's the will to prepare to win. And from what I see here—we're ready. (Applause.)

I see some familiar faces. (Laughter.) I've enjoyed following your progress, and when I visited you at the Olympic Training Center in Colorado Springs a while back, you all gave me an official warm-up suit. I've been using it just before meeting certain Members of the Congress. (Laughter.)

I also received a little gift from our ice hockey team. A hockey puck inscribed, "The puck stops here." (Laughter.) Believe me, I've put that one to good use, too.

I want you to know just how proud all of us are to have you representing us. And when you see us out on the stands waving Old Glory, you know that we're waving it for you.

The same spirit is evident all across this land. Back in the middle of May, I met the official Olympic torch carrier at the White House. As that flame has made its way across America, it's been greeted with cheers, accolades, and flags, by young and old, Americans of every race and religion.

Journalists have described and analyzed this outpouring of unity and positive feeling. They also noted that this year's Fourth of July celebrations were extraordinarily joyous occasions. There is a new patriotism spreading across our country. It's an affection for our way of life, expressed by people who represent the width and breadth of our culturally diverse society. And the new patriotism is a—not a negative force that excludes, but a positive force, an attitude toward those things that are fundamental to America, that draws together our freedom, our decency, our sense of fair play as a people.

In so many ways, you represent this new spirit. I know I speak for all your fellow citizens—no matter what political persuasion, no matter what race or religion, no matter if poor, middle class, or affluent—when I tell you that you are our team. And each and every one of you, we're with you 100 percent.

During these Games, you'll be competing against athletes from many nations, but most important, you're competing against yourself. All we expect is for you to do your best to push yourself for that fraction of—one more fraction of a second, or one notch higher, or one inch further. Each time you do that, you create a magic moment of beauty and excellence in which all of us will share.

The American ideal is not just winning, it's going as far as you can go. If by pushing yourself to the limit you set a record or win a medal, you'll hear us. We'll probably look a little silly expressing our pride in your accomplishment. But our affection and pride is something that you can count on. We'll be cheering, win, lose, or draw.

These Games are the culmination of the work and dedication of thousands of people. I think Peter Ueberroth has done an exceptional job. United States Olympic Committee President Bill Simon has assured me you're the best team ever. And Bill, himself, deserves our special thanks for all that he's done. And, of course, I'd like to mention your Executive Director, Don Miller, and all the coaches and managers who made this possible, and these captains who are here on these steps with us.

This has been a team effort all the way. Corporations have done their part. Individual contributions have played a major role. Those who couldn't give money, volunteered—I understand 50,000 volunteers here, backstage—to get these Games under way. They've been donating their time and energy to the success of the Games.

Special recognition should go to Rafer Johnson and Donna de Varona and their Olympic Spirit Team. These Olympians have put out an enormous effort on your behalf and on behalf of the Olympics. And today, you are joining this special fraternity of individuals who have competed in previous Olympics. It's an honor no one can take away from you.

Many years ago, believe it or not, I competed in sports, and coaches were known for spurring us on with some pretty punchy phrases and dialog—or monologue. And looking back now, I realize those coaches were just as excited at the time as we were. And the same is true right now, you can be certain of that. We're all in this together. And we know that we can count on you to push yourselves to the limit.

So set your sights high and go for it. (Applause.)

For yourselves, for your families, for your country—and will you forgive me if I just be a little presumptuous—do it for the Gipper. (Laughter.) (Applause.)

God bless you all. We'll be watching. (Applause.) Thank you all. (Applause.)

Note: The President spoke to members of the U.S. Olympic Team at Heritage Hall, Olympic Village, University of Southern California, Los Angeles, at 1:52 P.M. PDT.

Mondale's Tax Increases

August 4, 1984

My fellow Americans:

Lately, you may have heard a lot of talk about a so-called secret plan to raise your taxes. Well, I've made it clear that we have no such plan. But, apparently, such a plan exists, nonetheless. It's not our plan; it's not yours. It's the plan of the Democratic nominee for President.

When he accepted the Democratic nomination, he declared that he will increase your taxes. He said it several times since. But he still hasn't said exactly how. He has, however, come close to saying how much he would raise your taxes.

It takes a little calculation, but here's how it all adds up. The Democratic nominee has said he accepts deficit projections of over $200 billion a year, as far as the eye can see. Now, I don't accept them. And if we can keep our economy growing strongly, no one will have to. But he says he accepts them.

On top of those deficit projections, the Democratic nominee says he would add new government spending. How much? Well, he says his increases would total about $30 billion per year.

Senator John Glenn, on the other hand, said the cost of the Democratic nominee's promises would really come to somewhere between $90 and $170 billion. The Wall Street Journal reported estimates of experts that the amount of increased spending would come closer to $90 billion. So let's use that for working purposes.

The Democratic nominee says he will make some budget cuts. He says he'll cut defense, health care, and agriculture programs by a total of $55 billion to $65 billion. And although his plan isn't likely to produce them, he says he expects interest savings of $15 billion to $20 billion. Now, that would bring his total savings to less than $90 billion. So, when you add it all up, the Democratic nominee's savings, assuming he would achieve them, still don't quite add up to enough to pay for the likely cost of his promises. And the deficits would be even higher than he assumes, except for one thing. There's another element to all this, another promise.

The Democratic nominee says he'll cut those deficits by two-thirds. How? By raising taxes. He says he estimates increased taxes of "at least $60 billion." He says he would get these by doing such things as deferring indexation [*sic*], capping the third year of your tax cut, and adding a tax surcharge, all supposedly targeted at higher income taxpayers. Well, the truth is, he'd need an increase of more than twice his $60 billion, an increase of $135 billion to square with his promises.

That averages $1500 in increased taxes for every American household and, one way or another, that means you. It's the same tired old formula—tax and tax to spend and spend.

I think the Democratic nominee owes the American people not a partial explanation, but a full explanation of how and where he expects to get that $1500 more per household, over $135 billion in increased taxes. That's the secret that should be brought to light.

My approach to deficit reduction is entirely different, and it's no secret. We should reduce deficits first and foremost by continuing our economic growth and by reducing wasteful government spending.

Through the Grace Commission, for example, we've developed 2,478 recommendations of possible ways to reduce spending without hurting the needy. These recommendations are no secret. We've made them public. We've already begun to implement almost 20 percent of them. We're still completing our review of the rest, but they're there for all to see. And every one that is worth implementing will be implemented.

As for taxes, my approach there is well known and no secret. We have already reduced personal income tax rates for all Americans by 25 percent. That has not only lightened your burden, it's helped give us the strong economic growth, without inflation, that we now enjoy.

Our tax cuts have meant more money for you to spend and invest and for you to save and use as you wish, more money to create jobs and expand the economy. I mean to keep that growth going and not stifle it with a new burden of taxes. And I mean to simplify the tax system and broaden its base so that we can bring income tax rates further down, not up.

That, too, is no secret. I announced it in this year's State of the Union Address to the Congress.

Finally, let me tell you one more thing that should be no secret in case the Democrats' talk of so-called secret plans has you worried. I will propose no increase in personal income taxes and I will veto any tax bill that would raise personal tax rates for working Americans or that would fail to make our tax system simpler and more fair.

Until next week, thanks for listening. God bless you.

Note: The President spoke at 9:06 A.M. PDT from Rancho del Cielo, near Santa Barbara.

Equal Access Bill/Do-Nothing Congress

August 11, 1984

My fellow Americans:

I'm pleased to tell you that today I signed legislation that will allow student religious groups to begin enjoying a right they've too long been denied, the freedom to meet in public high schools during non-school hours, just as other student groups are allowed to do. This has been given a short-hand label, "Equal Access Legislation."

You might remember that I recently asked the House Democratic leadership to permit a vote on equal access and to permit votes on five other legislative measures important to you and your families that they, the Democratic leadership, had bottled up. Well, the Congress recessed yesterday, and the House Democratic leaders are returning to their districts. Some of these leaders and other Democrats have been campaigning on what they call their "new realism." But before they give too many speeches about all the wise things they promise to do for America, I want to give you a little report card on what they, in fact, did do—or, rather, did not do—as their new realism was put to the test. Of those six important pieces of legislation we requested, specific measures to help reduce deficits, reward hard work and thrift, make your neighborhoods and cities safer, and increase personal liberties, only one was voted on, the Equal Access Bill. Equal Access was only voted on after a majority of the House, led by the late Carl D. Perkins, defied the Democratic leadership, which continued to resist right up to the bitter end.

Of the remaining five proposals to test the new realism, not one was brought to a vote. So much for the test of the new realism. If the Democrats were given a report card, one out of six right would have meant a failing grade, a red-letter F.

When the Democratic leadership keeps saying no to America, they show how far they are from new realism and how far they've drifted from mainstream thinking. We asked for a vote on a Constitutional amendment mandating a balanced Federal budget. We will insist that the Congress move to a balanced budget, not by imposing new taxes on your families, but by spending within its means and allowing economic growth to continue.

The overwhelming majority of Americans agree with this position. But the House Democratic leaders don't. They don't want spending restraint because their party has made so many campaign promises, promises they intend to fund by raising your taxes more than $1500 per household.

We asked for a vote on our Enterprise Zones Bill to provide incentives for people to invest, work, hire, and start up new businesses in economically distressed areas. This measure has been passed twice by the Republican Senate. It's supported by a majority of Members in the House, including many Democrats, and by a broad coalition of community leaders.

We're ready to designate 75 zones to create opportunity, independence, and hope for our neediest citizens. But the Democratic leadership said no. We asked for a vote on our proposal granting spouses working in the home the same individual retirement right, IRAs, as spouses working outside the home. Each could save and exclude from taxation up to $2000 a year. The House Democratic leadership said no.

We asked for a vote allowing tuition tax credits for low- and middle-income parents who pay to send their children to parochial or independent schools while also paying their full share of taxes to support public schools. The House Democratic leadership said no. And we asked for action on our comprehensive anti-crime package to crack down on criminals through new restrictions on bail, tougher sentencing, and stricter enforcement of drug-trafficking laws. This bill passed the Senate 91 to 1, but the House Democratic leadership said no.

You might be interested to know what House Speaker Tip O'Neill has called these proposals for a balanced budget, expanded IRAs, Enterprise Zones, tuition tax credits, tougher law enforcement, and equal access for students. He says they're "a right-wing agenda." Does the Democratic leadership truly believe that common sense in budgeting and greater opportunity and security for people is a right-wing agenda?

The Presidential nominee of the Democratic Party and his running mate could have asked the Speaker to give democracy a chance. Could have, but didn't. They, too, said no.

All this has gotten me to thinking about a great Democrat. Just 36 years ago, Harry Truman called the 80th Congress the "do-nothing Congress." One thing is sure, Harry Truman wasn't afraid of the American people. He wasn't afraid of democracy, of putting issues to the test of a vote. Were he with us now, I think he would relish the chance to run against those who proclaim a new realism and then do nothing.

Until next week, thanks for listening, and God bless you.

Note: The President spoke at 9:06 A.M. PDT from Rancho del Cielo, near Santa Barbara.

August 18, 1984

My fellow Americans:

Something very bright and happy and hopeful has been happening across our country in recent days. We've watched a grateful nation shower its affection on those who showered us with glory—our Olympic athletes.

Theirs was a triumph of faith and hope. In honoring them, ours has been a celebration of the new patriotism. Nancy and I saw our athletes in Los Angeles the day after the Olympics ended. You could just feel their joy and energy. And when our famous gymnast, Mary Lou Retton, stood on her toes to give me a hug, I couldn't help thinking, "How can anyone not believe in the dream of America?"

Now, I've been accused of being an optimist, and it's true. All my life I've seen that when people like Mary Lou have a dream, when they have the courage and opportunity to work hard, when they believe in the power of faith and hope, they not only perform great feats, they help pull all of us forward as well.

Somehow the idea that American progress begins with spirit and a willingness of the heart was ignored during the 1970's. The intellectual establishment was so busy demanding more power for government, more bureaucracy, regulation, spending and—oh, yes—more and more taxes, they forgot all about the secret of America's success—opportunity for people, for all the people.

When the economy reached the point of collapse by the end of the '70's, they began talking about the crisis of spirit, about our malaise. But we hadn't given up hope; we just hadn't been allowed to hope.

So, when we came to Washington in 1981, we said, "Let us renew our faith and our hope. We have every right to dream heroic dreams." We put together an economic recovery program that made a radical break with past policies. For the first time since the administration of John Kennedy, we cut tax rates significantly for every working American. We told the people, "America's destiny is back in your hands. If you work harder and earn more than before, your reward will be greater than it was."

But from the beginning, the Old Guard establishment—people who still make policy from abstract statistics, theories, and models rather than looking at the reality of human behavior—have filled the airwaves with gloom, predicting our program couldn't meet our goals.

And from the beginning, they've been wrong: When they said inflation and interest rates wouldn't come down, when they said recovery wouldn't come, when they said the expansion wouldn't last, and when they said the deficit wouldn't come down.

Recently, many liberal analysts have been reviewing our record and our prospects. Their message remains, "Hasn't worked, can't be done." So when the Urban Institute came out with a study a few days ago, it was only natural that some of the press would look for the same old doom and gloom. For example, they didn't report that the study also said elderly Americans have clearly done better under our policies with real gains in disposable incomes, nor that the social safety net is still largely intact for the non-working poor. Even the Urban Institute said there is no evidence that working welfare mothers who have been eliminated from the rolls are quitting their jobs to requalify for benefits, and that, despite all the furor, it finds surprisingly few changes from 1980 with respect to the environmental, public lands, and water resources activities of the Federal Government.

And no one seems to mention that the centerpiece of our policy, the tax cut, was not fully in place until 1983. Our program has just begun. But let's look at the record since it has.

Over 6 million jobs created. A surge in investment and productivity, a record 600,000 business incorporations, the biggest increase in real after-tax personal income since 1973, and, perhaps most important, a new spirit of optimism and confidence about America's future. It's clear that, once people get a chance to show what they can do, well, America got well and got strong.

What isn't so clear is why those pessimists, with so little faith in people, so little understanding of incentives, and so many bad predictions, are not more humble and not treated a little more skeptically by the media.

In 1984, we face an historic choice. Will we heed the pessimists' agenda of higher taxes, more bureaucracy, and a bigger welfare state leading us right back to runaway inflation and economic decay, or will we continue on our new road toward a true opportunity society of economic growth, more jobs, lower tax rates, and rising take-home pay?

I believe the spirit we've seen during and after these Olympics reveals something very important about America. We believe in ourselves, we're hungry for real opportunity, and we're up to any challenge.

Until next week, thanks for listening, and God bless you.

Note: The President spoke at 12:06 P.M. EDT from the Oval Office at the White House.

Goals for the Future

August 25, 1984

My fellow Americans:

The campaign of 1984 is under way. This campaign is about what it was like four years ago and what it's like today.

But even more important, it is about the future. I believe our Republican Party is the true party of the future because our vision, ideas, and proposals seek to bring out the best in America by challenging the best in our people. The "Great Opportunity Party" believes in challenging people to do better. The Democratic leadership still insists on challenging government to grow bigger.

Our vision of a strong, secure future rests on our confidence that Americans can continue making progress toward four specific goals: strong, steady economic growth; developing the frontiers of science, high technology, and space; strengthening our community of shared values; and building an enduring peace.

As a Nation, we've already begun meeting the challenges we set forth four years ago. I won't rehash all the problems we faced; but, from a collapsing economy to weakening defenses, to rising rates of crime and poor educational performance, it was clear that America was in deep trouble. We were being led by a group of pessimists whose ideas had been threadbare for years and they hadn't even noticed. The realities of a changing world had long since passed them by.

We said, "If America is to be a successful leader in the world again, we must face up to the problems that have dragged us down. And we must begin doing that by trusting the people again." We said that together we must meet the challenges of reducing the growth of government, bringing down inflation and interest rates, and cutting tax rates to create jobs and get our economy moving again. And America has.

We said we must restore America's ability to defend itself and fulfill its responsibilities as a trustee of freedom and peace in the world. And America has.

We met our challenges before. And we can meet them again.

As for our first goal, economic growth, our position is clear. We've seen from the mistakes of the past and from the recent recovery that our economy grows best when earnings flow not to government, but stay with the people and in the economy. That's why we must meet the challenge of simplifying our tax system, making it more fair, easier to understand, so we can bring personal tax rates further down, not up.

With strong economic growth, we'll continue bringing down deficits. We must also control spending, and one tool is a Constitutional amendment mandating that government spend no more than government takes in.

Another is a line-item veto, so that a President can veto specific spending requests without vetoing an entire appropriations bill.

Until the leadership of the Democratic Party supports these two long-overdue reforms, they should close their mouths forever about budget deficits.

Our second goal—developing America's next frontiers in science and high technology and into the far reaches of space—will enable us to surge forward on the crest of progress and peaceful change.

We have it within our power to make astonishing advances in technology and medicine. And that will make us a more competitive, successful, and healthy people. Our greatest resources and hope for the future are the minds and hearts of our people.

That's why our third great goal is to help revive America's traditional values: faith, family, neighborhood, work, and freedom. Government has no business enforcing these values, but neither must it seek, as it did in the recent past, to suppress or replace them. That only robbed us of our tiller and sent [*sic*] us adrift.

Helping restore these values will bring new strength, direction, and dignity to our lives and to the life of our Nation. It's on these values that we'll best build a future.

Finally, we must continue meeting the challenge of working for a more peaceful world in which individual liberty can flourish. Today we're at peace, and this is good. I've seen four wars in my lifetime. I remember Pope Paul VI, saying to the United Nations, "No more war. War never again."

To continue the peace we enjoy, we must show clear support for our allies and exhibit strength and steadiness to those who wish us ill. Setting goals, meeting challenges, striving for excellence are keys to the endless possibilities the future holds in store for America. It's not for the Federal Government to set those goals, but we can help challenge Americans to challenge themselves in all areas of their lives; and, like our Olympic athletes, to reach for greatness.

I'll be speaking more to you about this in the days ahead. Until next week, thanks for listening, and God bless you.

Note: The President spoke at 12:06 P.M. EDT from Camp David.

Labor Day

September 1, 1984

My fellow Americans:

This weekend marks the 90th observance of Labor Day, a well-deserved tribute to the working men and women whose dreams and hard work helped build America into the greatest Nation in the world. We know that what is good for the American worker is good for America. And as we prepare for a new season of work, I believe there's good reason for giving a hopeful thumbs-up.

The outlook on Labor Day Weekend 1984 is for a continuation of strong, steady economic growth, more jobs, and low inflation. We still have great challenges to meet which I'll speak about in a moment. But we should also recognize the progress we've made together. It's an important source of confidence and inspiration for our future.

In the last 19 months, the jobless rate has fallen further and faster than any recovery in the last 30 years. We've seen the creation of six and a half million new jobs. The United States has created on average more jobs each month than all the Common Market countries combined in the last ten years. The Europeans are calling our success the American miracle.

A case in point is the automobile industry. Unemployment peaked at 28 percent in 1980. By this July, auto industry unemployment was down to 6.1 percent, and there were 153,000 more people at work in auto industry jobs than four years ago.

A key reason the job growth has been so strong is our success in keeping inflation down. We haven't seen unemployment and inflation drop during any term since the Kennedy administration. And we're determined to bring inflation further down, just as we're determined to simplify our tax system so we can bring your tax rates further down, not up, as my opponent would do, harming the growth and progress we've made.

With inflation and tax rates down, the American miracle can continue. Interest rates can come down further, people's earnings can continue to buy more, investment and productivity can keep on growing, new businesses can develop new products and markets. More jobs can be created, and all Americans can share in a dynamic, exciting future.

Our future can be one of boundless opportunity if we challenge the limits of growth through reforms like tax simplification and fight inflation by passing two long overdue reforms, the balanced budget spending limitation amendment and the line item veto.

We must also meet the challenge of pushing back our newest frontiers of science, high technology, and space. It's been estimated that high technology industries create jobs eight times as fast as low technology industries. Just as important, the knowledge we gain from the technological revolution enables our older industries to modernize their plants and equipment, increase their ability to compete in the world, and maintain and expand their work force.

Our citizens need training to step into these jobs, and that's why we initiated the Job Training Partnership Act. That act will train more than one million people a year to become productive, self-supporting citizens in the private economy. One sure way to spur jobs through new technology is by promoting more research.

On Thursday morning, I visited the employees of Goddard Space Flight Center and assured them our administration will continue its strong support for research and development, particularly in our universities. Between 1981 and '85, Federal investment in basic research will have increased by almost 30 percent in real terms. The importance of research work in universities reminds us that we must go forward with our agenda for excellence in education so today's students at the elementary and secondary school level can go on to college and acquire the knowledge to work in our rapidly changing world.

At the same time, we must stimulate economic development in inner city areas that have not benefitted from technological innovation or the economic expansion. We've proposed enterprise zones, offering strong incentives for people to start up new businesses in up to 75 areas of high unemployment, and a youth employment opportunity wage to open up job opportunities and reduce the high levels of teenage unemployment, especially among black youth.

Both enterprise zones and the youth employment opportunity wage would reduce dependency, providing new hope for millions. And they're supported by a broad coalition of minorities.

But both have been blocked by the Democratic House leadership, the very people who profess compassion. Americans aspiring to lift themselves up should never be held down by partisan politics. We will keep our economy strong, and we will not rest until it can bring a job to the home of every American.

Until next week, thanks for listening. God bless you.

Note: The President spoke at 12:06 P.M. EDT from the Oval Office at the White House.

Education

September 8, 1984

My fellow Americans:

Young people across the country returned to school this week. The approach of autumn marks the end of the year; but somehow it always seems to be a time of new beginnings in the home and the work place and in the classroom.

We've seen a great resurgence of interest in how our public schools run the past few years. We've seen a new seriousness about the importance of education in our lives. You may remember when a commission we appointed almost three years ago to study the state of our schools concluded that, if another country had done to our schools what we ourselves did to them, we would be justified in calling it an act of war.

But already things are beginning to turn around. It's been one of those great American stories, a little like how neighbors used to band together to raise a house out of the wilderness. Teachers and school principals and school boards have joined with parents and local community leaders to turn things around. Scholastic Aptitude Test scores are turning up. Academic performance is up, and more parents are now showing confidence in the schools.

Forty-two percent of Americans now grade their local schools with an "A" or "B," and that's up 11 percent since last year. A number of schools are leading this academic renewal. Katahdin High School up at Sherman Station, Maine, was named by the Department of Education as an exemplary school. At Katahdin, they encourage students and teachers to work together and understand each other's problems. They have firm disciplinary rules. Teachers feel they have a say in how the school is run. They can get the supplies they need. And they're looking to the future. This little school of 260 students has seven computers.

Then, there's Jefferson High School in Los Angeles, a big city school with 2,000 students, most of them Hispanic or black. Principal Francis Nakano came to Jefferson two years ago and found walls full of graffiti and halls full of unruly youngsters. But Nakano turned it around. He started with discipline—fast, firm and fair. He overhauled the buildings to create a climate for learning. He encouraged learning, recognizing and giving honors to the school's best scholars and helping slow learners with a special program that has them sign a personal contract accepting responsibility for their own progress in return for special individual instruction.

These are just two schools that are a part of our national renewal in education. But what we're doing isn't enough. We've got to do better. I propose that this week the young people starting school and their parents and future employers accept some challenges, and they'll be tough challenges, the type you have to meet by yourself.

First challenge, before this decade is out, we should regain at least half of what we lost in the sixties and seventies on Scholastic Aptitude Test scores. As I said before, those scores are inching their way up, but not fast enough.

Now, if you think that I can't do anything to help, you're wrong. If you're a student who will take the Scholastic Aptitude Test this year, study hard and do your very best. You can help lift our national average.

Second, violence and disorder have no place in our schools. Parents worry about it, and so do many children. Before this decade is out, we should reduce crime in the schools so much that it becomes a mere anecdote in studies about our schools.

Third, there's the problem of dropouts. Our high-school dropout rate is now 27.5 percent. I propose that before this decade is out the public schools of this country reduce the dropout rate to 10 percent or less.

You know, when a girl or boy drops out of school, we tend to think the child failed the system. But I wonder sometimes if it isn't also true that the system failed the child. Sometimes they just need that extra little bit of care and motivation.

There's one other great challenge I want to speak to you about— watching too much TV. Now, I don't want to sound like a scolding parent, but time given to a television show that ought to be given to a school book is time badly used. TV is entertaining and sometimes educational. It's part of the fabric of our lives. But, watching TV is passive—it's not living life.

Life involves effort and growth. You won't grow by watching a situation comedy, though you can grow by reading a book. I hope we aren't becoming a Nation of watchers, because what made us great is that we've always been a Nation of doers.

A dynamic and secure American future requires keeping today's economic expansion strong for tomorrow. And to meet that challenge, we must begin meeting these crucial educational challenges today.

Until next week, thanks for listening. And God bless you.

Note: The President spoke at 12:06 P.M. EDT from Camp David.

Clear Choice for Voters

September 15, 1984

My fellow Americans:

When I set out on this campaign, I said this election would offer one of the clearest choices in 50 years. One major element in that choice is simply this: whether America will continue to champion the great, driving idea for your future—economic growth through individual opportunity—or whether our nation will return to the past and stifle that growth.

We're determined to keep the mighty engine of this Nation revved up to build a future of lasting economic growth without inflation that reaches every American from the Bronx to Birmingham to San Francisco Bay. All that we've done and all that we mean to do is to make our free country freer still, to bring to each of you greater opportunities to build that stronger future.

We believe opportunity is the true engine of progress, the captain of great endeavors. And that's why we asked you in 1981 to give America a new beginning, why we fought for and won a 25-percent tax rate reduction for everyone, tax indexing to keep inflation from pushing you into higher tax brackets, estate tax reductions for family farms and small businesses, a reduction in the marriage penalty tax, an increase in the child care tax credit, deregulation of banking—allowing a higher rate of return for small savers and new incentives for IRAs and Keogh contributions.

These incentives are sweeping fresh winds of progress across America. Along with restraints on government spending and regulating, they're bringing America the strongest surge of economic growth, jobs, business investment, and spendable income since the 1950's. We're no longer talking about promises but about progress, but while that progress is a welcome change from the past, it won't be good enough until everyone can share it.

So, when people ask, "Where do we go from here?", my answer is, "Forward, with more opportunity for more growth for all Americans." We're seeing proof that rewarding people who work and invest and save to get ahead is creating a stronger growth and, in turn, helping still more people to find jobs and build a better life.

So, we want to take this idea of incentives a big step further. We want to enact an historic simplification of our tax system, make the system more fair, easier to understand, so we can bring everybody's income tax rates further down, not up.

Next, we want to put the power of incentives to work in distressed areas of our cities and countryside. We want to establish enterprise zones where taxes and regulations would be cut for anyone starting up or expanding a business.

Imagine ghettos across America with people off welfare working to support their families. Imagine their families living in more secure neighborhoods with less crime, feeling hopeful again about their future. Enterprise zones can do this for America.

To make a free country freer still we want to ensure that those who produce our food and fiber have markets for their products. We've made a good start. Already, we've ended the last administration's disastrous grain embargo, restored grain sales to the Soviets with over 23 million metric tons sold in the last year, given them the go-ahead this week to buy up to 10 million tons more, and reached an agreement with Japan to virtually double our beef exports over the next four years.

So you have a clear choice in 1984. To every American, we offer new opportunity, lower tax rates, more jobs, rising take-home pay, and a brighter future for everyone. My opponent offers the biggest tax increase in our history, $85 billion per year, he says—but really much more if his promises are fully funded. All tolled [*sic*], his tax increase could amount to an additional tax of $1,800 per household, a giant stop sign that would bring America's economic growth and your opportunities for the future screeching to a halt.

His plan would take us back to the worst misery index of the past. Ours would enable all of us to go forward together and build new opportunity for the future.

We're really talking about two different worlds. They see America wringing her hands. We see America raising her hands. They see America divided by envy, each of us challenging our neighbor's success. We see America inspired by opportunity, each of us challenging the best in ourselves.

We believe in knowing when opportunity knocks. They seem determined only to knock opportunity. I think Americans are saying, don't hold us back. Give us a chance and watch how high we fly. And that's just what we want to help you do.

Until next week, thanks for listening, and God bless you.

Note: The President spoke at 12:06 P.M. EDT from the Oval Office at the White House.

Help for Steel and Agriculture

September 22, 1984

My fellow Americans:

When we took office in 1981, our goal was to help all of you build a new era of lasting economic growth without inflation. And we're getting closer.

For the first time since the 1960's, America is enjoying strength in economic growth, business investment, productivity, and the creation of new jobs—six million in the last 20 months—while at the same time, we're keeping inflation down.

Yesterday, we learned that inflation for the last 12 months remains at 4.2 percent, only a third of 1980's 12.4 percent. We're enjoying an historic economic renewal. We can be proud of our accomplishments. But we can't and won't be satisfied until this expansion reaches every sector of our economy.

Two sectors in which millions seek their livelihood, steel and agriculture, have not shared fully in the recovery. This week, we took additional action to help people in both steel and agriculture help themselves so they can work their way out of difficulty and become full partners in our economic expansion, helping all of us build a stronger future.

The American steel industry, as you know, has been struggling through hard times in recent years. The steel companies and their workers have been trying hard to save their industry by cutting costs and modernizing their aging plants and equipment. And we've been trying to help. Our tax reduction, passed in 1981, encourages just such business investments to modernize smoke-stack America.

The industry is beginning to recover; but it's still climbing uphill on the international playing field. In some cases, new technology has simply reduced the need for steel products. But the industry has also been hurt by foreign subsidies and an overproduction of steel worldwide, with foreign imports biting into the U.S. steel industry's share of our domestic market, making the United States a kind of steel dump for the rest of the world.

Well, that simply isn't acceptable. So we've designed a comprehensive plan to cover the entire steel industry and enable us to take swift, effective action to keep the U.S. from being foreign countries' dumping group [*sic*].

I've instructed Ambassador Bill Brock, our International Trade Representative, to meet with representatives of those nations dumping steel and to seek their agreement to stop such practices. And I've made it clear that, as necessary, we'll initiate strong counteractions to defend American firms and workers from predatory practices of other nations.

Taken together, these actions can be expected to bring down the percentage of steel imports from its current 26 percent to about 18.5 percent, excluding semi-finished products. And they'll enable our steel producers to continue their modernization and compete on a level playing field again.

One thing I'm not doing, for it would damage our economy more than it would help, is imposing import quotas. That kind of protectionism is my opponent's policy, and just like his tax increase, it's the wrong policy.

The lessons of history are clear. The costs of protectionism for one group would automatically be passed on to another. Inflation would be reignited, jobs would be destroyed, not saved, and foreign countries would retaliate against our exporters like our farmers. And America doesn't need that kind of help.

I'm confident our plan will help steel producers rebuild and become stronger, more competitive, and profitable again. And that's how we're trying to help our farmers as well. We've ended the last administration's grain embargo, restored grain sales to the Soviet Union, and we've been able to bring down interest rates and sharply reduce inflation.

Unfortunately, our success against inflation, while helpful to farmers in most respects, has caused them some special problems. Many farmers took out loans in the late 1970's when inflation was soaring, and they assumed the value of the land they were pledging as collateral would keep rising with inflation. Well, now that inflation has plunged, those loans have become very difficult for some of those farmers to carry.

So, in the last three years, the Farmers Home Administration has more than doubled its regular operating loans for farmers. This week we announced another major initiative to assist farmers trying to cope with debt burdens. Farmers Home will permit a deferral for five years of up to 25 percent of principal and interest payments owed by farmers who need breathing room. The deferrals will be made on a case-by-case basis. For those not participating in FmHA, we're making available $630 million in guarantees of loans by private banks as part of rescheduling plans for troubled farmers.

The road back isn't easy. But by resisting quick fixes and helping those in steel and farming help themselves, we'll make sure all of us can, and will, go forward together.

Until next week, thanks for listening. And God bless you.

Note: The President spoke at 12:06 P.M. EDT from the Oval Office at the White House.

U.S.-Soviet Relations

September 29, 1984

My fellow Americans:

This has been a busy week of diplomatic activity for America. I've addressed the United Nations and the International Monetary Fund and World Bank meetings, and met with a dozen world leaders. Among them were the new leader of our neighbor to the North, Canadian Prime Minister Brian Mulroney, and, as you know, Soviet Foreign Minister Gromyko.

To the delegates at the UN, I emphasized America's dedication to world peace through confident and stronger alliances, and a constructive dialog with our adversaries. I told them of the importance we attached to seeking peaceful solutions to regional conflicts plaguing many nations, and the need for democratic principles and human freedom as the foundation for a more prosperous, peaceful world.

At the IMF and World Bank, I reported that an American economic renaissance is under way, leading the rest of the world from the darkness of recession toward brighter days of renewed hope and global prosperity.

World economic growth today is nearly twice what it was four years ago. And inflation in the industrial countries is half of what it was. The growing economic interdependence of our world is creating a ripple effect of good news for those countries committed to sensible policies—policies which allow the magic of the marketplace to create opportunities for growth and progress, free from the dead weight of government interference and misguided protectionism.

But we can't build an enduring prosperity unless peace is secure. Our relations with the Soviet Union have been at the center of my attention, and yesterday I met with Foreign Minister Gromyko at the White House for a thorough exchange of views. I've said from the outset of my public life that a successful U.S. policy toward the Soviet Union must rest on realism, strength, and a willingness to negotiate.

Last January, I spelled out clearly for—our goals for U.S.-Soviet relations—to reduce and eventually eliminate the threat and use of force in resolving disagreements, to reduce the vast stockpiles of armaments in the world, especially nuclear arms, and to establish a working relationship between our two countries marked by a greater understanding.

In our meeting yesterday, we covered all issues which separate us. And while I told Mr. Gromyko of our disappointment that his country walked out of the Geneva nuclear arms reduction talks last year, we remain ready to discuss the entire family of arms control issues as soon as they are. It's in both our interests that these talks commence promptly and that progress be made.

Our two countries have no more solemn responsibility than to reduce the level of arms and to enhance understanding.

Mr. Gromyko and I also discussed major trouble spots in the world. And I told him that it's vital for us to exchange views and help find lasting solutions to these regional disputes. We didn't seek to gloss over the hard issues that divide our two countries. We were not looking to paper over these differences. Indeed, I made plain to Mr. Gromyko what it is about Soviet behavior that worries us and our allies.

But they were useful talks. I made it clear that we Americans have no hostile intentions toward his country and that we're not seeking military superiority over the U.S.S.R. I told him, "If your government wants peace, then there will be peace." And I said that the United States is committed to move forward with the Soviet Union toward genuine progress in resolving outstanding issues.

Pursuing peace, prosperity, and democracy are not new goals. They've been at the heart of an American foreign policy that down through the years has sought to promote individual freedom and human progress in the world.

I think one great change has taken place in the world over the last four years: The tide of freedom has begun to rise again. Four years ago, American influence and leadership were ebbing. Our defenses were neglected, our economy was collapsing, and other countries were being undermined by Communist-supported insurgencies. Today, our economy is vibrant, our strength is being restored, our alliances are solid, and peace is more secure.

Now, the Soviets will return home to ponder our exchanges. And while they know they will not secure any advantages from inflexibility, they will get a fair deal if they seek the path of negotiation and peace.

Until next week, thanks for listening, and God bless you.

Note: The President spoke at 12:06 P.M. EDT from Camp David.

Mondale's Initiatives to Combat Drugs

October 6, 1984

My fellow Americans:

This week my opponent unveiled with great fanfare his plan to combat dangerous drugs, a plan comprising what he called "four new initiatives." Well, forgive me, but his so-called "new initiatives" aren't new. Every one of them is by now an old initiative, begun by us more than two and a half years ago when we first started the South Florida Task Force.

Then, a year later, following the success of the Task Force, we extended these initiatives nationwide and set up a National Border Interdiction System known as NNBIS.

Consider my opponent's first new initiative: "Create a high-level drug coordinator." Well, perhaps he hasn't heard, but we already have drug interdiction coordination at the highest possible level of government. The Vice President has been in charge of the South Florida Task Force and NNBIS from the start. And under his direction nearly two dozen Federal agencies have been brought into the war on drugs. Many, including the Army, Navy, Air Force, and Marines, are more involved in fighting drugs than ever before. Working with the Coast Guard and civilian law enforcement agencies, the military has contributed directly to the interdiction and seizure of major quantities of marijuana and cocaine in the past two years.

The Vice President has worked closely with the Attorney General who has created 13 new organized crime and drug enforcement task forces. And those task forces are bringing record numbers of indictments against the leaders of drug trafficking.

His second new initiative undertakes "broad international initiatives." Well, we're already working with other governments, as no administration before has, to stop the flow of drugs into our country. Bolivia and Peru recently began cocoa [*sic*] plant control programs. Pakistan has reduced its apium—or opium, I should say—poppy cultivation more than 90 percent. And Burma continues to expand its opium eradication effort. Columbia [*sic*] has begun spraying its marijuana crops and in the last year has located and destroyed major cocaine factories.

This past summer the Vice President met with the Presidents of five Latin American countries to discuss further efforts. And, as you saw this past week, expert cooperation between our Justice Department and the Italian government led to the arrest of Mafia leaders in the United States.

My opponent's third new initiative: "Step up American enforcement efforts." Well, someone should tell him that we've included $1.2 billion in the 1985 Federal budget for drug law enforcement—a 75-percent increase over the last budget of his administration.

During his administration, drug enforcement agencies and FBI agents were reduced by 10 percent. In our administration, the Department of Justice has added 1,200 new agents and prosecutors, and we've increased the special agents in Customs from 600 to 1,000.

Apparently he hasn't heard about the increase in radar balloons, and Navy and Air Force surveillance flights to track planes attempting to slip across the Gulf of Mexico and the Mexican border—not to mention the Coast Guard which is moving forward with its improved detection and surveillance program.

Finally, his fourth new initiative: "More State and local support." State and local officials are involved in the drug war as never before. Forty-seven States are now eradicating domestic marijuana. State and local law enforcement officials have expressed their satisfaction with the new high level of information sharing and cooperative efforts with the Federal Government.

At home and abroad we've seen record drug busts and convictions, and we've seen that, in each of the last two years, serious crime has dropped—the first time that's happened in consecutive years since the FBI began keeping statistics.

Let me mention something else, because for all the so-called "new initiatives" my opponent is proposing—that we've already begun—he did admit—omit—one very important one. We're not just increasing our efforts to limit the supply of drugs, we're also trying to limit the demand for drugs. And that's why Nancy's been joining with concerned parents and citizens all across our country to put out the word to young Americans: stay away from drugs; they hurt and kill.

And we can all be proud of the way our young people have responded. In 1979, one in nine high-school seniors used marijuana on a daily basis. By 1983 the number had dropped to one in eighteen—still too high, but a great improvement.

Just as Americans have pulled together to turn around so many problems we inherited four years ago—inflation, record interest rates, taxes, no growth, falling test scores in school, and low morale in our military—so, too, we're coming together as a Nation to tackle the drug problem.

So the question I keep wondering about my opponent is: Where's he been?

Until next week, thanks for listening, and God bless you.

Note: The President spoke at 12:06 P.M. EDT from Camp David.

Clear Choice for Voters

October 13, 1984

My fellow Americans:

The 1984 campaign is in full swing. And no matter who you are—student, construction worker, farmer, nurse, or high-tech entrepreneur—this election offers you the clearest choice for your future in many years.

The central economic issue in this campaign is growth. Will we have policies that give each of you opportunities to climb higher and push America to challenge the limits of growth, policies like those that in the [*sic*] 22 months have given this Nation the strongest economic expansion in 30 years? Or will we go back to those failed policies of the Carter-Mondale administration that inflicted unprecedented hardship on our people?

Our vision of strong economic growth is not a pipe dream. It's a living accomplishment. And it can continue to get better, offering new hope for everyone, including all of you who have not yet recovered from the Carter-Mondale past.

We came to Washington with a pledge to make a new beginning by putting more power, earnings, and decisions back in your hands. That's why we passed the first tax rate reduction for everyone since President John Kennedy's program 20 years ago. And it's no coincidence that once those tax cuts took hold the American economy woke up with a roar from years of economic slumber.

Think about this success because you're the ones who made it happen and who can and must keep it going. Twenty-two straight months of economic expansion, and yet inflation is only one-third what it was when my opponent was in office.

Six hundred thousand new business incorporations last year—an all-time record. Over 6 million new jobs created. In fact, more jobs created on average each month than were created in all the Common Market countries combined during the last ten years.

But we can't and won't be satisfied until every American who wants a job can find a job, until inflation is down to 0.0 and interest rates have been brought down more, until the farm community has fully recovered from the legacy of record interest rates, inflation, and the grain embargo—and until we modernize and make our older industries more competitive with new technologies. In other words, all of us have made great progress, but even greater challenges lie ahead.

We want to go forward with exciting new opportunities to help America challenge the limits of growth. For example, an historic simplification of our tax system, making the entire system more fair and easier to understand so we can bring yours and everybody's personal tax rates further down, not up.

My opponent has a very different vision—a gloomy vision of weakness that doesn't look to you with confidence or challenge you to dream great dreams and make America grow but that places its trust in bigger government. We must ask ourselves one question: What has he ever done or said to suggest, let alone convince us, that his vision can do anything but fail?

The record is clear. In his administration, the only things that went up were inflation, interest rates, and taxes, while everything else—investment, productivity, earnings, savings, confidence, optimism, and growth—all fell apart.

Then, when we came along, he predicted our tax reduction would be "murderously inflationary." That was just before inflation dropped dramatically. He said there was no hope of recovery. Then economic recovery began. He said recovery would be anemic at best. That was before the strongest economic expansion in 30 years.

Now he says the deficit cannot be brought down without new tax increases. And at this very moment, the deficit is coming down without new tax increases.

My opponent puts government first, which is why his policies fail and his predictions are wrong. We trust in you, and that spells success through economic growth. Nor has he learned from his mistakes. He has proposed to raise taxes by $85 billion. In fact, he would have to raise taxes the equivalent of $1,890 per household to pay for his promises.

And just this past week he began to reveal the rest of his plan. He said he would repeal indexing, the reform we passed to keep you from being taxed when inflation pushes you into higher and higher tax brackets. Now he says he goofed. Well—whatever. We do know he has a basic two-part plan: raise your taxes, and then raise them again.

Asking you to buy his failed policies is a little like someone expecting you to go to a used-car lot to buy back the lemon you got rid of four years ago. But you don't have to. You can stick with leadership that's working, leadership that trusts in you and offers growth and opportunity so all of us can go forward together to build a better American future.

Until next week, thanks for listening. God bless you.

Note: The President spoke at 12:06 P.M. EDT from Camp David.

Foreign Policy Issues

October 20, 1984

My fellow Americans:

Tomorrow, my opponent and I will debate foreign policy in Kansas City, so I'd like to talk to you about the foreign policy choice for our future as I see it.

In speaking about his economic policies, I've said my opponent is a man of the past whose administration's domestic policies failed and made America weak. Well, that goes for foreign policy as well. Mr. Mondale as a Senator, later as understudy to Jimmy Carter, and still today has seemed possessed with one simple but very wrong idea: American strength is a threat to world peace. And he's devoted a political career to opposing our strength, exposing us to dangerous, unnecessary risks.

As a Senator, he voted time and again against American strength, against technological advances meant to better protect our security. He voted against the cruise missile, the B-1 bomber, the Trident submarine, and against salary increases for the military. Yes, he did vote for certain things. He voted for cutting U.S. troops in Europe, for cutting our military manpower, and for cutting our defense budgets.

How could a politician even face the young people who protect our freedom after he's voted to deny them the equipment and protection they need? My opponent's Senate voting record on defense was so weak, he ranked right next to George McGovern.

The Carter-Mondale administration echoed this defeatist spirit. By the late 1970's, the policies of unilateral concession were giving the Soviet Union military advantages over the United States and the West. The Soviets installed missiles that created new vulnerabilities in Europe and put new strains on the NATO alliance. During those years, the Soviet Union expanded its influence in Africa, Asia, the Middle East, and here in our own hemisphere. They overturned or took control of a new country every year.

Meanwhile, the Carter-Mondale administration negotiated an arms agreement so weak they couldn't get it approved in a Senate controlled by their own party. My opponent talks about the Carter-Mondale years as a period of relaxed tension. Well, it's true they relaxed—but the Soviets didn't.

What troubles me most is how little he seems to have learned about the dangers of weakness and naive thinking. I don't question his patriotism; I do question his judgment. In 1968 he said that the days of Soviet "suppression by force" were "over." Then, the Soviets invaded Czechoslovakia. But he didn't learn. He voted against American military strength during the 1970's, even as the Soviets were embarking upon the most massive military buildup in history.

After the Soviets invaded Afghanistan in 1979, Mr. Mondale still hadn't learned. He said, "I cannot understand. It just baffles me why the Soviets these last few years have behaved as they have. And why do they have to build up all those arms?" Well, today he still advocates unilateral cuts in important weapons systems, still argues for a freeze, which his own running mate admits is not fully verifiable and Mr. Carter's former National Security Adviser describes as "a hoax."

Senator Glenn, a Democrat, has warned that "Walter Mondale's defense policies would emasculate America." Senator Hollings, a Democrat, said, "Walter Mondale thinks the Soviet Union would never violate an arms agreement. I think he's naive."

Well, to borrow Mr. Mondale's expression, he seems baffled by so much. He was confused about the rightness of freeing our students on the island of Grenada. He said that liberation took away our moral authority to criticize the Soviets about Afghanistan. Yet, he could not bring himself to repudiate the Reverend Jesse Jackson after he had traveled to Cuba and said, "Long live Cuba, long live Castro, long live Che Guevara."

Well, in the past 3½ years, our administration has demonstrated the true relationship between strength and confidence and democracy and peace. We've restored our economy and begun to restore our military strength. This is the true foundation for a future that is more peaceful and free.

We've made America and our alliances stronger and the world safer. We've discouraged Soviet expansion by helping countries help themselves, and new democracies have emerged in El Salvador, Honduras, Grenada, Panama, and Argentina. We have maintained peace and begun a new dialog with the Soviets. We're ready to go back to the table to discuss arms control and other problems with the Soviet leaders.

Today we can talk and negotiate in confidence because we can negotiate from strength. Only my opponent thinks America can build a more peaceful future on the weakness of a failed past.

Until next week, thanks for listening, and God bless you.

Note: The President spoke at 12:06 P.M. EDT from the Oval Office at the White House.

October 27, 1984

My fellow Americans:

When I was asked recently what's been the greatest highlight of our campaign, I said the tremendous number of young people at our rallies and the tremendous outpouring of their spirit for America and our future.

To all of them, I just have to say, your generation really sparkles. In my travels I have met you by the thousands, and I've seen enthusiasm and patriotism in your eyes that convince me you get high on America. Historians may look back at the strength of your spirit and common sense as key to the great American renewal in the 1980's.

Our generations are separated by more years than I care to admit; yet I feel a special bond of kinship with you. I think we share not only a great love for America but also an appreciation for the secret of America's success—opportunity.

America works best when we unite for opportunity, reaching for the stars and challenging the limits of our potential. And America's greatest progress for everyone—whites, blacks, young, and old—begins not in Washington, but in our homes, neighborhoods, workplaces, and voluntary groups across this land.

We weren't meant to be a Nation divided; we weren't meant to be a Nation second-best. We were meant to be, as our Olympic athletes showed last summer, a people with faith in each other, courage to dream great dreams, opportunities to climb higher, and determination to go for the gold.

Providing opportunities for all of us to make this great, free Nation greater and freer still is what we've been trying to do since we made a great sea change in 1981—a change to reverse the flow of power to Washington and begin restoring sovereignty to the people.

We knew that inflation and the highest interest rates since the Civil War were making it impossible for people to buy homes, start up businesses, or, for that matter, even find jobs. So, we reduced spending growth and cut tax rates for everyone. We knew that our defenses had become dangerously weak. So, we started rebuilding to be strong again.

We've only begun to clear away the debris from decades of bad policies. Many people still need help. Nevertheless, America already has made a great comeback. Inflation, taxes, interest rates, and crime are down, but confidence, jobs, investment, growth, and achievement in our schools are up. And unlike 4 years ago when the Soviets were gaining influence and spreading instability throughout the world, since 1981 not one square inch of territory has been lost to Communist aggression. That's what makes the world a safer place.

Today, our nation is at peace and our economy is in one piece. We're poised to meet great challenges for the future. We can reduce personal tax rates further, creating new jobs and opportunities for every American with nobody left behind. We can pass initiatives like enterprise zones to rebuild the distressed areas of our country and push on toward much greater progress in education, science, technology, and space.

This month an American woman, Kathryn Sullivan, made history walking in space, then returned to the space shuttle in which some of the great scientific and medical advances of the future will be made. That's why we support the space shuttle and why we've committed America to build a permanently manned space station within a decade.

And by keeping America strong and prepared for peace we'll have the best chance to begin reducing nuclear weapons and, one day, God willing, banish them entirely.

But before we do anything, you must choose: Will we keep moving forward on a new path toward a better future, or will we turn back to my opponent's philosophy—weaker defenses, inflationary spending, and huge tax increases?

The difference between us is that we look at a problem and see opportunity, and he looks at opportunity and sees a problem. We see a tax system that rewards work and investment and stimulates growth. Mr. Mondale would bring back the very policies that destroy incentives, destroy opportunity, and destroy economic growth—policies that would cause enormous hardship and send many of you from the graduation line to the unemployment line.

We can do better, much better. We want you to have an America every bit as full of hope, confidence, and dreams as our parents left us. Come November 6th, I hope millions of you will make history by voting for your future—voting for opportunity, voting for leadership that trusts in you and the power of your dreams. If you do, we'll bring this Nation together with new strength and unity. We'll make sure America's best days are yet to come.

Until next week, thanks for listening, and God bless you.

Note: The President spoke at 12:06 P.M. EDT from Camp David.

November 3, 1984

My fellow Americans:

In 3 days, this election campaign will be over, and America's future will be in your hands. As you discuss the election with family and friends in your homes and neighborhoods, I think there's one thing we can all agree on. We all want to vote for something, not against something. We want to vote for a better America, for a stronger country with our people pulling together; a future of peace, filled with hope and new opportunity, a future where our progress is limited only by our own dreams and determination and where Americans are working because America is working.

So, it seems to me the question to be asked is a straightforward one: Which team's record and proposals stand a better chance to enable you and your families to enjoy a strong and successful future? Well, our opponents don't spend much time speaking about their record. And that's understandable. Their record speaks for itself.

After 4 years of controlling the White House and both houses of Congress, they left America weaker, both at home and abroad. They would have us forget their legacy of an America second-best, double-digit inflation, record taxes and interest rates at home; growing instability and threats to peace abroad. I'd be willing to forget that record, too, if they weren't so bound and determined to give us some more of that medicine that made us sick.

As for their new proposals, they differ from their old ones in only one respect: They've promised more. They will spend more, and they will raise your taxes much higher, the equivalent of $1,890 per household, more than $150 per month.

Now, my opponent wants very badly to make you believe his enormous tax increase proposal won't hurt your families. That's what his commercials say. And those commercials are every bit as believable as the ones he ran portraying himself as a person committed to a strong national defense, standing on the deck of a carrier, even though he voted against them, with F-14 fighters, which he also voted against, and beside American enlisted men, whose salary increases he opposed.

Our opponents are determined to bring back even more big taxing and spending than before. And if they regain control of this government, Americans may look back on our term as one brief oasis of prosperity in an endless desert of worsening inflation and recession.

Yes, their intentions are good. But good intentions aren't good enough. Their policies made America weak before. They would make us weak again today, and even weaker still in the future.

America can do better, much better. And the fact is, America is doing better. The principal difference is, our vision for America will let the eagle soar. Theirs will return us to the days of the sore eagle.

We still face great problems, but today our economy is stronger than 4 years ago because we've cut your tax rates, brought inflation and interest rates down, and created 6 million new jobs. And America is more secure, because we're rebuilding our defenses and our alliances to ensure peace through strength.

Today, the United States expansion is leading the world into recovery, and that contributes to a safer, more prosperous world. Respect for America and confidence in America are rising again. And unlike 4 years ago, the United States is deterring, the Soviets aren't advancing, and all this, too, contributes to a safer world and a better future.

We've made a good start, but it's only a start. We want to lower your tax rates further to create more jobs and opportunities for every American, with nobody left behind. And nobody left behind means we must continue our efforts to modernize our older industries and to rebuild our inner cities and distressed areas of America, so every American who wants a job can find a job.

We've sponsored enterprise zone legislation, to encourage business development and creation of jobs in distressed areas. But from day one, our enterprise zone proposal has been held hostage by the House leadership, the very people who act as if they expect black and Hispanic Americans to march in lockstep with the Democratic Party.

I can assure all of you who want the opportunity to begin climbing the economic ladder, to build a better life: If you give us your support, we will never take your votes for granted.

I believe Americans are coming together with new strength, confidence, spirit, and unity. From the bottom of my heart, I thank you for allowing me the honor of serving you these past 4 years. I urge you to vote on Tuesday, and I hope you'll cast your votes for our team, our entire team, so we can make even greater progress in building a strong, secure future of opportunity for all of you.

Until next week, thanks for listening. God bless you.

Note: The President's remarks were recorded at the White House on October 31 for broadcast at 12:06 P.M. EST on November 3. This was the last radio address of his first term, despite the "Until next week" sign-off. Mr. Reagan resumed the talks on January 26, 1985.

INDEX

Abortion, adoption as option, 220; congressional legislation against, 67
Academic Fitness Awards, 210
Adams, John, quoted, 3
Adams, John M. G., 3
Adoption, 166, 220
Advisory Committee on Women's Business Ownership, 198
Aeroflot, 141, 144
Afghanistan, refugees from, 59; relieving suffering in, 62; Soviet aggression in, 5, 19, 45, 62, 63, 76, 217, 254
Africa, 152; Soviet influence in, 217, 253; U.S. economic progress in, 5, 57; Voice of America broadcasts to, 139
Agriculture, 193; Mondale's cuts in, 232
Air Force, and budget cuts, 85; retention rate in, 174; tribute to, on Armed Forces Day, 13, 14; tribute to, on Veterans Day, 157; in war on drugs, 249, 250
Air Force One, 215
Airline industry, deregulation of, 174
Air pollution, 226
Alabama, employment in, 146; Nancy Reagan's trip to, 31; and wilderness areas, 112
Alaska, 172; Reagan's visit to, 207
Alcohol abuse, 32, 223, 224
Alcohol-related automobile accidents, 60–61, 169
Alexandria, Virginia, 172
American Family Institute, 165
American Federation of Teachers, 176
American Red Cross, 172; appeal for aid to, 108
American University, 121
Andrews Air Force Base, 95, 125
Andropov, Yuri, 184–85
Arab states, and Israelis in occupied territories, 136; in negotiations with Israel, 148–49, 168
Argentina, 254; and confrontation with U.K. [Falklands], 3
Arkansas, Nancy Reagan's trip to, 31
Arlington National Cemetery, 156
Armed forces (armed services, military), 89; in Beirut, 95, 96; low pay in, 14, 174; Mondale vote against salary increases for, 253, 257; morale of, 174, 214, 251; restore readiness of, 56–57,

214; right to pray in, 67; tribute to, on Armed Forces Day, 13–15, 104–06; tribute to, on Veterans Day, 157
Armed Forces Day, tributes to, 13–15, 104–06
Armistice Day, 156
Arms control, U.S.-Soviet, 19, 45, 121–23, 152-53, 162, 248, 254; agreements on, 57, 200, 253–54. *See also* INF talks
Arms race, U.S.-Soviet, 105, 155
Arms reduction, 106, 109, 118. 185, 216; U.S.-Soviet, 53, 64, 69, 76, 85, 105, 121–23, 152–53, 154–55, 162, 218, 248; agreements on, 105, 152, 186, 214. *See also* Geneva; Nuclear arsenals; Nuclear weapons
Armstrong, Neil, quoted, 228
Army (soldiers), pay raise for, 56–57; tribute to, on Armed Forces Day, 13, 14; tribute to, on Veterans Day, 157; in war on drugs, 249
Asia, 152, 205; Soviet influence in, 253; U.S. interest in, 57, 174, 177; Voice of America broadcasts to, 139
Astronauts, 103
Atlantic Alliance, 218
Attorney General, 224, 249
Australia, flights suspended to Soviet Union, 142; U.S. sailors in, 89–90
Automobile Dealers Association of Eastern Ohio, 8
Automobile industry, and anti-pollution standards, 226; calling workers back, 70, 72, 109, 146, 240; and high interest rates, 1, 8, 30, 35, 40, 87, 91, 109; increase in sales and production, 9, 37, 39, 56, 72, 84, 92, 161, 173, 193, 214; interest rates lowered for new car purchases, 8; layoffs in, 1, 23, 40, 72, 240; and local content rule, 110

Bailey, Ashley, need for organ transplant, 124–25, 126
Baker, Howard, 29, 185
Balance-of-payments assistance, to Caribbean Basin, 52; to IMF, 124
Baldrige, Malcolm, 138
Ballyporeen, Reagan's visit to, 215
Banks and banking, deregulation of, 174, 244; guarantees to farmers, 246
Barbados, Reagan's visit to. 3–4
Bastiat, Claude F., 15
Beijing, Reagan's visit to, 206

Beirut, 156, 157, 167; Marines writing
from, 58, 148; terrorist attack on U.S.
Embassy in, 95–96
Belgium, Bush's visit to, 63
Benham, Amy, 171
Bible, Reagan family, 101
Bioengineering, 173
Bolivia, and drug control, 249–50
Bombers, B-1, 253; B-52, 76; manned,
54; Mondale vote against, 253
Boston Tea Party, 93
Bracket creep, 38, 85, 86
Bradford, William, quoted, 27
Brezhnev, Leonid, 47, 152
Brock, William, 41, 246
Budget, federal, 15–16, 17–18, 38–40;
and constitutional amendment to
require balanced, 10, 22, 31, 38, 43,
234, 235, 238, 240; defense share of,
38; deficits, *see* Deficit(s); for fiscal
year 1981, 11, 12, 71; for fiscal year
1982, 11, 12, 71; for fiscal year 1983,
11, 12; for fiscal year 1984, 68–70,
72–74, 76; liberal Democratic,
84, 92; Mondale's cuts in, 232; non-
defense share of, 38–39; proposed by
House, 84–88, 92; reductions in,
120–21; Senate resolution to reduce,
16; support for bipartisan, 9–10,
17–18
Building permits, 41, 195
Bureau of Customs, and drug
control, 250
Bureau of Labor Statistics, 12
Burma, and drug control, 250
Buses, segregation in, 64–65
Bush, George, to Andropov's funeral,
185; and King tribute, 65; trip to
Europe, 63–64; and war on drugs, 32,
249, 250
Business failures, 41, 103
Business loans, 150
Business start-ups, 41, 56, 103, 109, 214,
255; new incorporations, 237, 240, 251

California, 108; as environmental leader,
111, 226; Reagan's reductions in
spending in, 180
Camden (NJ) High School, and students'
experiments in space, 113–14
Camp David accords, 135–36, 148
Camp Lejeune, 157
Canada, and Caribbean Basin Initiative,
3, 53; suspended Aeroflot, 141; U.S.

commitment to, 20
Canadian Air Traffic Controllers Associ-
ation, 141
Cancer, and space research, 228
Capital punishment, 225
Capital spending, 150–51
CARE, aid to Poland, 34
Caribbean Basin, 51; drop in world price
of products of, 51; high price of
imports to, 52; as our third border, 3
Caribbean Basin Initiative, 3–4, 23,
51–53, 129, 132, 162, 201
Car loans, 150
Carter, Jimmy, 54, 253, 254
Carter-Mondale administration, 251,
252, 253–54, 257
Castro, Fidel, 254
Catholic Relief Service, aid to
Poland, 34
Catholics, and tuition tax credits, 7, 67
Central America, Communist influence
in, 197; instability in, 89, 197; and
Kissinger Commission, 130, 177–78;
Soviet and Cuban intervention in,
131, 148, 196, 197, 202, 217; U.S.
assistance to, 131, 174, 183, 197,
201–03; as another Vietnam, 148. *See
also* Carribean Basin Initiative
CETA (Comprehensive Employment
and Training Act), 80, 147
Child abuse, 220
Child care, tax credit for, 166
Child pornography laws, 188, 220
Child Protection Act, 220
Childrearing, cost of, 165
Child support, enforcement of, 166,
198, 220
China (People's Republic), Reagan's visit
to, 205–07, 218; and Soviet aggres-
sion, 206; textiles agreement with,
129–30; U.S relations with,
206–07, 218
Christmas Day, remarks on, 58–60,
171–73
Chrysler Corp., calling workers back, 72
Civil rights legislation, in housing, 121;
and King, 65
Civil Service Retirement System, abuses
in, 133–34
Civil War, 28, 255
Clark, Esther, quoted, 100
Clark, William, 163, 165
Clean Air Act, 226
Clean air bill, 43

Coastal Barrier Resources Act, 163
Coastal barriers, 227; and Watt, 163
Coast Guard, in war on drugs, 249, 250
Cocaine, 223, 249, 250; in south Florida, 32
Cold War, 137
College education, no-tax savings accounts for, 82
Colombia, and Caribbean Basin Initiative, 3, 53; and drug control, 250
Commission on Organized Crime, 225
Committee on Disarmament meeting (Geneva), 63
Common Market, employment in, 221, 240, 252
Communications satellites, 113
Communism, 249, 255; upon our doorstep, 148
Communist influence, in Central America, 89, 132, 179, 197, 203; in El Salvador, 132, 196; in Nicaragua, 131, 196
Communist party, in Poland, 25, 34
Computers, 151, 173, 180, 242; and crystals manufactured in space, 228
Conference on Free Elections, 42
Congress, 152, 153, 159, 160–62, 177, 230; and aid to Central America, 197; and aid to El Salvador, 197, 200–01, 203; anti-abortion legislation, 67; anti-crime legislation, 26, 187, 188, 225, 235; approval of Marines in Lebanon, 147–48; big spenders in, 84, 88, 119, 161; bipartisan budget, 9–10, 17–18; and budget savings, 192; and Caribbean Basin Initiative, 3, 52, 53, 162; and child-support enforcement, 198, 220; clean air bills, 43, 226; constitutional amendment to require balanced budget, 10, 22, 31, 38, 43, 234, 238, 240; and contribution to IMF, 123–24; deficit-reducing measures, 11, 12, 13, 162, 195, 222; and deregulation of natural gas, 78, 79; "do-nothing," 234–35; efforts toward recovery, 138; and employment programs, 80, 212, 213; enterprise zones proposal, 43, 166, 234–35, 258; and entitlement programs, 69; and EPA budget, 227; equal access legislation, 234; fiscal year 1984 budget, 68, 70; and foreign policy powers, 201; funding to modernize international broadcasting, 140; and government spending, 43; and

highway program, 50; increase in confidence in, 160; jobs bill, 221; job training bill, 30; and Kissinger Commission, 177–78, 183; legislation to train more math and science teachers, 84, 98; and merit pay for federal employees, 134; MX missile basing proposal, 54; and national parks, 227; and neglected defenses, 76; and pension plan reform, 198–99; prayers said in, 28, 67; proposal to modernize intercontinental ballistic missiles, 104, 118, 122; and regulatory reform, 43; and Soviet attack on Korean airliner, 137, 142; and spending cuts, 183; and student loan defaults, 208; supplemental appropriations bill vetoed by Reagan, 22–23, 24; support for Scowcroft Commission, 106; tax-cut program, 1–2; and tuition tax credits, 7–8, 67, 82, 98, 162, 235; and voluntary prayer amendment, 66–67, 82, 190; and voluntary prayer measure, 28–29, 162; Washington's address to, 75; and wilderness lands, 112; and Williamsburg Summit, 109; and withholding tax on interest and dividends, 93, 94, 95
Constitution, 188; amendment to require balanced budgets, 10, 22, 31, 38, 43, 234, 235, 238, 240; First Amendment, 28, 188–89; voluntary prayer amendment, 66–67, 82, 190
Constitutional Convention, 189
Construction industry, layoffs in, 1; recovery in, 51, 70, 79, 146, 161
Consumer confidence, 92
Consumer incomes, 18
Consumer prices, 87
Consumer spending, 56
Contadora process, 203
Continental Shelf, 163, 164
Contras, U.S. sympathy for, 132
Corregidor, U.S. nurses captured at, 117–18
Costa Rica, 132, 202; Reagan's trip to, 51, 53
Cost-of-living pay increases, 68; freeze in, 69; and indexing, 16–17, 85, 86, 91–92, 134, 191, 205, 213
Court of Appeals, 189
Courts, not tough on criminals, 26
Craxi, Bettino, 153
Credit bureaus, 127

Credit control, 41
Criminal forfeiture laws, 26
Criminal justice system, reforms proposed in, 26–27, 186–88, 224–25, 235
Crime, 25–27, 100, 184, 186–88, 224–26, 244; anti-crime legislation, 25, 187, 188, 225, 235; in New York subways, 25; organized, 187, 225; in schools, 175, 211, 243; victims, 26, 188, 224, 225
Crime Control Act, 187, 188
Crime rate, drop in, 151, 187, 220, 224, 250, 255; rise in, 25, 238
Cuba, 103, 137; intervention in Central America, 131, 178, 196; Jackson's trip to, 254; U.S. broadcasts to, 140, 162
Czechoslovakia, invaded by Soviets, 254

Davis, Courtney, 125
D-Day anniversary, 21; and Reagan, 216, 217
Death benefits, 198
DeBolt, Dorothy, 100
Debt collection, federal, 127, 208
Declaration of Independence, 189
Defense, budget provides for, 18; erosion of, 56; and force modernization, 76, 84, 105, 106, 118, 122; George Washington on preparedness, 75; Mondale's proposed cuts in, 232, 257; restore by making savings in, 69; triad defined, 54. *See also* Department of Defense
Defenses, neglected, 69, 75–76, 84, 238, 249, 255; rebuilding, 258
Defense spending, 41, 135; cuts in, 17, 75–76, 84–85, 87, 183, 195, 214; effects of cuts in, 85, 87; and House budget, 84, 195; increases in, 38, 74, 75, 314; to keep up with Soviet capabilities, 45, 85; Mondale's proposed cuts in, 253; vs. that on education, 115
Deficit(s), federal budget, 1, 11, 71, 180, 190–92, 236, 252; causes of, 38, 69, 179, 209; downpayment on projected, 183, 191, 195, 222; and gross national product, 69; Mondale's projections for, 232; problem explained, 68; proposals to reduce, 11–12, 23, 85, 87, 104, 110, 194, 195, 238; reduce by bipartisan budget, 9, 18, 22; reduce by cutting spending, 87, 161, 191–92; wipe out by collecting unpaid taxes, 7

Delinquency, 166
Democratic vs. Republican party, during campaign, 238–39
Deng Xiaoping, 206
Department of Commerce, 87
Department of Defense (Pentagon), 115; fight against fraud and waste in, 126–27, 134, 209; and supplemental appropriations bill, 22–23
Department of Education, 82, 115, 176, 192, 242
Department of Energy, 78
Department of Health and Human Services, 39
Department of Housing and Urban Development (HUD), 121, 127
Department of Interior, jurisdiction of, 163–64
Department of Justice, 121, 176, 208, 209; and drug control, 250
Department of Labor, 43
Department of Transportation, 208–09
Depreciation allowances, 2
Deregulation, 174, 221, 244
Deterrence, paradox of, 104, 105; policy of, 53–54, 55, 122, 153, 154, 162, 174, 218, 258
Dewey, George, 156
Diabetes, and space research, 228
Dillon, Robert S., 96
Dirksen, Everett, quoted, 180
Disabled veterans, 157
Disadvantaged children, 82
Disaster relief, through Red Cross, 108
Discount rate, 22
Discrimination, fought against by King, 64; in housing, 121
Diseases, and space research, 228
Disney, Hursel C., 8
Divorces, 151
Dole, Elizabeth, 182; and drunk driving problem, 170, 175
Dollar, strong, 128–29, 150; worth something again, 85
Domestic spending, 69, 84
Draper, Morris, 96
Drinking age, legal, 61
Drug abuse, 100; administration's strategy for fighting, 27, 32–33, 166, 224–25, 249–51; letter from addict, 223; Mondale's proposed initiatives to combat, 249–51; Nancy Reagan's comments on, 31–32, 223–24; Nancy Reagan's interest in, 33, 250

Drug-influenced drivers, problem of, 60, 173

Drug Kingpin Law, 225

Drug pushers, 26

Drug trafficking, administration's strategy against, 26, 32–33, 187, 220, 225, 235, 249

Drunk driving, problem of, 60–61, 169–71, 173, 175; programs to combat, 61, 170

Dublin, Reagan's visit to, 215

Easter, remarks on, 88–90

East Germany, escape from, 89

Ecclesiastes, quoted, 44

Economic growth, 238, 239, 240, 244, 245, 247–48; as campaign issue, 251

Economic indicators, leading, 24, 70, 72, 79, 193

Economic recovery, 43, 56, 73, 84, 85, 88, 91, 92, 103, 109, 138, 145–47, 160, 192–94, 220–22, 236–37, 252; worldwide, 106–07, 109, 200, 216, 217, 258

Economic recovery program, 1–2, 9–10, 18, 24, 40–42, 55–56, 70–72, 73, 74, 79, 87, 100–01, 163, 173, 179–80, 204–05, 213–14, 236; Reagan's open letter to senator criticizing, 40–42

Economic Summit (London), 216, 217–18; (Ottawa), 45, 217; (Versailles), 18, 19–20, 106; (Williamsburg), 106–08, 109–10, 122, 128, 153, 160, 217

Economy, 21–23, 29–31, 35–37, 38–40, 83, 84, 87; news coverage of, 193

Education, 81–83, 97–99, 115–17, 209–11, 242–43, 256; amount of government spending for, 115–16; campaign to restore excellence in, 83, 98, 151, 209–11, 255; cost per pupil, 116; discipline in, 166, 175–77, 209, 242; and in-school crime, 175, 211, 243; and in-school violence, 175–76, 243; loans for, 4, 150; and problem of high-school dropouts, 243; quality of learning declining, 82, 97, 115, 117, 151, 209, 238; Reagan's challenge to students, 98–99, 242–43; and students watching too much television, 243; and support for university research work, 240. *See also* National Commission on Excellence in Education; Prayer in public schools; Tuition tax credits; Voucher system

Egypt, peace treaty with Israel, 149

Eisenhower, Dwight D., and D-Day, 21; and Lebanon, 168

El Camino High School (Sacramento), 176

Elderly (senior citizens), benefits to, 191–92, 237; and crime, 25; preserving value of pensions, 29; surplus food to, 120

Elections (1982), 38, 42–43; foreign observers of, 42. *See also* Presidential campaign

Ellis Island, campaign to restore, 163–64

El Paso, Texas, Reagan's visit to, 130

El Salvador, 148, 196, 254; Cuban and Nicaraguan guerillas in, 178, 197, 202; presidential elections in, 196–97, 200, 202; U.S. support of, 130–31, 132, 178, 197

Employment (jobs), at 100 million, 23; at 100.8 million, 174; at 100.9 million, 150; of blacks, 221, 258; full, 92; of Hispanics, 221, 258; improvent in, 119, 145–46, 150, 174, 193, 195, 218, 219, 221, 237, 240, 244, 245, 251–52, 255, 256, 258; in space-related businesses, 229, 240; of women, 146, 150, 198, 199, 221

Employment programs, 79–81. *See also* Job Training Partnership Act; Job training programs

Energy, 102–03, 164–65, 200; and U.S.-Soviet trade, 46

Engineering, encouraged by space shuttle, 113–14

England, and peacekeeping in Lebanon, 149; Reagan's trip to, 215, 217

U.S.S. *Enterprise,* officer writing from, 58

Enterprise zones proposal, 43, 103–04, 162, 166, 234–35, 241, 244, 256, 258

Entitlement programs, 69, 74

Entrepreneurs, 150, 251; importance of, 102–03; women as, 198

Environmental management, 43, 110–12, 165, 226–27, 237

EPA (Environmental Protection Agency), 111, 209, 226, 227

Equal Access Bill, 234, 235

Ethiopia, Soviet influence in, 45

Eureka College, Reagan's speech at, 19

Europe, 76, 216; Bush's trip to, 63–64; and economic recovery, 106; missiles based in or threatening, 6, 152,

Europe (*continued*)
154–55, 253; Mondale's cut of U.S.
troops in, 253; Reagan's visits to, 18,
19–21, 174; unemployment in, 18,
221, 240; U.S. commitment to, 20, 41,
57, 177; Voice of America broadcasts
to, 139
Evans, Clyde, 29
Exchange rates, 107
Exclusionary rule, 26, 225
Exports, 47, 124, 129

F-14 fighters, Mondale vote against, 257
Fair Housing Act, 121
Fair trade, 48
Family, 99, 239; outlook for, 219–20; as
top priority, 66–68; tribute to, 165–67
Family violence, 188
Farmers, 251; administration's help for,
246–47; going out of business, 1;
grain embargo against, 129, 191, 244,
246, 251; loans hurt by inflation, 247,
251; producing crops for exports, 47,
246; and U.S.-China textiles agree-
ment, 129–30; and U.S.-Soviet grain
agreement, 129, 142, 191, 244–45,
246; and U.S. trade with Japan,
159, 245
Farmers Home Administration, 247
Farms, reduction in estate tax on, 92,
103, 191, 198, 244
Father's Day, Reagan's remarks on,
219–20
FBI, and drug enforcement, 187, 250
Federal Aviation Administration, 141
Federal Reserve, 22, 41, 222
Federal Reserve Board, 72; reappoint-
ment of Volcker, 113
Fenton, Missouri, auto plant, 72
Finland, flights suspended to Soviet
Union, 142
First National Bank and Trust (Plain-
field, IN), 8
Fitzgerald, Garret, 194
Florida, and drug trafficking task force,
32, 225, 249; unemployment in, 146
Food assistance programs, 120
Food stamps, 68, 69, 73, 87, 120, 126
Ford Motor Co., 135; calling workers
back, 72
Foreign competitors, 39
Foreign policy, 18, 248; bipartisanship in,
162, 201; challenges in, 200–01; Rea-
gan's vs. Mondale's, 253–54

Foreign Service, 95
Forest lands, 164
Fort Bragg, 157
Foster care, 220
Founding Fathers, 28, 157, 189; quoted,
107
Fourth of July, 117, 230
France, 39, 135, 142; Bush's visit to, 63;
peacekeeping in Lebanon, 149; Rea-
gan's visits to, 18, 19–21, 215, 217
Franklin, Benjamin, 20; quoted, 189
Free markets, 51, 129, 200, 216
Free trade, 47–49, 107, 216
Friends Don't Let Friends Drive Drunk
campaign, 170
Furniture and fixtures industry, recovery
in, 146; slow-down, 40

Gallup, George, 198
Galway, Reagan's visit to, 215
Gander, 141
Gasoline, cost of, 9, 29, 59; and deregula-
tion of oil prices, 77, 78; and Middle
East oil, 148
Gasoline tax, to fund highway repair
program, 50–51
Gemayel, Amin, 95–96, 149, 174, 184
General Accounting Office, 150
General Motors Corp., calling workers
back, 70, 72
Geneva, meeting on Lebanese situation
at, 168, 174; U.S.-Soviet arms reduc-
tions negotiations at, 6, 19, 45, 54, 57,
63, 122, 123, 144, 152, 153, 154,
155–57, 248
George Washington Preparatory High
School (Los Angeles), 176
Georgia, unemployment in, 146
German immigration, 300th anniversary
of, 181
Gilder, George, quoted, 102
Glass industry, and auto industry lay-
offs, 40
Glenn, John, on Mondale, 232, 254;
quoted, 254
Goals for the future, Reagan's, 238–39
Goddard Space Flight Center, Reagan's
visit to, 241
Gompers, Samuel, quoted, 137
Goode, Nicky, 125
Government, reducing growth of, 238;
reducing waste and fraud in, 39, 74,
126–27, 133, 180, 183, 191–92, 207,
208–09, 214, 233

Government employees, pay and retirement for, 69, 133–34, 180; reductions in, 69, 133

Government spending, 7, 35–36, 84, 87, 119, 179–80; controlling, 15, 30–31, 43, 110, 182, 183, 222; on education, 82, 98, 115–16, 210; Mondale's, 232; in 1980, 1, 15; nondefense, 38–39, 195; overall freeze in, 69; rate of increase at 17 percent, 1, 15, 16; reducing rate of increase in, 1, 41, 69, 74, 88, 126; reductions in, 2, 21–22, 36, 71, 75, 218, 221; restraints on, 244; runaway, 30, 31, 44, 56; on social programs, 38–39, 191–92

Grace Commission, 180, 183, 192, 208, 233

Great Depression, 12, 37, 128

Great Society programs, 166

Greece, 142

Grenada, 156, 162, 174, 254

Groceries (food), cost of, 9, 29, 101, 150

Gromyko, Andrei, 247, 248

Gross national product, 38, 69, 214, 229

Guam, Reagan's visit to, 205

Guevara, Che, 254

Guilderland High School (Albany), 189

Gulf of Mexico, and drug control, 250

Habib, Philip, 96

Haig, Alexander M., Jr., 3

Handicapped persons, 100, 121, 220

Harris Poll survey, 160

Hartford, Reagan's speech in, 224

Hartman, Arthur, 185

Hawaii, Reagan's visit to, 205

Hazelwood, Missouri, auto plant, 72

Health care, 69; Mondale's cuts in, 232

Heckard, Michelle, 125

Helms, Lynn, 141

Help-wanted ads, 42, 56, 146

High technology, 84, 103, 193, 252; education needed for, 98–99; growth in, 161, 179, 218, 221, 229, 238, 239, 240, 256; research in, 103, 195; science and math needed for, 82

High technology products, 151; U.S.-Chinese manufacture of, 207; U.S.-Soviet trade in, 46

Highway and bridge repair program, 49–51

Highway construction, 209

Highway death rate, and drunk drivers, 61

Historic sites and structures, preservation of, 163–64

Hitler, Adolf, 75

U.S.S. *Hoel,* crew's aid to Australians, 89–90

Hollings, Ernest, quoted, 254

Home mortgages, at 9.9 percent, 132; at 11.9 percent, 22, 132; at 16 percent, 132; at 18 percent, 87; and high interest rates, 1, 30, 35, 40, 87, 213, 255; reduction in interest rates on, 8, 16, 132–33, 214

Honduras, 202, 254; U.S. interest in, 131

House of Representatives, budget proposal, 84–88, 92; opposing Senate budget resolution, 16, 17, 18

Housing assistance, for needy, 73

Housing industry, hit by high interest rates, 8, 9, 40, 87, 89, 109; increase in home sales, 41, 44, 79; increase in housing starts, 9, 39, 41, 70, 72, 79, 173, 193, 195; recovery in, 56, 84, 92, 109, 161, 179, 214; at a standstill, 71

Hu Yaobang, 206

Iacocca, Lee, 164

Illegal aliens, receiving government loans, 126

Illinois, unemployment in, 146

Illiteracy, adult, 84; among youth, 97

Import quotas, 246

Incentives, 52, 92, 110, 193; high taxes depriving people of, 1, 85; to hire unemployed, 80, 212; to invest and take risks, 103; to produce, 78, 237; to save, 56, 103. *See also* Tax incentives

Income, per capita, 39, 150; real after-tax, 237

Independence Day, Reagan's remarks on, 117–119

Indexing, 31, 70, 86, 92, 95, 103, 161, 219, 232, 244, 252; and cost-of-living pay increases, 16–17, 85, 86, 91–92, 134, 191, 205, 213

Indiana, unemployment in, 146; and wilderness areas, 112

Indianapolis Private Industry Council, 147

Indian Ocean, 58

Indian trust lands, 164

Industrial production, increase in, 79, 160, 193, 195, 221

INF (Intermediate-range Nuclear Forces) talks, 63

Infant mortality, 120, 151, 220

Inflation, 9, 35, 37, 38, 39, 68, 74, 81, 84, 85, 138, 145, 194, 236, 245, 251, 252, 255, 258; double-digit, 2, 10, 22, 29, 30, 40, 44, 56, 71, 87, 91, 119, 150, 213, 217, 257; policies to bring down, 48, 100–01, 103, 151, 195, 214, 218, 219, 221, 222, 238, 240, 251; and worldwide economic recovery, 106, 107, 109, 200, 248

Inflation rate, 87, 91, 101, 109, 128, 150, 160, 213; at 3+ percent, 72, 109, 119, 173, 179; at 4+ percent, 2, 44, 245; at 5+ percent, 22, 24, 30, 36; at 12.4 percent, 1, 15, 16, 22, 24, 36, 40, 71, 85, 91, 101, 109, 179, 221,245; at 12.5 percent, 165; at 14 percent, 71; at 18 percent, 29; in 1980, 1, 15, 29, 85, 87, 119, 179

Insanity defense, 27, 188, 225

Interest, exclusion of income on savings accounts, 92; on loans to farmers, 247; on national debt, 68; on savings accounts for college, 83, 98

Interest and dividends, withholding tax on, 93–95

Interest rates, 37, 174, 213, 214, 236; at 10.5 percent, 87, 109, 213; at 11 percent, 173, 179; at 11.5 percent, 39, 41; at 12 percent, 36, 41; at 13.5 percent, 22, 24, 30; at 20 percent, 71, 217; at 21 percent, 87; at 21.5 percent, 1, 15, 22, 24, 30, 36, 40, 41, 71, 87, 103, 109, 165, 179; in 1980, 1, 15, 87; bringing down, 151, 238, 251, 258; dropped by 20 percent, 2; dropped by 50 percent, 44, 72; high, 1, 2, 17, 18, 30, 35, 41, 44, 56, 71, 74, 81, 84, 85, 87, 91, 145, 150, 222, 240, 251, 257; holding back recovery, 2, 8; lowered for new car purchases, 8; prime, 1, 39, 71, 87, 91, 103, 109, 173, 179, 213; reduce by bipartisan budget, 9, 18, 22; and worldwide economic recovery, 107, 109. *See also* Home mortgages

Internal Revenue Service, 7, 93–94

International Civil Aviation Organization, 141, 144

International Court of Justice, 203

International Federation of Air Line Pilots Association, 141

International Monetary Fund, 48, 124; Reagan's address to, 247

Investor confidence, 39

IRA (Irish Republican Army) terrorists, 194

IRAs (Individual Retirement Accounts), 92, 198, 235, 244

Ireland, Republic of, 194; Reagan's trip to, 215–16, 217

Irish-Americans, 194

Israel, border agreement with Lebanon, 149, 167; military agreement with Lebanon, 135, 168; in negotiations with Arab states, 148–49, 168; peace treaty with Egypt, 149; and settlements in occupied territories, 136; U.S. commitment to, 136, 148; violation of northern border of, 149, 167

Italy, 153, 250; Bush's visit to, 63; peacekeeping in Lebanon, 149; Reagan's visit to, 20

ITT Corp., and job training, 147

Jackson, Graham Washington, quoted, 66

Jackson, Henry "Scoop," 177, 178, 183–84

Jackson, Rev. Jesse, quoted, 254

Jackson Plan, 178

Jamaica, Reagan meeting in, 3

Japan, 39, 135, 180; dependence on Middle East oil, 148; and economic relations with Soviet Union, 45; flights suspended to Soviet Union, 142; Reagan's visit to, 158–60, 174, 217; share of U.S. military in, 160; and trade with U.S., 41, 159, 217–18, 245; U.S. commitment to, 20

Japanese Diet, Reagan's address to, 158, 162

Jay, John, quoted, 189

Jefferson, Thomas, quoted, 28, 71, 77, 81

Jefferson High School (Los Angeles), 242

Jews, 89; Sandinista persecution of, 202; and tuition tax credits, 7, 67

Job training bill, 30, 166

Job Training Partnership Act, 70, 80, 146–47; 198, 212, 241

Job training programs, 30, 42, 80, 81, 146–47; retraining workers, 107

Job vouchers, 80

Johnson, Rafer, 231

Joyce, Billy, quoted, 114

Kampuchea, relieving suffering in, 62

Kansas City, Reagan-Mondale debate

in, 253
Katahdin High School (Sherman Station, Maine), 242
Kean, Thomas, 210
Kemp, Gary, 58
Kennedy, John F., 215; quoted, 92, 93, 118, 121, 142, 203; and space program, 182; and tax cut, 9, 16, 41, 91, 236, 251
Kennedy administration, 38, 240
Kentucky, unemployment in, 146
Keogh contributions, 92, 244
Key, Ernest, quoted, 9
King, Dr. Martin Luther, Jr., tribute to, 64–66
King, Martin Luther, Sr., 64, 65
Kirkpatrick, Jeane, 142
Kissinger, Henry, 130, 177, 183
Kissinger Commission, 130, 177–78, 183, 201
Knoxville, Reagan's visit to World's Fair in, 9
Korean airliner (KAL 007), Soviet attack on, 136–37, 139, 140, 141–42, 143–44, 158–59
Ku Klux Klan, 66, 188

Labor Day, 136; tribute to workers on, 23–25, 137–38, 240–41
Latin America, and drug control, 250; Soviet aggression in, 19; U.S. interests in, 135
Lebanon, and border agreement with Israel, 149, 167; and military agreement with Israel, 135, 168; peacekeeping forces in, 135, 162, 172, 174; situation in, 137, 147–49, 167–69, 184; U.S. commitment to, 57, 95–96
Libya, assistance to Sandinistas, 202; and PLO, 167
Licensed Beverage Information Council, 170
Life expectancy, 151
Lima, Ohio, Reagan's visit to, 29
Lincoln, Abraham, 72–73, 75; quoted, 28, 38, 74
Lincoln Memorial, 73; King rally at, 65
Line-item veto, 239, 240
The Living Bank (Houston), 125
Li Xiannian, 206
London, Reagan's trip to, 216, 217–18
Los Angeles Times, 42
Louis, Joe, 32

Louis XVI, 20
Lumber industry, and housing industry slow-down, 40; recovery in, 87–88, 146

MADD (Mothers Against Drunk Drivers), 170
Madrid, Miguel de la, 130
Mafia, 250
Magana, Alvaro Alfredo, 131
Make-work jobs, 41, 51, 193
Malnutrition, 120
Manpower, Inc., job survey, 146
Mansfield, Mike, quoted, 158
Manufactured durable goods, increase in, 79
Marijuana, 32, 223, 249, 250
Marine Corps, and budget cuts, 85
Marines, sent to Lebanon by Eisenhower, 168; stationed in Lebanon, 147–48, 149, 167, 168, 174; tribute to, on Armed Forces Day, 13, 14; tribute to, on Veterans Day, 157; in war on drugs, 249; writing from Beirut, 58
Marshall Plan, 35th anniversary of, 18, 20, 21
Maryland, schools in, 210; unemployment in, 146
Math. *See* Science and math
Mayflower Compact, 189
McGovern, George, 253
McMullen, John, quoted, 9
Meal subsidies, 73
Medicaid, 124
Medical assistance, for needy, 73
Medicare, 161, 191; driven into bankruptcy, 84, 87
Medicine, new frontiers in, 193, 228, 239, 256
Memorial Day, 106
Mexico, and border drug control, 250; and Caribbean Basin Initiative, 3, 53; Reagan's visit to, 130
Michener, James, quoted, 15
Michigan, unemployment in, 41–42, 146
Middle East, 152; efforts to bring peace to, 5, 95–96, 134–36, 148–49; foreign dependence on oil of, 148; Soviet influence in, 63, 253; U.S. efforts in, 57, 148, 168, 177, 184; Voice of America broadcasts to, 139, 140
U.S.S. *Midway*, sailor writing from, 58–59

Miller, Don, 231
Milwaukee Security Savings and Loan, lowers mortgage rate, 22, 132
Mineral rights, and wilderness lands, 111
Minerals, 200
Minimum wage, 80–81; youth opportunity wage, 80–81, 212, 241
Minneapolis, letter from lumber executive in, 87–88
Misery index, 245
Missiles, cruise, 19, 253; ground-launched, 19; INF, 152, 153; intercontinental ballistic, 105; intermediate-range, 6, 144; land-based, 54, 76, 144; Mondale vote against, 253; MX Peacekeeper needed, 54–55, 105, 118, 122; Pershing II, 19; sea-based, 54; single-warhead, 105; surface-to-surface, 149; and U.S. proposal (1977) for Soviets to reduce number of, 54–55. *See also* Europe; NATO
Missiles, Soviet, SS-4, 19; SS-5, 19; SS-18, 54; SS-20, 19, 152, 155; SS-21, 149
Missing children, 166, 220
Missing in action, 172; in Southeast Asia, 157
Mississippi, Nancy Reagan's trip to, 31
Missouri, and wilderness areas, 112
Mitterrand, Francois, 153, 216
Modernization, of industry, 245, 258
Mondale, Walter, foreign policy debate with Reagan, 253; quoted, 254; proposed initiatives to combat drugs, 249–51; Reagan's view of his foreign policy, 253–54; Reagan's view of his policies, 252, 256, 257–58; and tax-increase proposals, 232–33, 240, 245, 246, 252, 256, 257
Money market, 2, 8, 18
Money supply, 40, 41
Montreal, ICAO meeting at, 141
Mooney, John, writing from *Midway*, 58–59
Morgan, Patricia, 22
Mortgage interest deductions, 92
Mortgage loans, 150
Mortgages. *See* Home mortgages
Moscow, flights banned to, 141, 144
Mothers, tribute to, 99–101
Mother's Day, Reagan's remarks on, 99-101
Mulroney, Brian, 247

Nakano, Francis, 242

Nakasone, Yasuhiro, 159, 217
Narcotics policy. *See* Drug abuse; Drug trafficking
NASA, and private-sector investment in space, 182; space shuttle, 113, 114; space station, 181
National Anthem, 189
National Bipartisan Commission on Central America, 130, 177–78, 183–84, 196–97, 201
National Border Interdiction System, 249
National Center for Missing and Exploited Children, 220
National Christmas Tree, 171
National Commission on Excellence in Education, recommendations, 98, 115, 116, 117, 209–10; report, 97, 115, 116, 209, 242
National Confederation of Black Mayors, 212
National Crime Prevention Week, 188
National Drunk and Drugged Driving Awareness Week, 169
National Federation of Independent Business, 221
National Institute of Education, 175, 176
National parks, 226–27; and Watt, 111, 112, 163, 164
National Park Service, and Watt, 111
National School Safety Center, 176
National Security Adviser, 254
National Security Council, 137
National Wild and Scenic River System, 112
NATO (North Atlantic Treaty Organization), 18–19, 20–21, 63, 122, 174, 216, 218; flights suspended to Soviet Union, 142; missile force, 152–55; Soviet threats against, 153, 253
NATO summit (Bonn), Reagan's meeting with, 19, 20
Natural gas, deregulation of, 77–79; purchase of Soviet, 46
Natural resources management, 110–12, 226–27
Navy, in war on drugs, 249, 250
Nazi Germany, 185
Nazis, and First Amendment, 188
Needy citizens, 119; benefits for, 73, 74, 120, 121, 166, 191, 235
Neighborhood Watch programs, 186
Netherlands, Bush's visit to, 63
Nevada, 108
New Ireland Forum, 215

New Jersey, schools in, 210
"New realism," 234
New Year's Day (1983), remarks on, 60–62
New York City, subway crime in, 25
New York Times, 135
New Zealand, flights suspended to Soviet Union, 142
Nicaragua, Communist influence in, 196; Cuban influence in, 196, 202, 203; not restoring democracy, 177, 178, 196; pope's visit to, 89; Soviet influence in, 196, 202, 203; support to guerrillas in El Salvador, 178; U.S. dealings with, 131, 132, 201–03
Nixon, Richard, to China, 206
Nobel Peace Prize, won by King, 65; won by Sakharov, 122
Normandy, Reagan's visit to, 216, 217
North America, economic progress in, 57, 106
North Atlantic Treaty (1949), 20. *See also* NATO
North Carolina, unemployment in, 146
Northern Ireland, problem of, 194, 215
North Korea, 158
Norway, flights suspended to Soviet Union, 142
Nuclear arsenals, 122; reducing, 62, 105, 123, 144
Nuclear energy, U.S.-Chinese agreement on, 207
Nuclear forces, U.S. and Soviet strategic, 63, 105
Nuclear freeze, 6, 254
Nuclear war, prevent by deterrence, 105; reducing risk of, 200. *See also* Deterrence
Nuclear weapons, reductions of U.S. and Soviet, 5–6, 45, 105, 118, 123, 144, 152–53, 154–55, 248, 256
Nutrition assistance, for needy, 73–74

Office of Management and Budget, 17
O'Heocha, Dr., 215
Ohio, unemployment in, 146
Ohio State University, 29
Oil, dependence on Middle East, 148; finding by risk-taking, 102–03
Oil embargo, 148
Oil and gas equipment, U.S. embargo on Polish, 46; U.S.-Soviet trade in, 46
Oil prices, deregulation of, 77, 78
U.S.S. *Olympia,* 156

Olympic Spirit Team, 231
Olympic Training Center (Colorado Springs), 230
Olympics (Los Angeles), 229–31, 236, 237, 239, 255; Reagan's remarks to U.S. team, 229–31
Olympics (Winter), 186
Omaha Beach, 157, 216
O'Neill, Tip, quoted, 235
Opium, 250
Organ donors, need for, 124–25, 126
Organization of American States, 203
Outdoor Advertising Association of America, 170

Pacific Basin, 201, 206, 218
Pakistan, and drug control, 250
Palestinian problem, 135, 149, 168; refugees in Lebanon, 149, 167
Panama, 254
Panama Canal, 203
Parks, Rosa, and bus boycott, 64–65
Parochial schools, and tuition tax credits, 7–8, 67, 82, 162, 235
Passover (1982), remarks on, 88–90
Peace, Reagan's international broadcast on, 143–45
Pension programs, 173; employer-sponsored, 92; reform, 198–99
Pentagon. *See* Department of Defense
Perkins, Carl D., 234
Peru, and drug control, 249–50
Petroleum, world price of, 52
Pharmaceuticals, and space research, 228
Philippines, U.S. nurses captured in, 117–18
Physical Fitness Awards, 210
PICs (Private Industry Councils), 147
Pierce, Samuel R., Jr., 121
Plainfield, Indiana, 8
Pledge of Allegiance, 27, 189
PLO, 149, 167; assistance to Sandinistas, 202
Plymouth settlers (Pilgrims), 27
Pointe du Hoc, 216
Poland, 89; refugees from, 59; and Solidarity, 24–25, 33–34, 46; Soviet oppression in 5, 19, 35, 46, 62, 63, 135; U.S. relations with, 33–35, 46
Poor, programs to help, 120, 237
Pope John Paul II, Bush's meeting with, 63; Reagan's visit to, 20; visit to Nicaragua, 89
Pope Paul VI, quoted, 239

Poverty, 166; in Central America, 197
Poverty line (level), 120, 204
Prayer in public schools, 28–29, 82, 162, 188–90, 211; equal access legislation, 234; voluntary prayer amendment, 66–67, 82, 190; voluntary prayer measure proposed in Congress, 28–29
Presidential campaign (1984), 238, 243, 251, 255–58
Presidential Commission on Drunk Driving, 61, 170
Presidential Commission on Industrial Competitiveness, 129
Price, Elizabeth, 169
Price, Mr. and Mrs. Gerald, 169–70
Price, Timothy, 169
Prices, for Caribbean Basin imports, 52; for Caribbean Basin products, 51; going up, 24, 30, 150, 221
Private (independent) schools, 97; and tuition tax credits, 7–8, 67, 82, 162, 235; and voucher system, 82
Producer Price Index, 36, 195, 214
Productivity, 39, 252; increased, 2, 23, 44, 85, 87, 91, 92, 150, 179, 195, 221, 237, 240, 245; worldwide, 107
Prompt Payments Act, 103
Prostitution, 220
Protectionism, 48, 49, 107, 109, 110, 128, 129, 159, 216, 246, 248; local content rule, 110
Protestants, and tuition tax credits, 7, 67
Proverbs, quoted, 101
Public lands, 237
Public schools, and tuition tax credits, 7–8. *See also* Prayer in public schools
Public transit, capital needs of, 50
Purchasing (buying) power, 29, 41, 85, 92, 150, 204; devoted to military, 69; of families, 119, 138; of family of four, 24, 29, 101

Quality of life, 149–51, 218, 228
Quinn, Hazel, quoted, 9

Radio broadcasting, U.S. international, 138–40, 143
Radio Free Europe, 140
Radio Liberty, 139, 140
Radio Marti, 140, 162
RCA Corp., encouragement to schools, 114
Reagan, Nancy, 58, 171, 174, 194; on drug problem among children, 31–33,

223–24; interest in drug abuse prevention, 250; with Olympics team, 229, 236; and requests for organ donors, 125; and space shuttle return, 113; trip to Ireland, France, and England, 215, 216; visit to China, 205–06; visit to Japan and Korea, 158
Reagan, Nelle, 101
Reaganomics, 70–72
Realtors, going out of business, 1
Recession, 1, 2, 17, 24, 36, 39, 41, 56, 67, 68, 70, 71, 75, 79, 81, 88, 91, 103, 109, 146, 192, 193, 214, 247, 257; worldwide, 47, 48, 52, 107, 200
Reciprocal Trade Agreements Act (1934), 216
Recovery, full, 39. *See also* Economic recovery
Reform 88 program, 127, 208
Refugees, 58–59; from Central America, 52, 177, 197
Religion. *See* Prayer in public schools
Republican vs. Democratic party, during campaign, 238–39
Research and development, in universities, 241
Retail sales, 39, 193
Retired citizens, suffering from inflation, 36
Retton, Mary Lou, 236
Revenue sharing, 161
Revolutionary War, 117, 171–72
RID (Remove Intoxicated Drivers), 170
Ride, Dr. Sally, 113
Robotics, 173
Rock River, 203
Rogers, Bernard W., 154
Rome, Reagan's visit to, 20
Romick, Timothy, quoted, 157
Roosevelt, Franklin D., 66, 75, 135; quoted, 21, 37, 166
Roosevelt, Theodore, quoted, 189
Rosh Hashanah, tribute to, 27
Rossow, Rachel, 100
Rubber industry, and auto industry layoffs, 40
Ruckelshaus, William, and EPA, 111, 227
Rumsfeld, Donald, mission to Lebanon, 168

Safety belts, 61
Sailors, tribute to, on Armed Forces Day, 13, 14; tribute to, on Veterans

Day, 157
Sakharov, Andrei, 122
Salvation Army, 172
San Antonio, Reagan's speech in, 224
Sanctions, lifted against Soviets, 46
Sandinistas, 131, 196, 202–03; and pope's
    visit, 89
Savings and small savers, 31, 37, 119,
    173, 174, 244, 252; and exclusion of
    interest income, 92; increase in rate of
    personal, 9, 16, 41, 44, 72, 85, 87,
    92; not taxed for college education,
    83, 98
Scandinavia, Soviet threats against, 153
Scandinavian Airlines, flights suspended
    to Soviet Union, 142
Scholastic aptitude test scores, 81, 116,
    242, 243, 251
School children, letter from, 90
School lunch program, 74, 120
Science, 193, 195, 256; developing fron-
    tiers of, 238, 239, 240; interest in,
    encouraged by space shuttle flight,
    113–14
Science and math, and Commission rec-
    ommendations, 116, 210; legislation to
    train more teachers of, 84, 98; needed
    for high-tech future, 82, 84; program
    to honor teachers of, 84, 98
Scowcroft Commission, 106, 122, 201
Scripture, quoted, 101
Seaga, Edward, 3
Senate, and budget resolution to reduce
    deficits $358 billion over 3 years,
    16, 17
Senate Budget Committee, 11, 12
Senate Finance Committee, 195
Sexual assault, 188
Shanghai, Reagan's visit to, 207
Shanker, Albert, quoted, 176
Shultz, George, sent to Middle East, 96
Simon, William, 229, 231
Sinai Peninsula, U.S. peacekeeping
    forces in, 135
Single parents, 166
Singles, Rev. Bill, 172
Small business (family-owned), 174, 221;
    owned by women, 150, 199; and re-
    ductions in estate tax on, 92, 103, 191,
    198, 244; tribute to, 102–04
Small Business Administration, 198
Small Business Innovation Development
    Act, 103
Small Business Week, 102

Smith, William French, 26
Socialism, 91
Social Security, 2, 9, 11, 161, 191, 204;
    reduction in payments denied, 11, 74
Social Security Commission, 69, 74, 161
Solidarity labor movement (Poland),
    24–25; union declared illegal, 33–34,
    46
Solomon, quoted, 98
Somerville, Massachusetts, letter from
    school children in, 90
South America, 57
South China Sea, 58
Southeast Asia, Americans missing in,
    157; boat people of, 27
South Florida Task Force, 225, 249
South Korea (Republic of Korea), 76,
    141, 172; Reagan's visit to, 158–60,
    174, 217; and share of U.S. military
    in, 160; and trade with U.S., 159. *See
    also* Korean airliner
Southwestern High School (Detroit), 176
Soviet bloc, 172; Middle East incorpo-
    rated into, 148; and PLO, 167; Voice
    of America broadcasts to, 139–40
Soviet pipeline sanctions, 46
Soviet Union (U.S.S.R.), 5, 39, 103, 200,
    255; advantage in military forces, 84,
    152, 253; aggression in Afghanistan,
    5, 19, 45, 62, 63, 76, 217, 254; aggres-
    sion in Africa, 217, 253; attack on
    Korean airliner, 136–37, 139, 141–42,
    143–44, 159; balance of power
    between U.S. and, 5–6, 45, 47, 55;
    challenge to U.S. in Europe and
    Korea, 76; defense spending vs. that
    of U.S., 76, 105; economic relations
    with U.S., 45–47; influence in Africa,
    Asia, and Middle East, 63, 253; in-
    fluence in Ethiopia, 45; influence in
    Nicaragua and El Salvador, 131, 196,
    202, 203; intentions of, 138–39; inter-
    vention in Central and Latin Amer-
    ica, 19, 131, 196, 217; invaded
    Czechoslovakia, 254; massive buildup
    of nuclear weapons by, 54, 55, 62, 63;
    new leadership in, 62, 63; oppression
    in Poland, 5, 19, 35, 46, 62, 63, 135;
    Reagan's peace broadcast to, 143–45;
    relations with U.S., 62–64, 184–86,
    248–49, 254, 258; threats against
    NATO, 153, 216, 253; U.S. grain
    agreement with, 129, 142, 191,
    244–45, 246; and U.S. grain

Soviet Union (*continued*)
  embargo, 129, 191, 244, 246, 251;
  Voice of America broadcasts to,
  139–40, 143–45. *See also* Arms con-
  trol; Arms race; Arms reduction;
  Nuclear weapons
Space, 182, 256; anniversary of landing
  on moon, 228; goals for, 181–82;
  high-schoolers' experiments in,
  113–14; new frontiers in, 193, 238,
  239, 240; private-sector investment in,
  182, 228–29
Space shuttle, 113, 180, 256
Space station, manned, 181, 218, 228,
  256
Spain, joining NATO, 18, 21
Special-needs children, 166
Sputnik, 140
Standard of living, 39, 48, 150, 193
START (Strategic Arms Reduction
  Talks), 19, 63
State of the Union address, Reagan's, 68,
  69, 121, 181, 233
Statue of Liberty, 164
Steel industry, 40, 71; administration's
  help for, 245–46; and high interest
  rates, 87, 89, 109; modernization in,
  245; recovery in, 84, 92, 109
Stenholm, Charles W., 124
Stewart, Potter, 190
St. John, quoted, 139
Stock and bond market, 22, 37, 41, 44,
  92, 173, 179
St. Patrick's Day, tribute to, 194–96
St. Paul, quoted, 88
Strategic forces, 54, 63, 105
Student loans, decrease in amount for,
  3–4; defaults on, 192, 208
Substance abuse, 223
Sullivan, Kathryn, 256
Summer jobs for youth, 211–13
Superfund clean-up program, 227
Supreme Court, 224; prohibiting prayer
  in public schools, 188; ruling on abor-
  tion, 67
Surgeon General, and conference on or-
  gan transplants, 125
Surplus food, distributing, 120
Survivor's benefits, 198
Switzerland, Bush's visit to, 63; flights
  suspended to Soviet Union, 142
Syria, occupying Lebanon, 149, 167, 168;
  and Soviet advisers, 149, 167

Targeted Jobs Tax Credit program, 212
Tariffs, on Polish goods, 34; on products
  made in space, 229; on U.S. imports
  to Japan and Korea, 159
Tax credits, for child care, 92, 166, 198,
  244; for hiring unemployed, 80, 212;
  for private-sector restoration, 163
Tax cuts, 70, 71, 119; congressional, 1–2;
  in July, 2, 9, 16, 18, 36, 71, 85, 86; in
  1981, 22, 38, 71, 151; in personal tax
  rates, 103, 218, 219, 222, 236, 237,
  238, 240, 244, 245, 251, 252, 255, 256,
  258; proposed in 1983, 9, 16, 44;
  proposed over next three years, 22;
  protected in bipartisan budget, 18;
  third-year, 31, 71, 85, 86, 92, 103, 161,
  232. *See also* Indexing; Taxes, income
Taxes, capital gains, 92, 151; on charitable contributions, 92; deductions for
  state and local, 92; dependency exemption, 219; and education, 83; exclusion of interest income, 92; on
  fringe benefits, 92; gasoline, 50–51;
  high, 1, 35, 44, 56, 67, 74, 84, 85, 87,
  150, 165, 251, 257; income, 7, 35–36,
  56, 71, 90–93, 183, 195, 214, reductions and cuts in, 2, 91–93, 95, 138,
  150, 179–80, 204–05, 213, 233, 244;
  reduction in estate, 92, 103, 191, 198,
  244; reduction in marriage penalty,
  92, 198, 244; shortening depreciating
  schedules, 103; simplification of system, 222, 233, 238, 240, 244, 252;
  standby (1986), 69–70; withholding,
  93–95
Tax incentives, 9, 16, 91, 92, 103, 109,
  151, 219, 222, 229, 244; for U.S. investment in Caribbean, 52
Tax increases, 88, 91; and House budget,
  84, 85, 191; Mondale's proposed,
  232–33, 240, 245, 246, 252, 256, 257;
  Reagan's campaign promise not to
  raise taxes, 233
Tax loopholes, 183, 195
Tax reform, 220, 222; bipartisan bill for,
  21–22
Tax relief, for women, 198
Tax shelters, 7
Teachers, better pay for, 116, 210; merit
  pay for, 134; of science and math, 84,
  98
Technological revolution, 150. *See also*
  High technology

Television, news coverage of economy, 193; students watching too much, 243
Tennessee, unemployment in, 146
Terrorists and terrorism, 200; attack on U.S. Embassy in Beirut, 95–96; in Central America, 202; in Lebanon, 149, 167, 184
Textiles, U.S.-China trade agreement on, 129–30
Thanksgiving, first, 27
Thomas, Candi, waiting for transplant, 125, 126
Thomas, Stuart, 125
Thurmond, Strom, 26
Toxic-waste dumps, 227
Trade barriers, 218
Trade Ministers meeting (Geneva), 48–49
Trade relations, East-West, 45–47. *See also* Free trade
Trade wars, 48
Treasury Department, and tax loopholes, 183; and tax reform, 219–20
Treaty of Versailles (1783), 20
Trident submarine, Mondale vote against, 253
Truman, Harry S., 13, 235; quoted, 235
Tuition tax credits, 7–8, 67, 98, 162, 166, 211, 235
Turkey, 142; Soviet threats against, 153

Ueberroth, Peter, 231
Ullom, Madeline, 117–18; quoted, 117
Unemployment, 23–24, 36, 37, 39, 40, 41–42, 43, 56, 66, 67, 70, 71, 79, 103, 110, 146, 160, 166, 214, 240; of black teenagers, 80, 212, 241; causes of, 24, 40–42, 44, 87; cyclical vs. structural, 79–80; displaced workers, 70, 80; in Europe and Common Market, 18, 221, 240, 252; long-term unemployed, 70, 80; reduce by bipartisan budget, 9, 22; reemployment assistance, 80; relation to interest rates, 30; structural, 146; summer jobs for youth, 211–13; of young people, 70, 80, 81, 146, 211–13, 241. *See also* Job Training Partnership Act; Job training programs
Unemployment benefits, 68, 70, 80
Unemployment compensation, 73
Unemployment insurance, 2, 36, 56, 80
Unemployment rate, 1, 138; at 2.9 percent, 24; at 7+ percent, 24, 30, 71, 193; at 8+ percent, 166; at 9+ percent, 12, 13, 24, 119, 128; at 10+ percent, 43, 70, 71, 72; at 8 million, 1; at 11 million, 39
United Kingdom (Great Britain), Bush's visit to, 63; and confrontation with Argentina [Falklands], 3; and IMF, 124
United Nations, 153, 239; Reagan's address to, 247; and Sandinistas, 203; and Soviet denial of shooting down Korean airliner, 139
United Nations General Assembly, Reagan's visit to, 143, 144, 145
United Nations Security Council, Res. 242, 136, 148; Res. 338, 136, 148; and Soviet attack on Korean airliner, 137, 142, 144
United Nations Universal Declaration of Human Rights, 168
University of Michigan survey, 151
University of Minnesota Hospital (Minneapolis), 124
Unknown Soldier (WWI), 156
Urban Institute, 237
Utah, 108
Utah Beach, 216

Valley Forge, 28
Varona, Donna de, 231
Vatican, Bush's visit to, 63; Reagan's visit to, 20
Venezuela, and Caribbean Basin Initiative, 3, 53
Venture capital, 150, 179
Versailles, Reagan's visit to, 19–20
Versailles Peace Conference (WWI), 20
Veterans Day, tribute to, 156–58
Vietnamese refugees, rescued by *Midway*, 58–59
Violence, in-school, 175–76, 243
Virginia, unemployment in, 146
Voice of America, 139–40; Reagan's peace broadcast on, 143–45
Volcker, Paul, 113
Volpe, John, 170
Voting Rights Act, 65
Voucher system, and schools, 82, 98, 211

Wages (earnings), decline in real, 165; increase in real, 37, 39, 56, 72, 150, 179

Walesa, Danuta, 165
Walesa, Lech, 35, 165; quoted, 89
Walesa, Maria Victoria, 165
Wall Street, 22, 179
Wall Street Journal, 193, 232
War and peace, fundamental questions
    of, 104–05
Warren, Ohio, 8
Warsaw Pact, 21
Washington, George, 171–72; knelt in
    prayer, 28, 172; quoted, 28, 75, 105,
    117, 189
Washington Post, 42
Waste-water treatment, 209
Water policy, national, 164, 226, 237
Watt, James, 111, 112; praise for, 163–65
Weinberger, Caspar, 126–27, 134
Welfare, 73, 166, 237, 244
Western Alliance, 18, 20, 46
Western Europe, dependence on Middle
    East oil, 148
West Germany (Federal Republic), 39,
    89; Bush's visit to, 63; Soviet threats
    against, 153
West Virginia, and wilderness areas, 112
Wetlands, and Watt, 163
Wilderness lands, 226; and Watt, 111–12,
    163, 164
Wildlife refuges, 226, 227; and Watt, 111,
    163

Williamsburg, Reagan's visit to, 106–08
Wilmington, job training in, 147
Wisconsin, unemployment in, 146
Withholding tax, on interest and divi-
    dends, 93–95
Women, as business owners, 150, 199;
    contributions of, 101; and crime, 25;
    higher employment for, 146, 150, 198,
    199; opportunities for, 198–99; recog-
    nition of Ride, 113; tribute to moth-
    ers, 99–101; tribute to POWs in
    Philippines, 118
Woodrow Wilson High School
    (Camden), 113–14
World Bank, 180; Reagan's address to,
    247
World's Fair (Knoxville), Reagan's visit
    to, 9
World trade, 128–30
World War II, 41, 75; followed fall in
    world trade, 48, 128; U.S. nurses cap-
    tured in Philippines during, 117–18

Yellow River, 206
Younger, Edward F., 156
Youngstown, Ohio, 8

Zero growth, 217, 251
Zhao Ziyang, 206

FUNDERBURG LIBRARY
MANCHESTER COLLEGE